PROCEDURES
AND PREPARATION
for Counseling

Wm. C. COTTLE

*Professor of Education and
Director Counselor Education
& Counseling Psychology
Program. Boston College*

N. M. DOWNIE

*Professor of Psychology
Purdue University*

PROCEDURES

AND PREPARATION

for Counseling

Englewood Cliffs, N. J.
PRENTICE-HALL, INC.

Library of Congress Catalog Card No.: 60–9576

First printing .... June, 1960
Second printing .... January, 1963
Third printing .... January, 1964

Printed in the United States of America
72291—C

Preface

BEFORE A COUNSELOR SITS DOWN WITH A CLIENT, HE SHOULD HAVE SOME idea of the problems the client will present and the background from which they arose. The purpose of this book is to draw together from a number of sources the kind of information and the type of preparation the counselor will need prior to a series of counseling interviews. It is not intended to be a text in counseling theory as such.

It is important for a beginning counselor to learn how to select and organize data for counseling purposes from many sources. This kind of appraisal helps the counselor to understand the behavior of a given client *prior* to counseling and to check the validity of client statements *during* counseling in the light of societal evaluations of these same data. Obviously, some of these procedures will overlap counseling itself and should probably be considered a part of the counseling process.

The initial interview is an example of this. Such an interview is a part of the preparatory processes in counseling as well as a part of counseling itself. In like manner, a discussion of how information about client behavior is to be used in an interview cannot be separated completely from a discussion of how it is obtained, if the beginning counselor is to have a full picture of the process.

Most of the following chapters are organized in terms of the sequence in which the beginning counselor would encounter these data and need to use them; they summarize and review tools and techniques of counseling learned in a number of courses, and show how more general educational and psychological tools, such as statistics, are used in preparation for counseling and in interpretation of client data. For this reason both introductory and advanced materials are included.

Such a summary and the concomitant discussion of applications of those psychological appraisal techniques should serve well as a basis for the work of teacher-counselors, school counselors, personnel workers, rehabilitation counselors, employment service counselors, and in the intermediate training of the counseling psychologist who is at the point of synthesizing data for use in practicum courses.

Cases or persons described in this book are fictitious and any resemblance to those of actual persons is purely fortuitous.

The authors are greatly indebted to the following individuals and organizations who so generously allowed the use of their materials: Gordon Collister, Sidney Fine, E. J. Hankes, G. F. Kuder, The American Psychological Association, The American Personnel and Guidance Association, Columbia University Press, Henry Holt & Company, Inc., McGraw-Hill Book Company, Inc., Harper & Brothers, Educational Testing Service, Stanford University Press, the University of Minnesota Press, and the U. S. Department of Labor.

The writers are no less indebted to Mrs. Margaret Lehman who typed and retyped the major part of the manuscript.

W.C.C.

N.M.D.

Contents

PROCEDURES
AND PREPARATION
for **Counseling**

1

Preparation for counseling

INDIVIDUALS FROM MANY PROFESSIONS CONDUCT INTERVIEWS AND ADVISE others, but only an individual with special knowledge, skills, and education can prepare for and carry on a counseling interview. A unique combination of attributes is needed by the counselor in order to help a client make self-evaluations and changes in behavior based on these evaluations without telling the client what choices to make. Counseling interviews are conducted primarily with individuals who are within the normal range of behavior, but who need to understand themselves and their environment better. The principal objective of this book will be to show how the counselor uses special training and skills to prepare for counseling.

The first task of the counselor is to identify those who need help and make them aware of the means by which they can get such help. Here the counselor must help the client develop a desire for change without forcing such choices or changes. The client must not only be aware of needs, but also want to meet them if counseling is to be effective. This identification and the development of counseling readiness involves sources of information and procedures that are supplied by a number of people cooperating with the counselor. Whether these preliminary procedures are carried on in school or in some other community agency, they center about collecting and organizing information about the individual and the cultural subgroups in which that individual functions. Such a task requires an understanding of the physical and psychological forces which have produced the current behavior of the individual and also an understanding of how that individual wishes to proceed to change behavior.

The counselor does not always direct or carry on these procedures preliminary to counseling, but consequently must show others the kind of information needed and how it can be used in counseling. If the persons who collect such data are aware of this, their contributions will be more useful to the counselor and the client.

1

Usually educational and psychological data have been collected from and are intended for use with groups. The same information and the same procedures for collecting the information can be adapted for use with the individual, but this changed frame of reference must be kept in mind in order that the full signification of the data as it relates to the individual is preserved in the course of collecting it.

It is the purpose of this book, therefore, to discuss how the counselor and others use these procedures to prepare for counseling. The procedures are often referred to as tools and techniques of counseling. This simply means that a tool of counseling is a device used to collect information, and a technique is the way in which the information is collected or used by the counselor. These procedures will be discussed as nearly as possible in the sequence in which the counselor would utilize them.

Upon entering a counseling job the first move is to learn about those who will be the potential counselees. This is a problem of identification from records, observation, and measurement.

The first recourse a counselor has is to records maintained by the agency. In most instances these records have been made for administrative purposes. It is the job of the counselor to assess their value for counseling and institute any additional records or changes deemed necessary to give a more complete picture of the counseling clients. The counselor should devise some system of organizing this recorded information about individuals in terms of potential versus performance, so that those most in need of immediate help can be identified (Darley, 1945). This means the counselor must have some system of organizing information collected so that it can be evaluated in these contrasting terms. For the beginning counselor the *Minnesota Occupational Rating Scales* offer one frame of reference for organizing client data. (See Paterson et al., 1953.) Experienced counselors usually prefer to develop a system of their own. The important thing is that some systematic approach be developed.

It should be kept in mind that recorded information used in an interview with a client may need to be modified from the form used by the counselor alone in identification of potential clients. However, the counselor may wish to develop one system which can be used for both purposes.

Observational techniques used to identify individuals in need of help include direct observation by the counselor and others, as well as the use of information from observations which is contained in ratings and anecdotes. Observation by the counselor is directed toward finding evidences in an individual's behavior that counseling would be useful. Such observation needs to be carried on in a systematic fashion with some sort of mental or actual checklist of behaviors that would warrant a referral for counseling. Problems so identified may range from behavior indicating simple lack of specific information usually supplied by the counselor, to behavior indicating somewhat involved problems of adjustment.

Observation requires training of the persons who are to do the observing. These observers must become familiar with the techniques they are to use. They must reach general agreement among themselves about their objectives and the descriptive terms they will use, if their observations are to be stable and capable of being combined into composite observations. Important characteristics in the testing and interview behavior of a client must be described carefully if observations in these circumstances are to be usable to several staff members.

As counselors turn more toward use of longitudinal descriptions of behavior, rather than cross-sectional studies of the individual, the place of biographical information about the client assumes a greater importance. Such biographical data present a developmental picture of the client which is more stable and explanatory of current behavior than any cross-sectional techniques can produce. All that cross-sectional data can do is describe the client at a given time, but when compared with longitudinal data can serve as a check on the validity and usefulness of the former. Biographical data properly collected and interpreted can show how, and perhaps why, present behavior developed. These data can take the form of a personal record completed for the counselor; autobiographies, compositions, or essays for classroom purposes; case histories developed by social workers; and other forms of personal documents or collections of information about the individual maintained over a period of time. The personal documents prepared by the client have the added advantage of showing not only what client behavior was, but also how the client felt or still feels about such behavior. Counselors need to stress much more than they have this approach to understanding their clients. At the same time the counselor must guard against letting such information cloud or bias interpretations of current behavior. To do this the counselor must be aware of past behavior, but make only highly tentative assumptions from it which are easily modified by new information—for that matter every assumption the counselor makes about a client should be a highly tentative and momentary assumption.

Another part of the process of preparing for counseling is the initial interview. Here the counselor has a chance to validate assumptions made from data already a matter of record and to add new data through information collected during the interview. In this interview the counselor starts the groundwork for the relationships which are so necessary to successful counseling. In addition to making the client feel comfortable and wanting to participate in the interview the counselor is helping the client develop the idea that counseling is of value. The counselor can foster this idea by demonstrating a preliminary knowledge of the client and his environment which indicates competent preparation for the interview. After a brief period spent in putting the client at ease and developing a statement of the reasons why the client has come for counseling, the counselor can begin to verify and expand information about the client which has been studied prior to the interview. As far as possible the client should control the content of the material discussed and the counselor should be concerned with methods of helping the client express these needs or reasons for counseling. Then the counselor can indicate ways the client may receive help and begin to structure for the counseling interviews. Some counseling may take place in this initial interview, but primarily it is concerned with activities that are really preparatory to actual counseling (Bingham and Moore, 1959) (Kahn and Cannell, 1957).

In order to evaluate the data about groups and about individual behavior that are basic to any counseling activities, the counselor must acquire and use a knowledge of statistics (Downie and Heath, 1959). The frame of reference in which the counselor uses these statistics with individuals is somewhat different from that in which other educational and psychological workers use statistics. The counselor's purpose is to use statistics to help a client understand himself and the groups in which the client functions. To do this the counselor must be able to use statistics for organizing and explaining data about client behavior. This is ordinarily done in terms of location in or divergence from the average group. Such divergence usually is sufficient to show strengths and weaknesses that may need attention. However, this use of statistics also involves data about intra-individual comparisons; therefore these two frames of reference for statistics, a comparison to a group and meaning within a given client, must pervade each statistical inference the counselor makes. The chief purposes for which the counselor uses statistics in the ways indicated above are:

1. To use directly for counseling purposes with clients or for referral reports.

2. To interpret reports in the literature which will improve counseling effectiveness.

3. To carry on research which will contribute to evaluation of counseling procedures or improve counseling effectiveness.

Statistics should be applied to all procedures and preparation for counseling, not just to tests used in counseling.

Standardized tests are the most common medium in which statistics are used. Such tests have played a primary part in counseling up to the present time. Until counselors develop greater proficiency in using data from other sources, tests will continue to be a major source of information about clients. Actually the chief value of tests lies in the data they provide to confirm information about behavior secured from other sources. In a few instances, such as vocational interest inventories, they provide data which can be secured in no other practical manner. Tests that can be administered and scored with relatively little training can also save counselor time when they are administered by clerical or other nonprofessional personnel. The more of these procedures that can be adapted for use by technicians to collect data, the more effectively the time of the professionally trained counselor can be used. Tests are ordinarily used to support other sources of information about academic potential and performance, about special aptitudes, about vocational interests, and about personality traits and attitudes governing behavior. Tests will be discussed here as they provide cross-validation for other counseling procedures.

The counselor ordinarily evaluates academic potential in terms of school grades or marks, teacher judgments, tests of general intelligence, or multiple aptitude tests. The average of previous school marks is usually one of the best indicators of future school performance. Use of marks in a given subject matter area, however, is subject to considerable error and should be handled cautiously by the counselor. The use of teacher judgment by the counselor should be tempered by the counselor's knowledge of the professional background, objectivity, and behavior of that teacher. Most teachers are capable of giving a good estimate of the academic potential of their pupils, at least for their own subject-matter areas. Tests of general intelligence are subject to variation in terms of the kind of test used and the errors of measurement connected with a given test. Tests providing timed performance and a high level of vocabulary or reading skills may present a different estimate of an individual's academic potential from that presented by tests which are untimed and nonverbal. For these and other reasons the performance of an individual on tests of general intelligence will fluctuate and make an *exact* estimate of academic potential difficult or impossible. Teachers and counselors have been generally unsuccessful in getting this concept of variability in intelligence test scores across to parents and to the general public. It is vital that the counselor make sure *clients* understand these facts. Many of these same defects of tests of general intelligence are inherent in multiple-factor tests, although multi-factor tests have been designed to overcome the most common faults of group intelligence tests (Samler, 1958).

The counselor evaluates academic achievement also in terms of previous school marks and teacher judgments, but adds to these other information about school projects, contests, and achievement test scores. In the initial interview the counselor should also ascertain how the client feels about both academic potential and achievement. Frequently client feelings about this may be at considerable variance with the evidence the counselor has collected. At this point the procedures preliminary to counseling must include an attempt to understand client perceptions of academic performance which differ from the actual performance shown by the evidence. Such a process involves much more than just an interpretation of test scores. These differences between the indicated potential and the self-concept of the client and between perceived and actual client performance in a group may be the basis for considerable counseling. Until these discrepancies are clarified and accepted by the client, it is of little value to discuss the meaning of school marks, other school success or failure, teacher judgments, and achievement tests scores in an attempt to help the client evaluate future possibilities.

In like manner information about special aptitudes and abilities is collected and evaluated against the client's perception of special strengths and weaknesses. Sources of this information are all of the recorded data available to the counselor, including scores of previous tests. Again the counselor needs to use these in the initial interview as a background against which to compare client statements in this area.

After the counselor has made as realistic an evaluation of future potential as is possible, the evaluation of interests is undertaken in order to narrow areas of investigation. The counselor begins such an evaluation by collecting evidence from the above sources which will shed light on what the client likes to do. Usually these data, when coupled with the client's own statements about interests, are sufficient to give a fairly stable picture of interests and to point toward highly promising areas of educational, vocational, and leisure activities. Client statements of interest alone, however, are at frequent variance with evidence of that client's behavior and with results from measured interests. Thus it becomes necessary to know how a client feels about interests so the counselor can understand and guard against misinterpreting the effect of these client response sets or tendencies upon the total data about interests and the client's scores from interest inventories. When these all present a congruent picture, the counselor can feel the client is on safer ground in making future educational, vocational, and leisure choices.

Emphasis on the importance of client feelings and response tendencies highlights the need for the counselor to make tentative interpretations about the personality traits and attitudes of the client. Many research studies show that these are the real reason behind the success of an individual in most of the activities that he undertakes. Knowledge of them is vital in helping the client understand self well enough to anticipate and predict future behavior. Collecting data about the personality traits and attitudes of clients is complicated by the fact that many persons who contribute data to these evaluations either lack training in making such evaluations or let their own personality traits and attitudes distort the evaluations.

PREPARATION FOR COUNSELING

Thus the counselor's task of helping the client create a consistent picture of behavior becomes a process of trying to eliminate or control all the inherent sources of distortion and of training persons to make observations and collect data without introducing any additional distortion.

It is evident by now that two factors are paramount in determining how well the counselor is able to prepare to function in a counseling interview. One of these is the education and experience of the counselor. The other is his purpose in using the data.

From some discussions of counseling one gets the impression that successful counseling is a function of age—the older the counselor, the better the counseling—or that academic preparation is all that is necessary to become a counselor. Successful counseling is based upon a thorough knowledge of factors affecting individual behavior and the ability to help a client understand and accept these factors so that they may play an appropriate part in future behavior. The counselor acquires these knowledges and skills through education and experience, and the relative importance of education and experience is unique to each counselor. Some individuals who aspire to counseling may complete the necessary academic preparation, yet can never develop sufficient sensitivity to people or sufficient objectivity to become effective counselors.

The successful counselor must have enough academic preparation to use the procedures and preparation for counseling surveyed above and communicate the meaning of client behavior during counseling. In addition such a counselor must be able to relate to clients in a manner that inspires confidence and trust, that respects the integrity and capacities of the client, and that minimizes the experiential biases of the counselor during counseling. While it is still difficult to spell out in detail the attributes which produce a successful counselor, it is possible to consider absence of any of the above as negative factors that will prevent an individual from doing effective counseling.

The purpose for which the counselor intends to use the various kinds of data to be discussed in succeeding chapters will determine the precision with which the data are collected and interpreted. If the purpose is to use one or a few tools or techniques in prediction of a specific act of the client, greater reliability and validity are required. If the purpose is to help the client develop a global understanding and acceptance of behavior, less precision is required in any given tool or technique because each plays a lesser part in the synthesized picture of client behavior.

Thus it is evident that the importance of each of the procedures to be described in the following pages will vary according to the needs of the client, the needs of the counselor, and the activities undertaken to satisfy these needs.

REFERENCES

Bingham, W. V., and B. V. Moore. *How to interview.* New York: Harper & Brothers, 1959.

Darley, J. G., *Testing and counseling in the high school guidance program.* Chicago: Science Research Associates, 1945, p. 25.

Downie, N. M., and R. W. Heath. *Basic statistical methods.* New York: Harper & Brothers, 1959.

Kahn, R. L., and C. F. Cannell. *The dynamics of interviewing.* New York: John Wiley and Sons, 1957, pp. 3–91.

Paterson, D. G., et al. *Revised Minnesota Occupational Rating Scales.* Minneapolis: University of Minnesota Press, 1953.

Samler, J., Ed. *The use of multifactor tests in guidance.* Washington: The American Personnel and Guidance Association, 1958.

2

Records and personal
documents

THERE IS AN ENCOURAGING TREND IN COUNSELING TOWARD THE USE OF records and personal documents as longitudinal evidence of behavior, in contrast to the cross-sectional methods that have been used in the past, such as the information that has been secured from tests. But this has been because there has not been an adequate effort to keep records on individuals over their life span. Lack of adequate school records forces school counselors to resort to testing and estimates based on current behavior. Lack of adequate work records has made job promotion a hit-or-miss affair based on subjective judgments that often could not be verified through objective data. Placement of clients from various state and community agencies has often been based on the counselor's hunches after a brief interview. But now attention is turning to what usually has been referred to as the life history method. This should not be confused with the case history used in social work, which stresses environmental factors. The life history method stresses individual behavior.

Super (1957) talks about this as the developmental method or the theory of life patterns inherent in the Career Pattern studies. Dailey (1958) has pointed out the limits of the trait-factor or actuarial method and suggests that "the assessment of an individual should be organized around (1) collecting a detailed set of facts regarding his past behavior, (2) translating that 'chronicle' into an economic, specific and coherent 'theory' of the individual, and (3) basing the inferences of his future behavior upon a projection of these past trends as conditioned by probable future circumstances." Paterson (1957) lists a series of sources contained in records and personal documents from which developmental pictures of behavior have been secured and used in prediction of occupational success. It is the contention here that such an approach is the most reliable

and valid one for helping a client to make *all* life choices, not just occupational choices.

The premise behind the life history method is that present and future
behavior is best explained by previous behavior.   So this longitudinal approach is characterized by the collection, analysis, and summary of data
that show the development of behavior.   Allport (1942) refers to this as
the study of "latent trends" within the individual which are evidence of
major characteristics.   This shifts the emphasis to the use of records
and personal documents presenting data collected systematically over
the entire life span of the individual.   It also requires the education of
counselors in the collection and interpretation of such data and the
integration of the data with current cross-sectional techniques to help
a client understand himself, evaluate his environment, and make choices
in the future on the basis of this understanding and acceptance of what
has been done in the past.   So emphasis here upon records and personal
documents is the emphasis upon client evaluation *by the client* assisted
by the counselor.

This approach has another advantage for the counselor.   From these
idiographic data which are collected on each individual the counselor
can achieve what Allport refers to as nomothetic or group data.   When
the counselor collects information about the individual, it can be combined into nomothetic information about the various groups in which
this individual participates, and therefore both kinds of information the
counselor needs are available.

Historically the first use of this method of any importance to the
counselor is the study conducted by Sir Francis Galton (1892) of the outstanding families in England.   His purpose was to show that it was not
a matter of just one person, but a number of outstanding people in the
same family who made important contributions to English history.
Terman (1925) used the life history approach in studies of gifted children.

Another incident was the use of personal documents in a 1920 study of
Polish letters by Thomas and Znaniecki (1959).   *The Polish Peasant*
analyzes 763 selected letters to show typical family problems and individual problems.   Here personal documents were used in sociological
study and Allport (1942) refers to this as the first methodological use of
personal documents.   There have been a long series of psychological
uses of autobiographies.   Some typical examples are William James'
Varieties of Religious Experience (1929), Clifford Beers' *The Mind That
Found Itself* (1948), and Helen Keller's autobiography (1903).

Along with this use of personal documents and historical records came
the development of various forms of school records beginning with
Horace Mann and the Daily Register in the 1830's.   This is still one of
the major records of an individual's school history, even though it is only

a record of attendance. About 100 years later in 1930 came the first cumulative record published by the American Council on Education and developed by a committee headed by Ben D. Wood and E. L. Clark. It was most recently revised in 1940.

In the earlier 1930's a series of Employment Stabilization Research Institute studies was conducted at the University of Minnesota; these are discussed by Paterson (1957). They form the basis for approaches to mechanical, clerical, and business aptitude testing. These early studies also made use of all kinds of historical records and personal documents to predict occupational behavior. They had information on home background, education and training; a detailed work history; the claimed interests of these individuals; information about their attitudes and motivations; general and special aptitude tests; trade, achievement, interest, and personality tests; clearance reports from previous schools, from employers, and from social service agencies. Paterson compares this to the use of a biographical data form and a brief interview by Employment Service interviewers in the prediction of job success. The people using the life history approach had more effective predictions.

This use of records and personal documents to get a description of people in terms of their life patterns is only half of the picture. Both Roe (1956) and Super (1957) point out that along with this increased use of records and biographical data, some sort of a description of life activities is needed. The kind of descriptive information about typical behavior collected by Barker and Wright (1951), or the work that Fine and Heinz (1957) have been doing in studying worker requirements for occupations, provides an example of typical life activities. Barker and Wright have tried to develop descriptions of typical daily behavior to show life activities. Fine and Heinz have made an attempt to describe jobs in terms of worker characteristics and trait requirements. They have attempted to organize this into a three-dimensional description called the Functional Occupational Classification Structure, discussed in Chapter 5. When these descriptions of the individual on one hand and the description of the life activities on the other hand are fitted together, individuals are better able to understand themselves and to make choices about common life activities.

RECORDS USED FOR COUNSELING

The counselor uses records to build up the longitudinal or developmental picture of the behavior of an individual. Records maintained over a long period will show how an individual's present behavior developed and, if enough personal documents have been collected, can sometimes show why it developed as it did. In order to use records in this fashion, however, it is necessary to have clearly in mind the varying purposes for which records are kept, the content of records used with clients, and the way they are used in guidance and counseling. Records can be used to identify individuals who need counseling. Then in counseling they can be used to predict future behavior, or they can be used to understand behavior so that the client can be helped to make changes if this seems desirable.

Purpose of records

As indicated above, the prime purpose of the counselor is to use records as a developmental picture of the individual. The counselor does this in order to help a client understand the amount, the rate, and the direction of growth that has taken place. For the client who is considering a career in journalism, it would be important to have samples of writing collected over a period of years and a series of brief evaluations by teachers which would show growth in fundamental English skills and creativity. This as well as other growth would be evident if teachers saved typical samples of work from each year. With the present state of records in most agencies it would not be safe to assume that a person could not write well just because there is no evidence of this in the agency records. The counselor must show colleagues how information about a client's strengths and weaknesses needs to become a matter of record before individuals who have contact with that client will consider these data important enough to be collected and preserved.

If this emphasis on contributing to records as a developmental picture of the client were stressed continuously, teachers and others who have contact with that person would be more concerned about preserving information expressing a clear picture of behavior. This information could be used not only with the clients, but also with others who must work with him. Teachers could have a clearer picture of a pupil's behavior, which would permit them to make instruction more meaningful for a given pupil, whether this pupil were a retarded, an average, or an exceptional child. The relationships that developed between teacher and pupil as they worked together to produce these records could improve the psychological field within which instruction and learning take place. School administrators could see the various ways in which a given client needs help in order to make school and other learning situations a more successful experience. As the administrator sees how records provide a more complete understanding of the behavior of clients, the counselor would have to spend less time in explaining the need for different aspects of the counseling program. The administrator through this better understanding of records could provide more effective and understanding leadership for the record keeping activities of the agency. As parents and relatives become aware of the ways in which information from records is used to help members of their families, they would be more willing to furnish useful information for these records.

Understanding and purposeful contributions to records make the work of the counselor more precise either in dealing directly with client needs in the interview, or in making appropriate referrals to cooperating agencies. The data provided by records that have been collected with understanding of their significance are more useful in research into the effectiveness of counseling and into ways of improving services to clients.

The content of records

Traxler (1957) has provided one of the most comprehensive discussions extant in the use of records for guidance and counseling activities. Although Traxler emphasizes school records, the principles would apply to any agency. He lists the following set of principles to govern the establishment and use of such records:

1. A comprehensive and detailed system of cumulative personnel records is indispensable for the proper functioning of the modern school.

2. The most important purpose of personnel records is to improve the instruction and guidance of each individual pupil.

3. Records are needed that will be continuous over the whole school history from the kindergarten to the junior college, and that will follow the child from school to school.

4. The personnel records for all pupils should be readily accessible to the entire faculty of the school. . . . the freedom of use of the main records should not be impaired by the need for recording occasional confidential bits of information.

5. The records system should be simple enough and well enough organized so that the essential facts about any given pupil will be brought together on one central record card or set of cards in such a way that they may be grasped through a few moments of study by busy teachers and counselors who are not highly trained in interpreting records.

6. An attempt should be made to keep the records high in reliability and comparability by basing them as far as possible on objective data.

7. The records should be uniform in type throughout all the schools of the system.

8. The records system should provide for a minimum repetition of items.

9. The building of a personnel record system for a given school does not begin with a consideration of the records themselves; it begins with a study of the nature and purposes of the school and of the pupil.

10. If a school adopts one comprehensive cumulative form as its basic personnel record, it should not only plan this form with meticulous attention to detail, but it should also carefully plan the forms which are to be used in collecting data which will contribute to the main record.

11. A detailed manual of directions should accompany the personnel records for the guidance of persons filling out or using the forms.

12. There is a natural and logical relationship between the information on reports made to the parents and the information recorded for purposes of permanent record; this relationship should be taken into account in planning both types of forms.

13. There is also a natural and close relationship between cumulative records and transcripts of school records which are sent to colleges.

14. A system of personnel records must not be static; it must be revised frequently, as a school's theory of education changes.

15. It is imperative that a system of personnel records be associated with a program of teacher education in the use of these records.

If the primary purpose of records in guidance and counseling is to help the client grow in self-understanding, all records should be planned so that they present a clear picture *to the client* of the etiological aspects of behavior. If this is done, it will also be a relatively simple matter for teachers and counselors to interpret and use the records. It is probably best if records are maintained in three parts: an administrative set of records which contain those data summarizing briefly the information about each client needed to establish and maintain administrative policies of the agency; a cumulative collection of behavioral data available to all members of the agency; and a confidential file of materials on specific clients only to be released to others with the written permission of the client.

In establishing such a system of records the counselor and the agency need to do two things. The first of these is to spell out clearly the agency policy on how these records will be maintained and the rules governing the release of such information to personnel within and outside the agency. This is particularly important with records which are considered to be confidential. The second consideration should be for statutes governing the release of information from these records. A given state may have a law giving clients the right of privileged communication (Committee Report, 1955), but the agency needs a ruling that such a right applies to their clients. In practice few cases have developed which create a violation of an agency's promise about the confidential nature of records. At the same time the counselor should be aware that most records are subject to subpoena by a court and govern the content of those records accordingly. For all these reasons it is essential that all agency personnel participate in the development of such a record system in order that they understand the purposes and rules governing use of records.

Bristow and Proctor (1930) have presented a functional classification of high school records which illustrates the limited use most agency rec-

ords have for counseling.   They list records under the following headings:

1. Registration and classification forms
2. Attendance
3. Routine permits and passes
4. Parental reports
5. Health and physical education records
6. Special and cumulative records
7. Reports to other agencies and colleges

It is evident that these records will have quite restricted value in preparation for counseling.

A much more valuable description of materials which should be included in school records is presented by Troyer and others (1947).   This
report was constructed on the premise that understanding of certain
kinds of behavior is essential to pupil personnel work and lists the following areas of information which should be included in records:

1. The student's home background
2. General abilities
3. Special abilities
4. Progress in skills and knowledge
5. Work experience, community service and other activities
6. Quality of thinking
7. Special interests, attitudes and beliefs
8. Social competence and emotional adjustment
9. Health and physical growth and energy output
10. Genuineness of purpose, level of aspiration
11. Life values

These items are obviously more useful to the counselor and the client
than are the items from Bristow and Proctor's list.   The items can be
collected for the records from the following sources:

1. Personal data form completed by client
2. Autobiography of client
3. Other personal documents of the client, such as written school work,
   letters and diaries
4. Case histories of social agencies
5. Anecdotal records
6. School marks, ratings and follow-up reports

7. Records of excessive absence from school or work

8. Records of residuals of serious illness or accident

9. Employer reports and ratings

10. Reports and ratings by supervisors of community activities, such as scout or church leaders

11. Results of standardized tests and inventories

12. Sociometric data

13. Reports of specialists, such as psychologist or physician

14. Record of extra-class activities

15. Reports of conferences with parents and relatives

16. Reports of previous interviews

The sources of items included in the preceding list and the nature of items shown by Troyer and others indicate the differences between records prepared for use by a counselor and a client and those prepared for administrative purposes.   There is no reason why the agency records cannot embrace both purposes as long as the sources from which the records are collected provide for both kinds of use.

THE USE OF PERSONAL DOCUMENTS

It is obviously impossible for anyone to say or do anything which does not express something about self and form a basis for hypotheses about future behavior.   At the same time very little has been done with psychological data of this sort.   Casual conversation with friends and acquaintances reveals how little attention is paid to such data in daily life.   Even the student doing graduate work in counseling tends to neglect these data unless the data indicate evidence of highly abnormal behavior. This disregard of such personal or biographical data is partly a function of lack of training in their use and partly a distrust of the candidness of the persons who write these documents.

More emphasis is being placed on use of personal documents in current counselor education programs in conjunction with renewed stress of the life history approach to the study of the individual.   Counselors are being shown what these data indicate and how they can be synthesized with other data for use with clients.   Emphasis is being placed on the integration of personal documents into the rest of the cumulative record collected for a given individual.   More often now the counselor asks, "How do I discuss the meaning of these with a client?"

With the increased recognition of the importance of the relationship between counselor and client and more information about the dynamics of behavior, the candidness of the client is recognized as a function of the timing with which the counselor puts the client into situations requiring candor, such as the writing of personal documents. The personal documents themselves vary from the more common personal data or biodata form and themes or essay examinations through the autobiography, structured and unstructured, to the controlled diary intended for a given topic.

The biodata form

The biodata form is used more frequently as a new client comes to an agency. It deals with the more specific information about a client such as identification or census data about client and family, educational background and aspirations, leisure time activities, work experience and vocational plans. Form 2.1 is a biodata form adapted for use at the high school level. Form 2.2 is intended for use with college students. Information similar to that contained on each of these forms is collected by most agencies. In cases where the counselor does not have access to records collected previously on a given client, the biodata form is quite useful in making tentative hypotheses about the client prior to the initial interview.

If the counselor knows the area in which the client lives, a street address permits tentative estimates of client socio-economic status and background. In states where religion and race are omitted from these biodata forms by law, a preliminary estimate of this can often be made on the basis of a street address. Dependent upon geographical region and urban or rural address of a given client, tentative conclusions about background can be made on the basis of size of family and occupation of parents. Occupation of parents, together with the length of time the family has lived in the United States, can often be a check on the academic potential of a client. A person coming from native American stock in a low socio-economic area will probably be estimated to have less academic potential than one from an area of high socio-economic status. On the other hand no conclusion about this is possible with recent immigrants who may have come from almost any socio-economic level in their native country.

In this same fashion data about educational background can be analyzed. For instance more meaningful estimates can be made about a client who says he was tenth from the top in a high school class of 250 than can be made about a client who was fourth from the top in a class of five. Or biodata about activities can give useful information about the girl stating an interest in engineering when they show she spends her leisure time building and flying power model airplanes.

The counselor who spends time learning to use these biodata forms can find considerable validation for data collected by other methods, as well as new data which the personal documents provide.

The autobiography

The discussion that follows is specifically related to the autobiography, but much of the material applies to any client writings.

Autobiographies may be classified into two types—structured and unstructured. As Hahn and MacLean (1955) and Danielson and Rothney (1954) have pointed out, the unstructured form is most suitable in counseling when the major emphasis is upon social-emotional problems and the structured form is most useful when educational-vocational choices are to be made by the client. In the unstructured form, the client merely writes the autobiography in whatever form seems most suitable. For educational and vocational counseling usually more specific information is desired. To obtain this an outline is presented to the client and he is asked to do his writing within that framework. Exactly what is contained in this outline depends upon the intentions and point of view of the counselor. In general the client should be expected to cover such topics as vocational plans, economic problems, past work experiences, major likes and dislikes, and others. An example of such an outline is shown in Form 2.3.

The autobiography is more than a check list written by the client. It is hoped that in such writing the client will really describe pertinent behavior and values. For example when talking about vocational plans, it is hoped that meaningful information about level of aspiration will be given. Further it is expected that more personal data and even more intimate information will appear here than would normally be obtained in an interview. However, this is probably related to the personality make-up of the client and may be true for some and not for others.

If the autobiography is to gather material of the type just described, it is felt that it should be written at the suggestion of someone associated with the counseling program. In schools these have been written in English classes as a regularly assigned theme, sometimes corrected, then rewritten, and then sent to the file in the counseling section or they are often written in social studies classes. It seems that the introduction of the English teacher into the picture sometimes obscures and changes the material that is most suitable for counseling. It probably is more desirable to have valid autobiographies with a few grammatical errors and misspellings in them than literary masterpieces of no value to the counselor. It is hoped that the client will reveal things about himself. To do this the material covered should be handled in confidential fashion. In a counselor-client situation this is possible, in a classroom situation it may not be.

There is no agreement as to how long such autobiographies should be. Certainly this is a function of what the counselor wants to know and the use to which the writings are put. Probably the best thing to do is to

PERSONAL RECORD

Name:
Address:
Phone:

This information will be released to no one without your written consent. When you wish to leave something blank, write *none*.

1. Personal data:
   Sex: _____ Age: _____ Date of birth: _____ Place of birth: _____
   Religious preference: _____ Height: _____ Weight: _____
   Physical disability? _____ Married: _____

2. Family data:
   Parents still married: _____ Separated: _____ Divorced: _____

   Father   Mother
   Age: _____   Age: _____
   Job: _____   Job: _____
   Grade completed: _____   Grade completed: _____
   Birthplace: _____   Birthplace: _____
   Brothers and sisters:

Name	Sex	Age	Grade completed	Occupation

3. Education:
   Course taken: _____
   Approximate High School average: _____
   Subjects liked: _____ Subjects disliked: _____
   What do you plan to do when you complete High School? _____

4. What do you like to do in your spare time?
   a. Hobbies: _____
   b. Training in music or art: _____
   c. Clubs and organizations: _____
   d. Offices held: _____
   e. Do you like to read? _____
   f. What books do you read? _____
   g. What magazines do you read? _____
   h. What kind of group activities do you like? _____

   i. What sports do you play? _____
   j. Varsity or intramural? _____

5. What occupation would you like to enter?
           Job   *Reason*
   a.
   b.
   c.
   Is this what your parents want you to do? Yes: _____ No: _____
   What job would you like to be doing 10 or 15 years from now?

6. What kind of work have you done?   Mark on-the-job training "X."
   Job.   Time in months.   Did you like it?   Why?

7. What problems would you like to discuss with a counselor?
   a. Job: _____ b. Education: _____ c. Relation with
   others: _____ d. Finances: _____ e. Other: _____

8. Underline the traits in the following list which apply to you:
   Persevering, friendly, patient, stubborn, capable, tolerant, calm, impetuous, pessimistic,
   bashful, self-confident, jealous, talented, quick-tempered, cynical, tactful, conscientious,
   cheerful, submissive, excited, irritable, anxious, poor health, nervous, easily exhausted,
   unhappy, frequent periods of gloom or depression, frequent day-dreaming.

GUIDANCE BUREAU

Personal Data Form

Case No. _____

Counselor _____

Date Returned _____

The purpose of this blank is to secure background information about you for use with tests re-sults and interview information. Please feel free to answer as much or as little as you wish. However, the more completely you answer the items, the more useful the form will be for counseling. *No information about you will be released to anyone without your written consent.*

Final responsibility for decisions and plans always rests with the person being counseled. However, a discussion of your problems with a properly qualified counselor, coupled with such facts about your abilities, personality, and interests as can be gained by this blank, psychological tests and interviews may enable you to make your decisions and plans more wisely than you could make them unaided. It is not to be expected that all problems will be solved by these interviews. Adjustment in and after school is a continuous process because of the changes within you and the changing conditions you must meet.

Name _____

         Last   First   Middle   Sex _____

Present Address _____ Telephone _____

Home Address _____

Height _____ Weight _____ Age _____ Date of Birth _____ Place of Birth _____

U.S. Citizen: Yes _____ No _____ Religious Preference: _____

Marital Status: _____ Dependents: _____

Spouse: Grade completed _____ Age: _____ Occupation: _____

             Father   Mother

Name _____   Name _____

Job: _____   Job before marriage: _____

Grade Completed: _____   Job now: _____

Birthplace: _____   Grade completed: _____

Age: _____   Birthplace: _____ Age: _____

Parents still married: _____ Divorced: _____ Separated: _____

Brothers and sisters:

Sex (M or F)	Age	Highest Grade Completed	Occupation
_____	_____	_____	_____
_____	_____	_____	_____
_____	_____	_____	_____
_____	_____	_____	_____

Name of high school? _____ Date of graduation _____

Course taken: (check one)   Subjects Liked   Subjects Disliked

    General _____ _____ _____

    Commercial _____ _____ _____

    Vocational _____ _____ _____

    College Prep. _____ _____ _____

                  Size of high school senior class _____

                  Approximate high school average _____

                  Rank in high school senior class _____

Adapted by permission of the University of Kansas Guidance Bureau, Lawrence, Kansas.

Best subject _____ Mark _____
Poorest subject _____ Mark _____

College or special schools attended, including K.U., and also including special training in art, music, stenography, etc.

Name of School or College	Date Attended	Course Taken	Approximate Average

College Subjects Liked	Marks	College Subjects Disliked	Marks

What is (or was) your major? _____ What year are you in? _____

How many hours study do you put in during the week? _____

Are you engaged in any outside work while attending the University? _____

If so, what is the nature of this work? _____

How much time does it take per week? _____

Who is your employer? _____

Why did you decide to come to K.U.? _____

What other type of training have you considered besides a college education? _____

How does your family feel about college?

Sources of your financial support in college.

_____ Opposed to my going to college.   _____ Family
_____ Not interested in what I do.   _____ Savings
_____ Leave choice to me.   _____ Part-time work
_____ Wants me to go to college.   _____ Government Aid
                                                    _____ Scholarship
                                                    _____ Other?

What kind of group activities do you like? _____

What do you like to do by yourself? _____

List in chronological order all your work experience to date including part-time or summer jobs.

Nature of Work	From To (Give month and year)	Salary

Which of these jobs did you like best? _____
Why? _____

Underline any of the following words which describe your general make-up:
persevering, friendly, patient, stubborn, capable, tolerant, calm, impetuous, pessimistic, bashful, jealous, talented, self-confident, quick-tempered, cynical, tactful, conscientious, cheerful, submissive, excited, irritable, anxious, poor health, nervous, easily exhausted, unhappy, frequent periods of gloom or depression, frequent day-dreaming.

From what person or other source did you hear of the Guidance Bureau? _____

List any problems you wish to discuss with a counselor.

If the problem(s) you wish to discuss with a counselor is not of an Educational-Vocational Nature it is not necessary to complete the remainder of this blank unless you so desire. If you do wish to discuss an Educational-Vocational problem, please complete the remainder of the blank following.

List in order of preference occupations in which you would like to earn your living. Do not consider abilities or job opportunities. Just consider whether you would be happy in the work.

	Occupation	Reason for Interest in Occupation
1.	_____	_____
2.	_____	_____
3.	_____	_____
4.	_____	_____

What is your present vocational choice? _____
When did you make this choice? (give the year) _____
Why did you make this choice? _____
How certain are you that this occupation you have specified is the one you really want to prepare for:
Very certain and satisfied _____ Uncertain _____ Very questionable _____
How much information have you about the requirements of the vocation you are choosing?
None _____ Some _____ Extensive _____
What vocation do (or did) your parents want you to follow? _____
Why? _____
If you were free of all restrictions (if you could do as you wish) what would you want to be doing 10 or 15 years from now? _____

We are interested in determining why you have considered your present occupational choice. Below write all the things that have happened to you which you think might have influenced your vocational interests. If you need more room, use an additional sheet of paper.

_____
_____
_____
_____
_____

Explain any diseases or physical handicaps that may affect your occupational choice:

_____

This space is provided for any additional information not covered in this form which you feel may be pertinent to your problem.

_____
_____
_____
_____

develop the outline so that the autobiography can be accomplished in about three-quarters of an hour.

These may best be written at the same time as the client's first regularly assigned session with the counselor. Some counselors have used the autobiography as a homework assignment. It is probably best to have it written in consultation with the counseling staff. If the papers are to be used for screening, this can be done easily by going through a pile and scanning. The counselor soon develops a system of organizing such data. If they are to be used in counseling, they should be filed and the information synthesized with other data immediately before the client appears.

In summarizing the use of this tool Hahn and MacLean (1955) most precisely state: "The autobiography, sensibly used, offers the counselor in the secondary school and college a tool which meets most of the criteria of practicality and modest budget. It encourages counselee participation in the counseling process. It motivates serious consideration of common but troublesome problems. It imposes no heavy additional chores on instructional staff or counselor. It is low in cost. It aids in developing longitudinal histories so needed to implement our cross-section techniques of questionnaires and tests."

Riccio (1958) has listed arguments against use of the autobiography as:

1. There are questions about validity, reliability and use.
2. Many students are unable to be candid.
3. The material often becomes quite complex.
4. There are frequent problems connected with interpretations.

At the same time he lists as some of the advantages:

1. Opportunity for students to tell about themselves, if they feel free to do so.
2. Abundance of psychological material the autobiography provides.
3. Provides information about a student's attitudes.
4. The convenience with which the information can be secured.

Other personal documents

A number of writers have discussed the use of *themes* and *subjective examination questions* as a common source of material for evaluating individual behavior. These are probably most useful to reveal personality dynamics and information about interests, goals, values and attitudes unless these elements are repressed because of poor teacher-pupil relationships. The teacher can summarize these and put them in the cumulative folder after the counselor has pointed out the kind of material which would be useful. Sims (1948) has discussed the use of essay

Follow the topics on this outline and discuss them in detail to show things about you which would be useful in making educational and vocational choices.

I. My present vocational choice is _____.
   A. How long ago did I make this choice?
      1. What other choices have I made?
      2. Why did I make a change in my choice and how long ago?
   B. What things have influenced me in the choice of this occupation?
      1. Reading and other observation.
      2. Advice or suggestion of relatives.
      3. Advice of friends.
      4. Advice of teacher or counselor.
      5. It's the occupation of someone I admire.
      6. Good pay.
      7. I know I possess the aptitude to succeed in this job.
      8. It offers adventure.
      9. It will give me prestige in the community.
     10. Other influences.
   C. Why do I think I will be successful? What aptitudes and abilities do I have? Why do I think I possess these aptitudes and abilities?
      1. What about my scholastic aptitude? Where do I usually stand in my school or class group?
      2. Have I the ability to get along with others?
      3. Do I have skill with my hands? Have I won contests or awards?
      4. In what subjects do I do best? Poorest?
      5. What do my scores in aptitude tests indicate about my special talents?
   D. What do I know about this occupation and where did I get this information?
   E. What kind of education, training and experience will I need to enter this occupation?
   F. My first year in this field I expect an income of $_____ per month. Five years after I have entered this field I expect to earn $_____. At the peak of my earning power in this occupation my salary should be $_____ per month.

II. My Work Experiences
   A. What are the jobs I have had, how old was I, who was my employer, what was the income I received, what was the type of work I did?
   B. Have these jobs influenced me in making my present choice of occupation?

III. My Hobbies
   A. What are my hobbies and other leisure activities which may have had vocational significance?
   B. How have they influenced my present choice?

IV. What Vocational Interests Do I Have?
   A. In which of the following groups would I best fit from the standpoint of the things I like to do?
      1. Occupations involving mechanical and manual activities, such as mechanic, repairman, printer, farmer, occupational therapist, or dental technician.
      2. Occupations involving technical or scientific work such as engineer, physicist, draftsman, chemist, physician, architect, veterinarian, nurse, or dietitian.
      3. Occupations involving clerical or business detail activities, such as stenographic work, bookkeeping, cashier, or receptionist.
      4. Occupations involving business contacts with people, such as various fields of selling or politics.
      5. Occupations involving management, such as office or store manager, shop foreman, school administrator, or business executive.

6. Occupations involving social service activities such as teacher, Boy or Girl Scout executive, personnel worker, religious or social worker.
7. Occupations involving literary work, such as advertising agent, newspaperman, author, or lawyer.
8. Occupations involving special artistic or musical activities.

B. Why do I think I have these interests?
1. Occupations involving mechanical and manual activities.
2. My shop courses are interesting.
3. My hobby is building a hot rod.
4. I have a part-time job at a garage.
5. I like to repair things.
6. I read *Popular Mechanics.*
7. My interest inventory scores are high in mechanical activities.

V. What personality traits do I have which will help me to do these things? How do I get along with people? Do I prefer to be with a few friends that I know quite well or am I comfortable in large groups of people? Can I convince people to do what I want? Would I be happy working alone?

questions as a projective device, dealing with the ways an individual reveals valuable information which is usable in the life history method if collected in records.

Letters are another personal document that can be analyzed for idiographic and nomothetic data, as illustrated by Thomas and Znaniecki (1959).

The *diary* is more frequently used as a controlled diary limited to a client's observation about a specific kind of activity such as study or work habits. Except with younger children, diaries have to be used cautiously. They must always be treated as highly confidential material. Many individuals do not realize the extent to which they reveal themselves and need to be protected when such personal documents are used by others. Marbury (1948) discusses the use of diaries and themes with children. He says the diary should be a chronological account over one or two days covering what was done, with whom and where. Properly structured by choice of topics or instructions, diaries can reveal highly useful background information about activities and family life which will form an important supplement to other client data.

IDENTIFICATION OF POTENTIAL CLIENTS

It was indicated previously that the counselor's use of records and personal documents in preparation for counseling would involve the identification of clients in need of help. This might mean using such data from within the counselor's agency, such as the school; or it might mean recourse to other agencies. Identification on the part of the counselor requires the development of some systematic approach in the organization of data from records. Some sort of method contrasting various attributes needs to be devised.

Graphing data

Darley (1945) has presented one way of contrasting information about academic potential and academic performance which has been modified and presented in the graph shown in Figure 2.1. Reference to Figure 2.1 shows immediately that Individual A and Individual D are approximately equal in academic aptitude, but considerably different in academic achievement. To the counselor this suggests a number of tentative hypotheses worth investigation. Individual D may be a person for whom the method of evaluating academic aptitude was unsuitable, or the circumstances under which estimates of academic aptitude were collected may have been unusual in some way. If Individual D had limited reading skills and the estimates of academic aptitude required quite effective reading skills, and at the same time the estimates of academic achievement were based primarily upon performance in nonreading or nonverbal courses, such a discrepancy could occur quite easily. On the other hand, Individual *D* may be under considerably more pressure to make more effective use of academic potential than Individual *A*.   In the former case remedial reading procedures may be an outcome of counseling.   In the latter case counseling may involve learning to live under the psychological pressures contained in working at the top limit of capacity in academic situations.   Review of records should not only identify Individual *D*, but suggest reasons why such a discrepancy exists between potential and performance.

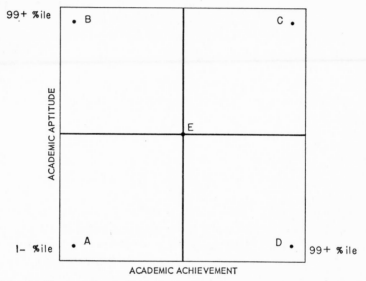

Fig. 2.1.   Positions of five individuals resulting from scores on tests of academic aptitude and academic achievement.

In like manner the reasons for Individual *B*'s failing to achieve at an academic level comparable to Individual *C* need investigation.   Do these reasons include physical or psychological factors, or both?   How can the counselor help?   Records are the first sources of answers to these questions the counselor should be asking.

While Individuals *B* and *D* present more clear-cut indications that their situation needs investigation, the counselor cannot afford to ignore Individuals *A*, *E*, and *C*.   They would appear to be achieving at an appropriate academic level, but contrasting data of another sort, such as that from social preference versus social behavior, or interest versus ability, may indicate ways in which Individual *A*, *C*, or *E* needs help from the counselor.   In addition to this method contrasting two variables for an individual in order to identify persons in need of counseling, information from sociometric devices may provide another way of extracting and organizing data from records to identify potential clients.

Sociometry

This means measuring social relationships. These techniques are useful to identify leaders, isolates, and rejects. Probably sociometric techniques have been used since people first began to study the behavior of the individual in groups. However, it was not until studies by Moreno (1934, 1953) were undertaken after World War I that any attempt was made to use these techniques systematically. Since that time Moreno, Jennings (1958), and Northway (1952) have been the leaders in producing an important amount of organized information on the subject. Two recent publications are those of Thorpe and others (1959) and that by Gronlund (1959). In the short discussion that follows an attempt will be made to show how the technique is used; how the data are collected and analyzed, and how the results of such sociometric evaluations may be used by the counselor to identify group leaders, isolates, and rejects who may need help in counseling.

General nature of sociometrics

As sociometrics are most frequently used, individuals are asked to respond to one or more very simple questions concerning other members in the group with whom they would like to carry on a specific activity. For example, suppose that a group is starting a project which is to be carried on by committees, or that the group is going to go on a trip, or going to have a party. Each person is asked to take a piece of paper and under his name place the numbers 1, 2, and 3. Then the person chooses in order the three members of the class with whom to carry on the proposed activity. If negative choices are to be indicated, it is best to do this in private orally to the person in charge. It is obvious that these sociometric techniques can only be used in groups that have been together for some time so that they can become acquainted with each other.

These data are specific to a single situation at a given time. The results of a sociometric test may be compared to a photograph. Status of each member of the group is shown as it existed on a certain day, perhaps even at a specific time during that day. Group relationships tend to shift and change, some groups more than others and certain aspects of groups more than others. Sociometry is useful in recording these group changes, but as Pepinsky (1949) has shown, this produces difficulty in demonstrating reliability of sociometric techniques.

For best results the questions that are asked should be related to something that the group is actually going to do. If any validity is desired in future sociometric tests, after the choices have been made by the group, effort must be made to see that the choices are carried out. The types of questions may vary, but most of them can be classified as involving social, educational, or physical attributes of the group.

There are two general methods used in analyzing such data for counseling use. The first consists of making a sociogram, as shown in Figure 2.2. In this figure are shown the choices of 13 fourth grade girls. In its simplest form the sociogram consists of a group of circles, one for each member of the group, drawn on a large sheet of paper. Then the responses of the group are taken singly and arrows drawn showing the member chosen by each individual. An arrow is drawn from Cloe, whose first choice was Martha, to Martha, and a 1 placed near the head of the arrow to designate that Martha was first choice. Cloe's second choice was Bessie; another arrow is drawn to her circle, this time with a 2 appearing near the head. Finally Cloe's third choice, Elizabeth, is drawn and a 3 placed on it. In this way the responses of each student are tallied. Different colors are sometimes used instead of numbers to show the sequence of the choices.

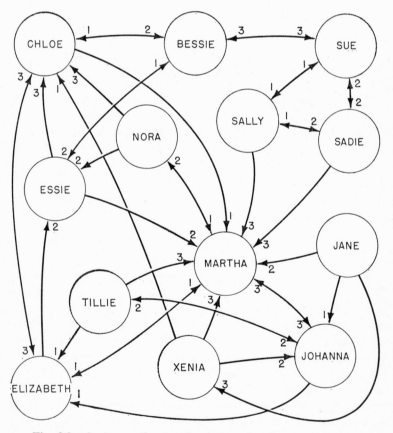

Fig..2.2.   Sociogram showing the choices of 13 fourth grade girls.

This sociogram presents a picture of the group choices in reference to the question asked. Notice that Martha has received more choices than the other girls. She is referred to as a "star of attraction" or a possible leader. No one chose Jane, and her status is referred to as being an isolate. If negative choices had been possible, Jane might have been a "reject." It will be noticed that there is also a small group within the group. This is in the upper right hand corner where Sadie, Sally, and Sue selected each other to as great extent as possible. This small group is referred to as a "clique."

When the size of the group is large, construction and interpretation of a sociogram become almost impossible. Such data are almost useless as far as studying them in relationship to other variables is concerned.

The other method for handling the data gets around these objections. With this method a worksheet similar to Figure 2.3 is set up on a large sheet of paper. Down the left-hand side are listed all the names of the members of the group. The same is done across the top. Under each

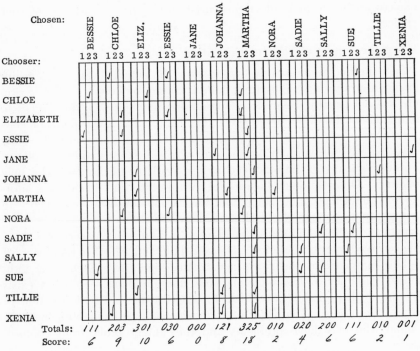

Chooser:	BESSIE			CHLOE			ELIZ.			ESSIE			JANE			JOHANNA			MARTHA			NORA			SADIE			SALLY			SUE			TILLIE			XENIA		
Chooser:	1	2	3	1	2	3	1	2	3	1	2	3	1	2	3	1	2	3	1	2	3	1	2	3	1	2	3	1	2	3	1	2	3	1	2	3	1	2	3
BESSIE							√				√																									√			
CHLOE	√								√											√																			
ELIZABETH						√					√								√																				
ESSIE		√					√														√																		√
JANE																	√		√																				√
JOHANNA						√													√																√				
MARTHA				√														√				√																	
NORA						√	√													√																			
SADIE																					√	√							√										
SALLY																					√				√			√											
SUE			√																						√			√											
TILLIE											√					√					√																		
XENIA				√													√				√																		
Totals:	1	1	1	2	0	3	3	0	1	0	3	0	0	0	0	1	2	1	3	2	5	0	1	0	0	2	0	2	0	0	1	1	1	0	1	0	0	0	1
Score:	6			9			10			6			0			8			18			2			4			6			6			2			1		

Fig. 2.3. Summary of the choices of 13 fourth grade girls.

name is a column headed with a 1, 2, and 3 to correspond to possible choices. The responses of the individuals are taken one at a time and entered into this chart. Suppose that Bessie's choices are considered.

Her first choice was Cloe, second choice, Essie, and third, Sue. A check mark is placed under the name of each of these girls in the column for the appropriate choice. This is continued until all the choices are entered. When this is finished, the results are summed and the number of first, second, and third choices for each girl appears at the bottom. These may be turned into a numerical score by multiplying each first choice by 3, each second choice by 2, and each third choice by 1. Notice now that the scores run from 18 for Martha to 0 for June. A check on the accuracy of the work is that the sum of these scores should equal the number of individuals multiplied by 6. In this case this comes to 78. It is possible to organize such a chart into quadrants to show boy choice of boy, boy choice of girl, girl choice of boy, and girl choice of girl.

Whether such choices are separated among first, second, and third choices and between sexes depends on the use to which the information will be put. There is evidence to show that such choices are temporary and less stable for socially extraverted individuals who know more people than for socially introverted individuals. The purpose for which these choices are made may affect the variability or the consistency of such choices.

Using the results of sociometric testing

Sociometric results merely tell or show the actual social relationships among a group. In the example Jane is chosen by no one. Such a situation is not usually desirable. One of the functions of counseling is to help a client develop a healthy emotional life. From this point of view Jane may be a girl who needs counseling help. It is necessary to study Jane more closely and try to find out why she is not chosen by others. To do this many of the other techniques available to the counselor may be used. Observation and anecdotal records, tests and inventories, information about the child's home, and the like could all be employed. In any group of average classroom size there are apt to be several of these isolates. In the group shown in Figure 2.3, Xenia had a score of 1, having received one third choice. She and Jane and all other isolates must not be lumped into one group and treated similarly. Each is an individual with her own individual needs and problems. So what exists for one, will probably have little to do with the cause of isolation of any of the others. The major use of sociometrics is *to identify* the individual who may have problems and thus might profit from counseling.

Perhaps it could be said that all this is unnecessary as any good observer knows the various types of leaders in a group and the ones for whom no one cares. This may be true, but research has shown that the opinions of many untrained observers are far from the actualities of the group structure and this is probably true for many other group situations.

Besides contributing to identification of individuals who may need counseling help, sociometrics provide information that is useful about group relationships to improve procedure in setting up groups. In addition to using this information to create group structure for projects and trips, data like these can be used in assigning individuals to halls and rooms in a dormitory, selecting adults for various types of work groups, or in any situation where individuals have to associate with others. But the main value of sociometric data to the counselor is as an indicator of persons with problems. Then the counselor can use other methods to explore causes of the problem.

Other means of identifying clients

Texts describing various kinds of behavior can be used to secure a list of the kind of characteristics the counselor should use in identifying clients who need a certain kind of help. An approach to this problem by devising a brief list of behaviors identifying various kinds of children at the elementary school level has been undertaken by Kough and DeHaan (1955). The counselor will need to supplement this with other sources, but it will serve as an initial list of behaviors to use when scanning records and personal documents.

The counselor can also make a checklist to use for this purpose. Even though the counselor has had considerable education in psychology and experience in counseling, it is well to have such a checklist. Whether it is actually checked or only covered mentally is the counselor's decision. Such a procedure tends to increase counselor reliability.

This checklist could cover the topics indicated in the list by Troyer and others (1947) in the beginning of this chapter. The counselor needs to ask such questions as the following:

1. What does the client's home background indicate about behavior?
2. What do records and personal documents show about level of abilities and achievements?
3. What do data about activities outside of school show about this client?
4. What interests, attitudes, goals, and values do they show?
5. What evaluation of social skills and personal adjustment can be made?
6. Are there any evidences of physical limitations or outstanding skills?

In these ways the counselor uses information from records and from personal documents to show the clients who may need help. The next problem is to check and see which ones want help and what can be done to promote readiness for counseling.

PREPARING COUNSELING DATA

The actual counseling use of data from records and personal documents may require a somewhat different system of organization than that for identification of those in need of help. Here the counselor has the choice of a system which has been developed like that proposed in the Minnesota Occupational Rating Scales or the counselor can develop a unique system of organizing these data. Both approaches will be discussed in Chapter 5.

SUMMARY

An attempt has been made in this chapter to show how the counselor's use of records to identify individuals in need of counseling and to help a client gain a greater self-understanding may require a different kind of information in such records. The work of Troyer and others points out the kind of information needed and possible changes in the way agency members contribute to agency records. Traxler has discussed the forms records may take to meet unique needs of a given school and has illustrated a number of these. Such an emphasis highlights the need for accurate, objective, directed observations on the part of all personnel contributing to records. The next chapter will consider how these observations are achieved and the conditions which should exist if the observations are to be useful to the counselor.

REFERENCES

Allport, G. W. *The use of personal documents in psychological science.* Soc. Sci. Research Council Bull., 1942.

Barker, R., and H. F. Wright. *One boy's day: A specimen record of behavior.* New York: Harper & Brothers, 1951.

Beers, C. W. *A mind that found itself.* Garden City, New York: Doubleday, 1948.

Bristow, A. B., and W. M. Proctor. Senior high school records and reports. *Junior-Senior High School Clearing House,* 1930, *4,* 410–432.

Committee Report, Joint report of the APA and CSPA committees of legislation. *American Psychologist,* 1955, *10,* 727–756.

Dailey, C. A. The life history approach to assessment. *Personnel and Guidance Journal,* 1958, *36,* 456–460.

Danielson, P. J., and J. W. Rothney. The autobiography: structured or unstructured? *Personnel and Guidance Journal,* 1954, *33,* 30–33.

Darley, J. G. *Testing and counseling in the high school guidance program.* Chicago: Science Research Associates, 1945.

Fine, S. A., and C. A. Heinz. The estimates of worker trait requirements for 4000 jobs. *Personnel and Guidance Journal,* 1957, *36,* 168–174.

Galton, F. *Hereditary genius.* London: Macmillan and Co., 1892. New York: Horizon Press, 1952.

Gronlund, N. E. *Sociometry in the classroom.* New York: Harper & Brothers, 1959.

Hahn, M. E., and M. S. MacLean. *Counseling psychology.* New York: McGraw-Hill Book Company, Inc., 1955.

James, William. *The varieties of religious experience.* New York: Longmans, Green, and Company, 1929.

Jennings, Helen H. *Sociometry in group relations.* Washington, D.C.: American Council on Education, 1958.

Keller, Helen A. *The story of my life.* Garden City, New York: Doubleday, 1903.

Kough, J., and R. F. DeHaan. *Teacher's guidance handbook, Part I: Identifying children who need help.* Chicago: Science Research Associates, 1955.

Marbury, F. W. Studying the child's social world. *J. Educ. Sociol.,* 1948, *21,* 535–543.

Moreno, J. B. *Who shall survive? A new approach to the problem of human interrelations.* Washington, D.C.: Nervous and Mental Diseases Publishing Co., 1934. Revised ed., New York: Beacon House, 1953.

Northway, Mary. *A primer of sociometry.* Toronto: University of Toronto Press, 1952.

Paterson, D. A. The conservation of human talent. *Amer. Psychol.,* 1957, *12,* 134–144.

Pepinsky, Pauline. The meaning of "validity" and "reliability" as applied to sociometric tests. *Educ. and Psychol. Measmt.,* 1949, *9,* 39–49.

Riccio, A. C. The status of the autobiography. *Peabody J. of Educ.,* 1958, *36,* 33–36.

Roe, Anne. *The psychology of occupations.* New York: John Wiley & Sons, 1956.

Sims, V. M. The essay examination is a projective technique. *Educ. and Psychol. Measmt.,* 1948, *8,* 15–31.

Super, D. E. *The psychology of careers.* New York: Harper & Brothers, 1957.

Terman, L., et al. *Mental and physical traits of a thousand gifted children— genetic studies of genius.* Stanford: Stanford University Press, 1925.

Thomas, W. I., and F. Znaniecki. *The Polish peasant in Europe and America,* 2 Vols. New York: Alfred A. Knopf, Inc., 1927. New York: Dover Publications, Inc., 1958.

Thorpe, L. P., et al. *Studying social relationships in the classroom.* Chicago: Science Research Associates, 1959.

Traxler, A. E. *Techniques of guidance.* New York: Harper & Brothers, 1957.

Troyer, M. E., et al. Essential pupil-personnel records. Committee Number V Report. *Teachers College Record,* 1947, *48,* 269–286.

3

Observation for counseling

purposes

OBSERVATION IS A BASIC TOOL OF THE COUNSELOR AND OF THOSE WHO furnish information for the counselor's use. Unless those who make the observations understand the frame of reference in which the observations are to be used, these data tend to be such a mixture of fact and subjective judgment that they are of limited value to the counselor.

Observations can be categorized in a number of ways, but perhaps the most useful categories for the counselor are finding observations and directed observations. *Finding* observations are those used in an exploratory or experimental situation to identify activities that are of importance to the observer. In counseling this means selecting activities that are important to the client being observed. When these activities have been singled out, any additional observations can be concentrated on such activities. These latter observations are then called *directed* observations. Thus directed observations are those where the observer's attention is pointed toward specific kinds of behavior. If the observations are described and recorded in a straightforward factual account, the counselor can use them to help clients become more aware of given facets of behavior.

Observations used in counseling come from many sources. The most important sources for the counselor are rating scales, anecdotes, psychometric situations, and initial interviews. These observations usually become a matter of agency records so that they are available to the counselor in preparing for interviews with clients. Unless sufficient preparation of observers has been carried out, the observations made are of limited effectiveness when the counselor is trying to piece together a picture of the behavior of a given client. A frame of reference is needed which will influence these observations in a way that makes them systematic and fairly objective. Such a systematic approach to observations can then be communicated to others during in-service training programs.

In order to secure uniform, factual records of behavior, the observers must have training. The purpose of making the observation and the use to which it will be put should be the first matters emphasized in such a training program. Those observers who are incapable of making accurate, factual, unbiased records should be eliminated from the training; this would include persons whose physical or psychological characteristics would prevent them from being trained to make usable observations. One simple way to demonstrate the error which can creep into such reports is for the leader to face away from the group *with eyes closed* and appear to be gazing out a window. If the group is asked to describe the leader's behavior, they will usually include the phrase "looked out the window." This procedure is a simple way of illustrating that the efficient observer only describes what can be *seen,* not what is inferred.

In the training of observers it is usually worthwhile to devote time to developing common agreement on the meaning of terms that will be used to describe behavior. Such agreement on terminology will make the observations more meaningful to all observers by producing a greater consistency in records of a given observer and among the group of observers. Reliability is also enhanced by using short time limits, by concentrating on one or a few individuals at a time and by the amount of control over the conditions under which the observations are made. Common agreement about terms used contributes to the observer validity involved in the completeness, simplicity, and clarity of the factual behavior description. Then the validity of the behavior itself becomes clearer and the validity of the counselor's interpretation of such behavior is increased. These different aspects of reliability and validity all operate to limit the usefulness of observations to the counselor and to the client.

RATING SCALES

One of the chief observational techniques used to secure information about clients preliminary to counseling is the rating scale, which can be used to describe many facets of individual behavior, either in self-evaluations or in evaluations by trained observers. The self-evaluations usually take the form of adjective or problem checklists and of structured interest or personality inventories. Rating scale evaluations by trained observers usually cover behavior for which more precise or more objective measures have not been developed, or the ratings are used as criteria for validating other measurement devices.

The counselor needs to be able to instruct raters, to organize and use

ratings by others, to construct or to use data from instruments of self
rating, and to construct rating scales and use them.

Since the time of Sir Francis Galton, rating scales have been used
to assess aspects of personality. After Galton's original work using rating
scales in the evaluation of the vividness of imagery, Pearson next developed one for the assessment of intelligence. Acceptance by psychologists increased slowly until World War I when scales were developed
for rating the performance of officers. After World War I rating scales
were increasingly accepted by both industry and education in appraising
various aspects of an individual's personality. Although today rating
scales are more widely used in industry than in education because more
precise evaluative devices and criteria have been developed in education, ratings still have many uses for the counselor, both in working with
clients and in carrying on research.

Types of scales

A discussion of all of the different types of rating scales is beyond
the present scope. The most comprehensive summaries of previous work
appear in Guilford (1954) or Symonds (1931). In the material that follows only the more frequently encountered types of scales will be covered.

Graphic rating scales

These represent one of the most commonly used types of scale. In
graphic rating scales a trait is considered as a continuum with descriptive terms placed along it as in the following examples:

How quiet is he?

Seldom speaks	Says very little	Carries on his part in a con- versation	Talks more than his share	Talks constantly

Does he do the best quality of work of which he is capable?

Almost always	Most of the time	Sometimes	Seldom	Rarely ever

In using a scale like those above, the rater considers the individual being
rated and places a mark along the line. This mark need not be placed
over one of the descriptive terms. In scoring these, a scoring scale with
intervals on it may be placed along the rating scale and the rater's mark
translated into a quantitative score. The gradations on this scoring scale
may be as fine as desired by the scorer. Some rating scales do have the
line divided into pieces or in line with the descriptive terms and each of
these segments or terms receives a value.

Construction and general use of graphic rating scales

Here are a few suggestions which have to be followed in making rating scales:

1. Reach agreement among raters about meaning of terms to be used. Such words as *usually, frequently,* or *often,* mean different things to different people. The best rule is to attempt to use quantitative terms rather than qualitative ones.

2. Keep the vocabulary as simple as possible. In making rating scales the same rules apply that are relevant when one is making a test or examination.

3. Build scales for traits that can be observed. Many of the troubles with rating scales arise because the builder of the scale asks the rater to do almost impossible things. The trait being rated should be of such a nature that evidence relating to the trait can be observed. Ratings require that the rater observe and then make a judgment about the individual being rated. These are both difficult tasks. It is much easier for raters to rate an individual on his promptness than on how his manners affect others. There are times when only very subjective ratings may be desired. Only skilled raters who are experts in the area should make such difficult ratings. There is some question whether even experts can carry on this type of rating with any sort of agreement.

4. It is probably best to have only one trait to a page. In practice this is rarely carried out, nor is the suggestion carried out that "desirable" and "undesirable" ends of the scale be alternated or randomized to prevent an individual's going down one side of the page marking all traits the same.

5. If possible, the use of extreme descriptive phrases or terms is to be avoided. When these are present, raters tend to mark nearer the middle and results are lacking in spread. The terms used at the end of the continuum should be of such a nature that they actually describe some individuals who are being rated.

6. The number of descriptive terms need not be the same for each scale. Sometimes fewer terms will function as well as many. These terms are merely guides to give an indication of what a mark at certain points on a scale means.

Use of the graphic rating scale

The use of these scales is usually rather easy, rapid, and straightforward. As with other observational techniques, any rater should have a period of training. In this training, major emphasis should be placed on the observation techniques used. Training two or more raters at once, having them carry on similar ratings, and then analyzing and comparing their results leads to more desirable ratings. The major problems that arise with the use of graphic rating scales are more or less common to all rating methods and are discussed below.

Errors in ratings

Usually in a discussion of rating methods several common sources of trouble are noted. Among these are:

1. *The "halo" effect.* Very briefly this is the tendency for a rater to rate an individual high on many or all traits merely because the rater considers the individual high on one trait. A student who is considered "good" by a teacher, that is, the student who causes a teacher little trouble, is apt to have spuriously higher ratings on other traits because of this attitude held by the teacher. A worker who plays poker with a foreman or supervisor may also be invalidly rated high on most traits for friendship reasons. The halo effect can, of course, work both ways. Another student for some personal reason annoys a teacher. Ratings of this student by the teacher would probably all be influenced in a negative fashion.

   Much has been written on how to avoid the halo effect. The usual recommendation is that individuals should be rated on only one trait at a time rather than one individual being rated on all traits at once. Other techniques such as paired-comparison and forced-choice techniques, which are discussed later, will reduce this type of error.

   Not all psychologists are in agreement that the halo effect is as important as some would have it. Johnson (1945) subjected a group of correlations obtained from a group of ratings to a factor analysis. In one of his studies the factor analysis of an industrial merit rating scale showed that almost all of the variability of the entire scale could be accounted for by one factor. The correlation among the traits is the result of this common factor rather than the halo effect.

2. *The error of central tendency* is the tendency for raters to avoid a rating at the ends of the continuum. Many judges dislike to make extreme judgments. This results in the persons being rated receiving evaluations near the middle. This can be reduced by avoiding extreme descriptive phrases at the ends of the continuum. Another possible method to reduce this error is to place the descriptive phrases at unequal intervals along the line. Those at the extremes can be closer together than those at the center.

3. *The error of leniency.* This is the tendency for raters to rate all individuals that they know above average or high on desirable or good traits. Guilford (1954) suggests that this type of error can be controlled by using only one unfavorable term and a series of favorable terms such as "fair," "good," "very good," or "excellent."

4. *Other types of errors.* Stockford and Bissell (1949) have discussed a *proximity* error by which they mean that the closer the position of two traits on a rating scale, the higher the intercorrelation between the traits. Murray (1938) proposed a *contrast* error by which he meant that raters tend to rate individuals in the opposite direction from the way in which they perceived themselves in reference to a trait. Thus a very precise or punctual individual would tend to rate others less precise or punctual. Raters low in a trait would tend to see others higher than themselves. Another type of error is referred to as the *logical* error. Certain groups of traits sometimes seem to be logically related in the minds of raters. Actually these traits are not related, but raters when rating individuals on

these traits produce results that are correlated. The effects of all of these different types of error may be reduced by the training of raters as indicated above or by the use of improved, specific rating methods.

Reliability of ratings

Since the 1920's the psychological and educational literature has contained many studies on the reliability of ratings. To review them in detail is of limited value. In general they may be summarized by saying that these earlier reliability coefficients tended to run between .40 and .60. Symonds (1931) concluded that the typical coefficient was .55. Most of this earlier research then proceeded to focus on how ratings could be improved by the training of raters and by increasing the number of raters. For it was shown that the reliability of ratings increased with the number of judges. This meant different judges, for usually two ratings by the same judge are no more reliable than one rating of this judge. Symonds in the reference cited stated that the pooled judgment of at least eight judges is needed to obtain high reliability. However, as Bradshaw (1930) showed, it is both the number of raters and the trait being rated that affects the size of the reliability coefficient. He used a rating scale issued by the American Council on Education in a study which produced the results shown in Table 3.1.

TABLE 3.1

NUMBER OF JUDGES NEEDED TO SECURE GIVEN RELIABILITY

Trait	.75	.80	.85	.90	.95
How does his manner and appearance affect others?	17	22	32	50	106
Does he need constant prodding or does he go ahead with his work without being told?	3	5	7	10	21
Does he get others to do what he wishes?	5	7	10	16	33
How does he control his emotions?	7	9	13	21	44
Has he a program with a definite purpose in terms of which he distributes his time and energy?	5	6	9	14	29

From F. F. Bradshaw, *The American Council on Education Rating Scale—Its Reliability, Validity and Use* (1930). Used by permission of the Columbia University Press and the American Psychological Association.

Bradshaw's study very specifically points out the fact that some traits are a lot easier to rate than others. Notice for trait 2 that only a small number of raters are necessary to produce pooled judgments of high reliability, whereas for trait 1 a large number of raters were needed to produce the same results.

At the present time, ratings are made with much higher reliability than in the past. It is not unusual to have ratings with reliabilities in the .80's and .90's. Such improvements have been brought about by the application of what has been learned on the use and construction of these scales and by the careful instruction of the observers who do the ratings.

Validity of ratings

Validity is studied by seeing how well the results obtained on one of these rating scales agree with some outside measure, referred to as a criterion. Validity is usually expressed in terms of correlation coefficients, in this case the correlation between the ratings and the criterion measures. The size of these validity coefficients tends to be between .40 and .60. All statements in Chapter 7 about validity coefficients apply to the use of rating scales. As in other types of observation, validity involves that of the observer, that of the individual being observed, and the activity being observed. All of these are involved in reported validities of rating scales.

OTHER TYPES OF RATINGS

Numerical rating scales are used to rate groups of individuals at the same time on a given trait. Usually at the top of a rating sheet different descriptive levels of the trait being rated are numbered on a scale of 1 to 5 or 1 to 7. Listed below this are the names of all of the individuals being rated with a series of numbers following each name. These numbers represent the levels at the top of the sheet. For a scale of seven levels, the rating sheet would be set up like this:

Edward	1	2	3	4	5	6	7
Jimmie	1	2	3	4	5	6	7
Paul	1	2	3	4	5	6	7
William	1	2	3	4	5	6	7

Then the rater considers each individual for the trait being rated and encircles the number that best describes the level for that individual.

Defined group scale

One modification of the graphic rating scale is the *defined group scales*. In this type of scale the raters are told what percentages of the sample should be expected to fall in each part of the scale. For example, a continuum may be divided into seven parts with a descriptive term for each part. Under each part is a percentage which gives the rater an idea of the approximate number of those being rated that should appear in each section when the rating is ended. With scales of this type the names of the ratees are listed under the trait and all are rated at the same time for a given trait.

Paired comparisons

The other major type of rating in current use is called the *method of paired comparisons*. The rater compares each individual separately with every other individual to see which of them has more or less of the trait than the other individuals. It is apparent that with a sample of any size, the number of ratings make completion of the rating scale a burden for the rater and the analysis of the results very laborious for the user of the scale. If there are 30 individuals being rated, the formula

$$\frac{N(N-1)}{2}$$

shows 435 judgments would have to be made. Even with small numbers there is a tremendous amount of work involved. McCormick and Bachus (1952) conducted an experiment in which 50 workers were to be rated. The 50 paired each with every other one would result in 1225 pairs. Patterns were developed for each person to be paired with 40, 35, 32, 25, 21, 17, 13, 9, and 7 members of the group. Performance rating indices were computed from these ratings and these indices were correlated with those obtained from the complete pairing. The correlation coefficients ranged from .994 to .858. From this it may be inferred that substantial reductions may be made in the number pairings without greatly affecting results. For example the correlation between 50 and 13 pairs per individual resulted in a coefficient of about .93.

In another study McCormick and Roberts (1952) again used the ratings of 50 employees by foremen for all possible pairs. Various patterns were developed reducing the number of pairings from 24 to 8. Reliability coefficients were computed and the following two findings reported:

1. The reliability of ratings obtained by partial pairings tends to decrease systematically with a reduction in the number of pairings.

2. For groups of 50, ratings based upon as few as 16 pairs per individual rater appear relatively stable (around .85). (Research since 1952 has made use of these findings and at present scales in actual use are so administered with good results.)

A rating technique closely related to the paired-comparison method is the *"forced-choice"* technique. One application of this type of rating most familiar to counselors is contained in the items of the *Kuder Preference Record, Vocational*. The items of this vocational interest inventory consist of groups of three or triads from which the individual selects the one liked most and the one liked least. These two choices must be expressed for each triad item, hence the "forcing." On some other inventories four items are presented and the subject selects the two that describe him most. There has been a considerable amount of discussion as to whether two, three, four, or more parts are best for each item. To date this has not been decided. Travers (1951) feels that forcing an individual to make a choice about the item which is most like him and that which is least like him puts the rater into an unrealistic position in which he has no logical reason for choice. Wittenborn (1956) criticized Edwards in his *Personal Preference Schedule* (1954) for using only two statements in each forced-choice item. Users of such inventories as the Kuder and the Edwards frequently notice that there is a resistance on the part of some individuals to complete items when they like none of the possible choices or none describes the individual. It is suggested that using three or more responses is the ideal way to handle forced-choice items and at the same time giving the rater instructions to select a statement that is most descriptive and one that is least descriptive of himself (Stewart, 1945). Jarrett and Sherriff (1956) reported that when subjects were permitted to leave items unanswered in forced-choice scales, many individuals actually do. They conclude that in the end substantially the same results are obtained as when clients are asked to answer all of the questions. This is open to question on several counts: 1, Leaving items unanswered may be a response set or personality trait in itself; 2, Leaving items unanswered may reduce reliability and validity; and 3, The effect of leaving items unanswered would vary with the affective nature of the items.

Users of forced-choice techniques claim that the various errors and biases discussed under graphic rating scales are controlled with this type of rating. In paper-and-pencil personality and interest inventories, which are actually self-rating blanks, it has been shown that the usual tendency is for the individual to make himself appear better than he actually is by selecting the items or marking the responses that are most socially acceptable. Frequently clients consciously or unconsciously distort the results by the response set operating when the inventory is completed. Edwards (1954) has attempted to control this by having all of the items on his inventory rated for social acceptability and by assembling pairs on the basis of equal social acceptability. Sisson (1948) noted that the use of these methods cut down on the ability of individuals to produce outcomes with either desired good or desired bad traits. In other words these methods are harder to fake. Linden (1958) attempted to demonstrate this by making two experimental forms of the *Guilford-Zimmerman Temperament Survey,* one made up of three-response and the other of two-response items. These, along with the regular form of the inventory, were administered under a real and "fake" situation to a group of university students over the course of a semester. While his conclusions were not clear-cut, he noted a trend that suggested that items in the forced-choice form, especially the three-response items, reduced the influence of bias and made it more difficult to distort than the conventional personality inventory.

Use of rating scales

It might be well to summarize here the uses that are made of rating scales. As just noted they are widely used in self-evaluations in both the areas of interests and of adjustment. This is one of the major uses in education. Another is the use of such scales as a criterion to validate other devices. In the past rating scales were widely used in education for ratings of adjustment of students to be made by teachers. This use has to a great extent disappeared except where instruction in making ratings has been developed. Much of this has been replaced by more precise objective methods.

Counselors and teachers frequently use rating scales in filling out application blanks used by universities, business, and industry. Often these blanks conclude with a short scale which summarizes the applicant as a student or as a possible employee. Many of the reports to parents used in schools also have scales built into them. These reports cover a student's growth in getting along with others, leadership, and other personality variables or traits typically evaluated by teachers by the means of simple rating scales. In industry and the Armed Services rating scales are extensively used in the rating of personnel by supervisors. Some corporations have all of their employees rated semi-annually or at least once a year. The results of these ratings are used for promotion.

Other rating scales besides personality inventories are useful for self-evaluation activities. When an individual uses one upon himself he is forced to analyze himself. A certain amount of thought is apt to occur and then it may follow that there is a redirection of efforts. Even when the individual does not fill out the scale, but is rated by others, much is to be gained by going over the ratings with the ratee. If this is done in a sound fashion and the ratee can accept the objectives of the ratings, this technique frequently encourages an individual to move toward more socially desirable or more effective behavior. A knowledge that there are to be periodic ratings is also desirable in keeping a work group at a higher performance or behavioral level.

Sometimes ratings are combined with brief anecdotes describing the behavior that has been rated. Such a method combines the two types of observation and highlights the need for factual anecdotal records as a basic tool in evaluation and in counseling.

ANECDOTAL RECORDS

Another device that implements the observational process is the anecdotal record. Beginning about 1940, teachers and counselors began to give serious attention to the use of the anecdote as a psychological technique (Jarvie and Ellingston, 1940) for appraising behavior. Since then much has been written discussing the best ways to use anecdotes and their limitations.

In its simplest form an anecdote is a record of some incident of significant behavior. Anecdotes are written by anyone who has contact with the individual. The anecdote may be considered as a verbal photograph of behavior. Usually the behavior is recorded on a form provided by the agency. A typical beginning for such a form is a factual statement of exactly what was said or done. Space at the bottom or on the back is usually provided for the observer's interpretation of the behavior. Anecdotes should contain pertinent background information.

Hamalainen (1943) noted that the purpose of anecdotes was:

1. To furnish the evidence needed for good cumulative records.

2. To substitute specific evidence for vague generalizations about human behavior.

3. To stimulate teachers to look for information that is useful in helping students achieve acceptable adjustments.

4. To contribute toward an understanding of an individual's basic personality.

Before a system of anecdotal records is instituted, a series of staff meetings should be held to discuss the purpose and use of these anecdotes. Understanding and acceptance by the staff is essential before such a system can be undertaken. When this hurdle is overcome, there should be sessions devoted to instruction in the actual writing of anecdotes. Writing anecdotes is not as easy as it sounds. Many staff members are prone to interpret a client's behavior in the light of their own attitudes and values. Actually then many anecdotes are more than records of behavior, because they tend to include a mixture of factual information, interpretation, evaluation, and condemnation. In the training session attention must be directed toward reports of significant behavior which are factual only. Instruction in writing anecdotes should emphasize that positive incidents are as important as negative ones. Frequently a system of anecdotes becomes nothing but a record of all the undesirable or antisocial behavior of individuals. Some agencies have gotten around this by insisting that for every negative anecdote written, a positive one must also be written. Sometimes, two different colors of paper are used for each of the two types of anecdotes.

Whenever a group discusses anecdotes, the question is always raised about how many anecdotes should be written and how often. There have been cases in which it was stated that each observer would write at least one anecdote per individual per week. This is probably not the best way to handle the writing of anecdotes. If the idea can be conveyed that when the observer sees significant behavior it should be recorded, then there is no major problem. Of course, there may be cases in which no apparent significant behavior is observed and no anecdotes written. In this case, the lack of significant incidents is important and should be noted in the records.

After the instructions in writing anecdotes have been handled, there arises an even larger issue about how the anecdotes themselves are to be handled. Unless something is done to treat the recording of anecdotes in a systematic fashion, the system will be mired under the weight of its own paper and paperwork. There are times when a teacher keeps anecdotes for personal use in evaluating students at periodic grade reporting. This use of anecdotes will not be discussed. Interest here centers on how anecdotes are used in an entire agency and how the results are made available and useful to the counselor.

There seems to be no question but that these anecdotes have to be forwarded to a central point. It is logical that this be the counselor's office. Many proposals have been made for the recording and summarizing of anecdotal data. To the writers it seems that one of the best methods is to draw up a summary record sheet on which are various traits, behavior patterns, or agency objectives. After each of these there are three spaces labeled "weak," "average," and "strong." As the anecdotes arrive at the office, each one is evaluated. It may be noted that any one anecdote may contribute evidence about one or more of these traits or objectives. Then the anecdote is further evaluated as to whether this evidence can be classified as "weak," "average," and "strong" as far as the trait under consideration is concerned. If this is the first anecdote for this individual, then a *1* is placed in the appropriate cell. Each anecdote is classified on a summary sheet for a given individual as it is received. A continuous behavioral record is set up in this way. Growth, or regression, over a period of time is made easily apparent by this summary sheet for a given client.

There frequently arises a problem of how long anecdotes should be retained. There is often concern about this, especially when the material in the anecdote is deemed to be confidential by the writer. As indicated in the previous chapter, confidential material should be kept in a private office. It is felt that material gathered from anecdotes which is not confidential should be made a part of the permanent record. Perhaps, at the end of a year, these summary sheets on which evaluations of the anecdotes have been made can be condensed into a brief verbal account of the individual's behavior over the year and this short summary entered into the cumulative record. It is felt that no attempt should be made to retain the complete anecdotes. After the initial evaluation of the anecdote has been made, all that remains is a note that the anecdote was evidence of the development or lack of development of a particular client trait.

Evaluation of anecdotal records

Anecdotes offer continuous evidence of growth and behavior. Instead of using a cross-sectional approach as is done with many personality inventories and projective techniques, use of anecdotes provides another longitudinal approach to the study of personality and adjustment. This is the more desirable type of information. Anecdotes include information from many sources. Not only does it provide information about classroom behavior, but also information from the playground, cafeteria, club, gymnasium, and all other facets of school life. Not only does the information come from many sources in the school or other agency, but it is gathered by varied personnel who have had opportunity to observe a given client. In terms of cost, anecdotal records are cheap when compared with other devices used in collecting information about behavior. Finally it seems that the evidence obtained by the use of anecdotes is highly valid evidence, provided the gatherers of such information have been trained and that this training was effective. One of the major problems in obtaining evidence on behavior is that of obtaining valid evidence. Since these anecdotes are records of what actually happened or did not happen, the validity of the anecdotes is contained in them. It should be noted here that the so-called "critical incident" technique being tried out in current research in industrial settings is a use of anecdote under another name.

On the negative side, there is no question that the writing of anecdotes is time consuming. Many agency personnel feel that they are overworked as it is. With increasing case loads there is no indication that the job of the personnel worker will become any lighter in the days ahead. There is the possibility that the writing of anecdotes might be substituted for some less worthwhile activity that such a worker has to carry on. Perhaps if these colleagues are really aware of the values that come from anecdotes, they might be more willing to produce and to use anecdotes. Perhaps the major obstacle in the use of anecdotes is that they require much staff time in recording and summarizing. This is certainly a valid argument. It is doubtful that ordinary clerical help is of much use here. To the writers it seems that the evaluation and summarizing of these anecdotes is the task for a trained worker, the counselor. Perhaps in the future, counselors will have less to do with administrative and clerical activities not directly related to counseling and will have more time to devote to their major work. Then certainly the daily batch of anecdotes could be readily disposed of in a brief part of each work day. Smaller case loads for counselors would also be useful in making it possible to set up a functioning system of anecdotal records.

OBSERVATION IN PSYCHOMETRY

The place in counseling where observation is very important and is most frequently conducted in a disorganized fashion is in the administration of tests. Psychometrics are often carried on by persons with limited training who do not realize the value of descriptions of client behavior during the testing situation. Such a person is often unaware that the test score may be more representative of affect than of any cognitive factor. If it is a test designed to measure cognitive factors, the entire interpretation of the counselor may be distorted by failure to describe adequately the circumstances under which the test was administered and the condition of the client while taking the test. For these reasons it is essential that psychometrists be trained as observers as well as in the mechanics of test administration.

The person in charge of such training should begin by pointing out how the agency intends to use its tests and the necessity of strict adherence to the instructions for the test given in the manual. It should be explained that unless the test is administered in as nearly the same way as possible each time, the results of testing may require a different interpretation each time and standardized, comparable results are impossible. In like fashion the person learning to administer tests must be shown that the counselor's interpretation of scores is based on how the client felt and responded while taking the test. If a description of client comments and behavior during testing accompanies a test score, the interpretation is much clearer to the counselor and can be explained to the client.

A simple observation, such as the time required to complete the *Ohio State Psychological Examination,* may be quite important for counseling inferences. Although the test is untimed, most individuals require from one and one-half to two hours to complete it. The counselor usually assigns a test of this nature when there is some question about the ability of the client to perform under speeded or timed testing conditions. Thus it is important for the counselor to know whether a client took one hour or three hours, if a really meaningful interpretation is to be made. For this reason psychometric observations should begin with an exact record of the day the client took the test, the time the test was started and when it was completed. Even if this information is not furnished completely in records given to the counselor, it is then available for reference in the agency files.

Irregularities during testing

Aside from these more mechanical observations which are an important part of ordinary testing, occasional irregularities in psychometric procedure need to be recorded so that the counselor can account for them in the test interpretation discussed with the client. A simple example of this would be a record of the number of items left unanswered in each scale of the *Guilford-Zimmerman Temperament Survey*. If more than three items of the thirty in each scale are left unanswered, it is difficult to tell what such a score means. However, if the counselor knows the number left unanswered, a tentative interpretation can be made. Assuming the raw score on the Sociability scale is 14 and that five items were left unanswered, the counselor can point out that the client's raw score is somewhere between 14 and 19 (a C-score of 3–5). This inference is possible because these items can only add to the raw score of 14 to the extent that they are scoring items; they are never subtracted to get a lower score. Since the profile of this test ranges from negative attributes attached to low scores toward positive attributes signified by high scores, information about omitted items can be quite important in interpreting the score. Other examples of irregularities during testing would be administering a test battery in the wrong sequence, using the wrong time limits for a test, giving erroneous instructions prior to the test, and sudden illness of a client during a test.

Other factors affecting interpretation

In the light of their effect upon test interpretation the counselor should also have observations showing remarks of the client, client attitude, and indications of tension during testing. The physical condition of a client during testing can also be quite significant.

Value of client remarks

Client remarks frequently indicate the approach the client made to testing and in this sense should become a part of the observations accompanying the test score or profile. If client remarks indicate a facetious approach to testing by joking with companions or ridiculing the tests, this may be a reflection of tension or a lack of interest in the testing program. Either of these attitudes would affect the counselor's interpretation of the results. Remarks showing a tendency to hurry through tests may be indicative of results which are an underestimate of client potential. Client remarks during testing can also give the counselor a different view of the reasons a client has come for counseling. Because the counselor is more skilled than the psychometrist at establishing rapport, the client may relax and be much less anxious in the interview than during testing. In these ways a psychometrist's record of client remarks during testing may become highly valuable to the counselor in achieving a fuller understanding of client behavior contained in a series of test scores.

While it may seem simple to record client remarks in a factual way which will recreate the meaning for the counselor, anyone who has attempted to reconstruct a counseling interview from verbatim typescript or tape recordings realizes how inadequate an actual record of remarks can be. The verbatim typescript does not show voice inflection and subtle meanings created by voice tone or emphasis. The tape recording adds these to the counseling record, but still does not contain the meaning added by bodily posture and gestures. Only a sound film of the interview can recreate the scene in enough detail so that full meaning can be inferred.

For these reasons the psychometrist needs to give sufficient description of the circumstances in which client remarks occur that the meaning of the remarks is clear to the counselor reading such a record. This means that the psychometrist should be an individual who can describe objectively not only the actual statements of a client and the setting, but who can describe the mood and more obvious feelings of the client at the time. Was the remark a gripe about the test or an attempt to be humorous with the psychometrist? Not only is this ability to infer mood or feeling important to the written observation, but it dictates the proper response by the psychometrist in order to maintain rapport with the client.

Such training in making observations about how a client seems to feel ultimately permits clearer records of client physical and psychological condition.

The fact that a client took a test while obviously distressed by a cold or some other physical deterrent may cause the counselor to check such data against more criteria and possibly arrange a retest if all data are not congruent. To know that a client was highly irritated by the items on a structured personality inventory may add immeasurably to the counselor's understanding of test scores and lead to a much less threatening discussion of results with the client. To know that a client is quite disturbed by failure to finish tests or by what seems to be poor test performance to the client will lead the counselor to a deeper insight into reasons the client is coming for help and to a better way of giving such help to the client. Evidence of other anxieties or tensions in the client during testing indicates other limits the counselor needs to place on test interpretation and interview activities with the client.

These are some of the ways psychometric observations can really enhance the counselor's interpretation of client behavior shown by test scores and perform a real service for the client.

Lack of agreement among test results

Another kind of observation which the psychometrist should learn to carry on is that of noting the extent of agreement among test scores which research and counseling experience have shown to be related. An example of this would be a standard score of 50 for a given individual on the *Dentist Scale*, 45 on the *Osteopath Scale* and 5 on the *Physician Scale* of the *Strong Vocational Interest Blank for Men*. Both statistical research and counseling experience have shown that these three scores tend to be high or low together. When the psychometrist notes that the *Physician Scale* is not in agreement with the other two, steps should be taken to check this observation. The obvious first step is to rescore the three scales to see that they have been properly scored. (This assumes that the initial scoring included a preliminary scanning of the answer sheet to see that the items were marked properly by the client.) In most cases such procedure will show an error in scoring. Occasionally the lack of agreement has explanation only in the unique behavior of a given client. Persons training psychometrists in observation should be aware of common checks for agreement among test results and point them out to the persons being trained. Through efficient observations of this nature much valuable counselor time can be saved.

OBSERVATION IN THE INTERVIEW

While counselor observation in the interview is continuous in effective counseling, it is of primary importance in the initial interview. When added to information from records, it is fundamental to the counselor's analysis and tentative hypotheses about the client. Initial impressions of both client and counselor can set the structure of future interviews and this first meeting often determines success or failure. The counselor needs to demonstrate to the client an ability to observe client behavior and integrate it into a coherent series of reflections and summaries which show that two-way communication is taking place. In this way client confidence and respect are established and the client learns through participating in the interviews in a more meaningful way.

Starting with such obvious factors as client appearance and dress, the counselor notes and records vocabulary level and grammar; alertness of client reaction to counselor statements; evidence of social sensitivity; ability to evaluate self in societal terms; balance of internal and external frames of reference; nervous mannerisms and degree of tension; flexibility versus rigidity of the client; obvious omissions or gaps in client topics during the interview; and inferences about client goals and values. The counselor is trying to determine congruence of client statements with the observed behavior of the client. This level of awareness of self and environment shown by the client will be a vital factor in the selection of the tools and techniques the counselor chooses to help the client. The question to be answered by these observations is, "How do the data already available coincide with what this client says about self?"

Client appearance

There are two reasons why observation of client dress and appearance is important to the counselor. Client dress can show awareness and concern of the client for reactions of others. It can also indicate how the client feels about self. In the first instance client dress is showing the amount of conformity the client is willing to express toward dress requirements and the importance the client places on the opinion of others. For example, suppose in a given school girls wear only white ankle socks and boys wear no ties and only black or white shoes. The girl who wears colored ankle socks and the boy who wears ties or brown shoes is differing enough from the group so that the counselor needs to know why. Is it because the client is unaware of these codes of behavior? Are parents the cause of this difference? Is the client's difference in dress an expression of hostility toward the group? These are some of the questions prompted by such a difference and the counselor needs to seek an answer to them.

The client's general appearance may also be indicative of the mood of the client toward self. A client sloppily dressed is frequently expressing actual inferiority feelings about self. Lack of concern about external appearance may be reflecting inner turmoil with which the client needs help. In many instances the counselor can secure cues to the success of counseling by observing progressive change in the client's dress or appearance. The counselor begins in the initial interview to establish a client norm for these external evidences of behavior and develops through succeeding interviews a picture of how the client conforms to the group, how the client differs in dress and the meaning this has in the global picture of client behavior.

Client vocabulary

The next aspect of client behavior which evidences itself in the interview is the way the client communicates with the counselor. How extensive is the client's vocabulary and what level of general intelligence does it indicate? What does client grammar indicate about family socio-economic level? How does client vocabulary indicate direction and extent of interests? What does vocabulary show about the nature and amount of client reading? The counselor who wishes to use client vocabulary as an indicator in making inferences about these questions would do well to be familiar with one or more of the common lists of word difficulty, such as that found in the *Thorndike-Century Junior Dictionary*. In such a list the number at the end of the definition indicates difficulty of the word. Usually, the lower the number, the easier the word.

A counselor gradually develops ability to evaluate vocabulary and make inferences about the academic ability of clients from such evidence. This may agree with other evidence from records and biographical data, or it may indicate need for individual testing as a further attempt to clarify the evaluation. The client's grammar may be a good indication of socio-economic status and give the counselor cues about family background which need to be investigated during the interview. If the counselor keeps in mind the general areas of vocabulary measured by a test like the *Michigan Vocabulary Test* and classifies client vocabulary into these areas, it is possible to develop a tentative pattern of client interests. Then it will be possible to get more detailed information about the way in which the client acquired such a vocabulary. Was it through reading, through audio-visual activities, or through actual participation in this type of activity? What does the client read and how extensive are reading activities? In present United States culture so many vocabulary building activities are of an audio-visual nature that spoken vocabulary is not necessarily a measure of reading or writing skills. The counselor needs to clarify this because a client with a reading or English handicap may function well in an interview, but not in a classroom situation. The same client may be much more alert in the interview where there is no struggle to understand the written word or to spell a word needed to express precise meaning. This alertness of the client may give completely different data from those secured through classroom information or standardized tests. A client who likes people but who does not like school is apt to be much more alert in an interview than in a classroom. Conversely the emotionally disturbed client may present a poorer picture in the interview than in the classroom, because this is a divergence from ordinary behavior requiring a greater effort to produce integrated behavior.

Client social skills

The initial interview presents the counselor with an opportunity to observe the social sensitivity of the client. Is the client poised and comfortable with the counselor, or ill at east and unsure of how to behave? Does the client make an effort to help the counselor develop a warm, friendly atmosphere, or must the counselor carry all this responsibility? Evidence that the client is aware of the counselor's feelings and of the physical comfort of the counselor can be an indicator that the client is able to relate well to people. Real social sensitivity is directly related to a client's ability to evaluate himself in societal terms and evidence of a client's balance of internal and external frames of reference.

The client whose conversation and thoughts center on the self to the exclusion of others is demonstrating too much concern about personal activities for good mental health. Good mental health usually requires a balance of interests and activities which involve others as well as self. The client who is preoccupied with self in the interview may be aware of societal values but frequently unable to apply them in self-evaluation. This is usually because there is too much threat to the self in facing these issues and not because of fear of the counselor's reaction. As the counselor helps the client understand the behavior in question, the client is able to reduce concern about self and develop more interest in relationships with others. This process eventually produces greater client awareness of the activities that must be carried on in effective social relationships and starts the client toward learning and practicing these skills. Before such a process can be initiated the counselor must observe the present status of the client and decide what steps to undertake to help the client make any changes indicated *and desired.* By evaluating client behavior toward the counselor in the initial interview and later in other relationships with the agency staff, the counselor is able to form tentative hypotheses about client social sensitivity and ability to relate to others.

Client tension

This process of evaluating client social skills leads to a related facet of client behavior. This is the first opportunity the counselor has to observe nervous mannerisms and the ways a given client indicates and responds to tension. The female client who becomes preoccupied with a topic and begins to twist her hair around her finger, or chew on her glasses or her pencil may be reflecting other behavioral needs than those she is describing to the counselor. In like fashion the male client who clenches the arm of the chair, or who perspires considerably, may be indicating tensions he is trying to conceal or control. The counselor needs to know how each client responds to tension in order to do an effective job of helping that client understand himself. The counselor also needs to have some concept of the reasons why a client is responding in this fashion. This means the counselor must be able to distinguish between less important client mannerisms like autistic gestures and the more important evidences the client displays of being under tension. Then the counselor is in a position to act to reduce this tension or to assume that the client is capable of handling it without counselor help. The writers see one of the chief functions of the counselor as controlling the amount of threat and tension in the interview. By doing this the counselor controls the climate or atmosphere in which the client functions and produces optimal learning conditions for the client. Only through observation directed toward this end can the counselor begin to form estimates of client behavior which indicate the degree of tension present at any given moment.

Interview topics

Usually the degree of tension is directly related to the topics the client is discussing at that time, although pauses in the interview for client thought may also be fraught with considerable tension and the omission of topics may show an area capable of arousing anxiety within the client.

Thus the counselor needs to note the relationship between the various topics discussed with the client and the amount of threat these topics present to a client. If a client is able to talk about relationships with every member of the family except one, this may be a cue that such an omission reflects a topic the client is afraid to consider. It could also indicate that the family member omitted is of little importance to the client, but this is less likely.

These topics covered in the interview also reflect client goals and values. The client who constantly refers to jobs, income and the things that could be done with money is presenting different goals and values than the client who is engrossed with interest in scientific activities such as experiments in a home chemical laboratory or in collecting and classifying beetles. The client who shows an avid interest in mechanical activities such as building and flying model planes or reconditioning old cars is evidencing goals and values in considerable contrast to the client who is engrossed with an interest in people and in helping them through activities of a social service nature. These interests are reflecting behavorial tendencies as well as probable educational and vocational choices. The counselor should investigate them to see that they are fundamental to the client's personality and not temporary goals and values foisted upon the client by excessive persuasion of others. No matter what the topics discussed in the initial interview, they reveal something about the personality of the client. The counselor by observation and classification can collect data of value for diagnosis and counseling further with the client.

A comprehensive observation of the extent and nature of topics covered in such an interview can also contribute to a tentative hypothesis about the flexibility or rigidity of the client. If the client is rigid, this limits the approach of the counselor and the tools and techniques which can be used to help the client. If the client is more flexible as indicated by the topics which can be accepted and discussed in the interview, the counselor has a less difficult problem of controlling threat. It is easier to create an interview climate in which the client is freed to make positive changes in behavior, whether these changes are clarification of educational-vocational choices or changes in attitudes and values.

These are some of the ways in which observations in the initial interview can contribute to more successful choice of ways by which the counselor can help the client deal with problems. They begin with an estimate of client readiness for counseling and progress to a counselor evaluation of the congruence between the content and the meaning included in client statements, and how this agrees with other data. These observations carried on in systematic fashion with the understanding and cooperation of the client can lead to a diagnosis which provides more effective procedures by the counselor and lead to more effective modification of behavior by the client. The more time the counselor spends in observation in the initial interview, the more time the client has to contribute information of value to the counseling process, because understanding of client behavior by the counselor usually develops more from client talk than from counselor comments. This is a chief purpose of the initial interview.

SUMMARY

The observations used by the counselor, whether made personally or secured from others, are only useful to the extent that they are based on factual information. The observer must be capable of making realistic, factual observations, and be trained in proper observational procedures. To be valid, observations must center on determining specifically what is to be observed and the methods by which this is to be accomplished. The observations of greatest value to counseling are those secured through use of rating scales and anecdotes, and those recorded during psychometrics and the initial interview. The counselor needs to convey to observers the kind of information needed about client behavior and the way in which this information will be used.

REFERENCES

Bradshaw, F. F. The American Council on Education rating scale: Its reliability, validity, and use. *Archives of Psychol.*, 1930, *18*, 1–80.

Edwards, A. L. *Personal Preference Schedule manual.* New York: The Psychological Corporation, 1954.

Guilford, J. P. *Psychometric methods.* New York: The McGraw-Hill Book Company, Inc., 1954.

Hamalainen, A. F. *An appraisal of anecdotal records.* New York: Bureau of Publications, Teachers College, Columbia University, 1943.

Jarrett, R. F., and A. C. Sherriff. Forced-choice versus permissive techniques in obtaining responses to attitude questionnaires. *J. Gen. Psychol.*, 1956, *55*, 203–206.

Jarvie, L. L., and M. Ellingston. *A handbook of the anecdotal behavior journal.* Chicago: University of Chicago Press, 1940.

Johnson, D. M. A systematic treatment of judgment. *Psychol. Bull.*, 1945, *45*, 193–224.

Kuder, G. F. *The Kuder Preference Record manual.* Chicago: Science Research Associates, 1949.

Linden, J. D. *The development and comparative analysis of two forced-choice forms of the Guilford-Zimmerman Temperament Survey.* Unpublished Ph.D. Dissertation, Purdue University, 1958.

McCormick, E. J., and J. A. Bachus. Paired comparison ratings, I: The effects of ratings on reduction in the number of pairs. *J. Appl. Psychol.*, 1952, *36*, 123–127.

McCormick, E. J., and W. K. Roberts.   Paired comparison ratings, II: The reliability of ratings based upon partial pairing.   J. Appl. Psychol., 1952, 36, 188–192.

Murray, H. A.   Explorations in personality.   New York: Oxford University Press, 1938.

Sisson, E. D.   Forced-choice—the new army rating.   Personnel Psychol., 1948, 1, 365–381.

Stewart, Naomi.   Methodological investigation of the forced-choice technique, utilizing the Officer Description and the Officer Evaluation Blanks.   AGO, PRS Report no. 701, July 6, 1945.

Stockford, L., and H. W. Bissell.   Factors involved in establishing a merit-rating scale.   Personnel, 1949, 26, 94–118.

Symonds, P. M.   Diagnosing personality and conduct.   New York: D. Appleton-Century, 1931.

Travers, R. W. M.   A critical review of the validity and the rationale of forced-technique.   Psychol. Bull., 1951, 48, 62–70.

Wittenborn, J. R.   A review of the Edwards Personal Preference Schedule.   J. Consult. Psychol., 1956, 20, 321–324.

4

The initial interview

THE INITIAL INTERVIEW HAS AT LEAST FOUR PRIMARY PURPOSES. ONE OF these is to establish a good working relationship between the counselor and the client which will last throughout counseling. Another is to validate and expand the data about the client collected prior to the interview. Still a third is to observe the client directly and to collect information which will show client feelings about values, interests, attitudes, and goals. In addition this first interview is used to establish the structure within which counseling will take place.

Counselor and client interaction is a function of movement toward the answers to two simple, basic questions each must answer. These questions which determine the personal and counseling frame of reference of client and counselor, are:

1. Who am I?
2. What am I doing?

For the counselor the answers to these questions determine the personal and professional values which cause his choice of counseling orientation and influence his counseling proficiency. These in turn affect client activity and the process of counseling.

The counseling process is dependent on consistent awareness, organization, and control of these counselor values if the client is to be helped to become more aware of the conflicts or uncertainties in client values which created the need for counseling, and to carry on the reorganization of these values. That is the primary purpose of counseling. Thus awareness of values on the part of both counselor and client is a major factor in readiness for counseling. It involves a recognition of such values and the desire to control or to change them.

COUNSELOR VALUES

Both Fiedler (1950) and Strupp (1955) have discussed the effect of experience upon the therapist, indicating that experience reduces differences among therapeutic orientations. Strupp further emphasizes the effect of therapist personality upon the therapeutic process. Both writers indicate that the effect of therapist personality is more variable with neophytes than with experienced therapists.

The question must be asked, however, as to the importance the counseling psychologist can attach to research data derived in a therapeutic setting; many of his clients are not concerned with the extensive personality changes inherent in the therapeutic situation. "Who am I?" to these clients means, "How am I different from other people in ways which will affect the life choices I must make?" This does not usually involve deep therapy, but rather clarification, synthesis, and different emphasis of known data.

Hence what Rogers (1957) has termed the "congruence" of the counselor may be of infinitely greater importance in its effect upon the client whose attention is less concerned with the internal activities of self and directed more toward external factors in the environment. Bandura (1956) has found a significant negative relationship between anxiety level of the therapist and therapeutic competence. How much more important then are counselor understanding and acceptance of self in a *counseling* psychology setting!

Thus emphasis upon the personal experiences of the counselor and the values these experiences have developed within the counselor center about the interaction of the counselor with environment. Every reaction the counselor has ever had to family, school, church, and community has produced unique effects that determine the personal values with which a counselor enters the interview. The depth of the counselor's insight into, *and acceptance of,* these reactions, and their subsequent effect upon personal values, in turn determines the control that can be exercised during interactions with a given client. The vividness of a counselor's feelings about individuals with certain patterns of behavior, or certain ethnic, religious, or racial characteristics can influence his interaction with them. The values the counselor attaches to religion or race and the objectivity with which the counselor can view the values limit the acceptance of differing values in the client. The control the counselor exercises over them is a part of the climate in which the client works during counseling.

These counselor personal values not only limit the relationship with a client in counseling, but also determine the kind and amount of formal education (learning) the counselor brings to professional practice. If the counselor's frame of reference is in the authoritarian direction, a Rogerian orientation will not only be somewhat objectionable, but usually professionally impossible to understand or achieve. Hence the controversies of a decade ago. If the counselor's personality produces the choice of working toward being a Rogerian, the use of eclectic counseling tools and techniques becomes difficult and sometimes impossible. It should be noted that Strupp (1955) found this more true of neophytes than of experienced Rogerians. The degree to which the counselor has been able to clarify, organize, and control these personal values in himself influences the effectiveness of innate potential for learning and therefore how much is learned about counseling, as well as what is learned.

Consistency in exercise of these counselor personal and professional values with clients whose behavior is within the normal range may be a more important factor than the nature of the values. Butler (1956) in a study of democratic and authoritarian college social fraternities found that consistency of orientation had more effect on success or failure of the fraternity and its members than whether it was of a democratic or authoritarian nature. Observation in classrooms and counseling settings also supports such an hypothesis. A given client learns in a variety of settings, but usually in the direction and to the degree that he determines. The counselor seems to function more in the nature of supplying a climate that promotes or retards this learning rather than a climate that creates or controls it.

Success in an initial interview therefore may be determined less by the specific nature of these personal and professional values than by the manner in which a counselor is able to control and use them in a systematic fashion. The counselor's personal needs and values and professional frame of reference developed during the theoretical and applied phases of counselor education must be consistent to reduce bias effect in the interview. The way these are blended into the personality of the counselor determines the approach the counselor will use in establishing a working relationship with the client and will also determine many of the things which do or do not occur during an interview.

CREATING A COUNSELING RELATIONSHIP

The first move in an initial interview, after the client has been greeted and made physically comfortable, is to ascertain what the client may have had in mind by undertaking counseling. During this discussion a brief general description by the counselor of the possibilities available through counseling will serve to make the client more aware of these. This attempt by the counselor to make a client comfortable and somewhat relaxed is the first step in the process of developing a good counseling relationship.

The counseling relationship

The most important element in counseling is the relationship established between the counselor and the client. Sometimes it seems that this relationship alone, without any of the other tools and techniques at the counselor's disposal, can account for much of the change that takes place in the client. Creating this relationship is a complex matter difficult to define. It is a professional relationship different from that which exists between friends or relatives. It is based on the client's understanding that the counselor is a relatively unbiased person with professional preparation and experience fitting the counselor to help with the client's problems. On the counselor's part it is based on a sincere desire to help by accepting the client as a person worthy of respect and as a person who possesses unused capacities for change, if the counselor can create a climate where this change can begin. Thus the relationship in the initial interview starts with the counselor and client adjusting to one another.

Usually the client comes to the interview with little concept of what actually will occur. The client wants to know how the counselor will try to help, but may be quite reluctant to relax and discuss the circumstances which have culminated in this meeting with the counselor. The counselor is trying to put the client at ease, so that discussion and learning can take place. The counselor wants to learn in what ways it may be possible to help the client. The client wants to learn how the counselor can help and what this help will involve. Each needs to learn enough about the behavior of the other so that these questions can be answered and the behavior of each will be modified by the goals set by both client and counselor.

The counselor may approach this by observing ordinary courtesies. After introductions the counselor invites the client to have a seat in the office. Then the counselor may talk about common interests noted in the information collected prior to the initial interview which do not appear to have a strong negative emotional value to the client. Usually some light remark or humorous comment begins this conversational part of the interview. The counselor's general rule in phrasing comments or in asking questions is ordinarily, "How would I like someone to say this to me?" or "How would I feel if someone said this to me in this way?" This is a good method of judging the amount of threat involved in comments and questions.

After the client has been made reasonably comfortable physically and psychologically, the counselor begins the process of creating a climate of confidence and trust. Whether or not the term "rapport" is used to describe this, or whether this goal is stated as providing a "warm, permissive atmosphere," the relationship must be based on *mutual* respect and willing cooperation. This involves two moves on the part of the counselor. The first is a statement about the persons who will have access to the information discussed in the interview. This can have considerable effect on the topics discussed in the interview. The second is a brief description of counseling facilities available to the client and the mechanics of the process that will be carried out during counseling.

While this process is going on, the counselor is also conveying to the client by everything that is said and done that the client is being accepted as a person worthy of respect and help. The counselor must therefore be able to like most people well enough to carry out the functions required in interviews. If the counselor cannot feel this way about a client, the client should be transferred to another counselor immediately, for these feelings about the client will pervade the interview and obstruct the development of the counseling relationship. Whether it is at a high level of awareness or not, the client will sense dislike and fail to react positively in the interview. For this reason the counselor needs to identify in the initial interview those clients with whom it is not possible to work. It is often possible to reduce those negative feelings if the counselor can recognize that the client acts in a given way only to maintain his present self-concept. It is the unusual client who deliberately acts at variance with society. The acts of the client are carried out because they are the best possible choice he can perceive at that moment. If they are unsuitable, the counselor must help the client perceive this and through an understanding of the conflicting values which cause them want to make a change to behavior more in harmony with society and with a changed self-concept, for this is the focus of the counseling process. As Hahn and MacLean (1955) have pointed out, it is the job of the counselor to open new doors with the client so that alternative solutions to problems are evolved. However, the counselor should never try to push the client through these doors.

To do this the counselor must help the client grow in capacity to solve problems. The experienced counselor will readily admit that most clients are better able to solve these problems than would be expected. Such a client may not be highly aware of these things, but actually knows more about his own personal attitude toward environment and reaction to environment than the counselor can hope to know after a number of interviews. The acceptance by the counselor of the client's capacity to solve these problems in a fashion most suitable to the client is the essence of a sound counseling relationship. It makes possible the sharing of responsibility by the client and the counselor in these interviews.

Counselor responsibility

The major responsibility of the counselor in the initial interview is thus to prevent a situation where the client is so threatened that it is not possible to function well. At the same time some threat must be present, or the client will fail to progress. This control of threat and anxiety by the counselor presupposes training and experience of such a nature that the counselor can estimate closely the amount of threat a client can handle and increase or decrease it by the techniques used in the interview. Rogers (1951) has pointed out that mere recognition of feeling can frequently make those feelings easier to bear and to discuss. Often if a counselor says to a client, "You find it pretty difficult to talk about this," this simple indication of awareness of client anxiety operates to reduce such anxiety. Acceptance of client and of client statements by the counselor in a matter-of-fact way can reduce the amount of threat the client is under. The choice of words used in phrasing counselor statements and reflecting client meanings can have considerable effect on the increase or decrease of threat. To say to a client, "You are very determined," is much different in the amount and kind of feeling it produces than to say, "You are pretty stubborn about this." The term "resolute" is a synonym for both, yet "determined" and "stubborn" have positive and negative meaning, respectively, to most clients. This choice of words is especially important in the initial interview because it helps set the tone of the relationship between client and counselor which usually pervades succeeding interviews.

A simple thing like the counselor's looking interested in what the client is saying improves client participation in the interview. If the counselor nods or tries in some other way to show understanding of what the client is trying to say, this seems to make it possible for most clients to relax and talk more freely. Conversely, if the counselor looks around the office, out the window, or stares at the bridge of the client's nose, the client may think the counselor uninterested, and begin to tense and have difficulty in talking. For this reason the counselor needs to show in every way possible that the data the client is presenting are the primary center of attention. This in turn focuses client attention on the material being discussed. As Tyler (1956) has pointed out, these same techniques of acceptance also help to prevent reinforcement of negative feelings the client may be expressing. Because they convey to a client only that the counselor understands what is said, they permit the expression of client feelings without signifying counselor approval.

In the initial interview the phrasing of questions is of utmost importance. Usually the counselor wants the client to talk and expand on data already available. To do this the questions the counselor asks must be precise and properly worded. One kind of phrasing will produce a "yes" or "no" answer, and another kind causes the client to talk at considerable length. The counselor must decide which is desirable and phrase questions to produce this effect. For example, the counselor may wish to ask why the client came for counseling. If the counselor says, "Would you care to tell me why you came here?" the client frequently responds by telling why he came to a given city, agency, or school. Whether this misinterpretation on the part of the client is a function of emotional factors is immaterial. The concern here is with phrasing. If the counselor had said, "Would you mind telling me why you came for counseling?" the phrasing of the question is more specific and precise. It should secure the desired response. The function of the counselor in asking questions and in making responses in the interview should not be just to make these statements understood. It should be to make questions and responses impossible to *misunderstand*.

Robinson (1950) has attempted to classify counselor remarks under the following headings which he refers to as techniques of leading:

1. Silence
2. Acceptance
3. Restatement
4. Clarification
5. Summary clarification
6. Approval
7. General leads ("What do you mean?")
8. Tentative analysis
9. Interpretation
10. Urging
11. Depth interpretation
12. Rejection
13. Assurance
14. Introducing new (and apparently unrelated) aspects of a problem.

Another way of classifying counselor statements is that proposed by Porter (1950). He suggests that the nature of these might be classified as reflective, supportive, probing, interpretive, and evaluative.

Some of the counselor leads which should produce client answers of considerable length are:

"Tell me about the kind of subjects and activities you liked in high school." (This can be contrasted against grades shown on the counselor's copy of the client's transcript.)

"Tell me how you got along with your brothers and sisters." (If this is asked toward the beginning of the interview, it will usually produce only positive statements. If it is asked toward the end of the interview, it will produce both negative and positive responses.)

"What sort of things do you like to do for fun?" (This usually leads to client statements which permit the counselor to ask further questions about group activities and solitary activities.)

"What sort of thinking have you been doing about the kind of jobs you would like to have?" (The counselor can check this against records of previous work experience, and against measured and stated interest.)

"Tell me about the hobbies that have interested you most." (This could offer leads into discussion of possible educational and job considerations. It could also offer leads to areas of re-education for new jobs for the client with a disability.)

"Tell me about any suggestions your physician may have made about limitations on the kind of work and recreation you should consider." (In general the use of a question beginning with "Can you tell me . . ." produces a response at length. If the counselor had said, "Has your physician made any suggestions about the kind of work and recreation you should consider?" the client has a chance to give a "yes" or "no" answer.)

Conversely, if the counselor desires short answers, the same questions should probably be phrased as follows:

"What subjects and activities did you like in high school?" (If the counselor asks, "How do you feel about high school?" the client is apt to reply by asking for clarification of the question.)

"How do you get along at home?" (This usually produces the response, "Fine!")

"What do you do for recreation?"

"What kind of job would you like?"

"What hobby do you like most?"

Thus the way the counselor phrases leads determines much of the client response. This is a vital part of the method by which threat is controlled and used in the interview.

Client responsibility

The client also has some responsibilities in this counseling relationship. The first of these has been described by Robinson (1950) as counseling readiness. This counseling readiness involves two things. The first is a knowledge that certain client behavior is unsatisfactory and the second is a sincere desire to change such behavior. This requires a willingness to change on the part of the client and an acceptance of the counselor's ability to promote such a change. The counselor can increase counseling readiness, but cannot create it. This is why it is usually easier to work with clients who come voluntarily for counseling. They tend to make more rapid progress than those referred to the counselor by some authoritative source.

Much has been made in discussions of the interview about the need for "frankness and honesty." Perhaps a clearer and more accurate term would be "candor," which implies frankness and an unreserved relationship without the value judgment implied by the term "honesty." Most clients are not deliberately deceitful with a counselor, but they may be under too much tension to be completely candid with the counselor— or with themselves, for that matter. Until several interviews have occurred the relationship may not be established enough for the client and counselor to be really candid with each other. The client actually may be more concerned with hiding from himself than with revealing himself candidly to the counselor. It takes time to learn that the interview is a place where it is no longer necessary to hide from himself or from another. Until this insight occurs it is difficult to examine goals, values, and attitudes in the interview and realize that the situation is free from criticism or the need for fear. When this situation occurs in the initial interview, both client and counselor must curtail other activities and concentrate on this aspect of the counseling relationship.

The client has to recognize that the matters being discussed are not the responsibility of the counselor. A part of the development of a successful counseling relationship is the working out of these areas of responsibility between the client and the counselor. Topics discussed and the extent of discussion are usually the responsibility of the client. The way in which these topics are discussed, the tools and techniques used, and the limits established within the interview itself are the responsibility of the counselor. If this division of responsibility does not emerge as the interview progresses, the counseling relationship is apt to be affected negatively.

Communication

These responsibilities are a part of the structure developed during the initial interview and are a direct outgrowth of the ability of client and counselor to communicate with each other. Communication in the interview involves meaning expressed to one another by speech, gestures, facial expression, or bodily posture. Such communication is affected by words used and voice inflection, but the meaning expressed reflects deeper elements of goals, values and attitudes. This is why it is difficult to understand and evaluate all that happens in an interview unless one is actually present in that interview. A typescript misses the physical interactions and the nuances of meaning contributed by voice inflections. A tape recording preserves the audible meanings communicated in the interview, but still misses physical interactions between client and counselor which modify the spoken words. Even a film or closed television broadcast can only present those aspects of an interview which seemed important to the person operating the camera. Frequently the whole scene is not presented and part of the total meaning is lost.

A part of the process of communication is involved in the phrasing of counselor leads, but in addition the counselor must note the way in which the client responds to these leads and the information this provides about client behavior.

It is important that the counselor check constantly on meanings abstracted by the client. This is an exceedingly difficult phase of the interview, but a vital one. The counselor has to develop a dual skill as indicated previously. This skill in communication requires ability to present material precisely to a client to produce a desired result. It also requires the ability to understand surface content and the meaning behind what the client is trying to express. This is one of the reasons why extensive actual and vicarious experiences are necessary before the counselor can really understand what the client is saying and see the world as the client sees it. On an oral basis it means that the counselor must be a person with many levels of vocabulary. Professional terminology must be used in communication with colleagues in education, psychology, medicine, social work, and rehabilitation. The same meanings often must be translated into the language of a factory worker or a seventh grader in an initial interview. Successful counselors tend to develop a method of expressing meaning to clients which is simple and clear enough for every client to understand, yet does not inadvertently communicate an intent to be patronizing or condescending on the part of the counselor. Such terminology also contributes to consistency of counselor behavior during the interview and ease in remembering interview statements for case notes. If the counselor cannot develop a common terminology, the level of vocabulary used in the interview changes like the colors of a chameleon to meet the needs of each succeeding client.

VALIDATION AND EXPLORATION OF PREVIOUS DATA

Planning the interview

In order for the counselor to use the initial interview to validate or expand and elaborate on data already collected on a given client, it is necessary to have some system of organizing client information, such as those described in Chapter 5, that will show easily the current knowledge about a client and the inadequacies or the discrepancies. Preliminary planning can only take into account counselor hypotheses about a given client's behavior based on knowledge about similar clients and limited specific knowledge taken from the client's records. The counselor must plan the interview in terms of the tentative hypotheses these data indicate for such a client after a comparison with counselor knowledge about the various groups within which the client must function. Along with validation of these data the counselor will need to observe the unique ways in which a client differs from group norms of behavior and modify perceptions of the client and tentative hypotheses about the client in the light of these unique differences. The beginning stages of the initial interview will usually produce statements about client purposes in coming for counseling. These client statements may vary considerably from what the counselor anticipates on the basis of preliminary data. They may also vary considerably from the real purposes that are revealed as this first interview progresses.

The counselor's system of organizing client data determines the tentative hypotheses he develops about the client and indicates the kind of planning he must do in preparation for the interview. The counselor must form some estimate of the level of general intelligence indicated by these data. This in turn establishes the communication methods and limits that are to be used in the interview. The questions a counselor can ask and the information that can be given are partially determined by the intellectual level of the client as well as by the emotional impact they may have for the client.

Another limiting element in interview planning would be the preliminary estimate of the way in which the client views himself. If the preliminary data indicate preparation for occupations involving working with people and the client sees himself as one who has been unsuccessful in relating to others, this limits the approach the counselor can make in presenting and discussing these data. If the data indicate a need to help the client with personal problems and the client sees the interview as a place to discuss only educational or occupational data, this also limits the counselor. In similar fashion the client's demonstrated readiness to accept or reject new ideas and the general adaptability of the client may limit the degree to which the counselor can accomplish plans for the initial interview. If these preliminary data also evidence what the client hopes to accomplish in the interviews, this, too, can be a limiting element.

At the same time the counselor compares the adequacies of the preliminary data to see if they are consistent with client purposes. If data are inadequate, then part of the initial interview must be devoted to checking this to see whether it is a matter of incomplete information, or whether there are real discrepancies between client goals and case information. If client goals include activities involving meeting and dealing with people, and client data indicate behavior antithetical to this, the interview plans must take this into account.

Most of the initial interviews the counselor will conduct will center about problems of an educational or vocational nature. This does not imply that these problems do not involve some rather strong feelings or that they are divorced from the rest of the client's field. It simply means that most client data must be organized to solve rather mundane, practical problems. To do this the counselor usually follows some convenient outline and fills in data collected prior to the interview. Then, no matter in what order validation data and new data are presented in the initial interview, it is organized later under these various topics. The client may present information about academic performance near the beginning, middle, and end of the interview as topics develop logically and merge one into another in the natural sequence of a conversation. Or the client may be able to make only positive statements about family members in the beginning of an interview and is able to be much more candid in expressing negative feelings about family toward the end of the initial interview.   Later the counselor gathers and lists this academic or family information with the rest of such data that have been collected previously from records and personal documents into a synthesis of case data about a given client.

Any convenient list or outline of topics that suits a given counselor can be selected.   One possible list which is similar to topics indicated in Chapter 2 is as follows:

1. Elementary or High School Background
   a. Subjects liked best and marks
   b. Subjects liked least and marks
   c. Total grade point average
   d. Number in graduating class and client's position in this group
   e. Extracurricular activities

2. Family data
   a. Marital status and dependents
   b. Age, education, and occupation of spouse
   c. Present living conditions
   d. Present financial status with respect to schooling
   e. Age, education, and occupation of parents
   f. Exact nature of father's business
   g. Age, education, and occupation of siblings
   h. Interaction with family

3. Leisure time activities
   a. Social life (actual and preferred—this includes religious activities, but do not ask about these: let client volunteer them.)
   b. Sports, participating and spectator
   c. Reading—books and magazines—be specific
   d. Hobbies—any consistent activities
   e. Organizations joined—current and past
   f. Experience in music and art

4. Course taken in college or technical school
   a. Subjects liked best—marks
   b. Subjects liked least—marks
   c. Grade point average or honor point ratio
   d. Extracurricular activities

5. Work and service experience
   a. Approximate number of months at each job
   b. Specific nature of job and duties
   c. Oral trade questions

6. Health and physical status
   a. Present disabilities, whether corrected, and how
   b. Long term illnesses—residuals

7. Client feelings about environment
   a. Important areas above which were avoided in the interview
   b. Topics above which seemed to produce tension in the interview
   c. Feelings about home and family
   d. Feelings about school and teachers
   e. Feelings about job and fellow workers
   f. Readiness to participate in community social groups
   g. General attitude toward solitary versus group activities

8. Would client be classified within the normal range of behavior?
   a. Diagnosis
   b. Suggested procedure
   c. Predicted results

All of the foregoing discussion about planning for the interview is based upon the counselor's breadth and depth of knowledge about people as individuals and the way they behave in groups. Knowledge like that is acquired through experience with all kinds of people and groups. It involves scientific knowledge achieved in academic courses in the social and natural sciences, but it also includes vicarious and direct knowledge acquired from group work and group recreational experiences. The greater this background of understanding experiences with people which the counselor has developed, the better the preparation to understand what a client is trying to say. This understanding sensitivity to people is a part of the empathic skill of every successful counselor. It should be noted, however, that this empathic skill is employed in a one-to-one counseling interview and does not necessarily mean that the counselor successful in the interview is also successful in group activities.

DIRECT OBSERVATION OF THE CLIENT

As indicated at various points in this chapter, one of the primary purposes of the initial interview is to explore the unique ways in which a given client differs from others in behavior and in personal interests, goals, and values. These individual differences in behavior are the factors that have brought the client to this first interview. The variance of these from societal values or the unique needs they indicate are the reason for counseling. The counselor uses the initial interview as the first opportunity for direct observation of these differences and as an opportunity to collect new data on client behavior.

This first interview furnishes a places where the counselor can begin to combine prior evidences of behavior and current observations of behavior to form an impression of *what* the client is doing. Usually the initial interview also furnishes the first opportunity the counselor has had to understand and explore the *causes* of client behavior. In this interview the counselor begins to experience with the client the feelings about self and environment which have resulted from the life values, interests, attitudes, and goals that the client has developed. In consequence the counselor encourages the client to express these feelings and minimizes the amount of counselor talk during this information-getting process.

Combining interview observations and other data

Until the initial interview counselor observations have been concerned with looking through records and observations made by others to see how the client differs from the group. Now it is possible to make direct observations and see from client behavior and from client talk what some of these differences are and why they have developed. As a counselor in beginning practicum once said, "I have had that boy in two classes, but this interview sure gave me a chance to get a different picture of him." Many clients reveal feelings in an interview which they have learned to conceal in other life situations. At the same time the counselor has learned to make a different kind of professional observation in the interview from that practiced with colleagues, friends, or family.

The counselor through experience can learn to translate data from records into a picture of a client, but the face-to-face situation of the interview can add much to this picture. The notation on a folder that a high school sophomore is six feet, four inches tall and weighs two hundred pounds at age sixteen is somewhat different from seeing the student filling the door of the counselor's office. Physical presence emphasizes data from records to make them more meaningful.

A client may be quite friendly and relaxed when visiting with others in the outer office, but very tense and ill-at-ease in the counselor's office. The initial interview gives the counselor a chance to find out whether this difference is caused by inability to adjust in social situations involving peer versus adult groups, or whether it is related to the seriousness of the conflicts in values which have brought the client for counseling. These conflicts in values may produce tensions which diminish as the client learns that the interview is a place where no penalties are attached to the mention and discussion of the feelings involved in such conflict.

Alert observation by the counselor can uncover important areas for remediation by contrasting client talk and visual observations. The client who has a slight speech problem can pass unnoticed in many school situations, but not in the interview, where a trained observer notices it and explores with the client the possibilities for correction. Then referral to a speech specialist can be made and followed up by the counselor. This may seem an unreal situation in modern society, but actually happens too often. In two recent cases of speech defects when teachers were asked about the clients, they thought in one case that it was a regional difference in accent, and in another that it was an affectation for status purposes.

The initial interview gives the counselor a chance to get specific details about physical limitations. The notation on a health record of a high school senior transfer that he developed arthritis in grade six is not very useful to the counselor. Sight of this boy in the outer office with his stiff bodily movements can immediately raise questions in the counselor's mind. Closer observation of enlarged knuckles and hunched shoulders gives evidence of some physical impairment and the counselor needs to know more about this to furnish effective help to the client. As ordinary conversation makes it possible in the interview, the counselor asks the boy to tell about the arthritis and how it has affected his life. The boy indicates that there are certain sports such as golf which are difficult because it is hard to grip the golf clubs, so he participates less in sports than in such things as reading and study. Now the counselor sees as normal for this client the statement on the personal data form that he reads five or six books per week. For most high school boys this would be atypical and possibly evidence of lack of social skills and group activity. Another significant item which appears in the initial interview is the fact that no one in any of the other four schools this boy has attended in three different states has mentioned the services available to him under state vocational rehabilitation. (This latter finding illustrates the lack of coordination among various counseling agencies and referral sources—someone should have checked this much sooner. Nor is this an isolated incident; all too often counselors and other public school personnel are unaware of such referral sources.)

As Tyler (1956) has pointed out, this phase of the initial interview deals with "identifying psychological realities." In addition to the more obvious factors discussed above, this is the first opportunity the counselor has to find out how the client feels about himself and his environment. When a client says, "I came to find out what my I.Q. is," the counselor cannot just give a number. Professional responsibility indicates the necessity of finding out why the client wants this information. The client may be seeking a way to excuse poor school work, or to show the counselor that there are feelings of inadequacy present, or this may just be a screen to conceal the real reason for coming to the counselor. To give a number or a position in a normative group is *not* the response to this client statement. The counselor needs to ask the client to tell more about why the intelligence test score is important. This leads to expression of the feelings which caused the client to come for counseling.

The counselor needs to use the first interview to find out how the client feels, not just to collect a series of related facts which can be fitted into a case history, or to give out specific information without knowing how it will be used by the client. Unless a client can learn to understand and accept the effect these feelings have upon educational and vocational choices, consideration of any client activities is usually inhibited by too much anxiety for a satisfactory choice. A part of the counselor's job is to distinguish between the normal anxiety or tension needed for learning and the abnormal anxieties which prevent learning.

In this process of getting to understand how client feelings and values affect behavior, the counselor must make a tentative diagnosis that such behavior is consistent and integrated enough for counseling to continue, or that a referral to some other agency is necessary. Unless the counselor can help the client reduce anxieties to the point that new behavior can be learned, some other agency will need to be used to help the client handle the problems. As Drasgow (1956) has said, "Sometimes the client is so disturbed that he cannot be helped despite the fact that he presents problems which are usually dealt with in counseling. This distinction between the client and the problem he brings may explain why we are often successful in helping some clients with problems and fail to help other clients with the same types of problems." Of course there are many other factors besides client anxiety that determine success or failure of counseling, but Drasgow's point is a good one for the beginning counselor to note. Unless client anxiety is optimal for learning, counseling tends to be ineffective.

A part of this process of helping the client reduce anxiety may be the most important thing that happens in the initial interview. A client may need to spend most of the time in this first meeting with the counselor in a discussion of the feelings which prevent successful school work, before it is possible to reach a point where an approach to educational or vocational choices is feasible. This may take several interviews where counselor and client explore these feelings and their causes. On the other hand the chance to relieve these feelings in this first interview often makes it possible for the client to handle them alone in the future and they do not appear in succeeding interviews.

The counselor may also make a decision not to permit these feelings to be discussed or to limit the amount or kind of feelings which are discussed in the first interview. Sometimes a client will reveal too much in this first meeting and be unwilling to return. The decision the counselor must make about this will have to depend on tentative judgments about the client made on limited data. The result of this counselor decision is one factor which accounts for the all too frequent failure of clients to return for counseling. One of the problems the counselor faces is the decision to let these feelings emerge and to what extent, or to temporize and see what happens in succeeding interviews. These decisions are determined by the counselor's education and experience, the purposes of the agency, the needs of the client and the referral sources available. As Tyler (1956) has said, "In some ways the counselor's task is harder than that of the psychoanalyst who aims to open up everything. The judgment as to which feelings should be recognized and which ignored is a very difficult one. A lifetime of practice is not enough for one to perfect the skill completely, but all of us can with concentration perform it moderately well."

STRUCTURING

Some of the material on structuring which has been discussed previously will be considered only briefly here. Structuring occurs all through the initial interview. It may be overt (formal) or covert (informal) at the discretion of the counselor, in the light of client need and comprehension. Structuring begins when the counselor greets the client and tries to create a satisfactory physical and psychological climate for the interview. In the process of doing this the counselor ascertains the client's concept of what is going to happen and points out or implies what can actually happen. The counselor demonstrates, but usually does not explain, the way in which the interview is conducted.

Overt structuring

This usually takes place with the orientation of the client to the various counseling processes that will be used and any discussion of agency, legal and ethical limits of counseling. For example, the counselor usually points out the available sources of information about the client and sometimes indicates how they have been used prior to the initial interview. This permits the client to see what information the agency has and how it will need to be supplemented and expanded during counseling.

Within the limits created by differences between counseling orientations, the purpose of a counselor lead is more often explained or evident to a client in the parts of the initial interview centering about discussion of educational-vocational choices than in the parts dealing with feelings a client is expressing. The steps taking place after the initial interview are also more apt to be described with educational-vocational problems. These steps would include discussion of persons the client is to contact, a description of any tests the client is to take, additional information the client must provide and the purpose of succeeding interviews.

In the beginning of the initial interview the counselor usually tells the client about the routine the agency carries out with each client. If fees are charged these are explained. Forms which must be completed are explained and their use illustrated. Most agencies have a control card for each client like that illustrated in Forms 4.1 and 4.2 which shows the steps involved in guidance and counseling. This is a useful device to indicate to a client the processes the agency carries on. Then as the client describes the reasons for coming to a counselor, the counselor points out which of these processes shown on the control card is applicable. The control card in Forms 4.1 and 4.2 is designed to permit coding of the information it contains on IBM cards for use in various types of agency research.

If it appears that another agency may be involved, the counselor can indicate how relationships with that agency will be handled and the data that might be collected and released to any other agency. At this point regulations of the counselor's agency concerning release of information and release forms to be signed are often described to the client.

If the counselor has reason to expect that legal or ethical problems may come up in the interview, this can be explained to the client with a statement about the counselor's legal status which in most states does not give clients the right of privileged communication. The counselor should realize that privileged communication is not intended to conceal a crime and that the law requires the counselor to report contemplated or committed crimes revealed by a client under penalty of becoming an accessory to them. Unless a state grants privileged communication to the counselor's clients, the counselor can be required to testify in court about the content of counseling interviews, and agency records, including records of interviews, are subject to subpoena. The client should be informed of this as soon as the counselor gets an intimation that such a situation can develop. Then the client is in a better position to decide topics discussed during counseling, and the nature or extent of this discussion.

The counselor's agency itself may have established certain limits within which counselor and client must function. These need to be explained at the beginning of the initial interview so that the client can decide whether topics coming under these limitations should be discussed. These limitations are apt to vary according to the needs and purpose of the agency and therefore may not be clear to the client without an explanation.

For example, it may be agency policy to secure a written release from the client before sending information to another agency. Or the agency may require a request from a potential employer before sending out information about client aptitudes, instead of sending such statements to employers at the client's request. This cuts down correspondence to just those potential employers interested in the client, rather than sending information to every place the client applies for work. The same policy is usually followed in sending information to schools.

Ethical practices in counseling are fairly constant from agency to agency, however, and are usually demonstrated rather than explained. An example of this would be asking permission of the client before any recordings are made of the interviews. Sometimes it is necessary to make statements about the ethics involved in the way the counselor treats confidential data. The counselor should explain the differences between such things as test data collected by the agency for its own use or for referral purposes, and data collected by the counselor and the client solely for use in the interview. Usually data collected for client use is more confidential in nature and consequently handled differently from such things as scores on placement or selection examinations or data collected for upgrading in a job. Some tests may be given in order that the scores can be furnished another agency, such as services for the blind, or state vocational rehabilitation.

Overt structuring also includes a discussion of persons the client will need to contact in the process of counseling. The counselor may ask the client to write and request that test results taken previously be forwarded from another agency. The client may be asked to have sum-

Year	1	Case No.	2-5	Student No.	6-10	Name ....
Class	11 M F	Marital Status	12			Address ....
School	13 Changes	14	15	16	17	Phone ....
Age			18 19			Home Address ....
Veteran □			20			Referred by
			21-23			High School
H.S. Graduation	24-25 Entered K.U.		26-27 Progress		x27 Physical Disabilities	28

Counselor	Interview	Counselor	Interview	Counselor	Interview	
29-31 PI	32		51-52		71-72	Referred to ....
CI	33-34		53-54		73-74	77 ....
	35-36		55-56		75-76	
	37-38		57-58			Testing ....
	39-40		59-60			Method of Leaving School 79
	41-42		61-62			Rec'd Degree from 80
	43-44		63-64			Remarks:
	45-46		65-66			
	47-48		67-68			
	49-50		69-70			

78

(G-B Form, Rev. 57)

Adapted by permission of the University of Kansas Guidance Bureau, Lawrence, Kansas.

NAME..

Scholastic Aptitude Tests

.... American Council

.... Otis Self Adm.

.... Ohio Psychological

.... Wechsler-Bellevue

.... Miller Analogies

.... SCAT

Special Aptitude Tests

.... Minnesota Clerical

.... Psy. Corp. Clerical

.... O'Conner Finger-Tweezer

.... Minn. Spatial Relations

.... Paper Form Board

.... Bennett Mechanical (Form ....)

.... Dynamicube

.... Purdue Pegboard

.... EPSAT

Reading Tests

.... Coop. C2Y

.... Iowa Silent

Interest Inventories

.... SVIB-M

.... SVIB-W

.... Kuder Preference Record ....

.... Kuder Occupational Form D

.... Lee-Thorpe

Personality Schedules

.... MMPI

.... GZTS

.... EPPS

.... CPI

.... Study of Values

English

.... Coop. English ....

.... Michigan Voc.

Mathematics

.... K.U. Math.

.... Coop. Math. ....

Science

.... Chemistry Aptitude

.... Physics Aptitude

.... General Science

.... Natural Science

Foreign Language

.... Coop. Adv. Lang. ....

.... Coop. Elem. Lang. ....

.... Iowa Lang. Aptitude

History

.... Coop. Social Studies (Ach.)

Study Skills

.... Tyler-Kimber

.... Brown-Holtzman

.... Wren Study Habits

Batteries

.... Gen'l. Culture—I, II, III, IV, V

.... DAT—Verbal Reasoning
Numerical Ability
Abstract Reasoning
Space Relations
Mech. Reasoning
Cler. Sp. & Acc.
Lang. Usage

.... STEP—Read., Writ., Listen.,
Math., Sci., Soc. Stud., Essay
Writing

.... ITED—I, II, III, IV, V, VI,
VII, VIII, IX

.... Essential H.S. Content—Math.,
Sci., Soc. Study, Eng.

.... MAT—I, II, III, IV, V, VI,
VII, VIII, IX

Miscellaneous

....

....

Adapted by permission of the University of Kansas Guidance Bureau, Lawrence, Kansas.

maries of previous interviews held in another agency forwarded for use in current interviews. Information about potential schools or potential employers may need to be secured by the client from direct contact with these referral sources. The client may agree to write for educational or vocational information. Many rehabilitation agencies make it a practice to have the client make the initial contacts about further schooling or future jobs. Such agencies feel the client assumes more responsibility for progress if client efforts have secured the placement than if the counselor has assumed responsibility for making the placement.

During the initial interview and especially toward the end, the counselor discusses appropriate tests with the client. Ordinarily the counselor is in a position to suggest that certain tests will best meet client needs for further information about himself; these suggestions are made and the client then decides whether such tests are worth taking, and which of several alternatives is best. For example, the counselor may say, "The *Strong Vocational Interest Blank for Men* will show you whether your interests resemble those of men in certain occupations," and name the occupations on the *SVIB* in which the client has stated an interest. The counselor may explain further that the test contains 400 items which the client marks "Like," "Indifferent," or "Dislike," and that it takes from thirty to forty-five minutes, although it is untimed. Some counselors also like to point out to a client that for most useful results the client should do the test as rapidly as possible, because the more the client ponders responses, the more confused and possibly the less consistent and typical the resulting *SVIB* profile becomes. Scoring procedures for the *SVIB* may be pointed out to a client to indicate why there is a longer time lapse between testing and discussing these scores than for most of the other tests a client takes.

For the same reason given above for the *SVIB*, a counselor may point out that most of the personality and interest inventories a client takes will be more useful if the client completes them as rapidly as possible even though they are untimed. Conversely, the counselor explains that an intelligence test like the *Ohio State Psychological Examination* is intended to provide the best possible estimate of academic potential in untimed circumstances. Therefore the test will only be useful if the client takes as long as necessary to give a complete and thorough indication of client potential. Unless a client is willing to spend enough time on the Ohio test to give a good estimate of potential, it is a waste of time to consider or to do the test.

In like manner the counselor describes the purpose and general nature of any other tests that might be useful to the client. Which of these are assigned for the client to take is dependent on the client, as is the way in which client-counselor discussion of test results is handled. If the client is able to spend only one or two days in concentrated testing and counseling activities, the tests may be taken as one assignment. If the client is able to take them gradually over a period of time, one or two tests may be assigned and their results discussed before any other tests are assigned. This latter procedure gives the client a chance to see how a particular kind of information fits into his self-concept before a new and divergent kind of test information enters to complicate his thinking about himself and his test interpretations.

A part of this structuring concerning tests can be handled in a group orientation to testing and counseling, but this needs to be reviewed in the initial interview also. Experience with group procedures followed by individual interviews has indicated that group orientation alone is not enough. Tyler (1956) has also mentioned the use of a brief written explanation of how the counseling service operates. Examples of this are shown in Forms 4.3 and 4.4.

Toward the end of the initial interview it is usually wise to review the processes the client will follow later. If succeeding interviews have a stated time limit, this should be explained to the client. A counselor might say, "It is your job to make your next appointment as you leave each interview. Usually you will want to make it for the same time and same day each week, because this is easier to remember and it seems to be a good hour for both of us." Or the counselor might say concerning testing, "You can come in at your convenience and the girl in the main office will arrange for you to take these tests as you have the time. I have told you how long each one takes. You can come in when you have that much time available, because most of them will take less than an hour. After you finish the test (tests), the girl will make an appointment for you to see me and talk about it (them)."

These are some of the more obvious ways the counselor can structure during the initial interview.

Covert structuring

There are certain kinds of covert structuring which are also carried on. This takes place throughout the interview as the counselor's leads and behavior show the client the climate that will prevail during counseling. Usually covert or informal structuring will cover such things as division of counselor-client responsibilities; demonstration of counselor professional capacities; attitude of the counselor toward the client; the distinction between cooperative evaluation and making value judgments by the counselor, and presentation or discussion of client data.

One of the problems which is usually handled by covert structuring during the interview is the matter of division of responsibility between counselor and client. In most of the other instances where a client goes to consult some specialist about a problem, procedures involve de-

Instructions for Practicum Counselees./Form 4.3

This paper is to tell you of the procedure you will follow in your counseling program and remind you to be at the Guidance Bureau at _____ p.m. on _____.

The Guidance Bureau is in Room 116 on the main floor of Smith Hall (opposite the bus shelter). When you report there for your first interview, the counselor and counseling supervisor will review with you the material you have written on the enclosed Personal Data Form which you should bring with you to the first interview listed above. They will also go over with you any pertinent information which applies to your choice of education beyond high school or choice of a job after completing high school. After this is done, you will help them plan a testing program designed to help you answer questions important to you. The tests will vary according to the kind of questions you want answered and according to the college or job you are considering.

At the end of the first interview you can begin taking tests. The Guidance Bureau is open from 8 to 12 a.m. and from 1 p.m. to 5 p.m. You can take tests during these times as you desire. It is important that you complete these tests as soon as possible because the Guidance Bureau will be closed from August to September and your original counselor will not be here during that time. After you have completed the tests decided upon, you will return to discuss them with the counselor and counseling supervisor. At this second interview you will also be shown how to use the Occupational Information Library at the Guidance Bureau.

The total number of interviews will vary according to the information you wish. After these interviews we will send you a letter summarizing all the material we have covered. If you have no objection, we will send a copy of that letter to your high school. The information in your folder is considered strictly confidential and is released only with your express permission. Because you have volunteered in order to help us in our training program, *there will be no charge for these services.*

NAME _____

ADDRESS _____

PHONE NO. _____
_____

scribing a situation and letting the specialist decide what is to be done. For example, the person who is consulting a physician describes a series of symptoms and the physician prescribes treatment. Or the person with a legal problem goes to a lawyer for advice about how to handle the legal situation. Even parents and teachers have a tendency to tell children what to do, instead of letting them make their own decisions. For this reason most clients coming to a counselor are inclined to describe their problem and wait for the counselor to tell them what to do. It is difficult for the counselor to show the client that the interview is a sharing process. The counselor needs to get across the idea that counselor knowledge and skills are used to secure, organize, and interpret client data in some usable form, but the decisions about client behavior based on this have to be made by the client. Sometimes this is handled in overt or formal structuring, but usually it develops informally out of other initial interview activities.

For example, the client may be discussing several possible subject-matter choices for a given school year and turn to the counselor with the question, "Which ones do you think I should take?" The counselor has a choice of several responses here. One response might involve simple reflection, "You would like to have me (someone else) make these choices for you." Others might be, "What do *you* think you should take?" or "Which ones would *you* like to take?" Responses like these which either reflect feelings or shift responsibility back to the client are a way of showing that the client is the one who should make the choice without harming the basic counseling relationship between counselor and client.

Another example is the client who has been discussing a proposed plan of action and turns to the counselor with the question, "What do you think about it?" The counselor can respond, "You're wondering what someone else would do about this," or "Someone else's opinion about this is important to you." Usually the counselor will avoid saying something like, "What I think is not important, it's your decision." This latter statement may be true but may have a negative effect on counselor-client relationships. Instead the counselor who does not wish to reflect the matter back may respond, "Have you considered what will happen if . . . ?" This makes possible the interjection of other information for client consideration without making a decision for the client.

In these ways the counselor indicates to the client the division of responsibilities in the interview.

At the same time, these responses and other counselor statements are indicating that the counselor accepts the client as some one worthy of help. By leaving the interview choices to the client, emphasis is placed on counselor belief that the client is capable of such decisions as these and similar choices. Thus without saying so openly, the counselor con-

Orientation Leaflet Distributed/Form 4.4
to Clients.

The Guidance Bureau

The Guidance Bureau offers free counseling service to students. It is open from 8 a.m. to 5 p.m. on weekdays and until noon on Saturday. Any student may discuss his problems with a counselor. The counselor ascertains that the student can be profitably served by the Bureau or refers the student to the campus agency which is best equipped to help with the specific difficulty. Thus, there is little overlap with the regular academic advisement program, the Student Health Service, or other student personnel agencies.

The educational and psychological training of the counselors prepares them to help students collect and interpret information about themselves from many sources. These include tests, interviews, biographical information, and records. They vary with the needs of each student. Such sources provide information about abilities, aptitudes, interests and personality to aid in making adequate choices of college majors and fields of occupations. They may also aid in the solution of personal problems allied to success in the University. A knowledge of strengths and weaknesses will permit the student to make the optimum use of opportunities while in college.

In the interpretation of these data the staff of the Bureau exercises discretion and professional judgment. Decisions are not made for students. Rather, students are aided in making their own decisions. Information about the student is released to no one without written permission. Counselees must arrange with their counselor if they wish information given to anyone.

The services furnished to students by the Bureau include aptitude testing, personal counseling with problems allied to academic success or failure, and counseling in regard to the choice of a suitable major or vocation. To use these services all a student has to do is make an appointment with a counselor through the Guidance Bureau Office either in person or by 'phone. In the first interview the counselor and the student decide which of the services of the Bureau will best meet the student's needs. This interview may last as long as one hour. If tests seem advisable, they are planned to meet the specific requirements of each student. Average time for most testing programs is from six to eight hours, arranged so that the tests can be fitted into the student's schedule. Succeeding interviews of one hour each are continued until the student has reached his objectives.

If the student is interested in investigating specific occupational fields, the counselor explains and illustrates the use of the Occupational Information Library. Here the student will find books on occupations which can be taken out for study, as well as files of unbound material and periodicals which can be used only at the reading tables.

In addition to these services offered free to students of the University, the Bureau also offers its services to high school students and to adults interested in further education. The five dollar fee charged to high school students merely covers the cost of materials used. The services of the staff to high school students are considered a part of the free service offered to citizens of the state by the University. High school students should arrange for counseling through the principal of their own school. Adults pay a fee of twenty dollars, as do high school students from outside of the state.

Persons may apply by mail. Biographical information forms will be sent to them in advance so that they may complete the preliminary interview, testing, and the first counseling interview in two days spent at the Bureau.

Some of the questions asked about the Guidance Bureau are answered below.

1. What is the purpose of the Guidance Bureau?
   To counsel with University students who need assistance in making educational and vocational choices and in dealing with personal problems.

2. Does it cost the student anything to use the services of the Bureau?
   There is no charge made to regularly enrolled University students. High school students pay a five dollar fee and adults pay a fee of twenty dollars.

3. How may the services of the Bureau be secured?
   For vocational and educational counseling, it is necessary to register with the Guidance Bureau secretary for an interview. This interview will be held as soon as possible after registration. If a student has a particularly urgent problem, access to a counselor is usually possible on request. The student may ask for any particular counselor.

4. How long does it take to go through the Bureau?
   This depends upon the nature of the problem. Sometimes a single interview is enough. In other instances the counseling process may run over several montns. The average calendar time is 3 or 4 weeks. When tests or inventories are used the average time for this is 6 to 8 hours, arranged at the convenience of the student.

5. When, during his school career, should a student receive the greatest benefit from Guidance Bureau assistance in the choice of an occupation?
   The Guidance Bureau has assisted freshmen, sophomores, juniors, seniors, and graduate students. However, first-year students may find the services of the Bureau of the most benefit. If a change of course should be decided upon by the student, it can then be made with the least loss of time.

6. Does a student have to take tests if he wishes to use the services of the Bureau?
   Not necessarily. For adequate vocational counseling some tests and/or inventories are essential. In the case of personal problems often none are used.

7. What is the purpose of taking tests?
   To gain information about interest, abilities, aptitudes, educational background, adjustment, and personality.

8. What is the purpose of an interview?
   The first interview is primarily for the purpose of presenting the problem. Other interviews are to help the counselee understand his problem, understand any data developed through tests, inventories, or the counseling process itself.

9. Will the Guidance Bureau tell the student what occupation he should follow?
   No. It will assist in securing, analyzing, and interpreting data, but the choice is the student's responsibility.

10. What is the purpose of the Occupational Information Library?
    It is a special library of occupational information maintained by the Guidance Bureau. An effort is made to have available for current use the best available information on occupational trends, opportunities, remuneration, working conditions, and training requirements, for as many occupations as possible. When information needed by the student is not in the library the Guidance Bureau will make every effort to obtain it.

11. Who uses the Guidance Bureau?
    More than 10,000 students have come to the Guidance Bureau since its establishment for aid in vocational, educational, and personal problems.

Adapted by permission of the University of Kansas Guidance Bureau, Lawrence, Kansas.

veys the impression of confidence in the client and acceptance (but not approval) of what the client has said. For instance, if the client has just described some incident and expressed strong feelings about it, the counselor may say, "I can understand why you feel this way." Such a statement signifies successful communication between client and counselor, but does not usually indicate approval.

These counselor statements play as important a part in demonstrating counselor competence and responsibility as do any interpretations of client data or direction of the client to appropriate sources of information or other agency contacts. Properly done those responses convey to the client a knowledge of client strengths which the client then begins to investigate and use.

At the same time, such statements provide a distinction between the value-judgments the client has encountered in other life activities and the lack of such evaluations by the counselor in the initial interview. The use of such counselor phrases as "I see" or "I understand" not only reduces threat but creates a different atmosphere than the usual "That's good" or "That's bad" found in the rest of the environment. In a school situation the client is more used to being told that a score on a test is "good" or "poor." Where test scores are discussed in counseling as being "higher than," "lower than," or "just like" most of the people who take the test, the client begins to see strengths and weaknesses without psychologically cringing from someone else's value-judgments about them. Through this kind of cooperative evaluation where value-judgments are left to the client, acceptance of weaknesses is easier and emphasis of strengths begins more quickly than in most life situations. Here the client is not being told "you are (or are not) able to compete with someone else"; it is evident, and the client can accept it as other feelings make such acceptance possible. Such a process emphasizes the importance of client value-judgments.

These inferences in the initial interview about the various things the client will do play a part in indicating how these activities are a part of the counseling process without actually listing them in 1, 2, 3, 4 fashion.

Another place where the counselor usually prefers to avoid overt structuring is in the termination of the initial interview. One way to do this is to summarize briefly the procedures the client will follow and then lean forward as if about to rise. Usually if this is timed with some signal that the hour has ended, the client will begin to make preparations to leave and in succeeding interviews will assume responsibility for this. For the counselor who has someone to control appointments, a call from the outer office saying the next appointment is waiting usually serves as another way of terminating the interview. Only in extreme cases will the counselor have to say, "I'm sorry, but this is all the time we can take today," and stand up to signify the interview is ended. This termination of the initial interview on schedule is important in structuring for future interviews and helps maintain a professional atmosphere in counseling.

SUMMARY

This discussion of the initial interview has centered around a consideration of establishing a counseling relationship, confirming client data secured prior to the interview, getting to know how the client feels about self and environment, and methods of structuring the interview. Perhaps the best way to close is with a quotation from Tyler (1956) with which she ends her article about the initial interview. Tyler says, "I wonder if other counselors would agree with me that the initial interview is the hardest part of our task—the part that demands from us the most intensive concentration. Each person constitutes for us a new adventure in understanding. Each is destined to broaden our own lives in directions as yet uncharted. Each initial interview renews our appreciation of the challenge and the fascination of the counseling task." (P. 473.)

REFERENCES

Bandura, A. Psychotherapist's anxiety level, self-insight, and psychotherapeutic competence. *J. Abnorm. & Soc. Psychol.*, 1956, 52, 333–337.

Butler, W. R. *An analytical study of factors associated with scholastic achievement in high and low achieving fraternities.* Unpublished Ed. D. dissertation, University of Kansas, 1956.

Drasgow, J. Intake interviewing in counseling. *Personnel and Guidance Journal,* 1956, 35, 100–102.

Fiedler, F. E. The concept of an ideal therapeutic relationship. *J. Consult. Psychol.*, 1950, 14, 239–245.

———. A comparison of therapeutic relationships in psychoanalytic, nondirective and Adlerian therapy. *J. Consult. Psychol.*, 1950, 14, 436–445.

Hahn, M. E., and M. S. MacLean. *Counseling psychology.* New York: McGraw-Hill Book Company, Inc., 1955.

Porter, E. H., Jr. *An introduction to therapeutic counseling.* Boston: Houghton Mifflin Company, 1950.

Robinson, F. P. *Principles and procedures in student counseling.* New York: Harper & Brothers, 1950.

Rogers, C. R. *Client-centered therapy.* Boston: Houghton Mifflin Company, 1951.

———. Conditions of therapeutic personality change. *J. Consult. Psychol.*, 1957, 21, 95–103.

Strupp, H. H. An objective comparison of Rogerian and psychoanalytic techniques. *J. Consult. Psychol.*, 1955, 19, 1–7.

Tyler, L. E. The initial interview. *Personnel and Guidance Journal,* 1956, 34, 466–473.

5

Organizing an educational-vocational case study for a client

THE BEGINNING COUNSELOR FACES THE PROBLEM OF DECIDING WHAT MA-
terials properly belong in a case study, how the case study should be
organized, and how it should be used. The term *case study* as ordinarily
used refers to the organization of all information available on a given
individual which is used for any specific purpose. Actually the term has
been borrowed from social work, just as most of the other terms used in
counseling have been borrowed from other disciplines. The term *client*
has been borrowed from law; the use of the word *therapy* is from medicine, and the case study or the case work approach is from social work.
Many of the techniques used in preparing a case study also come from
a number of disciplines.

The first consideration of the beginning counselor concerns what information should be included in a case study. The amount of information
and the nature of the information varies according to the purpose for
which the case study is to be used. If it is constructed in a school situation where it is to be used in a staff conference with all the school personnel connected with a given individual to discuss how each may contribute to helping this individual function better in the school situation,
then certain kinds of information are collected. If it is in a rehabilitation agency and the purpose is to set up a rehabilitation plan for a
client, this may involve a psychologist, a physician, a social worker, various therapists, or a psychiatrist. This so-called "rehabilitation team"
may wish to use different kinds of information for the case study from
that of the school staff. The most common purpose of a case study,
as far as the counselor is concerned, is to collect information which can
then be organized in a fairly simple fashion to be discussed with the

client.   Much of this information that the counselor collects is designed for personal use in understanding the client, or for helping the client understand self.   Usually the latter information is not given the formal name *case study*.

Another factor that determines the content and scope of the case study is related to the competencies or skills of the counselor in collecting, organizing, and using the information.   The beginning counselor will obviously be more limited as far as this factor is concerned and must use more time to prepare and interpret data than the experienced counselor who has developed a systematic approach.   The purpose for which the case study is used has to be tempered by client needs, by counselor needs, and by the needs of so-called referral agencies to whom the case study may be presented.   Estimates of the kinds of case studies completed by schools and other agencies usually indicate that about 60 per cent of these cases in an agency dealing with the general public, such as the employment service, people engaged in student personnel work, or counselors in the public schools, are centered about educational-vocational questions.   There really is no such thing as a pure educational-vocational question, because each individual varies enough that a counselor must consider a number of other factors besides the educational-vocational problems.   For example, the counselor may need to consider how this client feels about going to work.   In a rehabilitation agency the individual may have been on county welfare for two or three years and this has been more comfortable than seeking a job.   The client has not had to worry about people seeing his disability or commenting on capacities needed to meet a work situation.   It is easier to stay home.   It becomes a simpler life to live than going out and competing occupationally.   So it may be pretty hard to talk about educational-vocational possibilities with this client until the point is reached when the client is ready to consider these.   If county welfare is paying for the client to live, the client may not be willing to do this.   A similar situation occurs in a school situation.   Until a given boy or girl gets to be a senior, no goals beyond high school or goals beyond graduation from college may seem to be worth considering.   This is something in the far distant future and graduation from high school as seen by a sophomore seems a long way off, as does graduation from college as seen by a senior in high school.   Therefore, readiness of the client may be a factor in indicating what materials are to be included in a case study and how much client feelings enter into educational-vocational considerations.

The techniques that the counselor uses in preparing a case study come from a number of disciplines and professions.   In psychology the counselor discovers techniques which will furnish information about individual behavior and its causes, because the function of psychology is the study of the individual.   From social work come the techniques which permit the counselor to gather together information about the client's environment or background and its impact upon that client.   From education come the series of techniques which show how an individual learns and which help the counselor in the process of helping the client learn. From medicine come the techniques that give information about physical capacities or restrictions which exist for a given client.   These are the major professions from which the counselor has borrowed techniques of gathering client information.

SYSTEMATIC CASE STUDY

After the techniques have produced information, some method of organizing it must be selected.   Williamson and Darley (1937) have suggested six steps in clinical counseling which Hahn and MacLean (1955) discuss also.   Those steps are analysis, synthesis, diagnosis, prognosis, treatment, and follow-up.   They would also apply to the other three methods described in the rest of this chapter.   *Analysis* is the process of first studying over the data collected in the case study.   *Synthesis* refers to the organization or the putting together of this information in some usable form.   *Diagnosis* is the making of some estimate of causation and of the approximate nature of the problem in the same sense that the physician makes a diagnosis.   *Prognosis* refers to how the counseling processes may be useful for a client or whether a referral should be made to another agency.   When the counselor in a prognosis decides that counseling can be of assistance, then the more specific questions concerning the techniques which will be useful depend upon the orientation of the counselor.   In *directive* counseling the counselor makes most of the decisions and bears a major part of the responsibility for counseling activities.   In *client-centered* or *non-directive* counseling the counselor bears less of the responsibility for interview topics and is more concerned with relationships with the client, the atmosphere in which counseling takes place, and with reflecting to the client the real meaning behind what the client is saying.   The *eclectic* counselor, who is somewhere in the middle of this continuum, would be choosing techniques and sharing responsibilities with the client according to that counselor's position on the continuum.   If the counselor is more inclined toward a client-centered orientation, the process will be more "Rogerian."   If the counselor is more inclined toward the directive approach, the tools and techniques chosen will be more in that direction and will consequently again involve more counselor responsibility for what is actually discussed in counseling, as well as what is done in counseling.   Perhaps this is an exaggeration of such differences, because Chapter 4 has shown that experienced counselors tend to be more alike than different.

The fifth point covers what happens in *counseling*.   This deals with the actual one-to-one process which the counselor and the client share. In more directive counseling it may be just a few interviews; in client-centered counseling it may be many interviews.

The last step in the Williamson and Darley series, *follow-up*, is the one that is most frequently neglected. What happens to this particular client after counseling? In rehabilitation agencies, follow-up becomes a necessity, because such agencies get their funds from state and federal appropriations and they need to provide information to those governmental units attesting that the job is being done. So they have to collect this information. In a school situation, there is not so much pressure to do this, although there is the same obligation to show what was done. If a school administrator is to get money for a guidance program, there must be evidence that the program is successful and is doing specific things. One function of the school counselor is to furnish this evidence, although when it has been neglected it is not altogether the fault of the counselor. If a counselor has to be responsible for 900 clients in a given year instead of 300 clients, not much time is available for follow-up. Some sort of follow-up is necessary, however, in order to justify the existence of a counseling program.

Whether the counselor uses Williamson and Darley's six headings for the systematic organization of case data, or whether the counselor uses some other system, such as the seven headings proposed by Paterson, Gerken, and Hahn in the *Minnesota Occupational Rating Scales* (1953), or some personal system, makes little difference as long as the system is effective. The important thing is that an organized way of collecting, presenting, and using information about a given client is developed which the counselor can use comfortably, as well as professionally. If the counselor feels at ease with this system in the counseling situation, the client will be more at ease also. Actually the four systems discussed here have considerable overlap.

A DEFINITION OF TERMS

Before discussing any kind of a system for organizing data, a definition of terms needs to be presented. Terms used in discussing educational-vocational case studies are quite varied, but they boil down to a discussion of abilities, aptitudes, and interests, and the way in which these are organized to help an individual choose an educational or vocational field and decide upon an approximate level within that field to which the client can aspire.

The first of these terms to be defined is *ability*. In Bingham (1937) and in English and English (1958) there are a number of definitions of ability. As defined in this chapter, ability represents the power to perform responsive acts. It is a skill which an individual possesses right now. Some writers use ability synonymously with the terms *pro-*

ficiency, capacity, capability, and *skill.* These have somewhat different meanings. For instance a *proficiency* is what a person can do right now. The *capacity* of an individual is the maximum he will be able to do, so this also includes the aptitude concept as well as ability. *Capability* is usually used to mean maximum achievable in the near, predictable future. The term *skill* reflects more ease and precision in performing complex motor activity. It is obvious from a cursory survey of terms why it is better to use the term *ability* as reflecting what an individual can do now and not get involved in the more varied meanings contained in the other four terms.

Aptitude is usually intended to mean potential ability. Bingham (1937) discusses a theory of aptitude, and in the process proceeds to confuse the terms aptitude and ability. The term aptitude becomes more confusing because people have used it to characterize a total testing program for educational-vocational purposes—the "aptitude testing" program. This is a broader use of the term because it includes tests of abilities, tests of aptitudes, and inventories of interests. The concern in this chapter is with the use of the term *aptitude* to mean a potential ability, and with Bingham's theory of aptitudes. Bingham in his discussion makes three points. His first proposal is concerned with intra-individual differences. Simply stated it means that an individual's potentialities are not equally strong. Garrett (1946) has presented evidence to show that differences in academic potential change from relatively equal strength in early childhood to demonstrated inequalities in adolescence and adult years. While there are some questionable points in his presentation, the data generally fit with observed phenomena. It is probable that aptitudes within an individual progress from a state of equality in childhood toward the condition in the adult years where there are as great differences in aptitude within an individual as there are between individuals.

The second point in Bingham's proposals is that individuals differ one from another in their potentialities, and that these differences are not usually any greater than the differences within an individual. This is basic to trait-factor theory. One person may be able to run well. Another person may be able to speak English well. A third person may be able to do mathematics well. Is one better than the other? The third point is that many of these aptitudes, both within and between individuals, are relatively stable. They appear again and again. A fourth point added by Hahn and MacLean is that these differences can be estimated. This in a sense paraphrases a statement that Thorndike (1918) made years ago. He said that things that exist, exist in quantity, and therefore can be judged, estimated, or measured. This fourth proposal is the basis upon which "aptitude appraisal programs" are started. These differences within and between individuals can be estimated, and therefore some system of organizing information about those individuals can be undertaken so that they can make educational-vocational choices.

A third definition concerns interests. The term *interest* refers to an individual's likes or dislikes for certain activities. It can refer to either vocational purposes or leisure activity. It is possible to subdivide interests further into *stated interest* and *measured interest*. Stated interest reflects an individual's "I want to be a physician," "I want to be an engineer," "I want to be an auto mechanic." Measured interest refers to information shown by scores on inventories which reflect these linguistic and nonlinguistic factors. This is discussed in detail in Chapter 10.

A fourth definition involves what Hahn and Brayfield (1945) called the *field and level* concept. *Level* refers to the place in an educational or vocational hierarchy to which an individual may aspire. *Field* is the area, occupational or educational, in which an individual appears to have the best opportunities for success. This means the best combination of abilities, aptitudes, and interests. Consequently, one way of organizing information about individuals would be under this field and level concept. The level should reflect whether the person should plan to be a semiskilled, skilled, technical, or professional level worker. The field should be considered in the light of the linguistic and nonlinguistic continua dealing with interests, academic areas, academic skill, occupations, leisure activities, and so on. *Field* includes the things of an educational-occupational nature which are carried out by an individual. Paterson, Gerken, and Hahn (1953) have proposed the use of the *Minnesota Occupational Rating Scales* as one way of describing field and level.

THE MINNESOTA OCCUPATIONAL RATING SCALES

This is a psychograph designed for organizing data about an individual under seven headings: academic, mechanical, social, clerical, musical, artistic, and physical. The counselor makes an evaluation of the data in terms of A, B, C, or D level of performance and in terms of one of the seven possible headings or fields. For example, in Form 5.1 John Doe estimated his high school average as "B." This item could be placed at the B level in the Academic area. However, after the counselor has considered all the other activities in which John has participated, and John's age, it might be advisable to evaluate academic potential at the A level. Form 5.2 shows how the information from Form 5.1 might be organized according to the *Minnesota Occupational Rating Scales*. Some of the information can be placed in a number of areas. Placement of specific items at the various levels may be questioned. This is subject to the judgment of a given counselor and as long as fairly general agreement about placement of items can be secured, preparation for counseling can proceed.

Reference to Form 5.2 shows that most of the recorded information

A Sample Personal Data Form Using/Form 5.1
Fictitious Data.

PERSONAL RECORD

Name: John Doe
Address: 1541 Main Street
Phone: 492256

This information will be released to no one without your written consent. When you wish to leave something blank, write *none*.

1. Personal data:
   Sex: _M_ Age: _16_ Date of birth: _10/2/43_ Place of birth: _Anytown, Kansas_
   Religious Preference: _Protestant_ Height: _5' 10"_ Weight: _165_
   Physical disability? _None_ Married: _No_
   School Grade _12_

2. Family data:
   Parents still married: _Yes_ Separated: _____ Divorced: _____
   Father   Mother
   Age: _38_   Age: _38_
   Job: _Tool & Die Maker_   Job: _Office Manager_
   Grade completed: _12th_   Grade completed: _12th_
   Birthplace: _Anytown, Indiana_ Birthplace: _Anytown, Kansas_
   Brothers and sisters:

Name	Sex	Age	Grade completed	Occupation
Henry	M	15	10th	Student

3. Education:
   Course taken: _College Preparatory No. and position in your class:_ 10th in 52
   Approximate High School average: _B_
   Subjects liked: _Math and Science_ Subjects disliked: _English_
   What do you plan to do when you complete High School? _Go to State University_

4. What do you like to do in your spare time?
   a. Hobbies: _Repairs on car - Build model train system - play chess or checkers_
   b. Training in music or art: _1 year piano - 2 years mechanical drawing_
   c. Clubs and organizations: _Hot Rod Club, Eagle Scout, Rifle Club_
   d. Offices held: _Pres.-Senior Class   Pres.-Hi-Y_
   e. Do you like to read? _Yes_
   f. What books do you read? _Biography - Science Fiction_
   g. What magazines do you read? _Popular Mech.- Hot Rod - Sports Illus. - World News_
   h. What kind of group activities do you like? _Scouting - Church - Sports_

   i. What sports do you play? _Track - Basketball_
   j. Varsity or intramural? _Varsity_

5. What occupation would you like to enter?

Job	Reason
a. Engineer	Like math
b. Skilled mechanic	Father's job
c. College teacher	Prestige

   Is this what your parents want you to do? Yes: _X_ No: _____
   What job would you like to be doing 10 or 15 years from now? _College teacher_

93

6. What kind of work have you done? Mark on-the-job training "X."

Job	Time in months.	Did you like it?	Why?
Newsboy	36	Yes	Exercise & Money
Grocery checker	5	Yes	Meet people
Gas station attendant	5	Yes	Learn about cars

7. What problems would you like to discuss with a counselor?
   a. Job: _____ b. Education: ___X___ c. Relations with
   others: _____ d. Finances: ___X___ e. Other: _____

8. Underline the traits in the following list which apply to you:
   Persevering, friendly, patient, stubborn, capable, tolerant, calm, impetuous, pessimistic, bashful, self-confident, jealous, talented, quick-tempered, cynical, tactful, conscientious, cheerful, submissive, excited, irritable, anxious, poor health, nervous, easily exhausted, unhappy, frequent periods of gloom or depression, frequent day-dreaming.

Information from Form 5.1 Organized/Form 5.2 According to the Areas of the Minnesota Occupational Rating Scales.

| | | | Areas of Activity | | | | |
Level	Academic	Mechanical	Social	Clerical	Musical	Artistic	Physical
A	H.S. Senior at 16 B average 10th in class of 52 Occupations vs. education of parents College Prep. course Reads biography Wants to be college teacher Age-grade of brother	Liked Math and Science Disliked English Plays chess Built model train system Wants to be an engineer	Pres. senior class Pres. Hi-Y Eagle Scout				5' 10" 165 lbs Varsity track and basketball in fairly large school
B	Wants college Parents support occupational choice Says he is "persevering and conscientious"	Repairs on car Hot Rod club Plays checkers Wants to be skilled mechanic 2 years mechanical drawing Gas station work Reads science fiction	Parents not divorced Hot Rod club	Grocery checker Newsboy	1 year piano	2 years mechanical drawing	
C		Reads *Popular Mechanics* and *Hot Rod*	Says he is "friendly and tolerant"				
D				Disliked English			

95

about John is evaluated at the A and B levels and in the Academic and Mechanical areas. This might warrant further investigation of these areas by the counselor prior to actual counseling. However, there is enough evidence of social skills and interest in social activities to indicate that the counselor should investigate and perhaps open up further possibilities in this area. If John should eventually have the opportunity of becoming an administrative engineer or sales engineer, such social skills may be of the utmost importance. As far as the other areas are concerned, they would appear to be of minor importance to John in evaluating himself and in choosing a course of action for his future.

It should be noted here that the system of organizing data to present to John as outlined above is based on use of ratings of worker traits needed for educational-vocational fields of activity as presented by Paterson, Gerken, and Hahn and the evaluation of an appropriate potential level of performance within such fields. This method is highly useful to the counselor for organizing data from records. The field and level concept will also be inherent in the system to be proposed next.

LINGUISTIC AND NONLINGUISTIC APPRAISAL

Human behavior can be evaluated on a series of continua. One of the most convenient ways of describing the major continuum would be to think of it as ranging from extreme "linguistic" activities at one pole through a point of balance to an extreme of "nonlinguistic" activities at the other pole.

Subordinate continua can then be arranged in any order the counselor chooses. Those selected in Form 5.3 cover "School Courses," "School Extra-class Activities," "Occupational Data," and "Leisure Activities." They illustrate one way in which the counselor could organize data in preparation for counseling, but because of the nature of Form 5.1 the topics are limited more than if all existing information were utilized.

Form 5.3 shows that most aspects of John's behavior are distributed about a central point or on the nonlinguistic end of the major and subordinate continua. Thus the counselor can see at a glance that most of the evidence at present points toward those educational-vocational choices that do not involve many linguistic factors. Now the evidence can be presented to John in an initial interview and the counselor can check to see the amount and kind of effect these data have upon John.

There may be no negative emotional elements if John sees himself as a potential engineer. There could be considerable psychological conflict if John sees himself as a potential clergyman or journalist. Actually most of the data in Form 5.1 and therefore in Forms 5.2 and 5.3 present a congruent picture of John and one which the evidence indicates he can accept.

Nonlinguistic	Balance of Both	Linguistic

School Courses

Liked math and science	10th in senior class of 52	
2 yrs. Mechanical drawing	B average in high school	
Dislikes English	College Prep curriculum	

School Extra-class

Scouting		Pres. Hi-Y
Rifle club		Pres. Senior class
Hot Rod club		
Varsity track		
Varsity basketball		

Occupational Data

Gas station attendant	Newsboy	
Wants to be engineer or skilled mechanic	Grocery checker	
	Wants to be college teacher	

Leisure Activities

Reads *Popular Mechanics* and *Hot Rod*	Reads *Sports Illustrated*	Reads biographies
Builds model train system	Reads science fiction	Reads *World News*
Repairs own car	One year piano lessons	Church group
Plays checkers and chess		

In such a case the counselor can make predictions of success in educational and occupational activities of nonlinguistic nature. The counselor can point out to John that all three occupational choices are possibilities, but that present evidence indicates greater chance for success in engineering or skilled mechanics than as a college teacher. It would also be possible for the counselor to explore with John the items in Form 5.1 that indicate this and what John could do if he wished to change his behavior to improve his chances of becoming a college professor or something not particularly indicated by present data. In these ways the counselor uses such data either for prediction or for helping a client understand and change behavior.

Although some of the factors dealing with linguistic-nonlinguistic concepts in evaluating interests have been included in the organization of data in Form 5.3 and in Chapter 10, it may be useful also to describe them here. Cottle (1950) has proposed five such interest factors. They are described below as five subheads or continua which should be synthesized with data about aptitudes and abilities.

INTEREST FACTORS

Linguistic	Nonlinguistic
1. People and communication	Things and processes
2. Business contact	Scientific activities
3. Abstract, creative activities	Routine, concrete, organized activities
4. Social welfare activities	Non-social, mechanical activities
5. Prestige or status activities	Tangible, productive activities

The following elaboration of a linguistic-nonlinguistic system of organizing case data is based on research and counseling experience. It proposes a number of tentative hypotheses about the relationships that may exist between individuals and educational or vocational phenomena which need to be verified by further research. These hypotheses are proposed here to illustrate the system rather than as established relationships.

1. The interest factor, "people and communication versus things and processes," actually presents a continuum ranging from the individual who deals only with people and communication types of activities, through individuals like a physician or a physical education teacher who deal with people from a scientific background which would be nonlinguistic, to the person like the engineer or various kinds of mechanics who would be placed somewhere near the nonlinguistic extreme of this continuum.

2. The second factor, "business contact versus scientific types of activity," appears time after time in studies of interest measurement and is self-explanatory.

3. The third factor, "abstract, creative thinking" on the one extreme versus "routine, concrete, organized activities" at the other end of the continuum refers to types of activity which do and do not require very much change or newness and these closely approximate descriptions of certain kinds of personality traits as well.

4. The fourth factor, "social welfare activities versus nonsocial, mechanical activities," is enough different from the first factor so that it needs to be considered by itself. An example would be the kinds of people-related activities a teacher does compared to the activities of the bookkeeper, custodian, or machinist.

5. The fifth factor, "prestige or status versus tangible, productive activities," represents the kind of thing a manager, a salesman, or a public relations specialist might do in contrast to the kind of thing that a machine operator might do. The former needs tangible evidence of success in contrast to the machine operator, because at the end of a day the latter knows he has produced his quota of units and he has more in his tool box or locker for tomorrow. The machine operator can count the things he produces, he has no need for mink or expensive cars to demonstrate that he is successful. The nonlinguistic worker can usually show the things that he does, the bridges he makes, the houses he builds, or the machines he produces.

These are different ways in which the interests needed by people in jobs can be systematically described.

In a like fashion in the academic area, illustration of abilities on the linguistic side of the continuum would be the languages, English and foreign, and the social sciences. On the other end of the continuum would be mathematics, physical sciences, and some vocational education as examples of nonlinguistic types of abilities. When academic skills are considered apart from academic subjects, such linguistic skills as reading, writing, spelling, and recitation might be listed in contrast to the nonlinguistic academic skills such as computation, drawing, laboratory work, and class demonstration.

In terms of occupations, such linguistic occupations as teaching, law, journalism, selling, or management are occupations dealing with people and communication versus the nonlinguistic skills of the natural scientists, the mathematician, the accountant, or the chemist. All of the latter group work primarily with things and processes, and use nonverbal symbols more frequently than words. It is also possible to think of a sub-sub continuum when considering occupations. Teaching is an illustration of an occupation that could be further subdivided on a continuum of its own from linguistic to nonlinguistic extremes. At the linguistic end would be the English teacher, the librarian, or the social studies teacher, with the math teacher, science teacher, or the teacher of auto mechanics at the other end of the continuum. Probably the physical education teacher falls somewhere in the middle of the continuum. In like manner the clergy or physicians could be placed along a continuum of linguistic to nonlinguistic jobs or specialties within the general professional classification. Probably more minute subdivisions are possible, but do not seem warranted by present data. The important point here is that customary occupational stereotypes actually vary considerably within an occupation.

In terms of leisure time activities, reading on the one extreme versus model-building on the other would be examples of linguistic or non-linguistic leisure activities, respectively. Or parties emphasizing meeting and dealing with people versus playing cards such as solitaire, or even playing bridge in a foursome, might be examples of classifying leisure activities as in Form 5.3.

These linguistic things are the kinds of activities that more women do than men. The nonlinguistic activities are the kinds of things that more men do than women. In the past this has been described in terms of masculinity or femininity but has been a more limited concept than the one proposed here as a major educational-vocational continuum. Besides, the counselor who tries to explain to a high school boy that the boy has masculine interests, or worse yet that he has feminine interests, will find the atmosphere can get thick and warm for a few minutes. It is much simpler to explain to a male that he has linguistic interests centering around relationships with people and communication with those people. It is also easier to explain to a female that she has nonlinguistic interests centering around activities dealing with mathematics, or with scientific processes, or the kind of manual activities that a surgical nurse might do. These are the more masculine types of activities and occupations as far as women are concerned, but when they are called nonlinguistic activities they have less emotional impact on the client and thus they are easier to explain or to accept.

U S E S FUNCTIONAL OCCUPATIONAL CLASSIFICATION SYSTEM

For a number of years the United States Employment Service through the activities described by Fine and Heinz (1957, 1958) has been working on a system for classifying occupations in terms of a number of components which make up a description of the occupations and which also include a description of the kinds of people who carry on these occupations. This constitutes still another system of organizing information about the individual in order to help in choice of education and a career. The 1957 publication by Fine and Heinz stresses the need for a single classification system for all workers and described a research program which culminated in the *Estimates of Worker Trait Requirements for 4000 Jobs.* Table 5.1 shows how the job description is presented. These estimates provide profiles of six worker trait components required for 4000 entry jobs. The components deal with training time, aptitudes, temperaments, interests, physical capacities, and working conditions. Table 5.2 is a special template prepared for use in reading Table 5.1.

It is placed across the page shown in Table 5.1 under the matching columns as an aid in interpreting the symbols. In the 1958 publication dealing with functional occupational classification structure itself, two additional components, industry and work performed, have been added to the previous six. Each of the components in the original description of 4000 jobs was rated separately by different raters. These raters were four experienced occupational analysts and six relatively inexperienced occupational analysts. All the analysts received 100 hours of basic training in the kinds of rating desired and in the background information and materials which would be used in analyzing this sample of 4000 jobs.

This system is basically similar to the previously described *Minnesota Occupational Rating Scales,* but, instead of covering 432 jobs, is covering a sample of 4000 jobs. It is anticipated that the system will be extended to cover all jobs descriptions presently included in the *Dictionary of Occupational Titles* (1949).

In describing the proposed Functional Occupational Classification Structure of the Employment Service, Fine and Heinz (1958:180–1), make the following statement:

> What workers do is done at various levels of complexity in relation to
> *Things, Data,* and *People.* All jobs involve some relation to all three.
> The ways in which workers function in relation to *Things, Data,* and *People* are unique and can be expressed in terms of separate hierarchies. In
> each hierarchy, the functions proceed from the simple to the complex
> with each successive function conceived as including the simpler ones and
> excluding the more complex ones. Thus by selecting the appropriate
> function from each of the three hierarchies that describes what the worker
> does in a given job-worker situation, it is possible to show the totality of
> the worker's relationships to *Things, Data,* and *People.*

This code describing worker activities is composed of three sets of three digits each. The first three-digit part of the code describing the job in terms of Worker Functions is made up of letters indicating the level of functioning required by the job and the amount of involvement of workers with things, data, and people. These are shown in Table 5.3.

TABLE 5.1

Excerpt from Estimates of Worker Trait Requirements for 4000 Jobs Showing Descriptions of Ten Jobs

Line No.	D. O. T. Job Title	Vol. II Code	Part IV Code	GED	SVP	GVN	SPQ	KFM	EC	1 2 3 4 5
				Train. Time		Aptitudes				Tempera ments
1	Key-Crimping-Machine Operator	8–04. 10	6–X4. 419	3	2	445	445	343	45	2 3
2	Key Floorman	1–38. 04	1–X2. 8	4	6	333	433	444	55	
3	Key-Punch Operator	1–25. 62	1–X2. 9	4	4	333	333	233	55	3
4	Kick-In Engineer	5–73. 330	4–X2. 493	4	5	345	345	443	34	2
5	Kick-Press Operator I	6–88. 640	6–X4. 419	4	5	334	334	343	45	2
6	Kick-Press Operator II	9–13. 28	6–X4. 409	3	3	345	445	343	45	2 3
7	Kiln Burner	6–66. 251	6–X2. 605	4	6	333	434	444	53	
8	Kiln Cleaner	6–66. 265	4–X6. 232	4	5	334	434	333	54	2
9	Kiln Operator	4–33. 911	4–X6. 625	5	7	233	433	444	54	
10	Kindergartner	2–43. 97	2–X3. 3	5	5	224	444	443	44	4 5

TABLE 5.2

Template for Use and Interpretation of Estimates of Worker Trait Requirements for 4000 Jobs

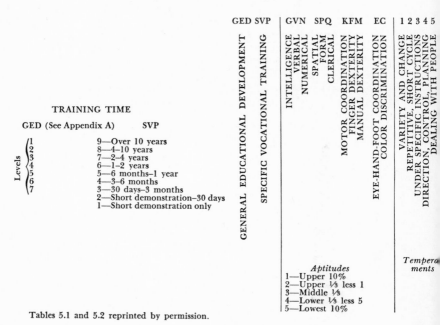

Tables 5.1 and 5.2 reprinted by permission.

TABLE 5.1 (Continued)

EXCERPT FROM ESTIMATES OF WORKER TRAIT REQUIREMENTS FOR 4000 JOBS SHOWING DESCRIPTIONS OF TEN JOBS

Temperaments					Interests										Physical Capacities						Working Conditions							Industry Code	OAP No.	OOH Page	Line No.
8	9	0	X	Y	1	2	3	4	5	6	7	8	9	0	1	2	3	4	5	6	1	2	3	4	5	6	7				
					1		3								L			4			I							214			1
																					I										
		0		Y	1								9		L			4		6	I							123			2
				Y	1		3								S			4		6	I							249	12		3
				Y	1								9		L			4		6	O							544			4
				Y	1								9		L			4		6	I							138			5
	9				1		3								L			4			I							138			6
				Y	1								9		L					6	B		3				7	178			7
				Y	1								9		M		3	4		6	B						7	178			8
		0		Y	1								9		M			4			B		3	4				008			9
								4				8			L			4	5		I							138			10

TABLE 5.2 (Continued)

TEMPLATE FOR USE AND INTERPRETATION OF ESTIMATES OF WORKER TRAIT REQUIREMENTS FOR 4000 JOBS

Temperaments
- 8 — PERFORMING UNDER STRESS
- 9 — SENSORY OR JUDGMENTAL CRITERIA
- 0 — MEASURABLE OR VERIFIABLE CRITERIA
- X — FEELINGS, IDEAS, FACTS
- Y — SET LIMITS, TOLERANCES OR STANDARDS

Interests
- 1 — THINGS AND OBJECTS
- 2 — BUSINESS CONTACT
- 3 — ROUTINE CONCRETE
- 4 — SOCIAL WELFARE
- 5 — PRESTIGE
- 6 — PEOPLE, IDEAS
- 7 — SCIENTIFIC, TECHNICAL
- 8 — ABSTRACT, CREATIVE
- 9 — NONSOCIAL
- 0 — TANGIBLE, PRODUCTIVE SATISFACTION

Physical Capacities
- 1 — STRENGTH
- 2 — CLIMBING-BALANCING
- 3 — STOOPING-KNEELING
- 4 — REACHING-HANDLING
- 5 — TALKING-HEARING
- 6 — SEEING

S—Sedentary
L—Light
M—Medium
H—Heavy
V—Very Heavy

Working Conditions
- 1 — INSIDE-OUTSIDE
- 2 — COLD
- 3 — HEAT
- 4 — WET-HUMID
- 5 — NOISE-VIBRATION
- 6 — HAZARDS
- 7 — FUMES, ODORS, ETC.

I—Inside
O—Outside
B—Both

TABLE 5.3

STRUCTURE OF WORKER FUNCTIONS

Things	Data	People
	A Observing	
	B Learning	
C Handling	K Comparing	R Taking Instructions-Helping
D Feeding-Offbearing	L Copying	S Serving
E Tending	M Computing	T Speaking-Signalling
F Manipulating	N Compiling	U Persuading, V Diverting
G Operating-Controlling	O Analyzing	W Supervising, X Instructing
H Driving-Controlling	P Coordinating	Y Negotiating
I Precision Working	Q Synthesizing	Z Mentoring
J Setting Up		

NOTES:

1. Each successive function reading down includes all those that precede it.

2. Feeding-Offbearing and Tending, Operating-Controlling and Driving-Controlling, and Setting-Up are special cases involving machines and equipment of Handling, Manipulating, and Precision Working respectively and hence are indented under them.

3. The hyphenated factors Feeding-Offbearing, Operating-Controlling, Driving-Controlling, Taking Instructions-Helping and Speaking-Signalling are single functions.

4. The factors separated by a comma are separate functions on the same level separately defined. They are on the same level because, although excluded from the one above it, usually one or the other and not both are included in the one below.

Fine and Heinz (1958). Used with permission.

TABLE 5.4

WORK FIELDS

001	HUNTING-FISHING	054	SHEARING-SHAVING
002	LOGGING	055	MILLING-TURNING-PLANING
003	CROPPING	056	SAWING
004	MINING-QUARRYING-EARTH BORING	057	MACHINING
005	BLASTING	061	FITTING-PLACING
011	LOADING-MOVING	062	FOLDING-FASTENING
012	HOISTING-CONVEYING	063	GLUING
013	TRANSPORTING		
014	PUMPING	071	BOLTING-SCREWING
		072	NAILING
021	STATIONARY ENGINEERING	073	RIVETING
		081	WELDING
031	CLEANING	082	FLAME CUTTING
032	IRONING	083	SOLDERING
033	LUBRICATING		
		091	MASONING
041	FILLING	092	LAYING
042	PACKING	093	TROWELING
043	WRAPPING	094	CALKING
051	ABRADING	101	STRUCTURAL FABRICATING-INSTALL-ING
052	CHIPPING		
053	BORING	102	UPHOLSTERING

Fine and Heinz (1958). Used with permission.

TABLE 5.4 (Continued)

WORK FIELDS

111	ELECTRICAL FABRICATING-INSTALLING	191	PRINTING
112	ELECTRONIC FABRICATING-INSTALLING	192	IMPRINTING
121	MECHANICAL FABRICATING-INSTALLING	201	PHOTOGRAPHING
		202	DEVELOPING-PRINTING
131	MELTING	211	APPRAISING
132	CASTING	212	WEIGHING
133	HEAT CONDITIONING		
134	PRESSING-FORGING	221	STOCK CHECKING
135	DIE SIZING		
136	MOLDING	231	RECORDING
		232	ACCOUNTING-RECORDING
141	BAKING-DRYING		
142	CRUSHING	241	LAYING OUT
143	MIXING	242	DRAFTING
144	DISTILLING	243	SURVEYING
145	FILTERING-STRAINING-SEPARATING	244	ENGINEERING
146	COOKING-FOOD PREPARING		
147	PROCESSING-COMPOUNDING	251	RESEARCHING
151	IMMERSING-COATING	261	WRITING
152	SATURATING	262	PAINTING
153	BRUSHING-SPRAYING	263	COMPOSING
154	ELECTROPLATING	264	STYLING
161	COMBING-NAPPING	271	INVESTIGATING
162	SPINNING	272	LITIGATING
163	WINDING		
164	WEAVING	281	SYSTEM COMMUNICATING
165	KNITTING		
		291	ACCOMMODATING
		292	MERCHANDISING
171	SEWING-TAILORING	293	PROTECTING
		294	HEALING-CARING
181	ERODING	295	ADMINISTERING
182	ETCHING	296	TEACHING
183	ENGRAVING	297	ENTERTAINING

The kind of information covered here would deal with aptitudes, interests, temperaments, and a general educational development evaluation. The second three digits of the code represent the work field which covers the kind of work that needs to be done in the job. This would include such things as machines, tools, equipment and work aids. It is illustrated in Table 5.4. The last three digits of the code represent the material, products, subject matter, or service with which the worker and the occupation interact. This is usually abbreviated as *MPSMS* and deals with the most important job content. This is shown in Table 5.5.

The way in which this system works is illustrated in detail in the 1958 article by Fine and Heinz. Therefore no elaborate description will be considered here. The counselor wishing to use such a system should study it thoroughly and check its use with the nearest state employment service office or with the United States Employment Service Regional Office.

SOME SAMPLE CASE DATA AND QUESTIONS

The data in Form 5.4 are presented to give the beginning counselor some working data. Some of the questions a counselor could ask and answer are as follows:

1. What data shown in Form 5.4 indicate that this person may not be a good reader?

2. Is it possible that this person may be unable to learn to read better, or is there evidence that his academic potential would permit him to acquire better reading skills than are evidenced here?

3. Is it possible that this person may be having difficulty in school because he does not know how to study?

4. Are there any evidences in these data that this person may be so emotionally disturbed that he is unable to perform well in school?

5. Does the information contained in scores from the interest inventories indicate the kind of profile that would be expected of a person that is enrolled in an engineering curriculum and one who is apt to be happy and satisfied in the kinds of academic work required of such a curriculum?

This case illustrates five common questions which are usually asked whenever any student is having difficulty in school. These questions center about academic potential versus academic achievement; the reading and other study skills of the student; whether emotional disturbance is affecting performance, and the part that interests play in motivation for school.

The most probable interpretation of the above data might answer these questions in the following way:

The student would seem to have sufficient potential to function at the college level, if reading skills were improved. Other study skills would

TABLE 5.5

SAMPLE SECTION OF MATERIALS, PRODUCTS, SUBJECT MATTER, AND
SERVICES CLASSIFICATION

080	FOOD STAPLES
081	Grain Mill Products
082	Meat Products, including Sea Food and Poultry
083	Dairy Products (Milk, Butter, Ice Cream, and Cheese)
084	Bakery Products
085	Oils and Fats, Edible (Margarine, Shortening, Table Oils, etc.)
086	Sugar and Syrup (Cane, Beet, Maple Syrup, etc.)
087	Canned, Bottled, Frozen and otherwise-Preserved Foods
088	
089	Food Staples, not elsewhere classified
140	LUMBER AND WOOD PRODUCTS
141	Logs, Rough Lumber, and Fuel Wood
142	Finished Lumber, Treated Wood, Shingles, and Cooperage Stock
143	Plywood and Veneer (Marquetry)
144	Prefabricated Wooden Buildings and Structural Members, Including Partitions (Stage Settings, except Scenery)
145	Millwork (Window and Door Frames; Doors; Mantels; Panel Work; Stairways; and Shutters)
146	Wood Fixtures (Shelving; Cabinets; Bar Fixtures; Butchers' Fixtures; Lockers; Display Cases; Racks, and Stands; and Telephone Booths)
147	Wooden Containers (Baskets; Laundry Hampers; Cigar Boxes; Crates; Cases; Shipping Drums; Barrels; Kegs; Box Shooks; and Wooden Trunk Slats)
148	Wooden Articles (Shoe Lasts; Hat Blocks; Mirror and Picture Frames; Kitchen Wooden-ware; Pipes; Toys; Pencils; Curtain Rods; Golf Clubs)
149	Lumber and Wood Products, not elsewhere classified (Excelsior; Caskets; Window and Door Screens and Weather Strip; Cork Products, etc.)
770	PERSONAL SERVICES
771	Barbering Services; Beauty Services
772	Lodging Services
773	Meal Services (Including both Food and Beverages; also Catering) except Domestic
774	Valet Services (Pressing, Alteration, Garment Repair; Shoe Repair, Shoe Shine, Hat Cleaning)
775	Laundry and Dry Cleaning Services
776	Child and Adult Care
777	Photographic Services
778	
779	Personal Services, not elsewhere classified (Funeral Services, and Porter Services; Social Escort Services; Clothing Rental; Steam Baths)

Fine and Heinz (1958). Used with permission.

Case of Male, Age 18, Freshman/Form 5.4 in Engineering.

A.C.E. Q. 64 Percentile National Coll. Fresh.
L. 5 "
T. 16 "

Coop. Reading C2 V. 27 Percentile Ent. Coll. Fresh.
S. 11 "
C. 20 "
T. 21 "

Coop. English U. 3 Percentile Ent. Coll. Fresh.
Sp. 11 "
V. 4 "
T. 6 "

Coop. Mathematics 31 Percentile Ent. Coll. Fresh.

Iowa Silent 20 Percentile Coll. Fr.
Grade Equivalent 10.9
Age Equivalent 16.0
Tyler Kimber
Study Skills 95 Percentile Jr. Coll. Students

Wechsler-Bellevue 98 Percentile Gen. Pop.
Full Scale I.Q. 128 15–19 yr. olds
Verbal I.Q. 128
Performance I.Q. 125

MMPI	T score
?	50
L	50
F	60
K	51
Hs	49
D	65
Hy	48
Pd	64
Mf	50
Pa	50
Pt	67
Sc	51
Ma	58
Si	61

Kuder Pref. Rec. B.M.
Adult Norms

Mech.	91	Percentile
Comp.	86	"
Sci.	91	"
Pers.	40	"
Art.	60	"
Lit.	5	"
Mus.	78	"
Soc. Serv.	10	"
Cler.	55	"

SVIB Men

A
Engineer
Prod. Manager
Printer
Math.-Sci. Tchr.
Policeman
Personnel Manager

Borderline B, B+
Carpenter
YMCA Phys. Dir.
Pres. Mfg. Concern

Rejects
Artist
City Sch. Supt.
Minister
CPA
Lawyer

B+
Chemist
Accountant
Office Worker
Purchasing
Public Admin.

O. L. 18 Percentile Stanford Freshmen
M. F. 83 Percentile College Males
I. M. 39 Percentile 18 yr. olds

appear to be adequate and interest in the curriculum in which the student is enrolled would seem to offer adequate motivational factors. There is some question about the meaning of the personality inventory scores shown on the *MMPI*. These may be reflecting the normal concern an individual would have who is not getting along as well in school as he would like. The *D* and *Pt* scores would be indicating this type of pressure. It is difficult to tell from these scores whether the high *F*, *Pd*, *Ma*, and *Si* scores are a reflection of other personality difficulties or the concomitant of academic difficulty. The program the counselor undertakes will be modified by the interpretation placed on these latter scores in the light of other case data and in conjunction with the weak reading skills shown above.

Counseling Case./Form 5.5

A.C.E. Psych.	Q. 74 Percentile Nat. Coll. Fr.
	L. 32 Percentile
	T. 54 Percentile

Otis S.A. Ment. Ability
I.Q.   117   70 Percentile Coll. Stud.
          93 Percentile Unselected
                    Adults

Coop. Reading C2	V. 6 Percentile Nat. Coll. Jr.
	S. 13 Percentile
	C. 22 Percentile
	T. 12 Percentile

MMPI

?	50
L	50
K	48
F	55
Hs	52
D	63
Hy	52
Pd	41
Mf	80
Pa	47
Pt	58
Sc	49
Ma	50
Si	48

Coop. English PM	U. 4 Percentile Nat. Coll. Fr.
	S. 1 Percentile
	V. 8 Percentile
	T. 2 Percentile

| Coop. Math B | 96 Percentile Nat. Ent. Fr. |

Coop. Gen. Cult. X Total	21 Percentile Nat. Coll. Soph.
Curr. Soc. Prob.	30 Percentile
Hist. and Soc. Stud.	28 Percentile
Lit.	2 Percentile
Sci.	75 Percentile
Fine Arts	2 Percentile
Math	82 Percentile

| Minn. Clerical | No. 7 Percentile Employed Clerical Workers |
| | Na. 5 Percentile |

| Minn. Paper Form Board | 91 Percentile Eng. Fr. |

Strong Vocational Interest Blank for Men

Kuder Preference
Record

Mech.	99	Percentile
Comp.	99	Percentile
Sci.	97	Percentile
Pers.	5	Percentile
Art	73	Percentile
Lit.	1	Percentile
Mus.	5	Percentile
Soc. Serv.	5	Percentile
Cler.	50	Percentile

A
Physician
Engineer
Chemist
Farmer
Carpenter
Printer
Math.-Sci. Tchr.

B+
Production Mgr.
Y. Physical Director

Rejects
Personnel Mgr.
YMCA Secretary
City Sch. Supt.
Minister
Sales Mgr.
Real Estate Sales
Life Ins. Sales

O.L. 3 Percentile Stanford Fr.
M.F. 78 Percentile Coll. Males
I.M. 23 Percentile 20 yr. old men

The information shown in Form 5.5 can be highlighted by a number of questions that the counselor might like to ask.   These questions are as follows:

1. What data from Form 5.5 would be indicating nonlinguistic factors as far as this individual is concerned?
2. If you had to discuss possible majors with this person in light of these scores, would you discuss engineering?
3. If you knew that this person was a second-semester college junior, would this make a difference in the possible majors you discuss?
4. When you look at the scores of the *MMPI* is there any scale which does not support choices of engineering or other nonlinguistic majors?
5. Would it help you to change the answer you made in question 4, if you knew that these data described a girl?
6. What additional data to support a nonlinguistic major are found in the Supplementary Data to Form 5.5?
7. What possible college majors would you suggest to this girl?

(Supplementary Data to Form 5.5)

This girl, who is a college junior with a math major, came in either for help in choosing another major or for confirmation of the major that she has already selected.

She states that her high school graduating class was a group of 20 and that she was 7th in this group with a B average. She then attended a junior college and maintained a B average there. In both high school and junior college she liked math best and English least. Courses which she took in high school and junior college in math include elementary and advanced algebra, plane geometry, general mathematics, trigonometry, college algebra, solid geometry, analytical geometry, calculus I and II. She received A's in all of these except a B in trig and in college algebra. She also has 12 hours of chemistry, 10 hours of physics, and is taking biology at the present time.

Activities that she likes are sports of all kinds. She reeled off a long list of all kinds of intramural sports which she likes to play rather than to watch. She would impress one as being a "tomboy." Other activities that she likes are dancing and reading books, mostly popular fiction. She lives in a sorority.

When discussing other types of activities at the end of the interview to get an idea of her social ability, she mentioned that she belonged to a card club which they had called a "poker club" but in which they played all types of card games.

Work experience includes work as a typist for one month, work as a packer in a soap factory for two months; work for two and half months in a powdered milk plant; and work as a girl scout and assistant girl scout leader. Her father, who is 70 and completed 8th grade, is a retired farmer. Her mother, who is 55 and completed 12th grade, is a housewife.

SVIB Women

A	Rejects	F.M. I—Percentile
Math Science Teacher	Home Economics Teacher	College Females
Physician	English teacher	
	Social Worker	
	Social Science Teacher	
	YWCA Secretary	

CASE OF WILLIAM ROE

Initial interview with William Roe

This student was graduated 2nd in a class of 20 from a 100 pupil high school (grades 9–12). He had a 90+ average, taking elementary algebra, plane and solid geometry, trigonometry, and college algebra. He also had general science and physics. He liked math best and physics least. The reason for his dislike of physics was that he had a war-trained teacher who was not a science major.

In high school he played varsity football (2 yrs.), basketball (4 yrs.), and baseball and track (1 yr. each). He went out for basketball in college and made the B team. He was a Star Scout in high school.

We began by discussing his reading. He stated that he had always been a very slow reader, that he was supposed to wear glasses for poor vision but had never done so. During the interview he decided that probably his first point of procedure should be to go over to the reading lab, have a further check on his reading to see if corrective or remedial work were necessary. If results seem to indicate this, he also thought it might be wise to take a trip to either an eye specialist or to student hospital for a check on the glasses that he has at the present time, as they are five years old.

Much of the time of this interview was spent in developing rapport. The boy was rather reserved and quiet and did not contribute too much unless continually stimulated. He stated that he is having difficulty in chemistry, doing about F work at the present time. This would raise a serious question, coupled with his dislike for physics, about continuing in engineering. Ability in math, however, seems to support some type of a mathematical background in further schooling and in occupations.

His college average at present is 1.4 (a "C+") with a D in inorganic chemistry. His math courses were A's and B's.

He doesn't work outside school, using P. L. 550 funds and some savings to cover living costs.

His father is at present a 2nd class Postmaster. Prior to this he was a superintendent of schools with a master's degree. His mother, a housewife, is a graduate of a 3-year teachers' college course with a permanent certificate for high school teaching.

He has three sisters. One, married, completed 13th grade. Another is in 14th grade at present. The third is in the 11th grade.

He doesn't like social activities, except such sports as tennis and swimming. He reads 1 book every 2 months and likes *Reader's Digest*. He gave no clear picture of his leisure time activities, either because he has no planned program, or because of reticence. This was the only serious gap in the information which was evidenced during the initial interview.

Here are some questions the beginning counselor might answer from the data on William Roe:

1. What nonlinguistic factors appear in the initial interview notes?

2. What data could be considered evidence of college potential?

Name *William Roe*	Unit *Engr.*	Class *Soph.*	Sex *M*	Age *21*
Name of Test Form	Score	Percentile	Norm Group	
ACE Psych '41 Q '41 L-57	R98*	37 (Q,50;L,32)	N. Coll. Fr.	
Coop. Reading, Total C2T	S54*	37	N. E. Fresh.	
Vocab.	49	20		
Speed	55	35		
Compre.	59	56		
Coop. English, Total PM	S41	6	N. E. Fresh.	
Usage	47	17		
Spell.	26	1—		
Vocab.	51	27		
Mathematics D-45	R60	73	E. Coll. Fresh.	
Wechsler Bellevue Full	I.Q. 123	95	Gen'l Pop.	
Verbal	127		20–24 Yr. Old	
Performance	113			
Coop. Gen. Cult X				
Sci.	20	38	N. Coll. Soph.	
Math.	35	89		
Rev. Pp. Fm. Bd.	R47	70	Engr. Fresh.	
Purdue Pegboard				
Right Hand	R12	8		
Left Hand	11	8		
Both Hands	10	17		
Total	33	3		
Assembly	8¼	65		
Minn. Clerical-Nos.	W82*	49	Adults Gainfully Occupied	
Names	61	32		
Iowa Physics Apt.	57	39	Engr. Fresh.	
Minn. Soc. Pref.	W125	34	Minn. U. Students	
Minn. Soc. Behavior	W144	67		

Kuder; Form BM, Adult Males.

Mech.	...........36 Percentile	Comp.	...........94 Percentile
Sci.	.............40 Percentile	Pers.	............87 Percentile
Art.	.............11 Percentile	Lit.	.............52 Percentile
Mus.	............22 Percentile	Soc. Serv.	.......77 Percentile
		Cler.	............20 Percentile

Strong:

	B+ on	B on	C on	
O. L. 28 Percentile	Prod. Mgr.	Printer	Artist	Minister
M. F. 35 Percentile	Math-Sci. teacher	Policeman	Psychologist	Muscian
I. M. 82 Percentile		Personnel Mgr.	Architect	Pres. (mfg.)
		Soc. Sci. Tchr.		Engineer
		Physician		Chemist
		Accountant		
		Dentist		
		Real Est. Salesman	City Sch. Supt.	

* R, S, and W show raw, scaled, and weighted scores.

3. If he transfers out of engineering, what other majors might be considered?

4. What does the family data contribute to understanding the values to which this client has been exposed?

5. What do you know about his social skills?

6. What additional evidence would you want from a testing program?

7. What tests would you select to give such information? Would you assign these all at once or gradually?

When the counselor inspects test data for William Roe, the following questions might be pertinent:

1. What evidence of poor reading skills exists? Do the scores on intelligence tests contribute to this?

2. Would you expect this client to be more successful at present in a Liberal Arts curriculum?

3. What about the ultimate choice of math-science teaching? Do the two interest inventories agree about this? What attitudes do you suppose the family environment has created toward teaching?

CASE OF EDWARD DOE

Initial interview record of Edward Doe

This student is a junior in the College of Engineering, taking power plant work in the mechanical engineering sequence with a grade point average of 1.3 (C+). This does not appear consistent with placement examinations taken in the spring of 1948. Nor is it consistent with the fact that he was an aviation cadet and had completed pre-flight training just before the war ended and then was separated from service. For that reason additional tests of academic ability, in particular the Wechsler Bellevue, were planned, as was a retake on the ACE. He was graduated in a high school class of 75 approximately midway in the class with a C average. He liked English least. He liked geography and math best and had only two years of math in high school. He played varsity basketball and participated in varsity track for three years. He has had no musical training to the present time and no inclination toward music. He took one year of manual training in high school which consisted of one semester of mechanical drawing and one semester of shop work.

Here at college he likes math and strength of materials courses best, although he failed the latter course last term. He likes English least.

Work experience includes work as an aircraft sheet metal worker for three years, work as a carpenter's helper for eight months, and Army training as an aviation cadet.

Leisure time activities include various types of mechanical hobbies. He states that he likes to "Mess around with mechanical things," such as building shelves, cabinets, and making photographic equipment for the new hobby of photography developed since a baby boy was born. He states that he has no darkroom, that he only takes photographs.

His father, who is 48, completed 4th grade in the United States (born in Czechoslovakia) and is a shovel operator in a coal mine. His mother, who

University Guidance Bureau, Summary Profile./Form 5.7

SUMMARY PROFILE

Name. *Edward Doe* . . . . School *Engrg.* . . . Class *1965* . . . . Sex *M* . . Age. *24* . . .

	Date	Name of Test Form	Score	%-ile	Norm Group	1	5	10	15	20	30	40	50	60	70	80	85	90	95	99
Placement Exams	9/59	ACE Psych. Total	72	11	Nat. Coll.															
		Q	35	37	Freshmen															
		L	37	6																
	9/59	Coop. Reading Total	45	8	"															
		C2T Vocab.	45	10																
		Speed	48	14																
		(level. J.) Compre.	44	7	"															
	9/59	Coop. English Usage	43	9																
		PM Spell.	52	43																
	9/59	KU Mathematics	49	46	K.U. Students															
Scholastic Aptitude	2/62	ACE Psych. Total	90	34	Nat. Coll.															
		Q	52	84	Freshmen															
		L	38	6																
			WS IQ																	
	2/62	Wechsler-Bellevue Full Scale	121 117	87	Gen. Pop.															
		Verbal	55 110		20-24 yr. olds															
		Perform.	66 121																	
	2/62	Otis S-A Mental Ability	52	53	Coll. Stud.															
		IQ	110																	
Achievement	2/62	Coop. General Culture Total																		
		I History-Social Studies																		
		II Literature																		
		III Sciences	24	50	Nat. Coll.															
		IV Fine Arts			Soph.															
		V Mathematics	30	84																
	2/62	Iowa Silent Reading		5	13th Grade															
Specific Aptitudes	2/62	Minn. Paper Form Board	54	81	Engrg. Sr.															
		Minnesota Clerical No.	185	94	Employ. Cler.															
		No.	166	90	Workers															
Personality	2/62	Minn. Soc. Att.																		
		Soc. Pref.	137	54	Minn. U.															
		Soc. Beh.	156	83	Students															
Misc.																				

Other Profiles   SVIBM *2/62*   SVIBW   Kuder *2/62*   MMPI   GZTS *2/62*

Used with permission.

114

Other Data for Edward Doe

Kuder Preference Record, Form C		Guilford-Zimmermann Temperament Survey	
	Centile		Centile
Outdoor	59	G – General Activity	80
Mechanical	99	R – Restraint	20
Computational	46	A – Ascendance	42
Scientific	75	S – Social Interest	55
Persuasive	55	E – Emotional Stability	35
Artistic	88	O – Objectivity	50
Literary	1	F – Friendliness	57
Musical	21	T – Thoughtfulness	50
Social Service	55	P – Personal Relations	50
Clerical	14	M – Masculinity	98

Strong Vocational Interest Blank for Men

Group I

Artist	C
Psychologist (rev.)	C
Architect	B
Physician (rev.)	B
Dentist	B+

Group II

Chemist	A
Mathematician	C
Engineer	A

Group III

Production Manager	A

Group IV

Farmer	B+
Math. Science Teacher	B
Forest Service	B–
Army Officer	
Aviator	

Group V

Y.M.C.A. Phys. Dir.	C
Personnel Manager	C
Vocational Counselor	C
Soc. Science Teacher	C
City School Supt.	C
Minister	C
Social Worker	

Group VII

C.P.A. Partner	C

Group VIII

Senior C.P.A.	
Junior Accountant	C
Office Worker	B–
Purchasing Agent	C
Banker	C
Pharmacist	

Group IX

Sales Manager	C
Real Estate Salesman	B–
Life Insurance Salesman	C

Group X

Advertising Man	C
Lawyer	C
Author-Journalist	C

Group XI

President (Mfg. Concern)	B

OL 36 %ile Stanford Freshmen
MF 91 %ile College males
IM 10 %ile 24-year-old men

is 43, was born in the U. S., completed 8th grade and is a housewife. He has one brother, 20, who completed one and one-half years at State Teachers College and is not in school at present; a sister, 22, who completed 12th grade and is now a secretary in Kansas City.

His own family consists of his wife who acts as a housewife caring for his boy who is 19 months old. She completed 12th grade, worked as a secretary, and operated a lathe in an aircraft plant during the war. She was very active in 4-H Clubs while she was in high school. He made this latter statement as if he were quite proud of the fact that his wife had achieved quite a bit of distinction in this work in the state.

At the close of this interview we discussed tests he might take, how they could be useful and when he would take them. He plans to investigate the power plant management and industrial engineering options of the mechanical engineering program. Problems in adjustment seem an outgrowth of his academic progress and problems of academic choice.

Some of the questions a counselor might ask after reading data about Edward Doe are:

1. How do data about potential for school coincide between initial interview and the first four scores on the Summary Profile? What does the Wechsler Bellevue Performance I.Q. indicate?

2. What tentative diagnosis about reading skills seems indicated? What data support this?

3. What test scores indicate problems of adjustment? Do these seem deep-rooted and serious? Why?

4. Do the interest inventory scores support continuance in engineering? Do they indicate possible choice of production engineering over research and development? How?

5. As counselor, what other data do you think this client needs before making a curricular choice to finish college?

6. Are there any remedial or corrective measures you would suggest?

SUMMARY

Thus, as the counselor through the use of records, biodata, observational techniques, or the initial interview studies the things which a client has done, a pattern of behavior develops which usually shows a preponderance of skills and a preference for activities toward the linguistic or the nonlinguistic end of the continuum. The counselor who can organize data in this fashion has a convenient and practical way of helping a client to understand behavior, to accept such behavior as a part of self, and to make sound educational and occupational choices as a result.

Such systems of organizing data from records will have to be developed by the individual counselor in the light of personal needs and skills. Beginning counselors will find that some system of handling data develops without deliberate effort. They should be highly aware of this process at first in order to evaluate how adequate their system is in terms of good counseling objectives and procedures. Only when this has been done can the counselor allow the process to take place at a low level of awareness.

REFERENCES

Bingham, W. V. *Aptitudes and aptitudes testing.* New York: Harper & Brothers, 1937.

Cottle, W. C. A factorial study of the Multiphasic, Strong, Kuder and Bell inventories using a population of adult males. *Psychometrika,* 1950, 1–5, 25–47.

English, H. B., and A. C. English. *A comprehensive dictionary of psychological and psychoanalytical terms.* New York: Longmans, Green and Co., 1958.

Fine, S. A., and C. A. Heinz. The estimates of worker trait requirements for 4000 jobs. *Personnel and Guidance Journal,* 1957, *36,* 168–174.

————. The functional occupational classification structure. *Personnel and Guidance Journal,* 1958, *37,* 180–192.

Garrett, H. E. A developmental theory of intelligence. *Amer. Psychol.,* 1946, *1,* 372–378.

Hahn, M. E., and A. H. Brayfield. *Occupational laboratory manual for teachers and counselor.* Chicago: Science Research Associates, 1945.

Hahn, M. E., and M. S. MacLean. *Counseling psychology.* New York: McGraw-Hill Book Company, Inc., 1955.

Paterson, D. G., C. d'A. Gerken, and M. E. Hahn. *Revised Minnesota Occupational Rating Scales.* Minneapolis: University of Minnesota Press, 1953.

Thorndike, E. L. The nature, purposes, and general methods of measurements of educational products. Bloomington, Ill.: *Seventeenth Yearbook, NSSE,* Part II, 1918.

United States Employment Service. *Estimates of worker trait requirements for 4000 jobs.* Washington: U. S. Dept. of Labor, 1956.

United States Employment Service. *Dictionary of occupational titles, Second Edition,* Vol. 1. Washington: U. S. Dept. of Labor, 1949.

Williamson, E. G., and J. G. Darley. *Student personnel work.* New York: McGraw-Hill Book Company, Inc., 1937.

6

Statistics used to describe groups and individuals

IN ORDER TO EVALUATE THE DATA ABOUT GROUPS AND ABOUT INDIVIDUAL behavior that are essential to any counseling activities, the counselor must possess a knowledge of statistics. In some ways the frame of reference in which the counselor uses these statistics is the same as that for other psychological or educational workers. Estimates of group behavior must be collected and interpreted so that a client is better able to understand the groups in which it is necessary to function. The client is helped to understand himself in terms of place in or divergence from the average group engaging in an activity. However, the frame of reference of the counselor differs also to the extent that part of the work with clients requires the use of statistics to organize and interpret data about intra-individual comparisons. Thus, it is essential that these two frames of reference for statistics, a comparison with a group and comparisons within a given client, are contained in almost every statistical inference the counselor makes.

These statistics should be used for all estimates of behavior in counseling and not just for test scores. The chief ways in which a counselor uses statistics may be summarized as follows:

1. Directly for counseling purposes with a client.
2. For referral reports about a client sent to other agencies.
3. In analyzing results of tests given to groups. These results form a large basis for counseling.
4. In interpreting reports in the literature so that such information can be used to improve counseling effectiveness.
5. In carrying on research which will evaluate counseling procedures or improve counseling effectiveness.
6. For reporting such research in the literature.

In this brief introduction to statistics, averages, measures of variability and measures of relationship will be considered. A short discussion of sampling theory and the testing of hypotheses as the counselor uses them in the frames of reference described above will compose the last part of the chapter.

AVERAGES

In statistics the counselor is usually concerned with two averages or measures of central tendency. These are the *mean* and the *median.* The term *central tendency* is used because it describes the activities of the middle of the group.

The counselor is concerned with helping a client identify and evaluate the distinctive characteristics or traits of the groups in which the client will function. To do this the counselor and client must decide which of these groups are appropriate. It is not usually appropriate to compare a twelfth grader with ninth grade groups unless some sort of retardation makes it so. On the other hand it is often logical to compare graduating twelfth graders with college freshmen, if this is the next group in which the twelfth grader will compete. To make these comparisons and to choose appropriate norm groups it is necessary to describe the groups in terms of their central or average tendency and their deviation from an average.

The mean

Suppose that a group intelligence test is administered to 40 individuals. The result of such an administration is shown in Table 6.1. There are two ways in which the mean can be obtained for these data. These

TABLE 6.1

Scores of 40 Individuals on the
Otis Self-Administering Test of Mental Ability

36	40	52	38	64	22	18	34
32	39	58	42	36	28	49	42
31	38	46	58	28	38	47	41
18	37	65	38	46	43	46	52
36	46	30	60	38	62	42	37

scores could be added together and their sum divided by the total number of cases. This result is a value which is already familiar to the counselor, namely the arithmetic average. If it is desirable to translate this operation into statistical language, it can be written as follows:

$$\overline{X} = \frac{X_1 + X_2 + X_3 + X_4 + \ldots\ldots X_n}{N}$$

Where:

$\overline{X}$ = the mean
X_1, X_2, X_n = individual raw scores
N = the number of cases or scores

However, instead of writing the formula as it is above, it is possible to summarize the terms in the numerator and then the formula for the mean becomes:

$$\overline{X} = \frac{\Sigma X}{N}$$

where:

Σ = Greek capital sigma and is read as "the sum of" and the other terms are as previously defined.   This is the usual formula for the mean.

Grouping data

Very often when there is a large number of scores, it is an advantage to use another method in calculating the mean.   To do this the data are set up in a frequency table as shown in Table 6.2.   To construct a table

TABLE 6.2

Computation of Mean and Standard Deviation
for the Scores in Table 6.1

		(1) f	(2) x'	(3) fx'		(4) fx'2
63–65	//	2	8	16		128
60–62	//	2	7	14		98
57–59	//	2	6	12		72
54–56		0	5	0		0
51–53	//	2	4	8		32
48–50	/	1	3	3		9
45–47	////	5	2	10		20
42–44	////	4	1	4		4
39–41	///	3	0	0	+67	0
36–38	//// ////	10	−1	−10		10
33–35	/	1	−2	−2		4
30–32	///	3	−3	−9		27
27–29	//	2	−4	−8		32
24–26		0	−5	−0		0
21–23	/	1	−6	−6		36
18–20	//	2	−7	−14	−49	98

$$\Sigma = 40 \qquad \Sigma = 18 \qquad \Sigma = 570$$

like this several simple rules should be followed.   In the first place, it is customary to have between 10 and 20 intervals or divisions in the frequency distribution.   In order to arrive at such a distribution, an adequate size for the interval must be chosen.   The interval size is determined by first obtaining the range of scores.   The range is defined as the

high score minus the low score.   In Table 6.1 the highest score is 65 and
the lowest score, 18.   The range then is 47.   The size of the interval may
next be calculated by trial and error.   If each interval had a size of 5,
this would result in a frequency distribution with about 9 or 10 intervals,
47 divided by 5.   If each interval were 4 there would be about 12 intervals, 47 divided by 4.   Another way to obtain the interval size is to take
the range and divide it by 15, half of the number of intervals between
10 and 20, the acceptable limits for the number of intervals.

After the size of the interval has been determined, the distribution is
arranged as shown in Table 6.2.   Suppose that for these data the table
has an interval of 3 ($i = 3$).   Work is begun at the bottom and the first
interval then starts with 18.   The next one starts with 21 and so on until
the one which includes the highest score is reached.   It is the usual
practice to construct these using numbers that are multiples of the class
interval.

After the table is completed the next step is to tally or list the frequency of the scores.   Then these tallies or frequencies are summarized
and this value is placed under column 1, labeled f, for *frequencies*.
This column adds to 40, which agrees with the number of cases in the
original group of Table 6.1.   This apparent agreement, however, does
not assure that there are no mistakes.   It is possible that every score
is placed in an incorrect interval.

How numbers are regarded in statistics

Before the mean is computed a digression to illustrate how each score
is considered seems essential.   Any number or score is thought of as
being on a straight line or continuum.   An example of this would be a
score of 8.   On this line or continuum the score 8 occupies the distance
beginning at 7.5 and continuing *up to* 8.5.   Each number has then a
lower limit and an upper limit.   The next number 9, really begins at
8.5 and continues *up to* 9.5.

Using the above idea, the bottom interval in Table 6.2, the interval
18–20, is interpreted as starting at 17.5 and continuing to 20.5.   The distance between these lower and upper limits is 3, which is the size of the
interval.   Each of these class intervals also has a midpoint, which is
midway between the lower and upper limit.   In this case if one-half the
size of the class interval—one-half of 3—is added to the lower limit—17.5—
19 is seen to be the midpoint of the bottom interval.   This is the way the
counselor interprets scores and class intervals of scores.   The score is
considered a band on the continuum rather than a point.

Computation of the mean for grouped data

The mean for the 40 intelligence test scores is computed by referring
again to Table 6.2.   The first step is to decide upon a starting place for

this operation. It makes no difference where such a start is made but if it is near the middle, the numbers that are used will remain smaller and hence make the work easier. Begin by selecting the interval 39–41 as the arbitrary reference point. A zero is placed in the row opposite this interval in the x' column. Each row in this column (x') above the zero has one more positive value (1, 2, 3, etc.) and each row below the zero has one more negative value ($-1, -2, -3$, etc.). It is possible to start with the zero in the bottom interval so that all of these values are positive. But the values become considerably larger and more unwieldly than by the method shown above. Next the fx' values in column 3 are obtained by multiplying the values in the two columns to the left. A positive score multiplied by a negative score in one of these two columns results in a negative quantity or product. Column 3 is then added. The easiest approach is to sum the positive values, and then to sum the negative ones. The difference between the positive and negative sums is the total for the column.

Now all the data are available to compute the mean. For grouped data the formula is as follows:

$$\overline{X} = M' + \frac{\Sigma fx'(i)}{N}(i)$$

where M' is the midpoint of the interval that was selected as the arbitrary reference point.

Then for the problem:

$$\overline{X} = 40 + \frac{18(3)}{40}$$
$$= 40 + 1.35$$
$$= 41.4$$

This mean that has just been computed is not quite the same as the one obtained if the scores were added and then divided by the number of cases. When data are grouped, it is assumed that the values of the frequencies in any one interval will, when averaged, result in the midpoint of that interval. If this does not happen, slight discrepancies enter into the work. These discrepancies usually cancel out, with that in one interval tending to balance that in another. To the extent that they do not, slight differences appear as a result of using the different methods.

The median

The other measure of central tendency frequently encountered in counseling practice and research is the median (Mdn). The median is defined as the point in any distribution with an equal number of cases on either side of it. It is the midpoint of any distribution.

The median for the set of intelligence test scores shown in Table 6.2

is computed in the following manner. Since the total number of scores is 40, the median will have 20 scores on either side of it. The first step in obtaining the median is to divide N by 2 or to take 50% of N. In Table 6.2 start at the bottom and begin counting cases upward. Twenty cases (one-half) are needed. This occurs in the interval 39–41 which has 3 cases or scores. There are 19 cases below this point. If the 19 cases and these 3 are added there would be 22 cases, which is more than the necessary 20. So it is necessary to interpolate from the bottom of interval 39–41. This is done as follows:

$$Mdn = 38.5 + \tfrac{1}{3} (3)$$
$$= 38.5 + 1$$
$$= 39.5$$

The numerator (1) in the fraction, $\tfrac{1}{3}$, is the number of additional cases needed in the interval. In this case it is 20–19. The denominator is the number of cases in the interval, and the multiplier, 3, is the size of the interval. It is assumed that these 3 cases are spread equally throughout the interval and that it is necessary to go through one third of the interval, which in this case is one third of 3.

The median can be checked by doing the same operation beginning at the top. Counting down as close to 20 as possible, the bottom of the interval 42–44 includes 18 cases from the top score. Two more cases are needed and the procedure is as follows:

$$Mdn = 41.5 - \tfrac{2}{3} (3)$$
$$= 41.5 - 2$$
$$= 39.5$$

This is identical with the value previously obtained. It should be noted that there is a minus sign in this operation. This is needed because computation must continue in downward direction.

Use of the median

The mean is used when the data take on the shape of the normal curve which is bell shaped, tapering off in both directions. When data do not take this form, extreme scores tend to pull the mean in their direction and the result is a mean that does not give a realistic picture of the middle of the group. The median is not affected by these extreme scores. The top score in Table 6.2 could have been any value, even in the millions, and the median would have been the same as the one computed. But such a high score would have pulled the mean in the direction of that high score. The mean is also used for other computations. The median is purely an end in itself. It is a basic landmark in the distribution, but little can be done with it other than to show the exact midpoint. It is useful in counseling when distributions depart from normal or when a quick estimate of an average is needed.

VARIABILITY

Suppose that there are two distributions. The first of these has a mean of 45 as does the second. Both contain the same number of individuals and both have been obtained by administering a test to these individuals. These two means tell very little about these two distributions other than that they have the same central tendency. Suppose that in one group the high score is 48 and the low score 42 and in the other group the high score is 68 and the low score 28. This gives an additional description of the two groups. One group has much variability or is said to be heterogeneous. The other has little variability or is said to be homogeneous. To describe a group adequately it follows that a measure of variability is needed as well as a measure of central tendency. The most widely used measure of variability is the standard deviation. The counselor needs to know how to compute the standard deviation in order to describe the variability of a group and to interpret a client's position in the group in terms of such variability. The standard deviation is expressed in equal units of variability. Thus, if the standard deviation of the Otis is 12 I.Q. points and that of the Stanford Binet is 16 I.Q. points, an Otis I.Q. of 112 is interpreted as equivalent to a Stanford Binet I.Q. of 116.

The standard deviation

To compute the standard deviation, refer to column 4 in Table 6.2. This column, fx'^2, is the product of the values in each row of the two columns to the left of column 4. This process produces only positive values.

The basic formula for the standard deviation is as follows:

$$s = \sqrt{\frac{\Sigma x^2}{N-1}}$$

Σx^2 is computed by the following formula:

$$\Sigma x^2 = i^2 \left[\Sigma fx'^2 - \frac{(\Sigma fx')^2}{N} \right]$$

From Table 6.2 we obtain the following:

$$\Sigma x^2 = 3^2 \left[570 - \frac{(18)^2}{40} \right]$$

$$= 9 \left[570 - \frac{324}{40} \right]$$

$$= 9 \ (570 - 8.1)$$

$$= 5057.1$$

Then substituting this formula in the basic formula for the standard deviation the values are:

$$s = \sqrt{\frac{5057.1}{39}} = \sqrt{129.67} = 11.4$$

Interpretation of the standard deviation

The standard deviation is always interpreted in reference to the normal curve, as shown in Fig. 6.1. Notice that if a standard deviation is marked off on either side of the mean, 34% of the area of the curve, or 34% of

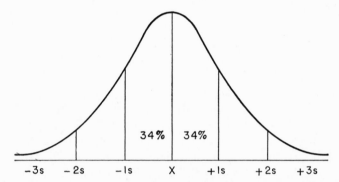

Fig. 6.1. Standard deviation units and the normal curve.

the cases are included between either of these points and the mean. A standard deviation from each side of the mean (2 standard deviations) includes 68% or approximately two-thirds of the area. Since it is assumed that the cases are equally spread over the entire area of the curve, one standard deviation taken on each side of the mean includes 68% of the cases. Two standard deviation units on each side of the mean (4 standard deviations) includes approximately 95% of the cases. Three standard deviation units on each side of the mean (6 standard deviations) includes practically all of the cases. Theoretically the tails of the normal curve never touch the base line but extend to infinity in each direction. Three standard deviations on both sides of the mean include 99.74% of the area. This means that there are 13 cases in each ten thousand in each tail of the normal curve out beyond three standard deviations.

In summary it is evident that six standard deviations cover the usual range of scores found in counseling. However, these relationships described above hold true only when the number of cases is at least two hundred. When the number of cases is smaller than 200, fewer standard deviations are needed to cover the range. As Dressel (1954) has indicated, in counseling it is customary to talk about being in, above, or below the average group. This average group is described in connection with the mean as the middle two-thirds or the middle two standard deviations, one on either side of the mean. It is also described as the distance between the sixteenth and the eighty-fourth percentiles. From this description it is easy to see why most people would fall in the average group on any given trait and why the best guess about the amount of a trait which a client possesses is "an average amount." This is one of the reasons why the mean is the more widely used of these two measures of central tendency discussed here. When the median is used, the average group is considered to be the middle fifty per cent of the distribution instead of the middle sixty-eight per cent.

MEASURES OF RELATIONSHIP

In dealing with test scores or academic grades it is frequently useful to determine the relationship between two or more variables or traits. The statistics used to measure these relationships are called correlation coefficients. In the work that follows two of the most frequently encountered coefficients will be discussed.

One of the questions a counselor is frequently called upon to answer is, "How are certain characteristics or traits related?" Another is, "How well will this estimate predict a given criterion of performance?" Still a third might be, "How consistent is behavior, or how stable is the characteristic?"

In order to answer such questions the counselor must compute or interpret coefficients of correlation. The size of a correlation coefficient indicates the degree of relationship that exists between two traits. Height may be closely related to weight, but they are not the same. This relationship means that the taller an individual is, the heavier he is. In like manner the coefficient of correlation shows how an estimate is related to a criterion of performance or how closely one estimate of behavior parallels another to show consistency or stability.

In size the correlation coefficient ranges from +1.00 through zero to −1.00. Both plus and minus one indicate a perfect correlation or relationship. Such relationships are pictured in Figures 6.2 and 6.3. In Figure 6.2 notice that individual A is in the lowest position on both the X- and the Y-axes. Individual B is in second position on the two axes. All other pairs of scores are arranged in the same way. The lowest on one test is the lowest on the second test. The second lowest on the first test is the second lowest on the second test. And so this goes for all of the other individuals. This illustrates a perfect positive relationship. Now notice Fig. 6.3. Here individual A has the highest score on the Y-axis and the lowest score on the X-axis. Individual B has the second highest score on the Y-axis and the second lowest on the X-axis. All the remaining individuals continue this pattern. A situation like this illus-

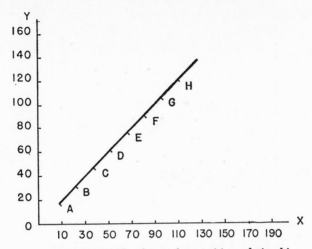

Fig. 6.2. An example of a perfect positive relationship.

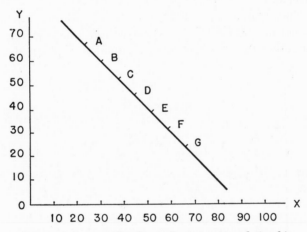

Fig. 6.3. An example of a perfect negative relationship.

trates a perfect negative relationship. Perfect relationships like these are not encountered in actual practice.

In educational and psychological estimates most of the relationships are of a positive nature, but they frequently are far from perfect. The tallies in Fig. 6.4 illustrate a fairly high positive relationship. Notice that the tallies no longer fall along a straight line as they did in the previous figures. One can still see the straight line relationship, but the tallies have spread out from it. The further they go from this imaginary line running through the center of them, the lower is the value of the correlation coefficient. When there is no relationship, the tallies are spread all over the diagram.

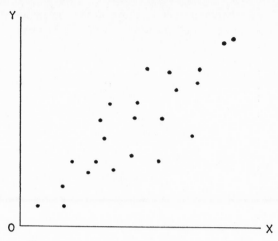

Fig. 6.4. A rather high positive relationship.

The correlation coefficients to be discussed below are associated with a straight line relationship. There are some situations when the relationship is not in a straight line. These relations are described as being curvilinear rather than linear. Such a situation is pictured in Fig. 6.5.

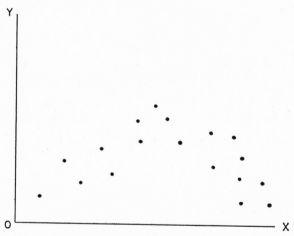

Fig. 6.5. An example of a curvilinear relationship.

If one were to plot on one axis the ability to carry on physical activities, and age on the other, such a curvilinear relationship would result. This means that as one gets older one improves in the physical skill up to a certain point, but with continued age, one becomes poorer and poorer in the skill as physical potential becomes more limited. When a relationship is found to be curvilinear, the two correlational techniques described below are not appropriate. The appropriate method for handling such data will be found in any elementary statistics book. It should be emphasized that curvilinear relationships are by no means rare and that it is always a good idea to do a little plotting of the pairs of scores before any correlational computations are made.

The Spearman Rank-Order Correlation Coefficient

The data in Table 6.3 will illustrate the computation of this statistic. This table contains the scores of 25 students on an intelligence test and

TABLE 6.3

COMPUTATION OF THE SPEARMAN RANK-ORDER CORRELATION COEFFICIENT

Indi-vidual	(1) Intell. Test Scores	(2) Algebra Test Scores	(3) Rank on Intell. Test	(4) Rank on Algebra Test	(5) D	(6) D²
1	62	58	1	6	5	25.
2	58	42	2	16	14	196.
3	54	66	3.5	2	1.5	2.25
4	54	60	3.5	4	.5	.25
5	52	68	5	1	4	16.
6	50	42	6	16	10	100.
7	49	53	7	10.5	3.5	12.25
8	48	37	9	22	13	169.
9	48	48	9	12.5	3.5	12.25
10	48	46	9	14	5	25.
11	46	53	11	10.5	.5	.25
12	45	48	12	12.5	.5	.25
13	43	56	13	7.5	5.5	30.25
14	42	59	14.5	5	9.5	90.25
15	42	63	14.5	3	11.5	132.25
16	41	40	16	18.5	2.5	6.25
17	39	32	17	25	8	64.
18	38	56	18	7.5	10.5	110.25
19	36	54	19	9	10	100.
20	34	42	20	16	4	16.
21	33	40	21	18.5	2.5	6.25
22	32	38	22	20.5	1.5	2.25
23	30	36	23	23	0	0.
24	29	38	24	20.5	3.5	12.25
25	24	34	25	24	1	1.

$$\Sigma = 1,129.50$$

on an algebra test. To determine the relationship between these two sets of scores the following steps are necessary:

1. Rank the individuals on the intelligence test. The first person, with a score of 62, is given a rank of 1. This is placed in column 3. All individuals can be ranked like this and there is no problem unless there are ties. Notice that individuals 3 and 4 each have a score of 54. Rather than assign one of these individuals a rank of 3 and the other a rank of 4, each of them is given the average of the two ranks, in this case 3.5. Individuals 8, 9, and 10 are also tied. In this case each of the three individuals is given a rank of 9 which is again the average of their ranks. This process is continued until all individuals are ranked.

2. Next the positions on the algebra test are ranked. Individual 5 has a score of 68 on the algebra test. Since this is the highest score on this test, a 1 is placed beside this number in column 4. Individual 3 with the next highest score of 66 receives a rank of 2. In like manner all of the scores on the second test are assigned a rank.

3. Column 5, headed D, is the difference obtained by subtracting one rank from the other. Since the differences are to be squared, only the absolute difference needs to be recorded.

4. Square each of these differences and place the squares in column 6.

5. Sum these values in column 6.

6. The Spearman Rank-Order Correlation Coefficient (*rho* or ρ) is then obtained by the use of the following formula:

$$\rho = 1 - \frac{6\Sigma D^2}{N(N^2 - 1)}$$

$$= 1 - \frac{6(1129.50)}{25(625 - 1)}$$

$$= 1 - \frac{6777.0}{15600.0}$$

$$= 1 - .43 = .57.$$

This value may be considered as being a moderately high correlation coefficient and also a rather typical one when two variables like these are correlated.

The above process is a rather simple one when the number of cases is not too large, that is, 35 or less. But if there are many individuals in the distributions, this technique would become an almost endless chore because of time spent in ranking the two sets of data. The second method, the Pearson Product-Moment Correlation, while it will probably seem rather difficult to the beginner, actually is not. It is considerably easier to compute, however, if one has access to a calculating machine or an adding machine.

The Pearson Product-Moment Correlation Coefficient

The computation of this statistic is illustrated with the same data that were used in finding the rank-order coefficient. This work is shown in Table 6.4. In column 1 are the intelligence test scores. These can be called X or referred to as the X-variable. In column 2 are the algebra scores, the Y-variable. Column 3 (X^2) contains the squares of all the scores in column 1. In practice, these are most easily obtained from a table of squares usually found in the appendix of a statistics or mathematics book. In column 4 (Y^2) are the squares of all the Y scores. Column 5 (XY), referred to as the "cross-products," is obtained by multiplying each X score by its corresponding Y score. Each of these five

TABLE 6.4

Computation of the Pearson Product-Moment Correlation Coefficient for the Data on 25 Individuals in Table 6.3

Ind.	(1) Intelligence Test Scores X	(2) Algebra Scores Y	(3) X^2	(4) Y^2	(5) XY
1	62	58	3844	3364	3596
2	58	42	3364	1764	2436
3	54	66	2916	4356	3564
4	54	60	2916	3600	3240
5	52	68	2704	4624	3536
6	50	42	2500	1764	2100
7	49	53	2401	2809	2597
8	48	37	2304	1369	1776
9	48	48	2304	2304	2304
10	48	46	2304	2116	2208
11	46	53	2116	2809	2438
12	45	48	2025	2304	2160
13	43	56	1849	3136	2408
14	42	59	1764	3481	2478
15	42	63	1764	3969	2646
16	41	40	1681	1600	1640
17	39	32	1521	1024	1248
18	38	56	1444	3136	2128
19	36	54	1296	2916	1944
20	34	42	1156	1764	1428
21	33	40	1089	1600	1320
22	32	38	1024	1444	1216
23	30	36	900	1296	1080
24	29	38	841	1444	1102
25	24	34	576	1156	816
	$\Sigma = 1{,}077$	$\Sigma = 1{,}209$	$\Sigma = 48{,}603$	$\Sigma = 61{,}149$	$\Sigma = 53{,}409$

columns is then summed and the correlation coefficient, r, is obtained by the use of the following formula:

$$r = \frac{N\Sigma XY - (\Sigma X)(\Sigma Y)}{\sqrt{[N\Sigma X^2 - (\Sigma X)^2][N\Sigma Y^2 - (\Sigma Y)^2]}}$$

$$= \frac{25(53409) - (1077)(1209)}{\sqrt{[25(48603) - (1077)^2][25(61149) - (1209)^2]}}$$

$$= \frac{1335225 - 1302093}{\sqrt{(1215075 - 1159929)(1528725 - 1461681)}}$$

$$= \frac{33132}{\sqrt{(55146)(67044)}}$$

$$= \frac{33132}{\sqrt{3697208424}} = \frac{33132}{60805}$$

$= .54$, which is approximately of the same size as was previously computed by the other method.

In actual practice all the values need not be copied down as in Table 6.4. If the work is done on the calculating machine, the sums of the five columns will be cumulated as one goes along and in the end all that one has to do is to copy the values from the machine.

Frequently it is useful to find the means and standard deviations when finding the relationship between two variables. For the data in Table 6.4 these can be obtained as follows:

$$\overline{X} = \frac{\Sigma X}{N} \qquad\qquad \overline{Y} = \frac{\Sigma Y}{N}$$

$$= \frac{1077}{25} \qquad\qquad = \frac{1209}{25}$$

$$= 43.1 \qquad\qquad = 48.4$$

To obtain the standard deviations it is necessary to find the Σx^2 and Σy^2 or the two sums of the squares as these are commonly called. The sum of the squares for the X-variable is obtained by the formula:

$$\Sigma x^2 = \Sigma X^2 - \frac{(\Sigma X)^2}{N} = 48603 - \frac{(1077)^2}{25} = 2206$$

Similarly the sum of the squares for Y may be obtained:

$$\Sigma y^2 = \Sigma Y^2 - \frac{(\Sigma Y)^2}{N} = 61149 - \frac{(1209)^2}{25} = 2682$$

The basic formula for standard deviation gives the following:

$$s_x = \sqrt{\frac{\Sigma x^2}{N-1}} \qquad\qquad s_y = \sqrt{\frac{\Sigma y^2}{N-1}}$$

$$= \sqrt{\frac{2206}{24}} \qquad\qquad = \sqrt{\frac{2682}{24}}$$

$$= \sqrt{91.9} \qquad\qquad = \sqrt{111.75}$$

$$= 9.6 \qquad\qquad = 10.6$$

The statistics discussed so far are referred to as descriptive statistics since they are the ones that are usually used to describe a distribution of test scores in terms of characteristics of a group. In the pages which follow some other uses of statistics will be discussed along with the use of statistics when dealing with individual cases rather than groups.

SAMPLING STATISTICS

Most of the counselor's work is actually concerned with samples. An intelligence test may be administered to an eighth grade class. This eighth grade class is actually a sample of all possible eighth grade classes in the local community, the state, or the whole United States. In like manner one or two eighth grade children could be held to be samples drawn from the population of all possible eighth grade children in the United States. As noted above statistics are used to describe these samples. Statistics in these cases are really sample values. When dealing with total populations, the numbers used to describe these are referred to as parameters instead of statistics. In much statistical work and research the sample group is of value as a tentative way of describing the larger group or total population from which it came. For example, if research is started on a new reading method or test, or developing a new interest inventory, the findings might be a description not just of the sample, but of the population from which the sample was drawn. There are a few cases in which it might be possible to deal with populations rather than samples. Actually in most cases it is impossible to describe total populations.

Standard errors

Suppose that to illustrate this concept an example is chosen that deals with the mental ability of all seventh grade students in one or more states, each with large over-all populations. To carry on this study it is necessary to develop and use a new intelligence test. For convenience suppose that the samples are limited to a size of 25. In one community, using sampling procedures that cannot be described here, the new test is administered to 25 seventh graders. Suppose that the mean and the standard deviation for this sample are now computed. These are found to be 101.5 and 14.7, respectively, and, since they are used to describe a sample, are referred to as *statistics*. Now another sample is tested. This time the mean is 97.2 and the standard deviation is 12.6. Samples of this same size are tested until there are 300 samples. There are now 300 means. These 300 means may be averaged and the standard deviation of the 300 means about the average mean computed. This average or grand mean may be taken as the best estimate that is available of the population or true mean. This standard deviation of the sample means about the population mean is given a special name and referred to as the standard error. All statistics have standard errors. To be specific this one is called the standard error of the mean and the symbol for it is $s_{\bar{x}}$.

In a similar fashion it is possible to take the 300 standard deviations, find the average standard deviation, and then the variability of these 300 sample standard deviations about this average. This standard deviation would be the standard error of the standard deviation.

In actual practice the value for the standard error of the mean is computed with the following formula, using the data obtained from one sample:

$$s_{\bar{x}} = \frac{s}{\sqrt{N}}$$

The size of the standard error of the mean is inversely related to the size of the sample. The larger the sample, the smaller the size of the standard error. This occurs because the larger the number of cases in any sample, the more reliable the statistics computed or the less they will vary from sample to sample.

Suppose that a test has been administered and the mean of the test is 48, the standard deviation 8, and N is 36. The above formula shows that the standard error of this mean is $8/\sqrt{36}$, or 1.33. Since standard errors are standard deviations, they may be interpreted in the same way. For this problem it is possible to say that 68 per cent of future samples would be expected to fall within 1.33 units from this mean of 48. If N in the sample were 64, $s_{\bar{x}}$ would be $8/\sqrt{64}$, or 1.00. This illustrates the statements of the previous paragraph about sample size.

As noted above all statistics have standard errors. Here are formulas for some of the more frequently used ones:

$$s_{\bar{x}} = \frac{s}{\sqrt{N}}$$ Mean

$$s_{Mdn} = \frac{1.253\ s}{\sqrt{N}}$$ Median

$$s_p = \sqrt{\frac{pq}{N}}$$ Proportion, where $q = 1 - p$

$$s_P = \sqrt{\frac{PQ}{N}}$$ Percentage, where $Q = 100 - P$

$$s_e = s\sqrt{1 - r_{tt}}$$ Standard error of a score or standard error of measurement. r_{tt} is the reliability of a test. This will be discussed along with reliability.

$$s_{xy} = s_x\sqrt{1 - r^2_{xy}}$$ Standard error of estimate. r_{xy} is the correlation of a test with another variable. This will be discussed along with prediction.

$$s_{D_{\bar{x}}} = \sqrt{s^2_{\bar{x}_1} + s^2_{\bar{x}_2}}$$ Standard error of the difference between two means when the scores are not related. When the scores are correlated, another formula is used.

Confidence intervals

As noted above one of the purposes of statistical methods is to make it possible to make statements or inferences about a population on the basis of sample values or statistics. This is generally done by setting up what is referred to as the confidence interval. To illustrate this, suppose that a test has been administered to 324 individuals resulting in a mean of 102 and a standard deviation of 16.   The standard error of this sample mean is calculated as follows:

$$s_{\bar{x}} = \frac{16}{\sqrt{324}} = \frac{16}{18} = .89$$

When dealing with statistical inference or making statistical tests, the two levels ordinarily used are the 1% and the 5% level.   If the 1% level is selected it means that the chances are 99 in 100 that such an inference is true.   At the 5% level the chances are 95 in a 100 that something is so.   Obviously the 1% level gives less opportunity for an event to occur by chance.   Associated with each of these levels are two standard scores.   Standard scores, known as z-scores, are scores that have been reduced to standard deviation units.   A raw score which is exactly one standard deviation above the mean will have a standard score of 1, a raw score two standard deviations above the mean will have a standard score of 2, and so on.   A standard deviation unit or score taken a certain distance from the mean in the normal curve always cuts off the same proportion of the area or the same number of cases.   When the sample size is large, a standard score of 2.58 cuts off 99% of the area of the normal curve.   One half of one per cent of the area remains in each of the tails. This standard score then is to be associated with the 1% level.   Similarly a standard score of 1.96 includes 95% of the area measured off on each side of the mean.   This score is associated with the 5% level.

The 5% confidence level for the mean in the example is established by the following procedure:

$$5\% \text{ interval} = \overline{X} \pm s_{\bar{x}} (1.96)$$
$$= 102 \pm (.89)(1.96)$$
$$= 102 \pm 1.74$$
$$= 100.26 - 103.74$$

It is now possible to say that the chances are 95 in 100 that the population mean related to this problem falls within this interval 100.26 — 103.74.

In a similar fashion the 1% interval can be computed:

$$1\% \text{ interval} = X \pm (s_{\bar{x}})(2.58)$$
$$= 102 \pm (.89)(2.58)$$
$$= 102 \pm 2.30$$
$$= 99.70 - 104.30$$

Now another statement may be made that the chances are 99 in 100 that the population mean lies within these two values.   Notice that the 1%

interval band, 99.70 — 104.30, is wider than the 5% band, 100.26 — 103.74.

The above technique works well when the size of the sample is large. But when the sample size becomes small, especially 50 or less, other values must be used for the 1 and 5 per cent levels. These are obtained from a table of t ratios found in statistics books. The appropriate t is found for the sample size under consideration at a given level of confidence and this value is put into the equations instead of 1.96 or 2.58.

MAKING STATISTICAL TESTS

Another very important and perhaps more frequently encountered use of sampling statistics is in the making of statistical tests. This is illustrated by the following data. Suppose that an experiment has been performed that produces the following statistics for two groups:

$$\overline{X}_1 = 78 \qquad\qquad \overline{X}_2 = 82$$
$$s_1 = 14 \qquad\qquad s_2 = 14.8$$
$$N_1 = 100 \qquad\qquad N_2 = 81$$

The two means differ, one being higher than the other. When there are differences, differences may be either chance differences or real and significant differences. Looking at the above data will not reveal whether a real or only a chance difference is present. A statistical test must be applied to these data to determine whether a difference exists.

In making a statistical test of this type a null hypothesis is proposed. This is actually an hypothesis that no difference exists. For this problem the null hypothesis is that "there is no difference between mean 1 and mean 2" or it can be stated that "mean 1 is the same as mean 2." It is also the usual custom to decide ahead of time whether one is going to test the hypothesis at the 1% or the 5% level.

Now to continue with the problem. First the standard error of the mean is calculated for the two distributions:

$$s_{\overline{x}_1} = \frac{14}{\sqrt{100}} = \frac{14}{10} = 1.4 \qquad\qquad s_{\overline{x}_2} = \frac{14.8}{\sqrt{81}} = \frac{14.8}{9} = 1.64$$

Secondly, the standard error of the difference between the means is computed using the formula for uncorrelated data:

$$s_{D_{\overline{x}}} = \sqrt{s^2_{\overline{x}_1} + s^2_{\overline{x}_2}}$$

$$= \sqrt{(1.4)^2 + (1.64)^2}$$

$$= \sqrt{1.96 + 2.6896}$$

$$= \sqrt{4.6496}$$

$$= 2.156$$

Finally, the standard score, z, is computed:

$$z = \frac{\text{Difference between the means}}{\text{Standard error of the difference between the means}}$$

$$= \frac{\overline{X}_1 - \overline{X}_2}{s_{D_{\overline{x}}}}$$

$$= \frac{78 - 82}{2.156}$$

$$= -1.855$$

The significance of z-scores of 1.96 and 2.58 has already been pointed out in discussion of confidence intervals. The z found here is evaluated by using the same two standard scores. If a z is equal to or larger than 2.58 the null hypothesis is rejected at the 1% level. This means that the chances are 99 in 100 that the difference in the data being studied is a real difference. Note, however, that there is still one chance in 100 that this difference could have occurred by chance. If the obtained z-score falls between 1.96 and 2.58, the null hypothesis is rejected at the 5% level. This means that the chances are 95 in 100 that the difference is a real one. This means there are 5 chances in 100 of being wrong about this real difference existing. Finally, if the z-score is less than 1.96, the null hypothesis is accepted for the experiment. Acceptance means that the data indicate that there is no difference between the two means.

In the problem a z-score of -1.855 was obtained. In interpreting this the minus sign is of no importance. With a z of this size the only conclusion that can be drawn is that "the null hypothesis stands." It was not possible to demonstrate any difference.

If the samples are small, less than 100 and certainly when less than 50, the technique is modified by making a t-test. This is done as above, t being the ratio of the difference between the means to the standard error of the difference between the means. For the problem worked here the t would be 1.855,. or the same as the z-score. However, this t statistic is interpreted differently. Instead of using the 1% and 5% values of 2.58 and 1.96, a t table is used to compare the computed value with the 1% and 5% values for samples of various size. Most statistics books include this table.

If for any reason the data are correlated, the above method is modified by using the formula for the difference between the means for correlated data. Data are correlated when there are two sets of measurements on the same individuals; when there are brothers in one group and sisters in the other; or some other relationship is known to exist between the groups. This formula is:

$$s_{D_{\overline{x}}} = \sqrt{s^2_{\overline{x}_1} + s^2_{\overline{x}_2} - 2rs_{\overline{x}_1}s_{\overline{x}_2}},$$

where r is the correlation between the two sets of data.

It is almost impossible to read the educational and psychological journals today without a knowledge of these statistical tests. Here is an example from a widely read journal. Wright and Scarborough (1958) compared scores on the Kuder Preference Record of 125 men who were first tested as freshmen and then retested four years later as seniors. The results of their study are shown in Table 6.5. This table demonstrates clearly what happened to the inventoried interests of these college

TABLE 6.5

COMPARISON OF INITIAL AND RETEST KUDER MEAN SCORES FOR SENIOR MEN (N = 125)

	Initial	Retest	Difference	t
Mechanical	34.09	32.49	−1.60	1.74
Computational	22.56	20.98	−1.56	2.08 *
Scientific	38.00	32.75	−5.25	5.64 **
Persuasive	44.02	46.34	2.32	2.11 *
Artistic	19.64	21.94	2.30	3.07 **
Literary	20.28	22.20	1.92	2.82 **
Musical	13.63	13.47	− .16	.30
Social Service	41.70	43.06	1.36	1.26
Clerical	37.78	36.74	−1.04	.96

* Significant at the 5 per cent level.
** Significant at the 1 per cent level.
SOURCE: Wright and Scarborough (1958:156). Used by permission of G. F. Kuder.

freshmen over a four year period. The greatest decline was in the scientific area. Here the difference was significant at the 1% level. There was also a decline in computational interests. This difference, however, was significant at only the 5% level. There were declines also in three other areas, but none of these was significant. As seniors these students showed more interest in artistic and literary activities (1% level) and in persuasive activities (5% level). The increase in social service activities was not significant.

In this chapter averages, variability, and measures of relationships were first discussed. These make up the part of statistics referred to as descriptive statistics. These statistics are used in describing samples or the relationships among samples. Next, a consideration was given as to how inferences are made about populations on the basis of a sample. Also, tests for significant differences among samples were discussed. These last two processes make up what is referred to as sampling statistics.

In the next chapter specific uses will be made of the statistics discussed in this chapter. Statistics form an important basis for counseling and personnel work.

REFERENCES

Dressel, P. L. Counseling caprices. *Personnel and Guidance Journal*, 1954, 33, 4–7.

Wright, J. C., and B. B. Scarborough. Relationship of the interests of college freshmen to their interests as sophomores and as seniors. *Educ. and Psych. Measmt.*, 1958, 18, 153–158.

7

Application of statistics

IN THE PREVIOUS CHAPTER THE BASIC TECHNIQUES THAT ARE USED FOR manipulating test scores or other quantitative data were considered. Every counselor must become skilled in the use of these techniques. In an over-all way the statistics just discussed are more frequently used when there is a large number of scores. Someone has to develop tests and set up norms. Means and standard deviations are most useful in doing this. With tests or other personnel instruments, information based upon groups must be obtained before such tests can be used with individuals. In this chapter attention shall be given to the use of tests with individuals, at least from the viewpoint of statistics. Here then will be considered the various types of test scores, what they are, and their advantages and limitations. Also when dealing with quantitative data, the reliability of the data must be considered. A discussion will follow of reliability coefficients, the various types, and how they affect the interpretation of test scores. Finally there is the matter of validity of measurements. Briefly here will be considered various types of validity, the validity coefficient, and the use of such coefficients in prediction. One of the basic tasks of the counselor is to predict future status or behavior on the basis of data which have been previously collected.

TYPES OF SCORES

In the educational and psychological world of today, many different types of scores are in use. It is impossible for all of them to be discussed in a book such as this. In the short discussion that follows age scores and quotients, centile scores, standard scores, and grade placement scores will be covered. This will be concluded with a short discussion of norms.

Age scores and quotients

Among the earliest scores to appear were the mental age scores that Binet used in the second edition of his intelligence scale appearing in 1908. With scales of this type each item on a test is given a value of so many months of mental age. An individual's score is merely the sum of the months of all of the items answered correctly. These may then be converted to years and months, as for example an individual may be said to have a mental age of 7-6, seven years and six months. These tests were so developed that a mental age of 7 would be the mental age of the typical or normal child of seven years. Such scales are difficult to develop and over the years have tended to disappear from the scene. They are found typically today in tests such as Forms L and M of Terman's *Stanford Revision of the Binet Scale*. There are also other types of ages similar to mental age, such as educational age, reading age, and the like.

Mental ages were divided by chronological ages to give the familiar *Intelligence Quotients* or *I.Q.*'s. In most cases the mental age, in months, is divided by the chronological age, also in months, and the quotient multiplied by 100 to get rid of the decimals. The average I.Q. is 100 and on Terman's *Stanford Binet* the average standard deviation for the different age levels is about 16. At the present time the I.Q. has a rather questionable status in American psychology. There are some who feel that it should be replaced with other types of scores. There are several reasons for this. In the first place I.Q. units are not equal units of measurement and therefore should not be manipulated mathematically. More important than this is that the I.Q. becomes something different as an individual gets older. Mental age increases up through adolescence. At some time in late adolescence mental growth is said to cease. At least this is the feeling of some psychologists. Then it follows that in the I.Q. ratio there is a numerator which has a limit and a denominator which continues to increase. To avoid getting smaller and smaller I.Q.'s, Terman uses a constant chronological age of 15 for all adults. Hence I.Q.'s of children are not the same as those of adults. Another problem is that I.Q.'s are available for different tests. These are sometimes all treated as if they were the same and interchangeable. In the last few years fewer and fewer tests have appeared using I.Q.'s. Some of the newer tests do use I.Q.'s, but these are a different type of score, namely a standard score, and will be discussed later. Form L-M, the 1960 edition of the *Stanford-Binet* uses this standard-score I.Q.

Centile scores

Centiles, or percentiles, as they are sometimes called, are among the scores most frequently encountered and used by the counselor. In the previous chapter one centile score, the median, has already been encountered. It may be recalled that this was defined as a point which has 50% of the scores on each side of it. Now any other centile point may be so defined. For example, C_{33}, the thirty-third centile, is defined as that point in the distribution with 33% of the cases below it. Each of these centiles may be computed in the same manner as the median was computed.   One could begin by taking 33% of the cases and then count up from the bottom, interpolate, and arrive at the value.   Admittedly this is a tremendous amount of work.   Rather accurate results can be obtained by setting up a cumulative percentage or ogive curve and reading the various points from this curve.

TABLE 7.1

SETTING UP CUMULATIVE PERCENTAGES

	f	cf	cP
120–129	1	159	100.
110–119	2	158	99.5
100–109	7	156	98.3
90–99	16	149	93.9
80–89	20	133	83.8
70–79	22	113	71.2
60–69	24	91	57.3
50–59	21	67	42.2
40–49	19	46	28.9
30–39	17	27	17.0
20–29	7	10	6.3
10–19	2	3	1.9
0–9	1	1	.6

$\Sigma = 159$

This will be illustrated by using the data in Table 7.1.   Here appear the scores of 159 individuals on a new test for which it is desired to set up centile norms.   In actual practice it would be desirable to have more cases before such norms are set up.   Some set an N of 500 as the highly desirable goal for such an operation, with 250 cases being the lower limit of acceptability.   In Table 7.1 a column labelled cf, for "Cumulative Frequency," has been set up.   This is obtained by starting at the bottom and for each interval listing the number of scores below the upper limit of that interval.   For example, the upper limit of the interval 30–39 has 27 scores below it.   The next column labelled cP, cumulative percentages, is obtained by changing each of the cumulative frequencies to per cents.   The easiest way to do this is to get a constant multiplier and then to multiply each of the cf's by this.   This constant is obtained by dividing 100 by the number of cases, in this case 100 by 159.   This results in a multiplier of .63.   The values in the last column have been rounded to the nearest tenth.

Next these cumulative percentages are plotted as shown in Figure 7.1. On the vertical or Y-axis are placed the percentages and the scores on the X-axis.   This is usually done with the ratio of the Y-axis to the X-axis about 2 to 3.   In putting the tallies into the graph, each of the cP's is placed above the value of the upper limit of its interval.   After all percentages have been tallied, a smooth curve is drawn.   This does not have to pass through all of the points.   Ideally some should be on it, and equal numbers on each side of it.

Reading of this graph is illustrated by showing how to obtain the median. Starting at 50% on the Y-axis a line is drawn to the curve using a straight edge. From this point another line is drawn meeting the X-axis at right angles. This point of intersection is the median. From the graph this results in a median of about 65 which is very similar to that obtained by using the method discussed in Chapter 6. In a similar fashion the other 98 centile points may be read. To do this with any accuracy, a large piece of graph paper, much larger than our illustration, must be used.

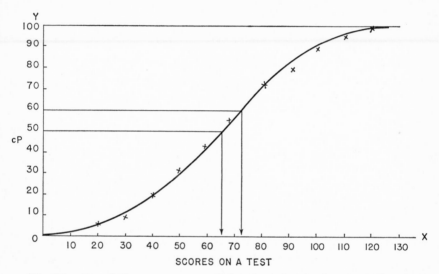

Fig. 7.1. Cumulative percentage or Ogive Curve for the data in Table 7.1.

Despite the widespread use of centile scores, they leave much to be desired. The basic problem with them is that they are by no means equal units of measurement. Most of the data that are used in counseling tend to take the shape of the normal curve, with a large piling up of scores at the center. Notice Figure 7.2; here a raw score of 72 is equal to the median. A score of 74 is the 60th centile. Actually there is no real difference or distance between these scores of 72 and 74 but in terms of centiles there is a difference of 10 centile points. Centiles then exaggerate differences at the center of the distribution. For all practical purposes, all of the various centile points in the center of a distribution may be considered as the same. On the other hand the centile points in both tails of the distribution are much more spread out, hence larger. Anyone familiar with such profile sheets as that used with the *Kuder Preference Record* has noted this peculiarity of centiles.

The counselor might then justifiably ask why he should use these scores. They do reveal something about an individual's position in a group.

But one must remember that many people use test results who know very little about tests and test scores. Centiles are rather similar to percentages in their appearance and are interpreted as such by the more naive test users. This is particularly true with the orientation tests or freshman testing scores used on most university campuses. From the viewpoint of research these scores should be avoided. The research worker must go back to the original raw scores if data that are to enter into the work are expressed in centiles.

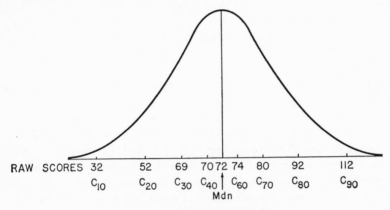

Fig. 7.2.   Distribution of centiles.

It might be noted that a few of the centiles have special names. C_{25} is referred to as Q_1, the first quartile, and C_{75}, the third quartile, Q_3. C_{10}, C_{20}, and so on, are also known as decile points, with C_{10} being referred to as the first decile.

Standard scores

The authors of more and more of the new tests are turning to this statistic for the reporting of results. A standard score, z, is obtained by the formula:

$$z = \frac{X - \overline{X}}{s}$$

where all terms are as defined in the past chapter. Suppose we illustrate this with a few test scores. In the distribution below, these scores are part of a larger distribution with a mean of 65 and a standard deviation of 10.

X	z
65	.00
75	1.00
55	−1.00
78	1.30
37	−2.80

The first of these scores has a deviation from the mean of 0. This results in a standard score of 0. The second score, 75, deviates by 10 from the mean. This divided by the standard deviation, 10, results in a standard score of 1.00. By the use of the formula, the remaining standard scores are computed.

A little thought will show that the standard score is merely the raw score transformed into standard deviation units. These scores on different tests then show an individual's position with reference to the mean equated for differing standard deviations. Thus the standard score indicates comparable *positions* in two groups, not the amount of achievement in a subject. The first z-score in the example is at the mean, thus having no deviation. The second score is one standard deviation unit above the mean. Its standard score then is a positive one. Since three standard deviations measured off on each side of the mean will include practically all of the cases, it follows that in most distributions z-scores will range between plus 3 and minus 3.

These z-scores have two characteristics which make them cumbersome to handle: in any distribution approximately half of them are negative, and they are all decimals. To avoid these drawbacks, the standard scores are transformed either linearly or using the normal curve. In a linear transformation, a new mean is decided upon and a new standard deviation. Suppose that it is desired to set up a system of standard scores with a mean of 50 and a standard deviation of 10. Each z-score would be multiplied by 10 and added to the mean of 50. The scores then would fall between 20 and 80 and all could be rounded to the nearest whole unit. If they are normalized, the tables for the normal curve have to be used. But the results are about the same if the size of the sample is made up of several hundred individuals.

One familiar with the tests used by the Army in World War II knows that these tests, such as the *Army General Classification Test,* have a mean of 100 and a standard deviation of 20. Tests used by the Navy had a mean of 50 and a standard deviation of 10. Other tests such as the "College Boards" and the *Graduate Record Examination* have means of 500 and standard deviations of 100. Wechsler's current test of adult intelligence, the WAIS, uses I.Q.'s. But these I.Q.'s are standard scores with a mean of 100 and a standard deviation of 15. Each of the subtests of this scale has a mean of 10 and a standard deviation of 3. Scores obtained with Form L-M of the *Stanford-Binet* also are standard scores with a mean of 100 and a standard deviation of 16. Series of group intelligence tests like the *Lorge-Thorndike* use similar-deviation I.Q.'s.

Standard scores may be manipulated mathematically. Perhaps more important than this to the counselor is the fact that any particular standard score always has the same meaning and one can interpret this if he is acquainted with the normal curve. For example, a standard score of minus one is at a point with 16% of the cases below it. By using the table of the normal curve, percentages for any other standard score can be so determined.

Grade placement scores

Many of the tests used in the elementary school have their results transformed to norms of this type. For example a certain child has a grade placement score of 4.2 in arithmetic, 5.3 in spelling, 4.8 in reading, 5.0 in social studies, and so forth. Suppose now that this child is in fifth grade and that it is at the end of October. He has progressed then two tenths of the way through fifth grade. His academic position is written as 5.2. Each of the above scores can then be related to this 5.2. This shows that his spelling is about the same as the group average, his social studies and reading are a bit below the group average, and that his arithmetic is one year behind the average performance for his group.

Such scores as these are very useful in making test results meaningful to both parents and students. These scores are based upon an assumption of equal growth through the ten months of the school year and no growth in summer. This assumption is not psychologically sound. Sometimes, too, a 5th grader secures placement scores such as 9.8 or 10.6. These are best interpreted by saying that he is very well informed or very adept in the subject tested; rather than that he is performing at the ninth or tenth grade level in any particular subject. The counselor will have little use for these norms, but they may appear on high school records if there is a continuous flow of information between elementary school and high school.

Fig. 7.3, from a publication of the Psychological Corporation, shows the relationships between these commonly used varieties of test scores.

Norms

After the counselor obtains a test score, the next move is to go to the manual accompanying the test and look for a table of norms that will help in interpreting the score on the test. An inspection of a few test manuals will show that the types and the adequacy of the norms provided by the various tests vary considerably. Many of the norms reported tend to be national in scope. A few of the newer tests present regional norms. Some provide norms for various types of high schools or the different academic curricula.

The counselor may wonder just what are good and adequate norms. This is a difficult question to answer. There are times when the national norms will be found most useful. But there are many other cases where local norms are much more to be desired. There is no question that communities vary. Even schools within a given city are apt to be quite different. Over the past thirty years there have been studies showing the

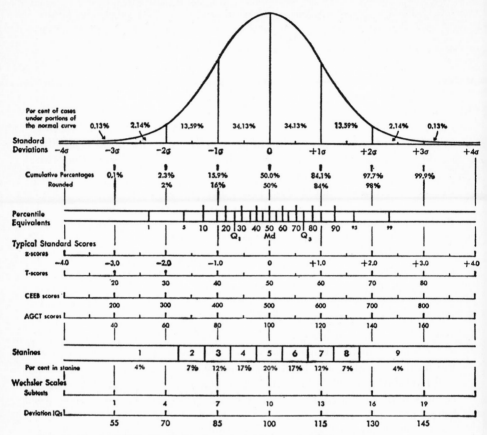

From *Test Service Bulletin No. 48,* The Psychological Corporation, 1955.

Fig. 7.3. The normal curve, centiles, and standard scores.

tremendous differences among colleges and universities in the mental ability of their students. Many schools and universities set up their own norms for tests that they use. Then new students are compared with previous and usually rather similar students. Selection, prediction, general evaluation, and the like, all seem to be improved when local norms are used. After enough cases have been collected, local norms may be set up using the centile or standard score methods as discussed above. The main concern of the counselor here should be that the individual is compared to an appropriate norm group whose members are most like this particular client.

RELIABILITY

A knowledge of statistics is basic to the understanding of the concept of reliability, whether this is applied to the use of tests or to other

types of data.   In the following brief discussion of reliability, the nature
of reliability will be discussed first, how it is usually measured will follow,
and finally the ways in which the counselor may use reliability information will be considered.

Perhaps the simplest definition that can be made of reliability is that
reliability is consistency.   A measuring instrument is reliable when it
gives consistent results.   Such a definition as this, while helpful, does
not get down to exactly what reliability is.   In modern test theory an
individual's obtained score is thought of as being made up of two components.   One of these is the so-called true score and the other the error
score.   The greater the error component in any test score, the less reliable
the measurement made by that particular test.

The commoner reliability coefficients may be classified into three types.
Reliability coefficients are usually correlation coefficients and may be
computed as described in the last chapter.

One of the simplest of these reliability coefficients is the *coefficient of
stability*.   This is obtained from a test-retest operation in which a test is
administered and then after a varying interval of time, the same test is
re-administered.   The size of this interval of time often has a significant
bearing on the size of the reliability coefficient.   If the first administration of the test is followed immediately by the second, then the individual
tends to put down the same answers on the second test as on the first
merely by remembering what those answers were the first time.   Then
if the period of time between the two testings is long, there may be much
growth and change on the part of the examinees and this will cause the
computed correlation coefficient to be lowered.   This type of reliability
coefficient is no longer encountered frequently in test development.

The second type of coefficient is referred to as a *coefficient of equiva-
lence*.   To obtain such a coefficient, equivalent, parallel, or comparable
forms of the same tests are necessary.   Two tests are said to be parallel
when they have equal standard deviations and means, are made up of
the same types of items measuring the same things, and correlate similarly with some other criterion.   The construction of such equivalent
forms of tests is common practice with test makers.   With the parallel-
form method, Text X is administered and this is followed by an equivalent form of Test X, Text Y.   Then a correlation coefficient is obtained
between the two sets of scores.   The memory factor is thus removed, but
again the time between the two administrations and familiarity in method
of doing the two tests are important.   In modern tests development this
is one of the most frequently used techniques for establishing reliability
coefficients.   It can be applied to many situations, and is the only legitimate method to be used with tests which are highly speeded or timed.

The third type of coefficient is referred to as a *coefficient of internal
consistency*.   A common example of this method is the so-called split-

half coefficient. When this method is used, each test has to be rescored. A common method is to obtain a score on the odd items and one on the even items. These two sets of scores are correlated and the resulting r corrected by what is known as the Spearman-Brown Prophecy formula. This is necessary because what has actually been obtained is the reliability of a test half the length of the original test, and the reliability of any test is a direct function of the length of the test. The longer the test, the higher the reliability, other things being equal. This correction consists of dividing two times the obtained coefficient by one plus the obtained coefficient.

Another coefficient of internal consistency is obtained by the use of the Kuder-Richardson formula number 20. To obtain this coefficient the difficulty of each item on the test must be determined. Here difficulty is defined as the proportion responding correctly to the item. The formula is as follows:

$$r = \frac{N}{N-1}\left[1 - \frac{\Sigma pq}{s_t^2}\right],$$

where:

N = the number of items on the test
p = the proportion answering each item correctly
q = 1 − p
s_t = the standard deviation of the test.

The numerator of the last term is obtained by finding the difficulty of each item, p, multiplying this by q $(1-p)$, and summing all of these products.

Coefficients of internal consistency must not be used with tests that are highly speeded. If they are, then the results obtained are an overestimation of the reliability of the test.

The size of any reliability coefficient is also related to various factors. It has already been noted that the longer a test is, the more reliable it is. Of course, there is a limit to the length that one can make a test. After a certain optimum length is reached, subjects become tired or bored, begin to guess or quit, and the reliability of the test decreases. Secondly the size of the reliability coefficient is related to the similarity or dissimilarity of the group tested. If a group consisting of students in grades 3 through 7 is tested and the reliability of this test computed and then compared with the reliability of the same test administered only to fifth grade students, the first coefficient will probably be much higher. Also test reliability is a function of similarity or homogeneity of the items making up the test.

If the counselor asks just how high a reliability coefficient should be, the best answer is that no particular value can be singled out as a minimum. With standardized tests of intelligence, special abilities, and achievement, reliability coefficients tend to be over .90. Actually, as will be noted later, it is not the size of the reliability coefficient that is most important, but that of the validity coefficient. Tests must be reliable, but this is not the most important characteristic of any test. The counselor should pay particular attention to the use of subtests. On many standardized tests, the subtests are apt to be made up of a small number of items. These subtests are frequently unreliable while the total test possesses high reliability. Diagnoses, predictions, and research made with these subtests are all apt to be worthless.

Finally it must be emphasized that tests are only pieces of paper and as such have no psychological properties. Whether a test is reliable or valid is to a great extent related to how, when, where, and with whom it is used. The author of the test usually does report a number of validity and reliability coefficients. But these were obtained when the test was used in a certain way. When the test user departs from the procedures outlined in the test manual for the use of any test, there is no telling what has happened to the reliability and validity of the test.

Some workers prefer to use the standard error of measurement in talking about reliability rather than to use correlation coefficients. These standard errors of measurement or standard errors of scores, as they are sometimes called, are not greatly affected by the variability of the group tested. They tend in general to stay about the same throughout the range.

The standard error of measurement is computed by the following formula:

$$s_e = s\sqrt{1 - r_{tt}}$$

where:

s_e = the standard error of measurement
s = the standard deviation of the test
r_{tt} = the reliability of the test

Let us now illustrate the use of this statistic. Suppose that Willie obtains a score of 49 on a test. The standard error of measurement is computed for this test and a value of 4 is obtained. This can be interpreted by saying that the chances are two out of three (remember that standard errors are standard deviations) that this score of 49 is within 4 raw score units of his true score. It follows then that the smaller the size of the standard error of measurement, the smaller the error component of an individual's test score, and then the more reliable any obtained test score will be.

VALIDITY

The most important characteristic of any evaluative device is validity. Unless our evaluating instrument has validity for a known purpose, it is of no use in the counseling program. Today psychology recognizes four types of validity: content, concurrent, predictive, and construct (A.P.A., 1954).

Content validity

Content validity is associated most often with achievement tests. For example, it can be said that a test constructed to measure plane geometry is valid when it measures both the objectives and the subject matter content of the plane geometry course in an adequate fashion. It is not difficult to achieve this type of validity, although care is necessary in the construction of the test (Downie, 1958, Ch. 6). Rating scales, checklists, and the like must also have this type of validity. Construction is important with these also.

Concurrent validity

A measuring device has concurrent validity when it separates members of a criterion group at the time of the testing. For example, a personality inventory that separates identified neurotics from normals tested in the same group or at the same time has this type of validity. Similarly tests which separate skilled machinists from unskilled or successful salesmen from poor ones possess this type of validity. A test of significance is applied to determine if there is a significant or real difference. A common test employed is the z or t test which was discussed in the last chapter. However, other tests such as the F test or chi square might be made (Downie and Heath, 1959). When any of these tests produces a significant result, concurrent validity is demonstrated.

Predictive validity

For the counselor, predictive validity is the most useful and the most frequently encountered type. To obtain validity coefficients of this type, a test or battery of tests is administered and these tests results are correlated with some other measure. This other measure, called the criterion, is that which the test is supposed to predict. The criterion in counseling usually involves performance in a given activity. For example, scores on an intelligence test administered to entering college freshmen are correlated with the grade average or index that each student made during his first semester. This correlation coefficient is called a validity coefficient. Notice here that the criterion scores or the criterion data are collected in the future. The only difference between this type of validity and concurrent validity is that the criterion data for the latter

are collected at the same time the test is administered. Other examples
of criterion measures frequently encountered are amount of sales, number
of units produced, supervisor's ratings, accident rate, or spoilage of materials.

It was previously noted that reliability coefficients tended to run above
.90 with standardized achievement tests. It may be stated here that this
is not the case with validity coefficients. The typical validity coefficient
for predicting academic grades is in the .50's. Very seldom is a validity
coefficient above .70 found. A little thought will show that the reason
for this is that these criterion measures that are used are far from perfect.
Take grades for example. Is mental ability the only factor that enters
into grades? Certainly interest and motivational factors are very important here. Then there are the idiosyncrasies of the various teachers,
the attitudes of the student toward the instructor and vice versa, and a
dozen other things that enter into the grade that any student receives.
The same is true of the criterion measures that are used in industry. Suppose that the criterion in a study is the number of units made by the
workers in a given period of time. First an assumption has to be made
that the motivation of each worker was the same. Of course, this is far
from the truth. Then there are the peculiarities of the different machines
as to speed, general state of repair, and the like. Light, noise, relations
with fellow workers, or the availability of materials each in its own way
may affect production. In all predictive or validity work of this type the
major problem is finding suitable criteria. Criteria themselves must be
reliable and valid. It might be noted here that content validity is used
with achievement tests because there is no adequate criterion available
either at the time of testing or at any reasonable future time.

As already noted, these validity coefficients are used in predicting
future performance. On the basis of an intelligence test score a college
freshman's first semester average is predicted. Or with a test of manual
dexterity a person's performance on a particular job may be predicted.
First the use of these validity coefficients in the prediction of individual
performance will be taken up. To do this it is necessary to use what is
known as a prediction equation (see Downie and Heath, 1959, or any
elementary statistics book). Little time will be spent here talking about
the derivation of these prediction or regression equations. In its most
useful form such an equation may be written:

$$Y' = \frac{r \, s_y}{s_x}(X - \overline{X}) + \overline{Y}$$

where:

$Y' = $ the predicted value of the criterion measure, in this case the predicted grade point average

$r =$ the correlation between text X and criterion Y, the validity coefficient

$s_y =$ the standard deviation of the criterion measures

$s_x =$ the standard deviation of the predictor scores; in this case the intelligence test

$X =$ the individual's obtained score of the predictor; his intelligence test score

$\overline{X} =$ the mean of the predictor, the mean of the intelligence test scores

$\overline{Y} =$ the mean of the predicted variable, the grade point averages

In order to set up such an equation as this, data have first to be collected and the various statistics computed; then the equation solved. For example, data might be collected on the entering freshmen of the current year and then this regression equation used on those who enter the following semester or the following year. It seems that most institutions tend to attract the same sort of students year after year; hence the prediction equation may be used in this way. It may be recalled that when the correlation coefficient between two variables using the Pearson r as described in the last chapter is computed, an assumption of a straight line relationship between the two variables is made. This prediction equation is the actual equation of a straight line.

Suppose that on the basis of data collected the proper values have been substituted into the equation noted above and the results simplified. Something like this results:

$$Y' = .041\,X + .24$$

Suppose that Y still stands for the predicted grade point average and X the intelligence test score. This is read by saying that the predicted grade point index (Y') is equal to 0.41 times the obtained intelligence test score plus a constant of .24. Suppose that on a certain intelligence test a student obtains a score of 100. Substituting this in the equation, his predicted grade point average is 4.34. Actually this is too simple to be true; it would only be correct if there were a perfect relationship between the two variables, that is, when r is equal to 1.00. To make predictions of this type, the straightforward approach has to be modified and a probability statement about the prediction made.

To do this requires that first a statistic known as the standard error of estimate be computed. The formula for this is as follows:

$$s_{yx} = s_y\sqrt{1 - r^2_{xy}}$$

where:

$s_{yx} =$ the standard error of estimate in predicting criterion Y from predictor X

s_y = the standard deviation of the criterion measure

r_{xy} = the validity coefficient

Suppose that as a result of substituting the proper values into this equation, a standard error of estimate equal to .3 is obtained. Remember that a standard error is a standard deviation and is interpreted as such. Then it can be said that, for any given X-score, the chances are two out of three that the predicted criterion score would be in the band made up of the Y' score obtained from the regression equation plus or minus the standard error of estimate, in this case three tenths. For the specific example, it follows that when a student has a score of 100 on this intelligence test the chances are two out of three that his predicted grade point average will fall between 4.04 and 4.64, the predicted value, plus and minus one standard error of estimate. A statistics book will show how this can all be done graphically by drawing the regression line and then constructing a parallel line on each side of this one standard error of estimate distance from the regression line. Then for any given X-score on the bottom of the graph, the range where two-thirds of the predicted values on the Y-variable for that score will fall may be obtained.

Sometimes counselors when they talk about the predictive capacity of a test refer to an index of forecasting efficiency (E). This is obtained by the use of the following formula:

$$E = 100 \left(1 - \sqrt{1 - r^2_{xy}} \right)$$

where all terms are as previously used. Suppose that for a specific situation a validity coefficient of .40 is obtained. By substituting in the formula:

$$E = 100 \left(1 - \sqrt{1 - .40^2} \right)$$
$$= 8.3\%$$

This is interpreted by saying that with this test predictions can be made 8.3% better than chance or 8.3% better than with no test at all. Values like this may be computed for each and every validity coefficient. A few of the more frequently used ones are listed below:

r	E
.80	40%
.70	28.6%
.65	24%
.60	20%
.55	16.5%
.50	13.4%
.45	10.7%
.40	8.3%
.35	6.3%
.30	4.6%

The counselor will find that for E to be large, in the 90's, the validity coefficient also has to be large. As already noted, this is seldom so.

Predictive ability is usually increased by using more than one variable for the predictor. Instead of using just intelligence test scores as the predictor, high school grade point averages, scores on a mathematics test, scores on an English or reading test, a score from an interest inventory, and the like might be used together. Usually four or five variables constitute the maximum number which are entered into this type of equation which is known as a multiple regression equation. See Guilford (1956).

By now the reader has probably felt that this is a rather bleak picture and has begun to wonder about the fundamental usefulness of tests. In most situations counselors are not concerned with the exact score or grade point average that a person might make on another variable. They are much more interested in questions such as, "Will this student pass or fail?" "Will this employee succeed on the job?" "Will this student become a superior student and thus merit a scholarship?" This is a sort of group prediction and standardized tests help very nicely in predicting when used in this manner. Any one who uses tests will soon see that tests are of limited use in telling whether a given person is going to score at the 40th, 50th, or 60th percentile on a test. Statistically there is little difference between these three centile points. But from these tests the odds are against a person who scores at the 5th centile on the test receiving a score at the 95th centile on the criterion, if the test is a valid one. The following material from Bulletin 45 of the Psychological Corporation (Psych. Corp., 1953) illustrates the effectiveness of tests. One hundred ninety-one eighth grade boys took the *Verbal Reasoning Subtest* of the *Differential Aptitude Tests* battery at the beginning of a school term. These measures of verbal ability were compared with grades received in a social studies class at the end of the term. Of these students 76 were found to have earned grades of D or lower. This was 40% of the entire class. Using chance estimates 40% of those at each test score level (low, medium, or high) would be expected to obtain grades of D or lower. The correlation between these two variables was found to be .61 which results in an index of forecasting efficiency of about 20%. The data in Table 7.2 show quite a different picture. Here it is seen

TABLE 7.2

CHANCE EXPECTATIONS AND ACTUAL PERFORMANCE IN A SOCIAL STUDIES CLASS
IN RELATION TO DAT-VERBAL REASONING SCORES

DAT Verbal Reasoning Test Score	No. of Pupils	% expected by chance to earn D, E, or F	% actually earning D, E, or F
26–up	19	40	6
18–25	49	40	14
10–17	60	40	36
2–9	63	40	73

SOURCE: Psych. Corp., 1953.

that this test is a good predictor of grades in social studies. Instead of 40% of the highest scoring pupils being found in the low grades group as would be expected by chance, only 6% are found there.

Some psychologists use expectancy tables (Tiffin and McCormick, 1958) to show the effectiveness of a test in prediction. In its simplest form such a table looks like this:

Intelligence Test Score	Per Cent Making C or better First term
140+	97
130–139	93
120–129	82
110–119	72
100–109	48
90–99	31
80–89	18
less than 80	4

An entering student with a score of 132 on this intelligence test would have then a sound prediction of becoming at least a C student.

In selection procedures using tests, a chart like Figure 7.4 may be set up. In this figure the test scores have been placed on the X-axis and

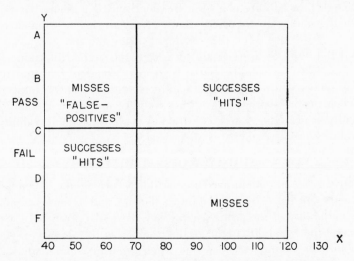

Fig. 7.4. An illustration of the use of a cutoff point in selection.

the criterion of "pass–fail" or "succeed–not–succeed" on the Y-axis. A line has been drawn above a score of 70 on the X-axis. This is referred to as the "cut-off point." Individuals above this will be admitted, those below this score refused admittance. The variable of success has been placed on the Y-axis. The horizontal line is drawn at the point separating success from failure. Any individual falling in either the upper right cell or the lower left one is classified as a success or as a hit. It was predicted that these individuals would succeed in one case or in the other case fail, and this they did. The lower right hand cells include the failures. Here success was predicted as these individuals scored above the cutting score, but they failed. Those in the upper left hand cell are also misses, but they are of a less serious nature. For these failure was predicted, but they succeeded. Such are referred to as "false positives." In actual practice the cutting score is moved around depending on the number that one wishes to select, the drop-out rate, or some other element. In industrial selection the number of job applicants would affect the location of the cut-off point. Again for a thorough discussion of this see Tiffin and McCormick (1958).

Construct validity

Construct validity will be of less concern to the counselor than are the others. Actually it is a major problem with the makers of various types of tests. A test that has been so shown to correlate with some previously determined factor, concept, or ability would be said to have construct validity.

Face validity

Although face validity is a term frequently used it really has nothing to do with validity as discussed above. A measuring instrument is said to have face validity when the individual taking the test goes away feeling that the test was appropriate for the reason he had in taking it. It really may have no validity, but it seemed reasonable, fair, and related to the examinee's future. Thus, it had face validity. This is most important when dealing with adults. Face validity and content validity are frequently confused. A test constructed to have content validity has true validity. Face validity is superficial.

SUMMARY OF VALIDITY

It must again be emphasized that validity coefficients, like reliability coefficients, are basically correlation coefficients and as such are affected by the variability of the group used in any particular study. In general, the greater the variability in the groups, the higher the validity coefficient. The counselor should consider this when he tries to evaluate validity statements found in the test manuals.

During World War II there was much research carried on in the construction of a test battery for the selection of aircraft pilots. To become a pilot, a trainee had to pass a series of hurdles made up of educational attainment, intelligence, and physical health and stamina. As a result of this testing, pilot trainees made up a rather homogeneous group. When the scores on these tests making up the battery were correlated with a criterion of success, the validity coefficients tended to be very low, some close to zero. At one time a group of unselected trainees was put into training. Validity coefficients for this heterogeneous group were of the usual size (Thorndike, 1949).

It was noted that validity coefficients tended to average about .50. Most of them reported in the research literature fall within the band .40–.60. The counselor might ask how large one of these coefficients should be to be considered useful. The best answer to this is that any that predict better than chance may be used (see pages 153–154). There are no absolute values for this. Also, as with reliability, test results are most valid when the test is used as recommended by the author. Any deviations from the instructions in the manual, such as using the test with a different group, changing the directions, or altering the time leave no other choice than to revalidate the instrument.

While on the subject of validity, reference should be made to another term that is being encountered more and more in research, and that is "cross validity." Very briefly this means to try the experiment or study again with another group and to see if the results are the same. Many of the studies in clinical psychology and some in counseling psychology are of no value chiefly because no research worker bothered to cross-validate them.

SUMMARY

In this chapter types of scores, norms, reliability, and validity were discussed. Each of these is important in selecting and using standardized tests and other evaluation instruments. In the next chapter the selection and use of tests will be discussed. The material in this chapter then provides an important basis for that which follows.

REFERENCES

American Psychological Association. *Technical recommendations for psychological tests and diagnostic techniques.* Washington: American Psychological Association, 1954.

Downie, N. M. *Fundamentals of measurement.* New York: Oxford University Press, 1958.

————, and R. W. Heath. *Basic statistical methods.* New York: Harper & Brothers, 1959.

Guilford, J. P. *Fundamental statistics in psychology and education,* Third Edition. New York: McGraw-Hill Book Company, Inc., 1956.

Psychological Corporation. *Better than chance.* Test Service Bulletin No. 45. New York: Psychological Corporation, 1953.

Thorndike, Robert L. *Personnel selection.* New York: John Wiley & Sons, Inc., 1949.

Tiffin, J., and E. J. McCormick. *Industrial psychology,* Fourth Edition. Englewood Cliffs, N. J.: Prentice-Hall, Inc., 1958.

8

The selection and use of
standardized tests

INTRODUCTION

MANY PEOPLE THINK OF TESTING AS SYNONYMOUS WITH A GUIDANCE OF counseling program. One of the most frequent questions asked in any discussion of guidance programs is "What tests shall we use?" There is no simple answer to this question. The most logical reply is to ask what the person wants to find out or what it is hoped a testing program can do.

Tests selected for a counseling program are limited by the unique needs of that program and by the available tests which will meet those needs adequately. These tests are designed to furnish information about a counselee's aptitude or potentiality, present skills or abilities, adjustment, and both avocational and vocational interests. They include tests of general intelligence, achievement, special abilities, and personality and interest inventories.

In general, people do not understand most of the problems involved in the selection and use of tests. Counseling and testing agencies get letters constantly from people in various government services, public schools, private schools, and community agencies seeking advice about test selection. The letters usually ask, "What *test* shall we use in our program?" but they do not give any information about what the school or the agency is attempting to accomplish. Testing services also get numbers of letters, not just an occasional one saying, "Please send us *The Aptitude Test*." These letters are from administrators and teachers in public schools and community agencies, who should have learned that there is more than one aptitude test. They usually indicate little or no awareness of the problems involved in the selection and use of tests.

LIMITATIONS OF TESTS

A major limitation in the use of tests is that errors associated with testing cause any obtained test score to be only an estimate of an individual's true score. Such errors may be classified into two types: chance errors and constant errors. These chance errors are associated with a single administration of a test. They are said to be nonreproducible. Suppose, for example, that a client being tested happens to be coming down with a disease which temporarily affects his test performance. This illness has a unique effect upon this single test administration. The chances are that the obtained score or scores would be lower than scores which might be obtained at another time when the client is in better health. In general, the larger this error component of an individual's score the less reliable is the test.

Other factors than health contribute to this error factor. Some common ones are the client's emotional condition, his state of fatigue, his motivation, and environmental factors such as heat, humidity, lighting, and amount of noise. Chance in knowing a particular fact, or luck in guessing, also contributes to this type of error.

While these chance errors are the most important ones affecting test scores, constant errors must not be overlooked. If men are being measured or weighed and the meter sticks or scales are out of order so that each individual when measured for height was given four centimeters over his true height, a constant error is present. This error is the same for every one and would be repeated as often as the same measuring instruments were used. In test practice a repetitive misuse of norms, of time limits, and certain directions in administration may produce constant errors.

Both of these types of error cause the obtained scores to differ from the client's true scores. All scores are unreliable to a certain extent. When using tests it is only possible to get an estimate of a person's true scores. The size of these chance errors of measurement is indicated by the use of the standard error of measurement or by the size of the reliability coefficient of the test.

Another problem is contained in this error concept also. A low test score is of less value in the prediction of what an individual can do than is a high score. For example, suppose an individual's score on the *School and College Ability Test (SCAT)* is at the 90th centile for college freshmen. There may be just as much error involved in this individual's score as there is with an individual at the 10th centile. But it is possible to predict more about what the person with the 90th centile score will do in college than about the person with the 10th centile score. The reason for this is that even though the score at the 90th centile is an underestimate, it is still possible to predict that this individual should get A's and B's with the appropriate motivation. What is apt to happen to the individual at the 10th centile is less clear. This latter individual may have been sick the day the test was given, or a fraternity brother may have said, "Don't make a good score on this or they'll expect you to get A's and B's." Any number of things may have happened to reduce the score unnaturally. So if the counselor predicted that this individual would not be able to do college work, the prediction could be in considerable error. Both predictions contain errors, but one is more usable for prediction of successful college performance than the other.

Here it would be advisable to refer to longitudinal data for validation of the test score, because over a long period of time the errors involved in longitudinal data are more apt to cancel out than they are in one short test. This is interpreted in the same sense that the average of all high school marks is a better index of what an individual should do, or a better predictor, than scores in a given subject. Actually then the trend in programs of guidance services today is toward the use of more longitudinal data properly collected and interpreted, supplemented by the judicious use of tests.

The judicious use of tests would mean a consideration of at least three stages through which a counselor passes in learning to use tests. The first stage is where the counselor discovers tests, jumps up in the air, and says, "Oh boy, this is it! This gives me all the information I need." Stage two develops when the counselor discovers tests will not do this and decides that tests are no earthly good. They will not give the information desired, so they are no good and the counselor will not use them. Some counselors never grow beyond this stage! The third stage occurs when the counselor learns what can and cannot be done with a given test. These stages might be called "discovery, disillusionment, and maturity" in the selection and use of tests.

In the third stage the counselor understands what tests can do, what they cannot do, and uses them properly to get the information wanted to help a client. In order to do this the counselor must go through a rather arduous apprenticeship in the use of individual and group tests. It is necessary to learn the theory involved and the practical, applied phases of psychometric techniques. Then the beginning counselor is ready to interpret tests to individuals in the practicum courses in counseling. This has to be done under supervision, if the counselor-in-training is to profit from it as fully as possible. Picking out a test in the agency situation and using it without instruction or supervision is fraught with too many perils for both the counselor and client. The counselor can pick up a test manual and read it, but it will not give all the background information that people who have used the tests professionally over a period of years can give.

People who use tests professionally often fail to write down their experiences, and many of these experiences involve subliminal cues. These experiences are such that counselors are hesitant to put them on record, because they are only very tentative hypotheses. For example, on the *"Psychopathic deviate (Pd)"* score on the *Minnesota Multiphase Personality Inventory (MMPI)* the test maker and the test user have only dealt with the meaning of a high score as indicating dislike of rules, regulations, and having to conform. They do not go on to point out, in the first place, that this person may conform, and that this high score may reflect covert resentment. This is more apt to be the case with girls, because they are used to being "good girls." A boy is more apt to react overtly and so this score may reflect with boys a tendency to rebel openly to rules and regulations; and with girls it may not. There is another element involved here, however—a low score on the *MMPI Pd* scale has no meaning as far as the test makers and the manual are concerned because the test was constructed to show only the meaning of a high score. Yet use has indicated that the individual who gets a score one standard deviation below the mean is apt to be a person who is pretty rigid. Such a person sets up high standards or goals for himself and his acquaintances. These individuals make their own lives and the lives of their acquaintances miserable, by the fact that they are always critical about not meeting such standards. A person who has rather strict moral or religious principles might fall into this category of getting low scores on the *MMPI Pd* scale.

These are the kinds of things that are not written in periodicals or manuals because they are considered too tenuous as hypotheses to be published without research validation or empirical data. Instead they are passed on orally in a supervised practicum situation.

Some of the other limitations involved with tests center around the kinds of information tests can give. Tests can give information about aptitude or potentiality or they can give information about present skills or ability. Actually tests of general intelligence today include both aptitude and ability. A certain amount of what is being measured by an intelligence test involves previous learning, and is therefore a measure of skill or capacity. It also involves seeing relationships which have not been encountered previously and this, of course, would deal with aptitude or potential. There is no measure of scholastic aptitude available at present which does not include some type of prior learning. When trying to predict future performance, the test is called scholastic aptitude. If the same test is used to measure present status, then it is a measure of ability or achievement. If the same test were used to diagnose weaknesses, it would be a diagnostic test. If used to show the need for or the results of remediation, it would be a remedial test. Thus the same test could be used for all of these things. That is why it is difficult to discuss this sort of material and information in a clear-cut manner. Included in these tests of achievement are structured personality inventories because these are a measure of current social skills—the ability to deal with people and the ability to live with oneself, both of which are aspects of social ability. A third kind of test is the interest inventory. These inventories are closely related to the structured personality inventory, but tend to be measuring different things than the structured personality inventory. Interest inventories are considered indicators of possible satisfaction in vocational or avocational activities.

TESTS AND BATTERIES

There are two types of tests available: the single tests, based on a specific norm group for each test, and batteries of tests which are based upon the same norm group for all the tests in the battery. These batteries are discussed in Samler, ed. (1958) and in Chapter 9.

Single tests include the kinds discussed above: aptitude, ability, achievement, and interest inventories. The most commonly used single tests are tests of general intelligence. These tests of general intelligence include four different kinds as will be shown in the next chapter. First is the speeded or time-limit test, an example of which is the *Cooperative School and College Ability Test (SCAT)*. On such a test an individual has to perform specific tasks within given time limits. These tests do not work well with the individual who is slow either physically or psychologically. These latter persons should be given a power test which is the second kind of general intelligence test. Examples of these are the *Ohio State Psychological Examination* or the *California Test of Mental Maturity*. No time limits are set on the power test so slow individuals may take as long as they require to do the best job they can. A third type of test is the oral, nonreading test read to a client by the examiner. A test like this is the *Binet* or the various forms of the *Wechsler*. A fourth type is made up of nonreading *and* nonverbal tests either for groups or for the individual. There are a number of tests which now have nonverbal parts. An example is the nonverbal part of the *Lorge-Thorndike Intelligence Test*. These nonverbal tests do not use words at all, instructions being the only verbal part and these are read by the examiner. Thus there are two kinds of tests of general intelligence that do not involve reading.

When batteries of tests are considered, their growth from the various factorial studies and the fact that all the tests in one battery are based upon the same norm group of representative samples from national population makes them more usable than single tests combined into a battery. For example, the *SCAT* has national college freshmen norms. The *Minnesota Clerical Test* has all kinds of norms, but those that are most commonly used are the norms for employed clerical workers or adults gainfully occupied. How can a score for employed clerical workers or a score for adults gainfully occupied be compared with a score for national entering college freshmen? How can the score on the *SCAT* for one group of entering college freshmen be compared with the score on some of the *Cooperative Achievement Tests* based on other groups of national college freshmen? Are the group samples from the same sort of groups, or are they different? This is unknown. There is no way of determining these relationships among the different norm groups except to *hope* that they are fairly similar. With a test *battery* this is no problem because the norms are established on the same group. These tests are mostly a result of factorial analysis and for the most part have limited overlap. In that sense they are better tests because the older tests developed singly had a considerable amount of overlap. Also these tests in new batteries have lower correlation among the parts of the battery and high correlation with a criterion. Sometimes the same criterion such as success in school would be used for a measure of numerical aptitude, a measure of verbal aptitude, and for a measure of spatial aptitude. This gives more comparable information per unit of testing time.

In summary there are three advantages in limited overlap among tests: lower correlation with other tests in the battery, a higher correlation with criteria, and more information per unit of testing time.

Another advantage, which is obvious but often overlooked, is the fact that these tests are created on a statistical rather than an empirical basis. The earlier tests were constructed on the basis of the kinds of items that the test author hoped might differentiate. New tests are a result of analyses showing the kinds of items that will differentiate for a given purpose. Thus it is possible to know when constructing the test that it will do certain things. Two examples of these batteries would be the *Differential Aptitude Tests (DAT)* and the *General Aptitude Test Battery (GATB)* of the United States Employment Service, both of which are discussed in the next chapter.

Actually there are different levels of professional competence and professional pride among the test producers. So it is necessary to evaluate the kinds of tests that are being put on the market (see Super, 1957).

HOW TO EVALUATE TESTS

Major uses of tests

From the viewpoint of the counselor, there are six major uses of tests. A very common one is the confirmation of diagnoses or decisions which have been made. For instance, a teacher considers a boy or girl in class as being capable of A's, B's, or C's, in terms of experience with that boy or girl. But this needs to be independently validated. So a test of general intelligence is administered to get some idea of how near right the diagnosis is. Or it may be obvious that a given pupil does a superlative job as far as the local school is concerned but it is hard to tell how that individual will compare with people in other schools over the nation. So the person is asked to take scholarship examinations to secure a comparison with pupils from other schools. These are two examples of the use of a test to confirm diagnosis, or judgment, or decisions that have been made.

A second purpose is to save time. If a counselor does not have time to sit down with a client and talk long enough to know whether psychiatric help is needed, an intermediate step might be to have someone administer the *MMPI*. This reduces the amount of time spent with that client, and the same thing is true with other tests. Rather than sit down and pick out piece by piece information about vocational interests from a client, it is simpler to give an interest inventory and check it against other case data. If the counselor does not have adequate school records it may be necessary to use tests to make up for information over the previous ten or twelve years which the agency did not collect or did not have available from other sources. The second purpose then is to save time or to correct errors of omission. Another example of this is in the community agency that may not have adequate records of what a client has done before being referred to that agency, or in the school that gets a new pupil with no accompanying records, and does not know what to do about placement or referral.

A third use of tests, the most logical and the least often suggested, is to get information that cannot be secured in any other way. If the counselor wants to know the status of an individual's inventoried interests the client can be given a *SVIB* or a *Kuder*. The easiest way to find out how this individual's interests compare to those of engineers is to give the client a *Kuder Form D* which has scales for mechanical and electrical engineer or give a *SVIB* which has a scale for engineer. Then it is possible to see how this client's interests compare with those of people working in that occupation. If the counselor wants to find out how this person compares with other scholarship candidates in a state or in the entire United States, the only way to find out is to give the client the same scholarship test taken by others in the state or the nation. The counselor may have a pretty good idea of how this person and others in the school compare with people across the nation, but unless they perform on the same test there will not be objective evidence. This is the most logical and justifiable use of tests.

A fourth purpose in testing would be to secure information for referral to other agencies. Very frequently other agencies prefer certain tests be administered before an individual is sent to them for help because they do not have the resources to handle such testing.

Fifth, tests are used in the prediction of future behavior. In educational and vocational counseling it is frequently important to predict what an individual will do or will be like. Many standardized tests are quite useful in developing such a prediction.

Sixth, and last, tests are used in evaluating a client's present status. This includes his achievement, abilities, and personality make-up. In general, it might be said that tests are basic in the evaluation of the strengths and weaknesses of the individual client.

Fallacies concerning tests

It probably would be a good idea to review briefly the fallacies concerning tests that are discussed by Hahn and MacLean (1955; used by permission). The first one listed is *belief* in tests. The competent counselor does not believe or disbelieve in tests. Such a counselor knows what a test can do and what it can not do. This is not a matter of faith but of professional experience and competence. The second is the fallacy of *simplicity*. Test results look simple. A series of scores on the *DAT* furnished by a state wide testing program appears pretty simple to interpret. But when the counselor starts thinking in terms of patterns of scores and differences between the scores on parts of the battery, the meaning that this has for a client in a given high school curriculum is nowhere near as simple as it looks.

The third fallacy is that of *test labels*. Just because a test is called a test of "critical thinking" does not mean that it is. A test labelled "achievement" may be used to indicate need for remediation and progress of remediation, rather than achievement. Allied to this is the matter of *named scales or keys*. For instance, on the *SVIB* one of the three non-occupational scales is a so-called "Occupational Level" score, which is supposed to show whether a client will perform at the professional level in occupations. Research has shown that engineers tend to score low and persons in managerial occupations score high. Such a score is a function of the field or area of the occupation rather than the level of the occupation. A high Occupational Level score is secured by marking few items in the "Indifferent" category. Another example of this fallacy of named keys is the "Interest Maturity" scale of the *SVIB*. It has been found that people score high on the Interest Maturity scale, if they like more things than they dislike (Rhodes, 1956). Engineers tend to score low on it. This does not mean that they are immature in their interests. It means they dislike more items than they like on the *SVIB*. Thus empirical observations during counseling and knowledge of published research are necessary to bring real meaning to the named scales of the *SVIB* (see Chapter 10).

A fifth fallacy centers about the *prestige* of the test author. Just because a prominent and accepted psychologist produces a test is not evidence that it is a good test. The chances are that it will be excellent as far as the statistics and the production of the test are concerned, but there is no guarantee that it is valid for the purpose for which it was constructed, until research showing validity is reported in the literature. It is probably safe to assume that it is a better test than an author lacking in measurement experience and training might produce.

Another fallacy is the matter of *generalizing* from a known test to a similar test or from a sample similar to the test norm group to one which is not like the standardization group. For example, the *SVIB* has been on the market for years and counselors have learned how to use it. Kuder has recently published what is called the *Kuder Preference Record-Occupational, Form D*. This interest inventory uses occupational criterion groups similar to the *SVIB*. Its ability to differentiate between people in a given occupational group and other groups *appears* similar to the *SVIB*. The test description seems as if it could be used in the same fashion as the *SVIB*, but when a counselor tries to use it in a counseling interview and compare interests of clients in mechanical engineering on the *Kuder* with those of the same clients on the engineering scale of the *SVIB* there appear to be discrepancies. This may be a function of differences in coverage of the two tests, differences in criterion groups, or differences in the interpretation of a score for a given individual due to error factors discussed earlier in this chapter. Research based on a study of the relationships between the two instruments is needed before a counselor can make statements to a client about this. A counselor cannot assume because of experience in using the *SVIB* that it is possible to move immediately into competent, effective use of the *Kuder-Form D*.

The other fallacy of generalization concerns a test developed on a given group. When it has been developed on this group, counselors often assume it will be useful with another group which actually may not be at all similar. When writing theses most persons state in the last chapter, "the results of this study apply only to the sample on which it was done or performed, and the generalizing to similar groups is dangerous, until the same information has been collected on those groups." The counselor cannot know what scores on such a test mean for freshmen in a given college or university until a sufficient, consecutive series of samples of such freshmen has been tested with the results reported and norms derived. If a counselor tests a ninth grade group and finds certain results, there is no guarantee that last year's ninth grade or next year's ninth grade will show the same results. Probably it will, but the counselor must check it to know this before making such statements or using the information for all three groups in a similar fashion. The counselor working in a rehabilitation agency will often assume that tests used with the general population apply equally well to the disabled clients with whom the agency deals, or that the scores of clients with various kinds of disabilities have the same meaning. This is not so. For example, Phillips and Wiener (1947) have presented evidence that various disability groups show a relationship between disability, disease and scores on the *MMPI*. The rehabilitation counselor may find that test scores indicating concern about physical health are a natural tendency with various disability groups and may not be "abnormal" concerns as interpreted for general population clients with similar scores. Tests used with the disabled may require separate standardization and frequently may need to be considered in light of the psychological disturbance accompanying the disability. Whether working with general population or specialized groups, the counselor cannot generalize that test scores derived on other groups apply until local use indicates that this is so.

The seventh fallacy Hahn and MacLean state is the point that *validity and reliability do not apply to tests alone.* These concepts apply to every tool the counselor uses in counseling and to the counselor also. Research should be conducted to show the validity and reliability of the counselor and of the tools used in a program of guidance and counseling.

CHARACTERISTICS OF TESTS

Validity

The first of these test characteristics and the most important, of course, is *validity*. No matter how long validity is discussed in classes, some counselors are still hazy about it. Validity as far as the counselor is concerned is how well this counseling tool predicts performance in a given activity (see Chapter 7). For example, the counselor is attempting to sit down with a client and on the basis of test evidence anticipate future behavior or predict future behavior. And how is this done? Usually the counselor does it on the basis of an instrument whose correlation with some criterion of future performance is known. The counselor knows the relationship between an intelligence test score and grades in school. The counselor knows the relationship between tests of ability and measures of interest. These relationships show the limits within which the counselor can predict performance. The other way in which validity can be shown is by tests of significance. If an experimental and a control group are compared in performance under specified circumstances, is the difference in performance of the experimental group greater than a chance difference? It should be noted here that it may be possible to show a statistically significant difference between groups which is not a *practical* difference usable in counseling.

The counselor needs to consider the percentage of forecasting efficiency for a given validity coefficient before deciding what predictions can be made. Suppose a correlation of .35 between a given instrument and a criterion is significant. The counselor still is not going to be able to predict much from it. This is a prediction that is six per cent better than chance (Bingham, 1937, 258–259, and Chapter 7 above). Chance should produce 50 right and 50 wrong predictions. Splitting the six per cent improvement in half and adding to the 50 right and subtracting from the 50 wrong will give the change in prediction with use of such an instrument. So the counselor would be right 53 times and wrong 47 times out of every 100 predictions made with this device. However, the counselor will not know which of the 47 times a wrong prediction was made until afterwards. It does not increase the counselor's predictive capacity very much and it is necessary to ask, "Is this worth while?". Cottle (1951) has discussed in detail these problems of forecasting efficiency and the selection of tests.

Counselors should memorize the percentage of forecasting efficiency for validity coefficients of .80, .70, .60, .50, .40, and so on (page 153). This tells the counselor quickly how much error is still involved in a prediction. Even though there is a correlation between an intelligence test and class grades of about .68, which results in a percentage of forecasting efficiency of 26 per cent, when the counselor tries to use this to predict grades, it only gives about 63 right out of every 100 predictions.

Reliability

Reliability gives the counselor an indication of how closely an individual's second performance approximates first performance on the tests, or how closely successive performances approximate each other. Are these scores dependable? This is what is meant when one talks about a person's reliability. How dependable or consistent is that person? The same thing is true with every test score. How much can this test be depended on to give the same information time after time? As was discussed in Chapter 7, reliability is actually determined in three basically different ways: test-retest, comparable forms, and the methods of internal consistency.

Probably the standard error of measurement is most useful in showing the reliability of scores. As was noted in Chapter 7, the statistic makes it possible for the counselor to make a probability statement about the relationship of an obtained score to a client's true score. Both the *Sequential Tests of Educational Progress (STEP)* and the *School and College Ability Tests (SCAT)* make use of this concept.

In the *STEP*, the test user turns to a table of norms and, opposite each raw score value, finds a centile band instead of a single centile. This is actually a distance of one standard error of measurement measured off on each side of the client's obtained score. To quote the *STEP* Manual for Interpreting Scores—Reading (1957):

> If the test interpreter assumes that students' "true" standings lie somewhere within the percentile bands corresponding to their obtained scores, in the long run he will be correct in his assumption about 68 per cent of the time.

The use of these bands should prevent any counselor from regarding scores more precise than they actually are.

Figure 8.1 from the student report form for *STEP* shows these centile bands for a student. The numbers below the figures represent the centile, 3 being the 30th centile. In using a profile like this, the counselor is reminded that, if the shaded areas overlap, there is no important difference in performance on the two tests, as in the first two in Figure 8.1. However, since there is no overlap between the bottom two, the counselor might conclude that the student did better on the bottom test than he did on the second one.

EXAMPLE

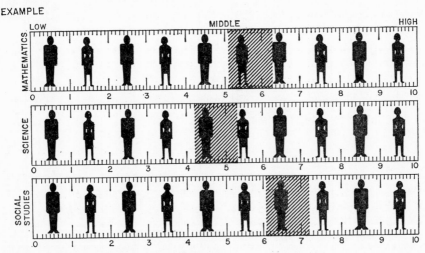

Used by permission of the Educational Testing Service.

Fig. 8.1. Use of the standard error of measurement in interpreting scores on the *STEP*. "The shaded areas for Mathematics and Social Studies overlap; there is no important difference in standings on these two tests. The same is true of Mathematics and Science. However, the shaded areas for Science and Social Studies do not overlap. The student is higher in Social Studies than in Science ability, as measured by these tests."

Another use of the standard error of measurement is shown in Figure 8.2, a form used at the University of Kansas for use with placement examinations given to entering freshmen. The raw scores in each of the columns are one standard error of measurement from each other. This may be used as follows. Suppose that a client has a raw score of 35 on the vocabulary subtest of the *Cooperative Reading Test*. A band could be marked off on each side of 35, extending from 32 to 38. The chances are two out of three that the client's retest score on this test would fall between these two points, each one standard error of measurement from his obtained score.

As is readily apparent, the smaller the standard error of measurement,

UNIVERSITY OF KANSAS

ACADEMIC PROFICIENCY
PLACEMENT EXAMINATIONS

NAME_____ SEX _____

COLLEGE_____ DATE_____

STEN SCORE	CENTILE RANK	T SCORE	ACE QUAN	PSYCH. LING	EXAM TOTAL	COOP READING VOCAB	SPEED	COOP ENGLISH USAGE	SPELL	KU MATH	T SCORE	CENTILE RANK
9		·84· ·82· ·80· ·78· ·76·	·79· ·77· ·74· ·72·	·109· ·106·	·176· ·172· ·168·	·57·	·78· ·76· ·73·	·160· ·156·	·45·	·77· ·74·	·84· ·82· ·80· ·78· ·76·	
8	·99· ·98·	·74· ·72· ·70· ·68·	·69· ·67· ·65· ·62·	·102· ·99· ·95· ·92·	·164· ·159· ·155· ·151·	·54· ·52·	·70· ·67· ·64· ·61·	·151· ·147· ·142·	·40· ·38·	·71·	·74· ·72· ·70· ·68·	·99· ·98·
7	·95· ·90·	·66· ·64· ·62·	·60· ·57·	·92· ·88· ·85·	·146· ·142· ·137·	·49· ·46· ·43·	·58· ·55· ·52· ·49·	·138· ·133· ·129·	·35· ·33· ·30·	·68·	·66· ·64· ·62·	·95· ·90·
6	·80·	·60· ·58· ·56·	·55· ·53· ·50·	·81· ·79· ·74·	·133· ·129· ·124·	·41· ·38·	·46· ·40· ·37·	·124· ·120· ·115·	·29· ·25·	·65· ·62·	·60·	·80·
5	·70· ·60· ·50·	·54· ·52· ·50·	·48· ·45· 42.98	·71· ·68· 64.05	·120· ·116· ·111· 107.08	·35· ·32· 29.57	·34· ·31· 28.32	·110· ·106· ·101· ·97· 92.24	·22· ·20· 17.19	·59· ·55· ·52· 49.18	·56· ·54· ·52· ·50·	·70· ·60· ·50·
4	·40· ·30·	·48· ·46· ·44·	·41· ·38· ·36·	·61· ·57· ·54·	·103· ·98· ·94· ·90·	·27· ·24· ·21·	·25· ·22· ·19· ·17·	·88· ·83· ·79· ·74· ·69·	·15· ·12·	·46· ·43· ·40·	·48· ·46· ·44·	·40· ·30·
3	·20·	·42· ·40· ·38·	·33· ·31· ·29·	·50· ·47·	·85· ·81· ·77·	·19· ·16·	·14· ·11·	·65· ·60· ·56· ·51·	·9· ·7·	·37· ·34·	·42· ·40· ·38·	·20·
2	·10· ·5·	·36· ·34· ·32·	·26· ·24· ·21· ·19·	·43· ·40· ·36·	·72· ·68· ·64· ·59·	·13· ·10·	·8· ·5·	·47· ·42· ·38·	·4· ·2·	·30· ·27· ·24·	·36· ·34· ·32·	·10· ·5·
1	·2· ·1·	·30· ·28· ·26·	·16· ·14· ·12·	·33· ·29· ·26·	·55· ·50· ·46· ·42·	·8· ·5·	·2·	·33· ·29· ·24·		·21· ·18·	·30· ·28· ·26·	·2· ·1·
0		·24· ·22· ·20· ·18·	·9· ·7·	·23· ·19· ·16·	·37· ·33· ·29·	·2·		·19· ·15· ·10·		·15· ·12·	·24· ·22· ·20· ·18·	

RECOMMENDATIONS :

HONOR ENGLISH_____ ENGLISH 1a _____ STUDY CLINIC_____ READING CLINIC_____

Fig. 8.2. Use of the standard error of measurement in reporting test scores.

the more reliable the test, and hence the more confidence a counselor can place in any single score. It is assumed that an obtained score is close to the client's true score on any test. Since it is impossible to know an individual's true score, the band cut off by the standard error of measurement about an obtained score gives an indication of the range in which the true score may be. It might also be noted that standard errors of measurement are approximately equal except in the extremes of the distribution. This statistic permits two things: the counselor can tell how much a client's score will vary on tests by the size of the standard error of measurement; and the counselor can compare tests of a similar nature to see which one is more reliable and, hence, which one would be better for use.

Baxter and Paterson (1940) proposed a statistic, the counselor's ratio, given by the formula $\sqrt{1-r}$, to be used as is the standard error of measurement. The range of scores is multiplied by this counselor's ratio and the result divided by 2. This latter value added to and subtracted from the obtained score will show the band in which repeated measurements of the same individual will fall.

Considerable time has been spent discussing certain aspects of validity and reliability. These are two characteristics a test must have above everything else. However, when the counselor is selecting tests for professional use, there are some other points which must be considerd. All of these other characteristics might be considered part of the practicality of a test. In the material which follows brief comments will be made about the more important phases of these characteristics.

Ease of administering

Tests used by the counselor should be of such a nature that they can be administered by an individual with a minimum of training and instructions. Frequently teachers and others with limited psychological training have to help in the collection of test data and other material used by the counselor. Any competent teacher can administer the modern group tests with valid results if willing to read the manual ahead of time and follow directions exactly. Most individual tests on the other hand require a trained and experienced administrator. These latter tests are frequently so time-consuming that they have limited use in the counseling program. A clerical worker who is conscientious can be trained in a limited time to administer most of the common group tests.

Ease of scoring

Many agencies do not have adequate budgets to facilitate the scoring of tests by either a rented scoring machine or sending the answer sheets for scoring to a test publisher or to a test scoring service. These tests have to be scored in the agency by agency personnel. One way to antagonize colleagues with reference to the activities of the counselor is to add to their already heavy schedule and duties the job of scoring group tests. One way to avoid this difficulty is to buy tests which are so-called "self-scoring." Such tests have carbons in them and to obtain a score all that one has to do is to open the test booklet or the answer sheet and count the number of marks that fall within the small blocks present or within other designated areas. At the present time, the California Test Bureau has a patented answer sheet called *Scoreze* and Houghton Mifflin and Company have had self-scoring tests on the market for many years. Even though these are a little more expensive, in the small school system the extra two or three cents expended per student for these special answer sheets will be repaid, and more, by the improved attitudes of the teachers toward the counseling program. The choice of machine scored tests whose stencils can be used for hand-scoring machine answer sheets also cuts down scoring problems. Another factor in ease of scoring is to have the hand-scoring key exactly opposite the answer space. Choice of tests without weighted scoring is a factor which can decrease scoring problems, if this is about the only difference involved in the test choice.

Ease of interpretation

The tests used by the counselor should be of such a nature that it does not require three additional psychology courses in order to find out what the results mean. Many tests have very straightforward and adequate information in the manuals to facilitate scoring and interpretation. The meaning of projective techniques and other individual tests is still highly controversial in spite of the amount of research and training that has been expended upon their use (Patterson, 1957). It is these techniques that require the most extensive training.

Probably the best way to begin learning how to interpret tests after basic instruction in evaluation is to take the test oneself and have it interpreted by a competent counselor. This will familiarize the beginning counselor with the items and a general interpretation. Then the beginning counselor needs to study the manual to see how the test author proposes the test be used and with what norm groups. At this point the counselor should begin to use and interpret the test under supervision.

Frequently the counselor will find that what appears to be an appropriate test has no norms for the individuals and the groups with which it must be used. The only recourse here is to collect scores on a large enough group so that appropriate norms can be developed. Until this happens interpretation must be delayed or must be highly tentative.

Costs

Most counselors find that they have to look in every direction in order to keep testing costs down. Saving can be most easily accomplished by purchasing the nonconsumable or reusable editions of tests with separate answer sheets. Then there is no telling how many times the test booklets themselves may be used providing the test administrator takes care to see that these booklets are handled as they should be. The counselor should determine ahead of time the maximum number that will be tested with a specific test at any given time. Then buy this number plus several extra test booklets. There are many tests that are used very infrequently. A couple of test booklets and a package of answer sheets is more than adequate for these. Also the counselor can cut costs by setting up a testing program that fits local agency needs rather than buying the packaged program offered by some publishers. This requires knowledge of tests and of the local situation. If the counselor cannot do this, it is better not to use tests until the counselor learns how to choose and tailor the testing program to fit local needs.

There is another point under cost that merits attention. There are times, especially after the counselor has gained some experience when it will be obvious that an inexpensive, short test will do as good or even better job than an expensive time-consuming battery. This is especially true with some of the tests used in the prediction of academic success or success on a job.

Time

Probably the best tests to purchase for a school are those that can be administered within a school period. Other agencies must judge this in terms of client and counselor time available for testing. This is important if either counselor or client must travel any distance for testing. The counselor must remember that there is more to this than just taking into account the amount of time needed to complete the items. The materials have to be passed out and collected, directions read, and often sample exercises are worked and corrected. The nature of the group or individual being tested causes the time spent on these preliminaries to vary considerably. Tests with parts having short time limits, such as four, five, eight and ten minutes, require use of a stop watch and still no two administrators get exactly the same timing. This produces part of the error factor involved in testing and reduces test validity and reliability.

There are some longer tests which have been constructed so that half of the test may be administered in one session of about fifty minutes' duration and the other half in another similar period at a later time. Some counselors do not like to break the test this way. They feel the individual is really not the same individual during each of the testing sessions. Also, when there are breaks like this, clients tested in groups are apt to talk about what was on the test.

Use of parallel forms

It is very useful to purchase tests with parallel forms available. Sometimes there is a question about whether a certain test score is a valid measure of an individual's ability. The first score may be verified by administering the second form of the same test. At the present time some test publishers have three or four forms of the same test. With parallel forms, one form can be used one year and another form with the same individual or group the next year. Often a certain test can be used at different levels.

Most of the newer tests are built in levels, the usual number being five or six. These levels usually cover measurement of aptitudes and abilities from kindergarten through high school, with several taking in a year or two of the university. There are two reasons for considering tests in these series. First there is apt to be a relationship between the scores made on the tests at the different levels that is higher than the relationships obtained when tests by different authors are used at different levels. This is true because the general structure of the test seems to be the same from level to level. Secondly there are times when it is convenient to have a more difficult test at hand to give to a client when the test given to a group of clients was too easy. If a test is too easy, especially a test like an intelligence test, the examiner does not get a measure of the real ability of the client tested. This works in the opposite direction, too. If a test is too difficult for some clients, a better measure of aptitude or ability may be obtained by using an easier test from a lower level.

Cautions on the use of tests

Some individuals come to the counselor to take tests believing that the tests themselves have all the answers to problems. "If I could take some of those aptitude tests and one of those interest inventories, my problems would be all over." This is not an unusual attitude to find but it should be apparent to the counselor by now that all tests are quite fallible instruments. As has been pointed out, there may be a wide difference in the performance of any given individual on the same or parallel tests from time to time. If then, only one evaluation of a personality trait is available for an individual and if this happens to be a test score, the counselor must be very cautious in the interpretation of this test score. In other words, the counselor should not place too much reliance upon one score. It is good procedure to use several intelligence tests, several interest inventories, and the like in the same counseling program or to validate test scores against other client data. The more information that can be obtained about the individual, usually the better the counseling tends to be.

Test scores are apt to be interpreted frequently without consideration of the motives of the individual who was tested. The counselor is apt to look at this in an idealizing fashion, assuming that each client is strongly motivated and did the best possible performance in the testing situation. Nothing is actually farther from the truth. There is all sorts of evidence that the motivation of test-takers varies considerably. Actually it is very difficult to know exactly what the individual has in mind when taking a test. There is strong evidence also that the social class status of an individual has a lot to do with motivation and performance on tests (Eells *et al.*, 1951). It seems possible to get greater motivation and thus more valid test results when dealing with children from middle-class homes. Taking tests and striving to do well on them is an accepted pattern of middle-class culture. The children copy their parents' attitudes and behavior in their daily activities. The reference above also contains evidence that many tests have a bias favoring middle-class children. As a matter of fact, one might generalize by saying that most of the tests used favor the urban, white, middle-class child.

Test scores certainly then cannot be interpreted singly or without other types of information. They represent pieces of the picture of an individual and a very important part of this picture, but they have to be integrated with the other information into what is hoped will be a meaningful whole. Too much reliance must not be put upon test data. The counselor must learn to accept the value, and even more important, the limitations of test scores.

Information about tests

Frequently the counselor has to purchase tests for professional use or needs to find some information about tests which appears in research or in the scores which appear on agency records. Many times the counselor is approached by others in the agency for information about the interpretation and selection of tests. The counselor then should have ready information about tests. Perhaps the best sources of this information are the *Mental Measurements Yearbooks* compiled under the direction of O. K. Buros (Buros, 1949, 1953, 1959). Although there have been five of these yearbooks published to date, with the earliest one appearing in 1938, the counselor will find that most of the information needed is found in the last three. These yearbooks are made up of sections covering the various types of standardized tests. For each of the tests discussed there is information about the content, level, forms, and other data concerning the basic structure and use of the test. This is followed by critical evaluations of the test written by several experts who are in a position to make valid remarks about the structure and use of the test. About the latter third of each of these yearbooks is made up of summaries of research using various tests. In using these yearbooks it is a good idea to start with the 1959 edition, the fifth one, and see if there is any information available on the test under consideration. There may be and there may also be references to similar entries in earlier editions of the yearbook about the same test.

In addition to Buros' books, information is continually appearing about tests in several journals with which the counselor should be familiar. *The Personnel and Guidance Journal, The Journal of Counseling Psychology,* and *Educational and Psychological Measurement* contain information and evaluations of new tests from time to time. Studies using tests in counseling research are often published in these journals as well. About every three years the *Review of Educational Research* contains an issue completely devoted to the research of the previous three years on intelligence tests. Similar issues cover achievement tests, personality evaluation, statistics, and other topics of interest to counselors. *The Journal of Applied Psychology* is another journal which is more or less devoted to research using tests or other evaluative techniques. However, the majority of the studies in this journal are related to industrial situations. Material on tests used in vocational guidance also appears in *The Vocational Guidance Quarterly.* The counselor should probably begin research on a topic pertaining to tests or testing by referring to the annual index in *Psychological Abstracts.*

Finally the information of the test publishers themselves about tests should be considered. Each of the large test publishers puts out an annual catalog which all agencies should receive. In these will be found the basic information about the tests published. All publishers offer specimen sets of their tests either for a nominal sum or free. It is best to obtain some of these specimen sets and look them over carefully before purchasing any test. These specimen sets usually contain a copy of the various forms of the test, a manual, scoring keys and often research information about the test.

The test publishers also put out from time to time short bulletins which contain much useful information about tests. The major ones are:

Test Service Bulletins—The Psychological Corporation

E T S Developments—Educational Testing Service

Test Service Bulletins—World Book Co.

Educational Bulletins—California Test Bureau

A postal card to any of these publishers will put the counselor on the publisher's mailing list and the agency will then receive new catalogs and bulletins as they appear. All of this material that the counselor will then receive should be read with the realization that these publishers are trying to sell something.

Listed on page 178 are the addresses of the major test publishers. These are their home offices. In their catalogs one will find that many of them list regional offices from which it is more convenient and less expensive to order materials.

Form for Evaluating Standardized/Form 8.1
Tests.

I. Preliminary Data: Name of test _____
   Author _____ Publisher _____
   Parallel forms available? _____ Is test part of a series? _____
   Cost per test _____ Type: Individual _____ Group _____
   Use suggested by author _____

II. Validity Indices	Number and Type of Subjects	Criterion	Adequacy of Criterion

III. Reliability Coefficients	Number and Type of Subjects	Method Used	Other Data

IV. Details of Administration: Untimed _____ Timed _____ Under 25 min. _____
   Under 45 min. _____ Under 90 min. _____ Over 90 min. _____.
   Materials needed: Stop watch _____ Electrographic Pencil _____ Special
   answer sheet _____ Punch board _____ Punch _____ Extra paper for
   working problems _____ Other materials _____
   Special training needed? Yes _____ No _____ Type _____
   Number of subtests and subscores _____ Purpose of these _____

V. Method of scoring: Hand scored _____ Machine scored _____ Either _____
   Self-scoring _____ Scoring stencil _____ Strip Key _____ Scoring time per
   test _____ Can it be scored by client? Yes _____ No _____ Weighting system
   used? Yes _____ No _____.
   Norms: Reported for what grades, groups, sex, and so forth _____
   _____. How reported? IQ's _____, Centiles _____, Standard scores
   _____ Other _____. Adequacy of these norms _____.

VI. Minimal interpretation needed:
   _____ By psychologist only
   _____ By counselor with psychometric training
   _____ By an instructor with no psychological training
   _____ By client with explanation
   _____ By client without explanation

VII. Recommendation: By whom recommended? _____ For what
   group? _____ For what purpose? _____
   References _____
   _____
   _____

VIII. On the back of this sheet write a short summary and evaluation.

Adapted from Cottle (1951:188–94); used by permission.

Acorn Publishing Co., Rockville Centre, New York.

Bobbs Merrill Co., 1720 E. 38th St., Indianapolis 6, Indiana (All Public School Publishing Co. Tests)

California Test Bureau, 5916 Hollywood Blvd., Los Angeles 28, California

Educational Records Bureau, 437 W. 59th Street, New York 19, New York

Educational Test Bureau, 720 Washington Ave. S.E., Minneapolis 14, Minnesota

Educational Testing Service, 20 Nassau St., Princeton, New Jersey

Houghton Mifflin Co., 2 Park Street, Boston 7, Massachusetts

Psychological Corporation, 304 E. 45th St., New York 17, New York

Science Research Associates, 57 West Grand, Chicago 10, Illinois

Sheridan Supply Co., Box 837, Beverly Hills, California

World Book Co., Yonkers-on-Hudson, New York

Much can be learned about tests by studying them systematically. The counselor should be well grounded in psychometrics. But practice with and the use of tests is basic to learning about them. It is a good idea to summarize information about tests on a form such as the one appearing on page 177. A large amount of the information concerning tests discussed in this chapter is summarized in this form. The beginning counselor may effectively learn about tests by taking them under the same conditions as a client would and by having a more experienced counselor interpret the scores. As he studies each test, pertinent information may be summarized from the manual.

In the next three chapters various kinds of tests are described and reviewed for the counselor approaching their use in counseling interviews. Whether tests are found in client records or taken between the initial interview and counseling interviews, or interspersed among counseling interviews, the following chapters of review information concerning tests should prove useful to the beginning counselor. These chapters should be considered a review of the more commonly used tests rather than a coverage of all tests available to the counselor.

REFERENCES

Baxter, B., and D. G. Paterson. A new ratio for clinical counselors. *J. Consult. Psychol.*, 1940, 5, 123–126.

Bingham, W. V. *Aptitudes and aptitude testing.* New York: Harper & Brothers, 1937.

Buros, O. K., Ed. *The third mental measurements yearbook.* New Brunswick, N. J.: Rutgers University Press, 1949.

———, *The fourth mental measurements yearbook.* Highland Park, N. J.: The Gryphon Press, 1953.

———, *The fifth mental measurements yearbook.* Highland Park, N. J.: The Gryphon Press, 1959.

Cottle, W. C.   A form for evaluating standardized tests.   *Occupations,* 1951, *30,* 188–194.

Eells, K., et al.   *Intelligence and cultural differences.*   Chicago: University of Chicago Press, 1951.

Hahn, M. E., and M. S. MacLean.   *Counseling psychology.*   New York: McGraw-Hill Book Company, 1955.

Patterson, C. H.   The use of projective tests in vocational counseling, *Educ. Psychol. Measmt.,* 1957, *18,* 533–551.

Phillips, E. L., and D. N. Wiener.   Relationships between selected disability and disease groups and the *MMPI. Amer. Psychol.,* 1947, *2,* 274.

Rhodes, G. S.   *An investigation of response sets in the Strong Vocational Interest Blank for men and response set effects on scores of selected SVIB scales.* Unpublished Ed. D. dissertation, University of Kansas, 1956.

Samler, J., Ed.   *The use of multifactor tests in guidance.*   Washington, D.C.: The American Personnel and Guidance Association, 1958.

Sequential Tests of Educational Progress.   *Manual for Interpreting Scores— Reading.*   Princeton, N. J.: Educational Testing Service, 1957.

Super, D. E.   The multifactor tests: summing up.   *Personnel and Guid. J.,* 1957, *35,* 576–577.

9

Evaluation of abilities and
aptitudes

THE WORDS ABILITY AND APTITUDE ARE FREQUENTLY ENCOUNTERED IN THE counselor's literature. In the past there has been considerable confusion between the two terms, which were used very loosely and often interchangeably. Aptitudes may best be considered in the words of Hahn and MacLean (1955) as: ". . . latent, potential, undeveloped capacities to acquire abilities and skills and to demonstrate achievement." Tests are constructed to measure these latent capacities, and on the basis of their scores, predictions are made of future performance or behavior. For example, an intelligence test, which in many cases is a measure of achievement, is used to predict scholastic performance or success. As an evaluation of an individual's current mental status, this test may be looked upon as a test of ability. When used to predict future behavior, this test becomes an aptitude test. Similarly there are tests of typing ability, musical ability, artistic ability, and the like. Many times, perhaps most typically, these are used as aptitude tests. Even an achievement test such as one constructed to measure high school mathematics is commonly used in the university to predict performance in mathematics, science, or engineering courses. The line which separates ability from achievement is a thin one. Both are probably the result of the developments of aptitudes by training and learning. In the discussion that follows tests which measure current status will be referred to as tests of ability or of achievement. The use to which these tests are put will determine whether or not they are aptitude tests.

A discussion of abilities may be separated into two parts. First there is general ability or intelligence. Theories as to the nature and components of this will be discussed below. The other abilities are referred to as special abilities. Of this type there are many. In the discussion that follows attention will be given only to those that are encountered in the usual counseling situations. These are mechanical, clerical, artistic, and musical ability. It should also be strongly emphasized that tests are only one method used in collecting information about these abilities. It is granted that they are very useful and even suspected that they are the easiest way of obtaining information about abilities. But they are not the only way, and the alert counselor is always looking for other bits of information with which to do a better job of evaluating abilities.

All information about aptitudes and abilities needs to be synthesized into a meaningful pattern for use with the clients in the counseling interviews. The cross-sectional data described in this chapter form an important part of the counselor-client evaluations which result in life choices. A central part of these data is that describing a client's general ability to perform life tasks. Thus it is essential that the counselor consider the meaning of general ability, ways of evaluating it, and how it can be used in the counseling interviews.

GENERAL ABILITY

Usually general ability is referred to as intelligence. Many have become dissatisfied with this term because it means different things to different people and thus becomes difficult to use. Frequently intelligence is called academic or scholastic ability, or even book-learning ability. There is justification for this when it is considered that these intelligence tests are used most typically in schools to predict how well an individual will learn in an academic situation, that is with books. Definitions of intelligence as made by psychologists have been many and varied. About sixty years ago Binet defined intelligence as the capacity to judge well, to reason well, and to comprehend well (Goodenough, 1949). In the *Journal of Educational Psychology* (1921) the editors published some definitions of intelligence in a symposium they conducted. Some of the various definitions are as follows: Dearborn, "The capacity to learn or profit by experience"; Henmon, "Capacity for knowledge or knowledge possessed"; Terman, "The ability to think in terms of abstract ideas"; Pintner, "The ability of the individual to adapt himself adequately to relatively new relations in life"; and Thorndike, "Intellect, as the power of good responses from the point of view of truth." Stoddard (1943) proposed one of the most comprehensive definitions by stating that "Intelligence is the ability to undertake activities that are characterized by difficulty, complexity, abstractness, economy, adaptiveness to a goal, social value, emergence of originals, and to maintain such activities under conditions that demand a concentration of energy and a resistance to emotional forces." Wechsler (1944) in the book about his intelligence test for adults described intelligence as the global capacity of an individual to act purposefully and to deal effectively with his environment. Garrett (1946) described intellectual capacity as the abilities demanded in the solution of problems which require understandings and the manipulations of symbols. Goddard (1946) conceived of intelligence as the availability and use of one's past experience for the solution of immediate problems and the anticipation of future ones.

All of these definitions may be classified into two general types. The first of these includes definitions related to the ability to carry on abstract thinking, the ability to manipulate symbols, or the ability to learn materials of a verbal nature. The other category includes the definitions that consider intelligence as the ability to adapt to one's environment. Stoddard's definition is the best definition of this type. It follows that, since a definition such as Stoddard's is so complex that it is all but impossible to construct a test to measure such a comprehensive concept, test makers have concentrated on measuring the other type of intelligence.

The early tests such as Binet's 1905 scale were based upon no theory of intelligence. They were essentially trial and error attempts that differed from their predecessors in that they seemed to work. This early test of Binet's was immediately followed by two revisions that were considerable advancements over the 1905 scale. Psychologists all around the world became interested in Binet's work and soon translations of his tests or adaptations began to appear in various countries. The most notable of these was Terman's *Revision of the Binet-Simon Intelligence Scales (1916).* This test was made up of items arranged in age levels. Each item was worth so many months' mental age and an individual's score on the test was the sum of the months received for responding to an item correctly. Such scale is referred to as an age scale. This mental age is divided by chronological age to give the I.Q.:

$$\text{I.Q.} = \frac{\text{MA}}{\text{CA}}\,(100)$$

The 100 was introduced to remove the decimals. A test like this is labelled an individual test because it can be administered to only one person at a time.

In 1917 the United States entered World War I and for the first time an attempt was made to measure extensively the mental ability and other characteristics of a large group of men. A group of psychologists was asked to construct a test which could be given to a number of individuals at once. The results of their efforts brought forth the first practical intelligence test, the *Army Alpha.* This test, which could only be used by draftees who could read and write English, was soon followed by the *Army Beta,* the first nonverbal group test designed for illiterates and non-English-speaking personnel. At the end of the war both industry and education began to use these intelligence tests, this use continuing to the present.

These early tests which are now referred to as "old-type" tests typically resulted in one score that was translated into an I.Q. The tests were made up of a series of items such as word meaning, arithmetic problems, number series, analogies, same-opposites, and the like. These items were arranged in random order as far as content was concerned but were usually arranged in order of difficulty with the easiest item first and each succeeding item more difficult than the one before it. Such an arrangement of mixed items in ascending order of difficulty results in a test described as a "spiral-omnibus" test. Tests which resulted in more than one score did not begin to appear until the 1930's when Thurstone's (1938) work was beginning to have effects. Since then the majority of these tests measure certain aspects of intelligence, or factors, as Thurstone called them. Instead of one score being derived from a test, a profile of several factors may result from this new type, or at least a total score that is broken down into parts: a verbal score and a nonverbal, quantitative, or performance score as this latter part has been variously labelled. Thurstone's original test was called the *Chicago Test of Primary Mental Abilities*. Other tests of this type are the *Cooperative School and College Ability Tests (SCAT)*, the *Army General Classification Test (AGCT)* administered to millions of draftees in World War II, the *Lorge-Thorndike Intelligence Tests*, and the *Holzinger-Crowder Uni-Factor Tests*.

Theories of intelligence

Spearman (1904) was the first to propose an acceptable theory of intelligence. His theory is referred to as the two-factor theory because he stated that intelligence was made up of a general factor, referred to as a g-factor, and other specific factors, s. According to this theory, two tests correlate because they both contain some of the g-factor, and the larger the amount of this factor in common between the two tests the larger the correlation between the two. Spearman stated that this g-factor was a particular type of mental energy that could be applied in making comparisons or in drawing inferences. In the years following, Spearman had to revise his ideas to make way for other factors that he referred to as group factors. Actually these group factors may be common to two or more tests but not to all tests under consideration at one time. These factors received labels such as mechanical, arithmetical, musical, logical, psychological, perseveration, oscillation, and will. Today Spearman's ideas are followed by British psychologists in describing and measuring intelligence.

In the United States, T. L. Kelley and L. L. Thurstone have been the pioneers in developing theories of intelligence. The approach in this country is to conceive of intelligence or of the organization of mental life, as it is sometimes called, as being made up of a group of factors. Thurstone (1938), after administering a large number of tests to a group of high school students, was able to identify statistically by factor analysis a group of factors that he called "primary mental abilities." These are:

V   Verbal: understanding ideas expressed in words

N   numerical: the ability to carry out the four fundamental arithmetic processes

R   reasoning: problem solving

S   spatial: the ability to perceive spatial relationships

P   perception: perceptual speed

WF word fluency: the ability to write and speak with considerable ease

M   memory

Six of the above factors (omitting P) are published as the *Chicago Test of Primary Mental Abilities.* The *SRA Primary Mental Abilities Test* contains only five of the factors, M (Memory) omitted as well as P (Perception).

Later research especially during and after World War II (Guilford, 1947, 1948, 1959) has resulted in the isolation of between 30 and 40 of these factors. Most American psychologists prefer this approach to that of Spearman, although actually there is not as much difference between them as some would contend. There are other theories of intelligence, but since they are not widely accepted they will not be discussed here.

The measurement of intelligence

In the past considerable confusion and disagreement existed as to exactly what these tests measure. If one looks at the types of items that appear on many of them, there is a very obvious conclusion. Consider the items: "If two pencils cost five cents, how many pencils can be bought for 35 cents?" "Who is the President of the United States?" "A word meaning the same as eulogize is . . . ." and the like. These items measure the results of learning or achievement. An intelligence test of this type then is an achievement test. The score that an individual obtains on such a test is greatly affected by his interaction with environment. It is important for the counselor to remember that background includes not only the school but the home and community as well, because much learning takes place in home and community activities for certain social classes and not for others. These tests then do not measure innate ability. They measure the effects that have been made upon this native potential or ability by learning. It follows then that the user of these tests has to make the assumption when using them that each child has had an equal opportunity to learn. A little thought reveals that this assumption is never fully justified, not only because of the inequalities of the schools, but also and chiefly because of the gross and glaring differences in the homes and communities from which children come. The psychological literature of the past is full of studies concerning the backwoodsmen of Kentucky and Virginia, the canal-boat children of England, and changes brought about in the measured intelligence of Negroes when they move to northern cities from the rural South. Children from these barren environments do poorly on intelligence tests mainly because they live in a different culture from the one upon which the tests have been standardized. Therefore the counselor must adjust the interpretation of a test score in terms of differing cultural backgrounds of clients.

Closely related to the above is the effect of parental occupation upon the intelligence tests scores of children. Terman (1937) in the manual of his revised *Stanford-Binet Scale* showed the effects of the socioeconomic status of parents on the intelligence test scores of children. For example he found that for children in the age bracket 10–14 the mean I.Q.'s for different social classes were as follows: Professional, 118; Semi-professional and managerial, 112; Clerical, skilled trades, and retail business, 107; Rural owners, 92; Semiskilled, minor clerical, minor business, 103; Slightly skilled, 101; and Day laborers, urban and rural, 97. The greatest mean difference here is 26 I.Q. points between children of professional people and those of farmers who own their land. Terman showed similar differences for children of three other age groups among these same social groups. Eells and others (1951) in a major study conducted at the University of Chicago evaluated the effects of social class membership on more widely used group tests. They found that on some of these tests every single item had a bias which favored the child from the middle class home. Their work resulted in a test known as the *Davis-Eells Games (1953)* which attempts to measure mental ability by ruling out the effects of class membership. Again the counselor must take this influence into account in interpreting and using test scores with a client.

In addition to the effect of background of the individual being tested on test results, there is also the effect of motivation. This is related to a certain extent to the social class to which the individual belongs, for the individual from the middle class comes from a background where the emphasis is on striving and attaining success. It might be expected that he will do his best to work up to capacity in a testing situation. For example, lower class children are apt to see little value in tests or in anything associated with school. There is usually no evidence about just what their test score measures. It follows then that a counselor has to use extreme caution in interpreting such test scores. The best thing to do is to interpret any such score in the light of all other information available about a student. Also the counselor must remember that there are error factors even in the best of intelligence tests. Actually these tests are most valid when they are used to measure the mental ability of urban, white, middle class American children between the ages of 7 and 16.

Scores from these tests are reported in I.Q.'s, centiles, or standard scores. I.Q.'s have been used longer than other derived scores and probably will continue to be used despite the clamor from some quarters for their abandonment. Exactly what is an I.Q.? As noted above it is not a measure of one's innate ability. Probably the best way to look at it is as a ratio that gives an indication of the level at which an individual may be expected to learn. As was pointed out in Chapter 7 where scores were discussed, I.Q.'s have little meaning when used with adolescents and adults. Another problem that has concerned psychologists for a long time is related to the constancy of the I.Q. In earlier times there were those who thought that it was stable or constant throughout life. Then there were the environmentalists who argued that placing any child in a desirable environment would bring about a significant increase in measured intelligence. Stoddard (1943) presents a good picture of the research basis of these ideas. The whole question was whether measured intelligence was the result of factors inherited from parents or the effect of being in a desirable environment. Today the argument has quieted down and most psychologists take a middle of the road approach saying that both inheritance and environment are important and that what is measured is the effect of both. As far as stability of the I.Q. or the intelligence test score is concerned, it is now felt that, if a child's intelligence is measured at age six or older, this measure is a reliable measure of what he will be like in later years. There will of course be variations, but these are slight and if the individual stays in the same sort of environment he will obtain about the same scores on subsequent forms of the same test, the variation being a function of the standard error of measurement. Even a great change in environment will bring about only increases of a few points. Tests administered before age six are apt to be more unreliable, and the younger the child at the time of testing, the more unreliable the test (see Cattell, 1947). It must also be noted that I.Q.'s from different tests are not the same. The means of all may be 100, but the standard deviations will vary. For example, the standard deviation of the Binet is 16, the Otis, 12. Thus the counselor interprets a Binet I.Q. of 116 as equivalent to an Otis I.Q. of 112.

Types of intelligence tests

The simplest classification that can be made of intelligence tests is that of group and individual tests. Of these two types group tests are by far the more common. Group tests may be administered to one or more persons at once. The responses to the items are recorded either on the test booklet or on a special answer sheet. An individual test on the other hand is administered orally to one individual at a time and responses to every separate item are recorded by the examiner. Most of the tests that the counselor uses are group tests.

Group tests of intelligence

Group tests may be further divided into two types, one-score tests and those which provide results in terms of many scores or a profile. The one-score type of test, as was previously pointed out, is the older of the two. Such tests as the *Otis Self-Administering Tests of Mental Ability,* the *Otis Quick-Scoring Mental Ability Tests,* the *Henmon-Nelson Tests,* and several short tests used in industry, such as the *Wonderlic Personnel Test,* and the *Purdue Adaptability Test* are of this type. The older of these tests produced results that were expressed in I.Q.'s. Some of the newer ones as the last two mentioned above use centiles in reporting scores. Such tests as these are usually short with about thirty minutes being the maximum testing time. Several such as the *Wonderlic* are very short requiring only twelve minutes of working time. They are very useful in working with groups in elementary, high school, and industrial situations, especially with the average individual. Brighter students or older individuals need more difficult tests. When these tests are used with college students, for example, there is a tendency for the students to cluster near the top score. Such tests are said to have low ceilings. Individuals who are considered dull or below the average group in mental ability cannot have valid estimates of their mental ability made with these tests, for these persons are slow or retarded in reading and speed is an important factor in the taking of such tests.

As was pointed out, the work of the Thurstones led the way in the construction of tests with more than one score. In the most general form such tests are composed of a verbal and a nonverbal part, resulting in two scores and a total score. A few of these tests go further than this and break mental ability down into component parts. It must be pointed out that all of these tests are not based upon the results of factor analyses as was Thurstone's *Chicago Test of Primary Mental Abilities.* In the next paragraphs several of the more widely used tests of this type will be mentioned.

In 1955 the Educational Testing Service issued the first forms of the *Cooperative School and College Ability Tests (SCAT)* to replace a test, the *American Council on Education Psychological Examination (ACE),* that had been used for many years with high school upperclassmen and entering college freshmen. This new test, the *SCAT,* differs from the *ACE* in that it covers five levels: intermediate grades, upper grades, junior high school, senior high school, and college freshmen and sophomores. The test is made up of four parts that result in a verbal score (V) and a quantitative score (Q). This test, like the *ACE,* is a good predictor of academic success.

Another test series that can be used throughout the school period is the *Lorge-Thorndike Intelligence Tests* issued by Houghton Mifflin Company. This test, like the previous one, consists of five levels: I, for kindergarten and grade 1; II, for grades 2 and 3; III, for grades 4 through 6; IV, for grades 7–9; and V for grades 10–13. The tests covering the first two levels are essentially nonverbal in nature. For the three highest levels the tests are made up of two parts, a verbal series and a nonverbal series. The authors recommend that Level IV be reserved for the general run of the population and Level V be used with high school graduates. Results are expressed in I.Q.'s, but these I.Q.'s are of the standard score type.

In 1957 the California Test Bureau released a revision of the *California Test of Mental Maturity*. This series consists of six levels: (1) Pre-primary, for kindergarten and grade 1; (2) Primary, for grades 1–3; (3) Elementary, for grades 4–8; (4) Junior High School, for grades 7–9; (5) Secondary, for grades 9–13; and (6) Advanced, for grades ten to college and adults. These tests are published in a "short form" which can be administered in the typical school period, and a "long form" that requires about two hours for completion. Results are given in terms of language, nonlanguage, and total mental ages and I.Q.'s. Also a detailed profile is presented that shows the individual's performance on each part of the test.

While these batteries with all their details and elaborate profiles seem ideal and useful, it must be remembered that the reliability of any test is directly related to the length of the test. On some of these tests the number of items in the various sub-tests is small. This results in sub-tests with low reliability or no reliability, whereas the total test score or the scores based upon the two parts, such as verbal and nonverbal, may have high reliability. In many cases these sub-scores are of no value and should not be considered in counseling. There is even evidence that the use of more than the total score adds little or nothing to the prediction of academic success (Super, 1956-d).

There are several tests that were constructed for the top part of the distribution of mental ability. Level I of the *SCAT* would be one example of this. Another test widely used with high school seniors and university freshmen is the *Ohio State University Psychological Examination* which is available from Science Research Associates. This test is almost unique in that it is a power test, that is, there is no time limit, but most individuals complete it in less than two hours. The test is entirely verbal in nature, being made up completely of verbal and reading items. It is an excellent predictor of the grades of college freshmen. Another test of an even higher level is the *Miller Analogies Test* (available through the Psychological Corporation to certain counseling and testing bureaus) which is made up of one hundred analogy type test items. Certain universities use this in the selection of students for graduate work. Validity coefficients resulting from the use of this test have tended to be very low. There may be two reasons for this, the fact that grades in the typical graduate school tend to be very restricted in their range, and the homogeneous nature of the graduate student group. It may be recalled that the more restricted the range of the group, the smaller the size of any correlation coefficient. Terman developed another high-level test, the *Concept Mastery Test* (available from the Psychological Corporation). This test resulted from his study of gifted individuals and is similar in part to the Miller in its make-up and use. Batteries such as the *Graduate Record Examination* and the *College Boards* also contain high-level intelligence tests of a verbal and quantitative nature.

Of all the tests mentioned and discussed above, the majority may be classified as being verbal or mostly verbal in nature. By this it is meant that to respond to the item the examinee has to manipulate words. The other type of group test is called nonverbal. When taking these, the examinee manipulates geometrical figures, mazes, figure analogies, and the like. These tests are used with those who have language or reading handicaps or in some cases with those who do not speak English, as was the *Army Beta* of World War I. At the present time these tests are used in the schools chiefly with children in the primary grades (see the *Lorge-Thorndike Tests* above) and with others who have reading problems or who have been raised in an environment of such a nature that taking an ordinary verbal test would be to their disadvantage. Similar in their function to these nonverbal tests are other tests known as performance tests. Usually these are individual tests in which the client has to complete tasks such as mazes, formboards, or building designs with colored blocks. Again such tests as these are usually reserved for the physically and mentally handicapped. While such batteries or tests do result in I.Q.'s, such I.Q.'s are apt to be considerably different from those obtained from verbal tests. A typical correlation coefficient between these two types of tests would be somewhere around .50. The counselor will have limited use of performance tests such as these.

Individual tests

As pointed out above, individual tests are administered to only one individual at a time. At present there are two widely used individual tests. The oldest of these is the *Stanford-Binet,* now in its third revision (1960). This battery consists of a series of tests that start at age two and go by either half-years or whole years up to the adult ages. Administration, scoring, and interpretation of the test requires special training in which tests are administered and scored under supervision. Results are either in mental ages or I.Q.'s. By nature the test is highly verbal. This and the fact that it was standardized upon children and adolescents in school limits its use, especially with adults. At the present time the test is most frequently used in clinics such as child guidance centers.

Wechsler (1939) introduced his *Wechsler-Bellevue Intelligence Scale,* an intelligence test for adults standardized upon adults. This scale was made up of two parts, a verbal scale and a performance scale, the latter being a collection of many of the performance tests that had been used by psychologists for many years. In 1955, a revision, the *Wechsler Adult Intelligence Scale (WAIS),* was produced; however, there is little difference between the two editions except that a few of the tests were lengthened. Wechsler also has developed the *Wechsler Intelligence Scale for Children* (1949), similar in content to his other scales and for use with children from ages 5 to 15. Since World War II these Wechsler scales have been widely used in both clinics and counseling centers. A lot of pointless research has been carried on with the sub-scales of these tests —pointless because it was based upon tests with such a small number of items that reliability was nonexistent. Many counselors have recommended that clients take the test. In some schools all clients were automatically administered this test when they appeared for counseling. The writers feel that such a practice is a waste of time and money. There is no evidence that the individual tests are any more useful or effective with the average client in educational and vocational counseling than any of the group tests. Until any real value is shown to result from the use of these tests with all clients, they should be reserved for those individuals who cannot be adequately appraised by the use of the group tests. This is a group composed of individuals at the extreme ends of the continuum of intelligence, and those with reading, language, or physical handicaps. A bright child has a chance to be more adequately measured on the Binet because of the higher ceiling of the test.

Use of intelligence tests in counseling

Intelligence tests along with other evidence of mental ability that shall soon be discussed probably find their greatest use in the prediction of educational and vocational success. This is not surprising when it is considered that one of the major goals of counseling is educational and vocational adjustment. These tests are also used in identifying the superior students for awards, scholarships, or for more advanced and strenuous academic programs. At the other extreme these tests are used in a diagnostic manner along with reading, study skills, interest, and personality tests to see if the reasons for a student's failure can be identified.

With intelligence tests there is a question about whether a client should be told his exact score. The general feeling on this is that it should not be done. But this refers only to the exact scores. What was said earlier about the standard error of measurement is one reason for not handing out these tests scores indiscriminately.   Each score is unreliable to a certain extent.   These scores then become too indefinite to be labels put on clients unless they are combined with other evidence.   Then the I.Q. is no longer the major factor.

However, if the counselor accepts as one of the major aims of counseling that clients obtain information about themselves and their own strength and weaknesses, it follows that they must have some information about where they stand on the continuum of intelligence.   It is hoped that on the basis of the information brought out in the counseling situation the client will be able to put all the details together and come to a logical decision about self and future.   This is impossible if the client knows nothing about his mental ability.   So instead of being told or given specific scores, the client should be informed about scores on rather broad bands into which the continuum of intelligence has been divided such as "in the top ten per cent of your freshmen class," "in the bottom twenty-five per cent of high school seniors," "very superior when compared to high school seniors in this curriculum," "below the average group" or "below the mean when compared to other engineering freshmen."   There is no need to be too threatening with the use of this method when the client is in the lower half of the average group or in the lowest sixteen per cent.   Usually the client knows this and a way can be found to say it, if the counselor is alert.   Less selective norm groups can be chosen which will be fairer and more meaningful comparisons for the client.   Then comparisons can be made without creating a feeling of despair in the client.

In using intelligence test scores it is a good idea not to place too much reliance upon scores from a single test.   In the ideal testing program the client is tested at different intervals and usually there are one or more scores from the same test series that can be evaluated to give a better idea of the client's mental ability than would be obtained from a single score.   The ideal use of intelligence tests in schools is to have administered such tests at the end of the primary grades, this followed again in grade five by another test to act as a check upon the previous test.   Then a test should be administered at the beginning of junior high school and at the beginning of senior high.   Also it is recommended that there be additional testing in the senior year when there is an intensification of the counseling process for both educational and vocational purposes.   In general, intelligence tests should be administered at the transition points in the educational program.   In other agencies sufficient intelligence test scores should be secured that together with other evidence of intelligence they will give a stable estimate for counseling purposes.

Again it is emphasized that these scores of mental ability must be interpreted in the light of other information collected about the client.   Psychologists consider individuals in parts or segments of behavior when testing and evaluating them. Often when results are considered there is a tendency to overlook the fact that information about some of these parts is not consistent with that about the whole individual.

Other evidences of mental ability

Considerable space has been devoted to the use of tests in the collection of evidence on mental ability. It must not be overlooked that there are other ways in which such information may be collected, very important among which is the use of observational techniques. Ratings are used to appraise how an individual solves problems, shows evidence of creativity and original thinking, or carries on any activity involving mental ability. Probably better than the use of these rating scales is the use of a system of anecdotal records (see Chapter 3). Well-written anecdotes are filled with information such as that which was mentioned along with rating scales. Another source of information about mental ability is in the questions that individuals ask. This is particularly true with younger children, for it seems that in many schools as children grow older they become conditioned to asking certain kinds of questions, or toward not asking questions at all. Also the judgments of competent teachers provide excellent information on students' mental ability. The use of rating scales and anecdotes includes these teacher judgments to a great extent.

There are many bits of additional evidence that the counselor might look at which offer suggestions as to the client's mental ability. Some of these are noted below. The client's age may be compared with his grade placement in school. The amount and the type of reading done offers valuable insights. Certain hobbies, such as playing chess and working complicated puzzles, aid in identifying the brighter individuals. The counselor may note the rapidity with which the client catches on in the interview. Samples of the client's writing containing material which offers a chance to be creative or to organize are also good indicators of higher mental ability. Rank in graduating class is also important, but the counselor must consider the size of the class. This information is very important when the client was graduating in a large class, but is of no value when the graduating class consisted of only a small number of individuals. A comparison of grades obtained with the number of activities carried on by a student is also useful. Finally such factors as socioeconomic status of family, occupations of parents and siblings, education of parents and siblings, and the like may also contain valuable information. The counselor must recognize that all of these may not provide valid information about the mental ability of all individuals. An individual from a minority group should not have some of these applied to him.

Another important source of information on this general ability is the grades that students receive in their academic courses. Earlier it was noted that marks in school correlate highest with these intelligence tests and for that reason the tests are known as tests of book-learning ability. The counselor must accept grades for what they are. By this it is meant that such grades are apt to be unreliable for there are any of a number of different things that go into the make-up of grades given by any one teacher. When one compares grades from one teacher with those of another, or compares grades among members of different departments or schools, the variability of the grades becomes even greater. However, when all grades are taken for any given individual, they tend to cancel out the idiosyncrasies of a given teacher and to give a rather accurate picture of the individual's mental ability. This is frequently limited by differences in motivation among individuals. Inequalities between academic potential and grades are most frequently encountered where contingency or motivational factors, such as attitudes and interests, play a vital part. It is not unusual to find one of the brightest individuals in a school, office, or factory failing or being dropped because of poor work. In such cases the counselor needs other evaluative devices. Grades are not the only measure of school achievement available, for there is a large series of standardized achievement tests that provide valid and reliable measures of academic attainment. Grades should be compared with achievement test scores to see whether the teachers' estimates coincide with a more objective measure of classroom performance. These achievement tests will be discussed next.

ACHIEVEMENT TESTS

Standardized achievement tests are the most plentiful of the many standardized tests. An achievement test is a test that is used to measure the outcomes of learning. While most of them are associated with classroom learning, this does not have to be the case. Achievement tests fall into two rather large groups, the elementary school batteries and the specific subject matter tests used in high schools and colleges. Especially important among the latter are reading tests. All of these produce highly reliable results when used correctly. They are so constructed that they possess content validity. Before such tests are purchased they should be carefully examined to see how well they cover the content and the objectives of the courses taught in the schools where they are being used. Many times there is a rather wide discrepancy between local practices and what the tests measure. The extent of this discrepancy governs the validity of the tests. In the discussion that follows several of the more widely encountered batteries and tests will be described. The counselor interested in others should see the catalogs of the various test publishers or Buros (1949, 1953, 1959).

Currently the widely used elementary school batteries are the *Metropolitan Achievement Tests, Stanford Achievement Tests* (both published by the World Book Co.), the *Iowa Every Pupil Tests* (Houghton Mifflin Co.) the *California Achievement Tests* (California Test Bureau) and the newest of these, the *Sequential Tests of Educational Progress* (Educational Testing Service). While these batteries, in general, cover the elementary grades up to junior high school, the last two differ in that they may be used with high school students and those in the first two years of college. Generally these batteries measure reading skills, language usage or communication skills, arithmetic skills, and work-study skills. Some of the older ones have tests on content, such as history, literature, and geography, but the trend is away from this to a concentration on the more permanent results of the educative process, such as the ability to use data and apply principles.

At the present time three series of achievement tests are used with students in secondary and higher education. One of the oldest of these is the group known as the *Cooperative Achievement Tests* (Educational Testing Service). These tests are of two types, test of general proficiency as in mathematics and the regular tests associated with specific academic course subjects like plane geometry. These tests have a reputation of excellent construction and norming. A second group is the *Evaluation and Adjustment Tests* (World Book Co.). This group is made up of a series of well-constructed tests for each of the secondary academic subjects. Finally there are the *Iowa Tests of Educational Development* (Science Research Associates). This series differs from the others in that no attempt is made to measure the various academic subjects. There are nine tests in this battery, bearing such headings as "Understanding of Basic Social Concepts," "Interpretation of Reading Materials in the Natural Sciences," "General Vocabulary Test," and "Uses of Sources of Information."

The results of such tests as these are useful to the counselor in various ways, an important one of which is prediction. A common problem of the high school and university counselor is assisting the client in making vocational plans. For example, achievement tests and course grades in mathematics and physical science would be most useful in making a prediction about success in engineering or even in discussing the feasibility of the study of engineering with a client who is considering engineering as a vocation.

Achievement tests are also useful in the diagnostic work of locating weak areas. This is especially true in the area of reading. It is not at all unusual to find that some students are doing poor or failing work merely because they are poor or slow readers. The counselor must not overlook this and in all such cases reading disability must be considered as a potential source of the difficulties. At other times mathematics and

English tests may serve a similar need in their respective areas. The counselor or teacher may also use an achievement test in a given subject to determine weak areas in need of remediation within the subject field. Thus achievement tests can be used for predictive, diagnostic, or remedial ✗ purposes. In general, the counselor should use these tests to evaluate with the client individual strengths and weaknesses in the academic subjects in the way that best meets the client's needs. Proper use of these would then result in better educational preparation and better vocational adjustment for the client.

SPECIAL ABILITIES

In contrast to general ability or intelligence there is a group of abilities equally important in counseling referred to as special abilities. The considerations that follow will include five of these: mechanical, clerical, artistic, musical, and physical ability.

FIELD AND LEVEL CONCEPTS

Order is introduced into the area of abilities and the use of them in predicting educational and vocational success by the use of what is known as field and level concepts. A little thought will reveal that it would be impossible to set up tests for the thousands of different occupations that exist in the United States. Many of these occupations can be classified as being in the mechanical area or field. To be successful in these occupations one has to have one or more of the mechanical skills or traits discussed above. Individuals with these skills, however, do not all work at the same level. Some are trained and perform at the professional level whereas others are said to be doing semi-skilled work. To a great extent the amount of general ability one possesses more or less determines at which of these levels he is going to perform.

In one of the earlier classifications of fields Paterson *et al.* (1941, 1953) constructed the *Minnesota Occupational Rating Scales*, in which they set up the following abilities:

1. ACADEMIC—the ability to understand and manipulate ideas and symbols.

2. MECHANICAL—the ability to manipulate concrete objects, to work with tools and machinery, and to deal mentally with mechanical movements.

3. SOCIAL—the ability to understand and manage people, to function well in social relationships.

4. CLERICAL—to handle numbers and names accurately and rapidly.

5. MUSICAL—to sense sounds, to image these sounds in reproductive and creative imagination, to be aroused by them emotionally, etc., and finally the ability to give some form of expression in musical performance or in creative music.

6. ARTISTIC—the ability to create forms of artistic merit and the capacity to recognize the comparative merits of forms already created.

7. PHYSICAL—the ability to perform physical tasks.[1]

The fields that are used with the *Minnesota Occupational Rating Scales* are named exactly as are the seven abilities listed above. Practically all occupations can be placed into one of the above fields or in a combination of two or more of them.

In respect to level the same authors set up four levels which may be generally classified as follows:

Level A (Professional, Semi-professional, and Executive Occupations—top 10% of the population except in the last three fields where it is 4%).

Level B (Technical, Clerical, Supervisory—15% of the population).

Level C (Skilled tradesmen, low level, low grade clerical workers and the like—middle 50% of the population).

Level D (Unskilled workers—bottom 25% of the population).

These authors describe the intelligence or academic ability associated with each of these levels as follows:

Level A—Superior abstract intelligence with training equivalent to college graduation from a first-class institution or two or three years of college, or to that of executive of a moderately large business. Ability for creative and directive work is implied.

Level B—High average abstract intelligence with training equivalent to high school graduation and/or technical school or junior college.

Level C—Average abstract intelligence with training equivalent to vocational high school. Work demanding specialized skill and knowledge; tasks mostly of a concrete nature requiring specialized training.

Level D—Low average or slightly below average abstract intelligence with training equivalent to eighth grade or less. Work demanding a minimum of technical knowledge or skill but may involve special abilities, such as dexterity in the performance of repetitive routine work.

Applying the concept of level to the area of mechanical ability examples of types of work in each level as listed by the same authors are:

Level A—machine designer, mechanical engineer, toolmaker, civil and electrical engineers.

Level B—draftsman, engraver, bricklayer, auto mechanic.

Level C—boiler maker, tire repairer, shoe repairer.

Level D—telephone operator, wrapper, bench assembly worker, day laborer, lawyer, writer, and public officials in non-mechanical occupations.

---

[1] This and the following lists of levels were adapted with permission from D. G. Paterson, C.d'A. Gerken, and M. E. Hahn, *Revised Minnesota Occupational Rating Scales* (Minneapolis: University of Minnesota Press, Copyright, 1953).

At this point the student should refer to Form 5.2, page 95, and the discussion of the use of these scales in a counseling situation. The main purpose of this chapter is to show the counselor how he can obtain information that will enable him to do an adequate and valid job in organizing information about clients in the fashion of Form 5.2. These *Minnesota Occupational Rating Scales* also enable the counselor to have ready access to an analysis of the minimum levels of these various abilities that are required for more than 400 occupations. For example an automobile salesman should have the following profile: Academic ability, B; mechanical ability, C; social ability, A; clerical ability, C; and artistic and musical abilities, both D's. This section of the Rating Scales is followed by a listing of jobs that require A and B levels in the different fields.

A similar device, though more elaborate, was developed by the United States Department of Labor (1956) and published under the title of *Estimates of Worker Trait Requirement for 4000 Jobs* (see Table 5.1, pages 102–103). Each of these jobs is analyzed under the following headings:

1. General Educational Development. Seven levels described, with level 7 being able to comprehend and express himself in precise or highly connotative meanings as in scientific journals and philosophical works and level 1 with no speaking, reading, or writing being required.

2. Specific Vocational Training. Nine levels ranging from Level 9—more than 10 years—downward.

3. Aptitudes. Here are listed the 9 aptitudes (noted on page 213) and the following five levels for the evaluation of each:
   Level 1—Upper 10%
   Level 2—Upper ⅓ exclusive of top 10%
   Level 3—Middle ⅓
   Level 4—Lower ⅓ exclusive of bottom 10%
   Level 5—Lowest 10%

4. Temperaments. Here are listed 12 different types of occupational situations to which workers must adjust such as variety and change, isolation, performing under stress, and dealing with people.

5. Interests. Ten items here based upon five bipolar factors. Examples-Situations involving a preference for activities dealing with things and objects versus situations involving a preference for activities concerned with people and the communications of ideas.

6. Physical capacities. Five categories ranging from S (sedentary) to V (very heavy).

7. Working conditions. Inside, outside, or both.

To illustrate how this is used, "industrial psychologist" is looked up and the estimated trait requirements for this position read from the chart. This is what is found:

1. General Educational Development is 7, the highest level of comprehension and expression.

2. Specific Vocational Training Time is also 7, meaning from 2–4 years of specific vocational training.

3. Aptitudes—top 10 per cent in general intelligence, verbal, and spatial ability, top third in numerical ability, middle third in form perception, bottom third in clerical ability, manual and finger dexterity, and motor coordination and in the bottom 10 per cent in eye-hand-foot coordination and color discrimination.

4. Temperaments—listed here are situations involving variety and change and those involving the evaluation of material against measurable or verifiable criteria.

5. Interests—both social welfare interests and interests in scientific and technical things are noted here.

6. Physical Capacities—sedentary.

7. Working Conditions—inside.

All of this when put together gives a rather good idea of what an industrial psychologist is like. The reader must remember that such volumes as these are not to be used as cookbooks. The title of the one just quoted used the word "estimates." These traits and characteristics are suggested for exploring in the counseling situation. One must not test the individual and then go looking for a profile that seems to fit best his test pattern and then make this the recommended vocational goal. Rather the complete picture of behavior collected for an individual includes possible educational or vocational placements at proper field and level.

MECHANICAL ABILITY

Over the past 30 years the psychological literature has included much speculation and theorizing as to the nature of so-called mechanical ability or mechanical aptitude. Actually no progress was made in pinning down the nature of this ability until applications of Thurstone's method of factor analysis were made to materials used to evaluate this ability. One of the earlier of these factor analyses was made by Harrell (1940). As a result of administering a battery of tests of mechanical ability and including information upon such variables as amount of schooling, ratings of job performance, and the like, he analysed mechanical ability into these factors: (1) verbal; (2) spatial; (3) agility (manual dexterity); (4) perception; and (5) youth (inexperience). Wittenborn (1945) in a similar analysis of test data collected at the University of Minnesota isolated six factors: (I) spatial visualization; (II) stereotyped movement (of the wrist and forearm); (III) scholastic ability; (IV) manual dexterity; (V) perceptual speed; and (VI) steadiness. Guilford (1947, 1948) showed that this ability on the basis of factor analyses of data used in the USAAF testing programs was made up to a great extent of two factors, mechanical information and spatial visualization. Other factors similar and more numerous than Harrell's were also present. Research carried on in the Division of Occupational Analysis of the War Manpower Commission (1945) based on the factor analysis of 59 tests revealed or suggested the following factors: (1) a verbal factor (V); (2) a numerical factor (N); (3) a spatial factor (S); (4) a factor designated O, apparently general intelligence; (5) a perceptual factor (P) involving the use of geometrical figures; (6) a second perceptual factor (Q), related to words and numbers; (7) an aiming factor, related to accuracy and exactness of movement (A); (8) a speed factor (T); (9) finger dexterity (F); (10) manual dexterity (M); and (11) a logical reasoning factor (L). Later work conducted in United States Employment Service continued using the factors V, N, S, P, Q, and M. The O factor above was replaced by one called General Intelligence (G). The speed factor (T) and the logical reasoning factor (L) were dropped. The aiming factor was replaced by a factor called motor coordination (K). Two other factors (E), eye-and-foot coordination and (C), color discrimination, were added. These are the factors which are used in the general category of "Aptitudes" in the U.S. Department of Labor's *Estimates of Worker Trait Requirements for 4000 Jobs* (1956).

Usually any discussion of mechanical ability is broken into several of these subdivisions or factors. Super (1949) has separate chapters on manual dexterities, mechanical aptitude, and spatial visualizations. Bennett and Cruikshank (1942) in their monograph set up three categories: (1) the capacity to understand mechanical relationships, (2) manual and finger dexterity, and (3) motor abilities of strength, speed of movement, and endurance. The discussion that follows will consider spatial visualization, dexterities, and mechanical information.

Spatial visualization or spatial perception

Tests that measure this ability require that the subject visualize the putting together or the taking apart of geometrical forms or objects. In the earlier tests this ability was actually measured by the speed and accuracy with which pieces were inserted into a board. To a great extent this technique has been superseded by tests known as paper form boards in which all the maneuvering is done mentally.

One of the earlier and more widely accepted devices used to measure this ability was the *Minnesota Spatial Relations Test* (C. H. Stoelting Co.). This instrument is made up of two sets of two boards each about three feet long and one foot wide. From these boards have been cut, usually in sets of three, circles, triangles, squares, and other objects of irregular shape. Boards A and B use 58 of these cutouts in common while the other two boards, C and D, are completed by the use of another set. The subject stands in front of the board and tries as rapidly as possible to insert each piece into its correct position. The four boards are completed and scored either by counting the results of the first board as practice and letting the score consist of the number of seconds required to complete the other three boards together or by counting the number of seconds required to complete all four boards.

As these tests are individual tests and require a half hour or more for administering, they have been replaced to a large extent by a test known as the *Minnesota Paper Form Board* (The Psychological Corporation). This 64-item group test has a time limit of twenty minutes. Each of the items consists of a geometric design which has been cut into pieces. Following this are five geometrical figures, one of which can be correctly visualized mentally from the pieces shown in the main part of the item. Another paper-and-pencil test is the *Space Relations Test* of the *Differential Aptitude Test (DAT)* (The Psychological Corporation). In this test the stem of the item consists of a two-dimensional design or pattern followed by a series of three-dimensional objects. The examinee has to decide how many of these latter objects are the result of the folding of the original two-dimensional surface.

Research with these tests has shown that they are useful in predicting success in courses in mechanical drawing, machine-shop work, dentistry, and art. Therefore, the chief use of these to the counselor is for counseling with clients about technical courses, engineering courses, and drawing and art training.

Dexterities

Under this heading are included the grosser arm movements referred to as manual dexterity and the finer ones known as finger dexterity. The measurement of both of these abilities is more or less restricted by the nature of the ability to performance tests of an individual nature. Super (1949) recommends the use of the term arm-and-hand dexterity to separate manual dexterity from wrist-and-finger dexterity or finger dexterity.

The most widely used measure of manual or arm-and-hand dexterity is the *Minnesota Rate of Manipulation Test* (Educational Test Bureau). This consists of a board about three feet in length and one foot across with 60 circles cut out in four equal, parallel rows. In the first part of the test, "placing," the subject is to place the circles from an arranged pattern on the table into the board. The second part of the test, "turning," requires that the subject using a standardized technique turn each of the circles the other side up. Usually four trials are administered for each part of the test with the first one being or not being counted as a practice trial. This test has been used to select bundle or parcel wrappers.

Finger dexterity is measured by the use of pegboards, two commonly used ones being the *Purdue Pegboard* (Science Research Associates) and the *O'Connor Finger-Tweezer Dexterity Test* (C. H. Stoelting Co.). A pegboard consists of a piece of wood or metal into which holes have been drilled. By either the use of the fingers alone or by the use of a pair of tweezers, pegs are inserted into these holes as rapidly as possible. The wooden *Purdue Pegboard* differs from most in that there is first a trial for the right hand, then one for the left hand, followed by both hands simultaneously, and finally an assembly test in which small objects are assembled out of pegs, washers, and collars.

Research with these instruments points out that they are most useful in the selection of individuals for semi-skilled jobs consisting of assembling small objects, packing, sorting, and the like. Their major use then has been industrial. However, in the counseling situation they may be used in negative fashion for advising students against considering technical training in courses such as watch-repairing, tool and die making, lens-grinding, typing, and even such professional occupations as dentistry and medicine.

Mechanical information

In the earlier days of testing and counseling, mechanical information was measured by the use of individual tests such as the *Stenquist's Mechanical Assembly Test* or later by the *Minnesota Mechanical Assembly Test*. In both of these the examinee was confronted with a metal box consisting of a series of metal bins in each of which a mechanical object such as a mousetrap, door latch, clamp, or bicycle bell was disassembled. The client was given a fixed amount of time to reassemble each object.

Currently these tests have been replaced by paper-and-pencil tests such as the *Bennett Test of Mechanical Comprehension* and *The Test of Mechanical Reasoning of the Differential Aptitude Tests* (both published by The Psychological Corporation). In both of these tests the emphasis is upon the general principles of mechanics, information about tools, and some of the elementary principles of physics. For example two shears are presented and the question asked which is the better for the cutting of metal. Or there are arrangements of gears and cogs with the direction of the rotation of one noted and the examinee has to figure out the direction in which another cog or gear is turning.

Counselors will find tests of this type useful in counseling students about technical or vocational training. In some agencies there has been the unwarranted assumption that if an individual can do nothing else academically, he can always be put into a shop course to be trained. In actual practice this makes no more sense than putting all individuals into any other field, or area, or curriculum. There should be appraisal and selection before individuals enter technical training because field and level determined by skills, aptitudes, and interests are just as important there as in any other area.

There are several tests available that cannot be classified into one of the three above areas; rather than measuring one of these aspects of mechanical ability, they tend to cut across abilities and measure two or more of them. Probably the most frequently encountered of these is the *MacQuarrie Test of Mechanical Ability* (California Test Bureau), a booklet made up of seven sub-tests measuring one-hand manual dexterity, spatial visualization, and perceptual speed and accuracy. Another one is the *SRA Mechanical Aptitude Test* (SR Associates) which has sections covering mechanical information, spatial visualization, and shop arithmetic.

Other sources of information

Very valid evidence of mechanical ability is available from sources other than these standardized tests. A very important one is the individual's hobby or spare time activities. It is obvious that the boy who tears down and rebuilds old cars, constructs scale models of vehicles or machines, or designs and draws mechanical things possesses this ability. Other evidence comes from grades in shop courses or certain academic courses such as physics and drawing. On-the-job performance on mechanical jobs or tasks is valid and useful information, if described in sufficient detail so that the counselor can evaluate it. A filling station attendant who just pumps gas does not get the same mechanical experience as one who also makes car repairs of various kinds. Closely related with this is the type of part-time job that a student might have in his spare time or during the summer vacation. In all of the above it is a good idea to ascertain whether or not the client has been free to make his own choice in taking jobs or courses and also as to whether or not other possibilities were available.

There are certain other characteristics and skills that should be considered with mechanical ability in certain types of vocational counseling. For example there is the entire problem of vision. Good eyesight has a lot to do with certain types of work. Then there is color blindness, the absence of which is basic to training in many skilled and unskilled occupations. This is usually measured by a series of plates like the Ishihara plates which consist of a background of small circles of one color, usually a light or pastel one. Into the center of this background a number has been traced in another color. The client goes through the plates reading these numbers. The presence and degree of color blindness is determined by the client's responses to these numbers. Another good test of color blindness is the *Farnsworth Test of Color Blindness* (The Psychological Corporation). It measures three kinds of color blindness.

Presence of color blindness will limit a person in mechanical work like telephone installation or welding where the telephone wires are connected according to colors or the welder tells how hot the flame is by the color of the flame. In a similar way hearing and tests for hearing are important in other types of vocational planning and training. They function as negative indicators. Lack of the trait measured will limit an individual in performing mechanical activities. Possession of the trait without defect does not insure success in mechanical tasks.

CLERICAL ABILITY

Clerical ability like mechanical ability is not a single unitary trait but a complex of different abilities, skills, and interests. One of the major components of this trait is the ability to handle or to manipulate words and numbers accurately and rapidly. Basically this is nothing but accuracy of perceptual speed. Along with this is associated skill in arithmetic, especially in the four basic arithmetical processes. Clerical ability also involves knowledge of good English usage, that is, the rules of grammar, punctuation, spelling, and sentence structure. In certain positions involving the use of clerical ability a good vocabulary is also essential. Since many clerical workers operate typewriters and various office or business machines, manual and finger dexterity are important in certain clerical tasks. There is no single test that measures all of these different abilities and knowledges. The following discussion will include several of the widely used tests of clerical ability along with some of the other evidences of this ability for which the counselor should watch.

Tests of clerical ability

Probably the most widely used test of clerical ability is the *Minnesota Clerical Test* (Psychological Corporation). This short test is made up of two parts—number checking (8 minutes) and name checking (7 minutes). Items like the following make up the entire test:

$$
\begin{array}{lll}
87694 & \text{X} & 87694 \\
5468926 & & 5469826 \\
\text{John J. Smith} & & \text{John F. Smith} \\
505\ \text{Lingle Ter.} & \text{X} & 505\ \text{Lingle Ter.}
\end{array}
$$

The examinee proceeds through the test as rapidly as possible placing an "X" in the space between the pairs that are similar. Obviously this test measures the ability of perceptual speed and accuracy that was mentioned above.

Norms are provided with the test for grades 8 through 12, gainfully employed adults, general clerical workers, and clerical workers in specific occupations as accountants, bookkeepers, and shipping clerks. Age seems to have little effect upon scores except for the usual slowing up in middle age. Research reported in the manual and by others shows that scores on the test are not affected to any extent by clerical experience. Sex differences in favor of women are significant on this test requiring the use of separate norms for men and women. An inspection of the norms shows that only twenty-one per cent of employed male clerical workers exceed the median of female clerical workers. Andrew (1937), the author of the test, reported a correlation of .66 between number-checking and name-checking. Darley (1934) reported the reliability of the two parts of the test to be .76 and .83, respectively. As Super (1949) has pointed out, since their intercorrelation is lower than their separate reliabilities, one of them is measuring something not so well measured by the other. Later this was shown to be intelligence and, of the two parts of the test, name-checking correlates higher with intelligence than number-checking, .37 vs. .12 with a homogeneous group and .65 and .47 with a heterogeneous group (Super 1949).

Another clerical test is the *General Clerical Test* (Psychological Corporation). This is a much more comprehensive test than the *Minnesota Clerical Test* and is made up of nine sub-tests. The first two sub-tests, "checking" and "alphabetizing," are measures of perceptual ability. The three subsequent tests, "arithmetic reasoning," "computation," and "location of error" produce a numerical score. The last four tests, "spelling," "reading comprehension," "vocabulary," and "grammar" provide a verbal score. Another simple short perceptual test is the *Clerical Speed and Accuracy Test* of the *Differential Aptitudes Tests* battery.

Validity studies of all of these tests produce values of the usual magnitude when results are correlated with such criteria as grades in commercial courses and accounting. Hay (1943) showed correlations of .51 and .47 between the two parts of the *Minnesota Clerical Test* and the speed of posting ability of bookkeeping machine operators. Blum and Candee (1941) showed correlations of the two parts of this same test with the output of packers in a department store to be .57 and .65, respectively. In summary these and other studies (Super 1949) show that clerical tests predict very well grades in commercial and related courses, success on business machine operating tasks, and various packing and inspecting tasks.

Just as with mechanical ability, there are other sources from which very valid evidence of clerical ability may be obtained to supplement that obtained from these tests. First among these is grades in commercial courses in high school and such specialized courses in commercial skills that might be learned in a commercial trade school or at the college level. Certain hobbies might also be evidence of clerical ability as keeping track of statistics on athletic teams. Other evidence might come from some on-the-job tryouts on various clerical jobs or part-time work programs in vocational education. Types of after-school or summer jobs held by individuals might also offer evidence.   There is also a group of aptitude and ability tests for specific types of skills such as shorthand and typing that can be administered for more specific information about clerical ability.

Use of evidences of clerical ability in counseling

The concept of level may be applied to the use of this clerical information just as it was with mechanical ability (Paterson *et al.*, 1941).   Before tests of clerical ability are used, measures of general ability must also be present.   The top level, A, requires superior general intelligence usually accompanied with a college degree.   Included here are such occupations as accountant, actuary, statistician, and top level secretaries (top 10% of the group).   In level B, the technical level, high school graduation or specialized training equivalent to this in commercial skills is required for those who operate at this level.   In this group are bookkeeper, secretary, and operator of various business machines.   Here the next fifteen per cent of the workers are included.   In level C (routine clerical level) very little training is needed to perform the jobs included here— file clerk, mail clerk, retail sales clerk, simple machine operator, as ditto machine or mailing machine.   Here is included the middle 50% of the distribution of clerical ability.   Many individuals possess sufficient ability to operate at this level.

In using data on clerical ability the counselor must associate general ability with it first keeping in mind that some of the top positions in the clerical field require a college degree or more.   It must also be remembered as Hahn and MacLean (1955) point out that this field of work is to a great extent a woman's world.   However, this does not preclude the entrance of males into this field of work, especially if these males are skillful in the field and possess high general intelligence.   Confidential secretaries to the presidents of corporations or to corporation boards of directors or trustees are filled most frequently with male clerical workers. The same writers point out also that since there is a rapidly increasing movement from hand work to machine operating in this field the counselor must be alert for new job openings.   It might be added that he should also be aware of the various types of clerical jobs that are disappearing because of the increasing use of business machines.   New developments in automated business processes are increasing jobs at the B level for programming of automated equipment, as well as more jobs at the B level in mechanics to repair such machines.   There is a tendency for a considerable decrease in C and D level clerical jobs as a result of automation.   For example, a plant at Camillus, New York, does practically all of the national clerical work for Sylvania Electric Company. This trend is also developing in the mechanical field.

ARTISTIC ABILITY

Artistic ability, like those previously discussed, is also made up of various skills and abilities (Meier, 1942). In the manual accompanying his *Art Judgment Test* Meier states that there are six factors involved in this ability: manual skill, energy output and perseveration, aesthetic intelligence (spatial and perceptual ability), perceptual facility (the ability to observe and reproduce sensory experiences), creative imagination, and aesthetic judgment. However, it is only the last of these that is measured by Meier's test. Hahn and MacLean (1955) consider aesthetic intelligence, as they label this field, to be divided into four parts each requiring a greater amount of this ability. These divisions are: appreciation, interpretation, creativity, and analysis. The latter includes the research scholars and high level critics.

Tests of artistic ability may be broken into two types, tests of artistic or aesthetic judgment and tests of creative ability. The most widely used test of the first type is the *Meier Art Judgment Test* (Bureau of Educational Research Services, University of Iowa or The Psychological Corporation). This test is made up of 100 items consisting of pictures of works of art from all parts of the world and of such a type that they can be generally considered as being timeless. Each of these items is made up of two parts, one a reproduction of the art as the author originally created it and the other the same piece of art but with a certain aspect of the work changed. The student's attention is focused on this part of the picture and he has to decide which of the two he prefers. His actual score is the number of times that he selects the work as the artist created it. Scores on this test have been shown to correlate in the .40's with grades in art school and similarly with ratings of creative artistic ability.

An older test, the *McAdory Art Test,* used instead of works of art such items as household furniture, interior design, or clothing, all of which made the test become dated and thus of limited use. Another approach was made by Graves with the *Design Judgment Test* (The Psychological Corporation) in which was used geometric designs and lines in shades of gray and black. Most of these are arranged in pairs as on the *Meier* and the examinee goes through the booklet marking the one preferred. Art teachers were used to judge which was the best drawing on each page. Little research has been done with this instrument. Downie in an unpublished study found that the correlation between scores on this test with those on the *Meier* for 45 university students in a course in psychological testing was approximately .40.

When tests of artistic ability are used, the individual is given various things to do to see if actual drawing, sketching, or painting skills are present. One of these tests, the *Knauber Art Ability Test* (The Psychological Corporation) contains seventeen parts in which the examinee has to reproduce a drawing from memory, shade compositions, draw objects asked for, create abstract designs, and do similar things. A similar test is the *Lewerenz Test in the Fundamental Abilities of Visual Art* (California Test Bureau). A different approach was made by Horn (1945) in which the chief part of the test consisted of twelve cards each bearing lines arranged in various ways. The examinee uses these lines as starting points about which he has to construct a picture on each card. The scoring of all these tests of artistic ability is very subjective as in most of them the work done by the examinee is compared with prepared scales and evaluated by finding the item on the scale that comes closest to the examinee's drawing. The drawing is then given this value.

Other evidence of artistic ability

It is felt by the writers that the best information about a client's artistic ability is obtained by having some of his work evaluated by an expert or two. Usually on university campuses there are such people in one of the schools who will be very willing in helping the counselor and the client in making such product evaluations. Two evaluations here are better than one for one is apt to contain biases of the individual judge that cause him to be overcritical of art that deviates from his own school or standards. Prizes and awards from art shows or even the showing of works in shows certainly indicate the presence of this ability. Tests of spatial relations, finger dexterity, and color blindness offer some evidence of various aspects of this ability.

Use of data on artistic ability in counseling

Using the *Minnesota Occupational Rating Scales* this field can be divided into three levels and a fourth, nonartistic. In level A, the professional level, a high degree of creative skill is required. This is the top 4% of the distribution and includes professional artists, sculptors, etchers, and art teachers. Level B, containing those in below these professionals but above the ninth decile in ability, requires that those in this band have a fairly high degree of artistic ability along with some originality. Commercial art workers as well as magazine illustrators, advertising lay-out men, landscape gardeners, interior decorators, and various types of designers are included here. Level C, crafts and mechanical work, includes all those above the first quartile in this ability. This is the level of the craftsman—sign painter, draftsman, potter, weaver, and others.

These tests of artistic ability may frequently reveal individuals who have hidden talents. They are perhaps *more useful* in pointing out those who have very little or no artistic ability. In general, it seems that very high scores or low ones should be considered as the significant ones when these tests are used.

MUSICAL ABILITY

Of the few tests which have been constructed to measure this ability Seashore's *Measures of Musical Talent* (The Psychological Corporation) has been most widely used and has had the largest amount of research conducted with it. Seashore started working with this test during World War I and spent the rest of his life while at the University of Iowa experimenting with it. Seashore (1939) considers the traits involved in musical ability as manual skills, energy output and perseveration, creative imagination, emotional sensitivity, and those abilities measured by his tests.

The Seashore battery consists of three 78 r.p.m. records, each having a test on both sides and measuring pitch, loudness, time, rhythm, timbre, and tonal memory, or one 33⅓ r.p.m. L.P. record with three tests on each side. The items on the tests are presented in pairs and the examinee has to evaluate if the second is louder than the first, the same as the first, or which note has been changed in a series of notes. These records may be used with individuals from grade five on up. When used with younger children, the results are frequently of no value because one has to attend carefully to the records in order to complete the test. Younger children have difficulty doing this as do some adults, especially those with little of this musical ability. The administration of the test requires about an entire class period. Practice is given at several points on each record until every one understands exactly what he is to do and then the test for the record is administered. Some counselors prefer to shorten this process by using the tests of pitch, tonal memory and rhythm as negative indicators and omit the balance of the tests.

Reliability of the different tests varies between the .60's and the high .80's. For example, with adults the lowest reliability coefficient is .62 (timbre) and the highest, .88 (tonal memory). The second lowest value for this age level is .74.

Validity has been mostly determined by correlating results with grades in music courses, completion of a period of training, and ratings of musical ability as criteria. Correlation of Seashore scores with grades in music courses have produced coefficients ranging between .30 and .59. The most noted study in reference to completion of training was that of Stanton (1929) who over a period of years administered the Seashore battery to more than 2,000 entering students at the Eastman School of Music. The results were filed unseen by members of the staff. Stanton set up a rating system on the basis of the Seashore scores, intelligence test scores, and teachers' ratings by which the students could be classified as "safe," "probable," and so on. Later she showed that 60 per cent of the "safe" group were graduated, 42 per cent of the "probable," 33 per cent of the "possible," 23 per cent of the "doubtful," and 17 per cent of the "discouraged." In this study Stanton made no attempt to isolate the importance of the intelligence factor. In general though this test seems able to select those who have musical ability from those who do not. It separates professional musicians from amateurs and beginners. Also as Fay and Middleton (1941) have shown those who prefer classical music make higher scores on pitch, rhythm, and time sub-tests than those who prefer jazz music.

As with the artistic field, the judgments of experts are most useful and important in evaluating the musical ability and potential of a client. In most cases it does not take long for one of these judges to decide whether or not an individual has the ability needed for professional training.

Use of musical ability tests in counseling

Only individuals in the top 4% of this ability can operate at the professional level in this field. In this small group are concert artist, composer, soloist, conservatory teacher, and director. The technical and lower professional level, making up the remainder of the highest 10% includes arrangers and critics of music, music teachers in grade and high school, orchestra members, and the like. Here is the average professional musician with average or above musical talent accompanied with a high degree of technical knowledge and well-developed musical discrimination. The third level from the first quartile to the ninth decile includes musical repairmen, instrument testers, clerks in music stores, and music retailer. A small amount of musical knowledge, but a greater amount of technical skill and general musical information must be possessed by those who operate at this level.

The counselor might use the results of these tests in the same way as the results of artistic ability tests. Low scores will point out those who have little musical ability. High scores may or may not be indicative of musical ability. But these high scores merit further investigation. Scores in between high and low scores are of limited significance.

PHYSICAL ABILITY

Information about physical abilities and health is most important to the counselor as it is logical that records of physical development and health reflecting the physical status of the client be available for every client counseled. In this case the counselor is a user of material collected by others, not an information gatherer per se. However, things may come up in the counseling interview that offer insights into physical status or show the need for proper referral to investigate or remedy conditions that have gone undetected. In the space below, the types of information that the counselor should have will be noted.

Physical or medical examinations

Examinations of this type are conducted by a physician and are usually of a periodic nature being given at the beginning of school, at the end of the primary grades, and at both the commencement of junior and senior high schools. In most places these are carried out by the family's personal physician and the results filed in the student's school folder. For other individuals these examinations are carried out more frequently. Among those examined more often are the members of athletic teams, individuals who work in the school lunchroom or cafeteria, those who have a record of a chronic disease or disability or who have been out of school a long time as a result of a long illness or an accident, and any other individual who in the judgment of teachers, administrators, or counselors should have it. Results of dental examinations conducted by the school dental hygienist should also be a part of the medical record. Reports of school nurses are also to be included.

Health histories

This record of diseases and disabilities is usually gathered from an interview with a parent at the time a child is starting school. Information is added to it as the individual progresses through school.

Screening tests

These are probably the most commonly employed practices used in evaluating health and physical status. In most schools these tests are an annual event, especially in the lower grades. They are conducted by both the teacher and the school nurse. Most typically these consist of tests of vision, hearing, and speech along with measurements of height and weight. The dental examination is usually conducted at this time also.

Physical tests

The physical education department has a large battery of tests that are useful in evaluating physical development. These consist of tests of strength, capacity, and endurance. While the results of these tests may not be available to the counselor in the cumulative record, there is no reason why they cannot be; better still, a summary should be included in the words of the physical education instructor of the evaluation of the physical development of each individual as revealed by these different tests.

Observational techniques

The classroom teacher is in the best position to gather information on physical health and to record and report such data. One method applicable here would be through the use of anecdotal records. In addition to this the classroom teacher becomes the source of most of the referrals in relation to the student's health.

MULTIFACTOR TEST BATTERIES

Both the factor analysis work of Thurstone and the experiences gained in the construction and use of tests in World War II in dealing with military personnel led to the development of what are known as multifactor batteries. Typically these consist of six or more of the various types of tests that have already been discussed. Usually the types of tests included in these batteries are representative of the various mental abilities and are comprehensive enough to be used in consideration of many different occupations. These tests may be constructed upon the basis of an analysis of the various worker requirements of different jobs. In using the tests the counselor or personnel worker works in terms of test battery profiles, this being merely an analysis of the client's or job applicant's strong and weak points. In some of these batteries the majority of the tests are the results of factor analyses. However, this is not true of all of them. Basically there are two types of multifactor batteries. One is of a general nature used in counseling individuals when all capacities and traits are being considered. This is the case with students and workers who are just entering the world of work. The other type is made up of batteries specific to a given purpose. For example, there are batteries constructed for the selection of students for medical school, law school, dentistry, teaching, and other professions.

Batteries such as these are expensive in both time and money. Usually they take a full day to administer and the cost is correspondingly high. Usually the cost of the battery for professional schools is born by the individual taking the examination. Another complicating factor is that there is evidence that shows that predictions as good or even better than those made with the multifactor tests can be made with a short intelligence test. On the positive side, there is no question that these are well-made tests and usually of an interesting nature to the examinee. Situations are offered which are unusual and intriguing. Some of them, such as the dental school batteries, have increased their validity through the use of manipulative tests that correspond to activities carried on by dentists. Specific evaluations of the different batteries will be made as each is discussed. The general type of battery will be discussed first.

GENERAL MULTIFACTOR BATTERIES

The most important of these batteries to the high school and college counselor are the *Differential Aptitude Tests* (*DAT*) which were made available for use in 1947 by The Psychological Corporation. This battery is made of eight tests assembled in seven separate booklets, the last two tests being combined into one (Bennett, 1955, 1956). These tests are: (1) verbal reasoning, understanding of and reasoning with words; (2) numerical reasoning, numerical computation; (3) abstract reasoning, reasoning by the use of designs and geometrical symbols rather than by the use of words; (4) space relations, visualization of three-dimensional figures from a two-dimensional pattern; (5) clerical speed and accuracy, a perceptual test similar to the *Minnesota Clerical Test;* (6) mechanical reasoning, similar to the *Bennett Test of Mechanical Comprehension;* and the combined language usage test—(7) spelling, and (8) sentences in which errors of grammar and punctuation have to be located. The first four of these are tests designed to measure Thurstone's factors, V, N, R, and S (see page 184). The clerical sub-test also measures a perceptual factor. The other three tests measure achievements, proficiencies, or learnings.

This test battery was basically designed as a tool in the educational and vocational counseling of high school youth. Norms are also provided for eighth grade students and some universities are employing the battery in their counseling activities using norms that have been developed locally. The tests are so built that any one of them may be administered easily in a class period. The manual recommends several sequences for the administration of the tests in giving students the entire battery. However, whether there is a reason for any sequence—other than the prevention of boredom—or whether any given consequences issue from not following these patterns, has not been demonstrated. In many situations there is now the practice of using only those pieces of the battery that the counselor and client feel are appropriate to the immediate needs of the client.

The 1952 revision of the manual contains a summary of about 4,000 validity coefficients. Super (1956-a) recapitulates all of these data by saying that the *DAT* tests do a good job in predicting grades in English, social studies, science, and mathematics. They seem to measure that which is needed for success in such courses, namely general ability or intelligence. In commercial courses, the number and language-usage sub-tests are good predictors in bookkeeping and typing courses. Scores on the space relations sub-tests were to some extent related to grades received in vocational shop courses.

Bennett (1955, 1956) summarized a long range study done with the *DAT*. Scores of about 1,400 students who had taken the battery when it was being developed or when it first appeared were reexamined in the light of their status seven and eight years later. He showed that those students who were graduated from college tended to be superior on the basis of all tests from the high school group of which they were a part. As might be predicted this superiority was most noticeable on the verbal reasoning, numerical reasoning, and language usage sub-tests. Students who had some years of college fell between the group that was graduated from college and that which had had no further education beyond high school. Students who attended special schools tended to score near the mean for their high school group and students who had no more education beyond high school were slightly below the overall average for high school students. Bennett also analyzed the scores of the individuals on the basis of the occupations that they were currently pursuing. His findings were in line with expectations—engineers were considerably above average on all tests. Individuals in the technical trades tended to fall around the mean, and those in the semi-skilled and unskilled occupations tended to fall a bit below the group average on the various sub-tests.

A second of these multifactor batteries is the *General Aptitude Test Battery (GATB)* issued in 1947 by the United States Employment Service (see Dvorak, 1947, 1956). The current revision of the battery consists of 12 tests that are used to measure nine aptitudes. These are:

G   Intelligence: Measured by tests numbered (3) Three-Dimensional Space, (4) Vocabulary, and (6) Arithmetic Reasoning.

V   Verbal Aptitude: Test (4) a vocabulary test.

N   Numerical Aptitude: (2) Arithmetic Computation, and (6) Arithmetic Reasoning.

S   Spatial Aptitude: (3) Three-Dimensional Space.

P   Form Perception: (5) Tool Making, and (7) Form Matching.

Q   Clerical Perception: (1) Name Perception.

K   Motor Coordination: (8) Mark Making.

F   Finger Dexterity: (11) Assemble, and (12) Disassemble.

M   Manual Dexterity: (9) Place, and (10) Turn.

Eight of the above tests are paper-and-pencil tests, the last four, 9, 10, 11, and 12 being individual performance tests. An examination of the sub-tests reveals that these cover the major factors and skills that are required to a greater or less extent in the majority of occupations. Lacking from the above are tests of rather specialized abilities such as art and music and also tests of mechanical information such as the *Bennett* or the *Mechanical Reasoning Test of the DAT.*

Norms are presented in terms of aptitude patterns for different occupations, giving cut-off scores for the three most important aptitudes required for any family of similar occupations. Suppose that a family of occupations requires G—intelligence, S—spatial aptitude, and P, form perception. Minimum cutting scores are then provided for these three aptitudes for different positions within the family of jobs. Profiles of individuals are compared. The United States Department of Labor's

Estimates of Worker Trait Requirement for 4,000 Jobs (1956) lists the different aptitudes, and the level of aptitude, required for each job.

Although this battery was developed for use in government operated employment services, especially as an aid in placing the new and young worker who has had no vocational experience, the battery has been offered for use with high school and college students. There are high schools in which the graduating seniors are given the battery as an aid in planning their life's work.

A third battery is the *Guilford-Zimmerman Aptitude Survey*, the GZAS (Sheridan Supply Co.) (Guilford, 1956). This battery is made up of seven sub-tests: verbal comprehension, general reasoning, numerical computations, perceptual speed, spatial orientation ("the ability to form an awareness of the spatial order of things perceived visually"), spatial visualization, and mechanical knowledge. Guilford (1956) showed that the first six of these have factorial validity (a type of construct validity) and the mechanical knowledge test was built to have content validity.

This test battery was constructed for use with high school and college students. When scores on different sub-tests of this battery were correlated with freshmen grades made in college, correlations of the following magnitudes were obtained: verbal comprehension, .46; general reasoning, .34; numerical computations, .28; perceptual speed, .16; space orientation, .10; spatial visualization, .17; and mechanical knowledge, —.07. Notice that the first three—the ones usually included in a test of general intelligence—were the important ones in predicting.

Other multifactor batteries are the *Flanagan Aptitude Classification Tests* (Flanagan, 1957; published by Science Research Associates), the *Holzinger-Crowder Unifactor Tests* (Crowder, 1957; World Book Co.), *Segal-Raskin Multiple Aptitude Tests* (Segal, 1957; California Test Bureau), and the SRA *Primary Mental Abilities* (Thurstone, 1957; Science Research Associates). In general these are similar in content and in recommended use to those already described.

EVALUATION OF MULTIFACTOR BATTERIES

Super (1949) wrote "The day of the publication of isolated tests of single aptitudes will no doubt soon be past." That he was not alone in holding this attitude is shown by other writers of that period (see Anastasi, 1954, and Cronbach, 1949). However, in less than ten years Cronbach was writing in the Annual Review of Psychology (Farnsworth and McNemar, 1956): ". . . while factorial scores may be useful for a theory of abilities, as soon as testers make inferences to behavior in significant situations, they encounter the same trouble as personality assessors." That these troubles are tremendous ones will be pointed out in Chapter 11. In a series of articles beginning in the September, 1956, issue of the *Personnel and Guidance Journal* and continuing with an article on and an evaluation of a particular multifactor battery in each of nine subsequent issues, and concluding in the September, 1957, issue of the same journal, Super and one of the authors of each of the batteries presented descriptions and criticisms of each battery. These will now be examined.

In the first of these articles Super (1956-d) offers a general discussion of multifactor batteries and what they should do. He notes that (1) they should describe the make-up of the student or client, (2) they should predict what he will be like and what he will do in the future, (3) they should be timeless, and (4) they should be multipotential. An examination of the current batteries reveals, he continues, that they do describe, they are timeless to a certain extent, and that they are multipotential. He feels that they fall down when it comes to prediction, especially differential prediction. In the construction of each of these batteries an attempt was made to arrive at factorial purity, providing for each battery factors or aptitudes, as they are called by some, of psychological meaning and importance. These different factors contribute to success in a variety of situations or occupations in any of which the factor in question may be related. Super states that these factorial tests are pure, abstract, and general in nature. In tests used in specific situations, when the test is a miniature of the job, the elements common to or specific to certain jobs give these tests higher validity coefficients than would be obtained from the general factor test in the same situation.

In his critique of the *DAT*, Super (1956-a) notes that grades in English are well predicted by scores on the verbal reasoning, numerical reasoning, abstract reasoning, and spelling and sentence sub-tests of this battery. The same sub-tests also predict grades in social studies, as well as grades in mathematics and science. In other words, the tests do an adequate job in predicting success in the usual academic grades, but not in any differential manner. This may, however, be a lack of clarity in the criterion rather than a defect in the tests. Those tests that measure intelligence predict success in the academic subjects. This was also true of the *Guilford-Zimmerman* above. Super further notes that numerical reasoning and language usage scores predict bookkeeping grades in addition to predicting typing grades. Scores on the spatial reasoning test also predict shop grades to a certain extent. Then if all that is desired is prediction of academic success, why not use a simple, short, and economical intelligence test which saves both time and money?

In the subsequent article Super shows that the other batteries are no better and frequently worse than the *DAT* in differential prediction (1956-b, 1956-c, 1957-a, 1957-b, 1957-c, 1957-d, 1957-e). In the final article (1957-f), he summarizes by stating that the *DAT* and the *GATB* are judged ready for use in counseling at the present time. He found the *FACT* perhaps ready for limited counseling. The *Guilford-Zimmerman, Holzinger-Crowder,* and *Segal-Raskin* batteries were judged to still be in the research stage. Two batteries, the SRA *Primary Mental Abilities* and the *Factored Series* (King, 1957), were dismissed as not having "stood the test of time or the scrutiny of science." In using these batteries the counselor must remember that validation is to a great extent still to be desired. Super notes that these tests and their publishers do a fine job of demonstrating content, concurrent, and construct validity, but have frequently not enough on the subject of predictive validity which is related to the counselor's chief job.

Another major study concerned with the use of the aptitude test batteries was conducted by Thorndike and Hagen (1959). The test battery used in this report was that given to aviation cadets in the Army Air Corps during World War II. This battery, made up of nineteen parts, yielded twenty scores covering areas that may be broadly grouped into five abilities: (1) general intellectual, (2) numerical, (3) perceptual-spatial, (4) mechanical, and (5) psychomotor. A Biographical Data Blank, in addition to yielding two of the above scores, provided data against which to analyze both test scores and criterion data. This battery in one form or another was administered to approximately one-half million Air Force personnel in World War II. Men taking this battery had to pass a stiff physical examination, score at or above a certain score on a test of general intelligence (The Aviation Cadet Qualifying Examination), be single, and between 18 and 26 years of age. It follows that the men completing these tests made up a select group.

Thorndike and Hagen selected a sample of 17,000 of these trainees who took the tests at about the same time during 1943. Approximately 12 years later these men were sent a short questionnaire covering educational and vocational activities since their separation from the Air Corps. The items on this questionnaire lead to the following criterion scores: monthly salary, number of men supervised, a self rating of success and one of job satisfaction, a rating of both vertical and lateral mobility, this latter being a measure of job stability, and finally, length of time in occupation. The ratings of mobility were derived by judges from responses made to items on the questionnaire. About 70 per cent of the sample returned the completed questionnaire.

As a result of their study, Thorndike and Hagen showed that there were real and logical differences among various occupational groups. For example, college professors were shown to be about 0.75 of a standard deviation above the overall mean on general intellectual ability, about 0.4 of a standard deviation above the mean on both numerical and perceptual ability, about 0.3 of a standard deviation below the mean on mechanical ability, and at the mean on psychomotor skills. Artists and designers were shown to have means very similar to the group means on all abilities except perceptual. For this ability their mean score was about 0.5 standard deviation above the group mean. Other occupations such as clergyman and real estate salesman showed profiles that were quite flat. In other words some occupations were shown to require very special abilities and others to have no special requirements in terms of the abilities studied in this research. It should also be noted that there was considerable variation within any specific occupational group in terms of the five abilities studied. (See Chapter 5.)

An analysis of the Biographical Data Sheet showed that the various occupational groups differed in background variables as well as on ability test scores. The item on this data sheet that made the most discriminations was the one that asked if the trainees had any previous college education. This single item differentiated 54 occupations at the .01 level of significance and ten at the .05 level. An analysis was made to see how well each of the 112 items on this sheet differentiated among the various occupations. For example, 74 of the items differentiated college professors significantly either positively or negatively from other occupational groups at the .01 or .05 level. College professors showed a history of verbal and intellectual activities (positive discrimination) and one of low activity in sports and mechanical activities (negative discrimination). (See linguistic-nonlinguistic discussion in Chapter 5.)

The final conclusion of the study based upon some 12,000 correlation coefficients was that success in an occupation cannot be predicted either by these aptitude tests or by the items on the Biographical Data Sheet when these data were analyzed against the criteria previously mentioned. This last finding is the one that created all the stir when the results of this study were first made public. It may be well to remember the limitations of the study pointed out by Thorndike and Hagen. They emphasize that the individuals in this study were a select group to begin with and present evidence to show that the more successful of these tended to return the questionnaire. Secondly, other aspects of personality such as interests, attitudes, and overall personal adjustment were not studied. These so-called nonintellectual factors may have much to do with vocational success. A third problem arose from the fact that, even if occupational groups bore similar titles such as college professor or lawyer, many different types of college professors and lawyers were included. Each of the different occupational groups was quite heterogeneous. Finally the authors discuss the criteria of vocational success used. It so happened that these criteria were those most readily available. It does not follow that they were the best or were collected in the most dependable fashion. They conclude their discussion of limitations of the study by saying:

> As far as we were able to determine from our data, there is no convincing evidence that aptitude tests or biographical information of the type that was available to us can predict degree of success within an occupation insofar as this is represented in the criterion measures that we are able

to obtain. This would suggest that we should view the long-range prediction of occupational success by aptitude tests with a good deal of
skepticism and take a very restrained view as to how much can be accomplished in this direction.

In the light of the limitations of the study that Thorndike and Hagen
themselves point out, the present writers wonder if it can really be said
that occupational success cannot be predicted. Perhaps a test battery
administered to predict occupational success rather than success in air-
crew training school used in conjunction with other nonintellectual predictors may present different results. The evidence is not yet conclusive
on this point.

BATTERIES FOR SPECIFIC OCCUPATIONS

As was pointed out earlier there are a large number of batteries that
have been constructed chiefly for selection purposes in admitting students to the study of medicine, dentistry, law, and the like. The counselor will have little opportunity to use these batteries, but it will certainly
fall upon him to advise others to take them. The distribution of these
tests is, as it logically should be, restricted. The test batteries are usually
administered one or more times a year at certain examination centers.
Individuals who plan to take them sign up in advance, pay a fee, and
at that time or later are sent an admission card to the testing session.
Sample items and a general discussion of the battery are given to the student at that time. These tests in their format and content are apt to
be very similar to the multifactor batteries just discussed, but they do
include materials or tests specific to the profession for which they were
constructed. In general they are made up of tests of abilities and
achievement tests. In the paragraphs that follow a few of these tests
will be described.

For many years the Association of American Medical Schools has supported the construction and use of a battery for the selection of medical
students. At the present time the *Medical College Admission Test*
(issued by The Educational Testing Service) is made up of two parts,
a test of ability and another of achievement. Part one is made up of
tests measuring verbal ability and a single test of quantitative ability.
The second part is made up of two sub-tests, the first measuring the
understanding of modern society and social concepts and the other part
covering premedical school science.

Similar to this are the batteries used in dental schools except they
are apt to have added a test of spatial relationships and manual and
finger dexterity. This is frequently done by having the examinee carve
objects out of a block of chalk. As might be expected, batteries used in
law schools emphasize the verbal aspects of mental life. Typically such

tests measure vocabulary, reading comprehension, interpretation of data, or evaluation of arguments. Tests used for engineers put stress on numerical computations, problem solving, formulation, and achievement in the basic physical sciences. *The National Teachers Examination* (The Educational Testing Service) is composed of a morning examination covering professional interests (educational psychology, child development, measurement, guidance, and so on), general culture (history, literature, fine arts, science, and mathematics), English expression, and nonverbal reasoning. The afternoon session is devoted to an examination covering the examinee's two major teaching specialties.

In addition to the above there are such batteries as the "College Boards" and the *Graduate Record Examination* used for selecting students for undergraduate and graduate training, respectively. These also are made up of measures of verbal and nonverbal intelligence as well as measures of achievement. The first one, the College Boards, is especially heavily weighted with achievement tests, including those that cover the major academic subjects studied in the high school. The *Graduate Record Examination* is made up of a verbal and nonverbal test of general ability and an achievement test covering the subject's undergraduate major. This last part is an optional test.

In the use of these specific batteries there is evidence that selection and prediction carried on by them could be just as adequately carried on with a good intelligence test. The *Graduate Record Examination* is basically this. Even in these specialized schools there are few activities carried on that are not related to general intelligence. The counselor should also note that there is a growing feeling that prerequisites for the various professional curricula are perhaps not valid. For example, a report in *The New York Times* for December 1, 1958, showed that of more than 1,000 men who were graduated from Harvard and who entered medical school, those with a major in the usual "pre-med" subjects did better in their first year of medical school but by the end of the third year were only slightly ahead of those who had a broad undergraduate background. In the Medical School of Harvard University those who majored in social relations, psychology, and anthropology actually ranked slightly higher at the end of the third year than their classmates who had had the "pre-med" background.

SUMMARY

Thus the counselor in reviewing the scores of aptitude and ability tests found in the record of a given client may wish to go over these scores during the initial interview and discuss with the client any additional information needed to supplement such data in later counseling interviews. This means the counselor must not only be able to interpret the test scores which are a matter of record, but must be in a position to recommend appropriate counseling tools which will provide the additional data needed during counseling.

In addition to test scores the counselor must be able to evaluate and use other evidences of aptitudes and abilities from agency records and from other community sources. This area has been largely overlooked in the past, but is coming to have increasing importance for the counselor and the client.

REFERENCES

Anastasi, A. *Psychological testing.* New York: The Macmillan Company, 1954.

Andrew, D. M. An analysis of the *Minnesota Vocational Test for Clerical Workers, I and II. J. Appl. Psychol.,* 1937, *21,* 18–47; 139–172.

Bennett, G. K. The *DAT*—a seven year followup. *Test Service Bulletin* No. 49, The Psychological Corporation, November 1955.

Bennett, G. K., *et al. The Differential Aptitude Tests:* an overview. *Personnel & Guid. J.,* 1956, *35,* 81–91.

Bennett, G. K., and R. M. Cruikshank. *A summary of manual and mechanical ability tests.* New York: The Psychological Corporation, 1942.

Blum, M. L., and B. Candee. The selection of department store packers and wrappers with the aid of certain psychological tests, II. *J. Appl. Psychol.,* 1941, *25,* 291–299.

Buros, O. K. *The third mental measurements yearbook.* Brunswick, N. J.: Rutgers University Press, 1949.

———. *The fourth mental measurements yearbook.* Highland Park, N. J.: The Gryphon Press, 1953.

———. *The fifth mental measurements yearbook.* Highland Park, N. J.: The Gryphon Press, 1959.

Cattell, Psyche. *The measurement of the intelligence of infants and young children.* New York: The Psychological Corporation, 1947.

Cronbach, L. J. *Essentials of psychological testing,* 2nd ed. New York: Harper and Brothers, 1960.

Crowder, N. A. *The Holzinger-Crowder Uni-factor tests. Personnel & Guid. J.,* 1957, *35,* 281–286.

Darley, J. G. Reliability of tests in the Standard Battery. *Bull., Empl. Stab. Res. Inst.,* No. 4, University of Minnesota, 1934.

Davis, A., and K. Eells. *The Davis-Eells Games.* Yonkers-on-Hudson, N. Y.: World Book Company, 1953.

Downie, N. M. *Fundamentals of measurement.* New York: Oxford University Press, 1958.

Dvorak, B. J. *The General Aptitude Test Battery. Personnel & Guid. J.,* 1956, *35,* 145–152.

———. *The new USES General Aptitude Test Battery. Occupations,* 1947, *26,* 42–44.

Eells, K., *et al. Intelligence and cultural differences.* Chicago: University of Chicago Press, 1951.

Farnsworth, P. R., and Q. McNemar, Eds. *Annual review of psychology.* Stanford, Cal.: Annual Reviews, 1956.

Fay, C. J., and W. I. Middleton. Relationship between musical talent and preferences for different types of music. *J. Educ. Psychol.,* 1941, *32,* 573–583.

Flanagan, J. C. *Flanagan Aptitude Classification Test. Personnel & Guid. J.,* 1957, *35,* 495–503.

Garrett, H. E. A developmental theory of intelligence. *Amer. Psychologist,* 1946, *1,* 372–378.

Goddard, H. H. What is intelligence? *J. Soc. Psychol.,* 1946, *24,* 51–69.

Goodenough, F. *Mental testing.* New York: Rinehart, 1949.

Guilford, J. P. Factor analysis in a test development program. *Psychol. Rev.,* 1948, *55,* 79–94.

———. The discovery of aptitude and achievement variables. *Science,* 1947, *106,* 279–282.

———. The *Guilford-Zimmerman Aptitude Survey. Personnel & Guid. J.,* 1956, *35,* 219–223.

———. Three faces of intellect. *Amer. Psychologist,* 1959, *14,* 369–379.

Harrell, T. W. A factor analysis of mechanical ability tests. *Psychometrika,* 1940, *5,* 17–33.

Hahn, M. E., and M. C. MacLean. *Counseling Psychology.* New York: The McGraw-Hill Book Company, 1955.

Hay, E. N. Predicting success in machine bookkeeping. *J. Appl. Psychol.,* 1943, *27,* 483–493.

Horn, C. A., and L. F. Smith. The *Horn Art Aptitude Inventory. J. Appl. Psychol.,* 1945, *29,* 350–359.

"Intelligence and Its Measurement" (symposium), *J. of Ed. Psych.,* 1921, *12,* 123–147.

King, J. E. The *Factored Aptitude Series of Business and Industrial Tests. Personnel & Guid. J.,* 1957, *35,* 351–358.

Meier, N. C. *The Meier Art Tests: I, Art Judgment.* Iowa City, Iowa: Bur. of Ed. Res. Services, 1942.

Paterson, D. G., C. d'A Gerken, and M. Hahn. *The Minnesota Occupational Rating Scales.* Chicago: Science Research Associates, 1941.

———. *The Minnesota Occupational Rating Scales* (revised). Minneapolis: University of Minnesota Press, 1953.

Seashore, C. H. *The psychology of music.* New York: The McGraw-Hill Book Company, 1939.

Segal, D. The *Multiple Aptitude Tests. Personnel & Guid. J.,* 1957, *35,* 424–431.

Spearman, C. General intelligence objectively determined and measured. *Amer. J. of Psychol.,* 1904, *15,* 201–293.

Stanton, H. W. *Prognosis of musical achievement.* Eastman School of Music, Studies in Psychology, No. 1, 1929.

Stoddard, G. D. *The meaning of intelligence.* New York: The Macmillan Company, 1943.

Super, D. E. *Appraising vocational fitness.* New York: Harper and Brothers, 1949.

———. Comments [on the *DAT*]. *Personnel & Guid. J.*, 1956(a), 35, 91–93.

———. Comments [on the *GATB*]. *Personnel & Guid. J.*, 1956(b), 35, 152–154.

———. Comments [on the *GZAS*]. *Personnel & Guid. J.*, 1956(c), 35, 223–224.

———. The use of multifactor test batteries in guidance. *Personnel & Guid. J.*, 1956(d), 35, 9–15.

———. Comments [on the *Factored Aptitude Series*]. *Personnel & Guid. J.*, 1957(a), 35, 358–360.

———. Comments [on the *Flanagan Aptitude Classification Test*]. *Personnel & Guid. J.*, 1957(b), 35, 504–507.

———. Comments [on the *Holzinger-Crowder Unifactor Tests*]. *Personnel & Guid. J.*, 1957(c), 35 287–288.

———. Comments [on the *Multiple Aptitude Tests*]. *Personnel & Guid. J.*, 1957(d), 35, 432–434.

———. Comments [on the *Tests of Primary Mental Ability*]. *Personnel & Guid. J.*, 1957(e), 35, 576–577.

———. The multifactor tests: summing up. *Personnel & Guid. J.*, 1957(f), 36, 17–20.

Terman, L. M. *The measurement of intelligence.* Boston: Houghton Mifflin Company, 1916.

———, and M. A. Merrill. *Measuring intelligence.* Boston: Houghton Mifflin Company, 1937.

The Stanford-Binet Intelligence Scale: Manual for the Third Revision, Form L-M. Boston: Houghton Mifflin Company, 1960.

Thorndike, R. L., and Elizabeth Hagen. *10,000 Careers.* New York: John Wiley and Sons, 1959.

Thurstone, L. L. *Primary mental abilities.* Psychometric Monographs, No. 1, 1938.

Thurstone, T. G. *The Tests of Primary Mental Abilities.* *Personnel & Guid. J.*, 1957, 35, 569–577.

U. S. Dept. of Labor, Bur. of Employment Security (USES). *Estimates of worker trait requirements for 4000 jobs.* Washington, D.C.: Government Printing Office, 1956.

War Manpower Commission, Division of Occupational Analysis. Factor analysis of occupational aptitude tests. *Educ. Psychol. Measmt.*, 1945, 5, 147–155.

Wechsler, D. *Adult intelligence scale (WAIS).* New York: The Psychological Corporation, 1955.

——. *The measurement of adult intelligence.* Baltimore: Williams and Wilkins, 1944.

——. *Wechsler intelligence scale for children.* New York: The Psychological Corporation, 1949.

Wittenborn, J. R. Mechanical ability, its nature and measurement, I: An analysis of the variables employed in the preliminary Minnesota Experiment. *Educ. Psychol. Measmt.,* 1945, 5, 241–260.

10

Interests

THE COUNSELOR PREPARING FOR A SERIES OF COUNSELING INTERVIEWS MAY use the material covered in this chapter in several ways. Data about interests may already be included in the client's record; this necessitates synthesizing these data into a form usable with the client, and requires counselor skill in interpretation of such data, for which this chapter can provide a review. The counselor and client may discuss in the initial interview the need for collecting further data about interests in addition to that already available; hence the counselor needs to point out the process and instruments by which further interest data will be collected. A brief discussion with the client of the instruments to be used and vital points in the client's approach to completing them may make the data produced by the instruments more usable and is apt to produce a more candid response by the client. Again this chapter should provide a review of pertinent material used by the counselor in this process.

The counselor may wish to discuss with the client the value of interest data in broadening an understanding of client behavior and in providing an insight into client motivation. With college bound clients and clients from upper levels of general intelligence, interest data may provide the only useful differentiation of educational or vocational possibilities. With other clients interest data may provide a clue to specific areas of further investigation before making further life choices.

These are some of the ways in which information about client interests can be useful in preparation for counseling interviews.

BRIEF HISTORY OF INTEREST MEASUREMENT

The measurement of interests closely parallels that of mental ability in its development. Early in the twentieth century when Binet was making the first scientific attempts to measure intelligence, other psychologists were attempting to do the same for interests. The history of this is covered in Fryer's *Measurement of Interest in Relation to Human Adjustment* (1931). This volume of Fryer's is considered the basic landmark in the history of measuring interests because of the fact that it is a comprehensive summary of the theorizing and experimenting that went on in this area of human personality up until about 1930. At the present time a good share of this early work is found to be of little more than historical value because of the lack of statistical techniques possessed by these early workers for handling data, ignorance of sampling techniques, and poorly designed experiments. The reader of Fryer's volume will be impressed though by the fact that all of the problems that confront the appraiser of interests today are mentioned in one manner or another by Fryer.

Fryer considered that there was a dual approach to the appraisal of interests, a subjective and an objective one. The subjective aspect was evaluated by the use of inventories, questionnaires, and rating scales, just as are used today. The objective approach was a measurement of one's observable reaction to stimulation. Some of these objective measures that Fryer considers are information tests, free-association tests, learning tests, and distraction tests. It might be noted that little has been done with this objective approach to the measurement of interests since the time of Fryer's writing except for isolated instances such as the development of the *Michigan Vocabulary Profile Analysis* which measures interests on the basis of one's knowledge of the vocabularies of the different fields of interests, and some limited attempts at vocational information tests.

Another rather interesting aspect of Fryer's ideas is that he separated motivation from interest. In the course of his writings Fryer (1931:349) derives a theory of interest that states: "Objective interests are acceptance reactions and objective aversions are rejection reactions. It may be that the acceptance, or turning toward stimulation, and the rejection, or turning away from the stimulation, are correlated with pleasant and unpleasant experiences. Subjective interests, or likes, would appear to be acceptances of stimulation and subjective aversions, or dislikes, would appear to be rejections of stimulation. At any rate, they may be regarded as acceptance-rejection experiences." In spite of this, it is only recently that users of interest inventories had begun to interpret them in terms of patterns of acceptance and rejection.

The second landmark in the history of the measuring of interests is Strong's *Vocational Interests of Men and Women* (1943). In this large volume Strong summarized the vast amount of data that had been collected over the years through the use of the *Strong Vocational Interest Blank* (*SVIB*). Much of this work will be discussed later when the *SVIB* is taken up in detail. In the 1930's Kuder began developing the *Kuder Preference Record, Vocational*. After World War II this came into common use in the appraisal of vocational interests. Kuder's approach differed from Strong's in that instead of developing keys for different occupations on the basis of the inventoried interests of successful individuals in various occupations, he developed an inventory on the basis of statistical analysis which resulted in an individual's interests being reported in fields or areas of interests such as mechanical, artistic, clerical, and the like. Forms A, B, and C were of this type. Form D, Kuder's latest contribution, is similar to Strong's in that keys are available for specific occupations.

In 1931 Allport and Vernon published their *Study of Values*. This high-level inventory was revised in 1951 and is now known as the Allport-Vernon-Lindzey *Study of Values*. Over the years it has been widely used both in carrying on research and in counseling with university students. In the 1940's Lee and Thorpe published their *Occupational Interest Inventory*. A novel approach appeared in Weingarten's *Picture Interest Inventory* (1958). All of these will be discussed later.

THEORIES OF INTERESTS

As psychologists measured interests they also began to speculate and hypothesize on the nature of interests. As noted above Fryer developed his theory of acceptance-rejection. Early in his major book, Strong (1943:6) reverses Fryer's stand and says that interests are aspects of motivation. A few pages on (10), he states that since interests involve the reactions to specific things, they must all be learned. This is his major theory, but as the book goes on and as he considers his research data various amendments are made to this theory. Presently (333) he shows that there are significant relationships between mental ability and vocational interests. Most of these correlation coefficients fall between plus and minus .40. He continues:

> Are interests inherited as are physical traits? The first answer to this question is "No." Interests are related to objects and activities in the environment in quite a different sense from height or color of eyes. Interests are learned. Liking to be an aviator and disliking gardening are reflections of experience. The second answer to this question is that interests are inherited to a certain degree. An interest is an expression of one's reaction to his environment. The reaction of liking-disliking is a resultant of satisfactory or unsatisfactory dealing with the object. Different people react differently to the same object. The different reactions, we suspect, arise because the individuals are different to start with. We suspect that people who have the kind of brain that handles mathematics easily will like such activities and vice versa. In other words, interests are related to abilities and abilities, it is easy to see, are inherited. There is, however, a pathetic lack of data to substantiate all of this. (682–683)

Strong seems to be saying here that interests are partly a function of innate potential and partly a function of learning through encounters with the environment.

Other theories have considered interests as arising from the development of personality. Carter (1940) considers the choice of a vocation to be the practical adjustment to the environment. Solutions possible for any individual are limited by his own capacities, needs, motives, and by his and his family's socio-economic status. If there are no major discrepancies between these factors and the requirements of a vocation, an individual will tend to continue in an occupation. If there are discrepancies, the individual seeks another vocation. In this way as time goes on a pattern of vocational interests forms that is closely identified with the individual.

Darley (1941) on the basis of Strong and Carter's work suggested cautiously that the data support the hypothesis that occupational interests emerge from the development of one's personality. . Darley's theory was based upon studies made with the three so-called non-occupational scales of the SVIB: Occupational-Level, Interest-Maturity and Masculinity-Femininity. Later research with these scales and other developments led Darley himself to see defects in his own ideas (Darley and Hagenah, 1955:147). Super (1949) criticized the ideas of Carter and Darley for unwarranted interpretations of the data, fragmentary evidence, and even for making assertions that are no way related to the basic research data.

Bordin (1943) stated that the vocational goals and aspirations of an individual form one of the mainsprings of his actions. He notes that the older an individual is, the more likely he is to be vocationally situated and the less likelihood that he will need a change of vocation. Finally, he stated: "In answering a Strong Vocational Interest Test an individual is expressing his acceptance of a particular view or concept of himself in terms of occupational stereotypes." (53)

Super, a strong critic of the ideas of Strong, Carter, and Darley proposed his own theory of multiple causation (1949). To quote him:

Interests are the product of interaction between inherited aptitudes and endocrine factors, on the one hand, and opportunity and social evaluation on the other. Some of the things a person does will bring him the satisfaction of mastery or the approval of his companions, and result in interests. Some of the things his associates do appeal to him and, through identification, he patterns his actions and his interests after them: if he fits the pattern reasonably well, he remains in it, but if not, he must seek another identification and develop another self-concept and interest pattern. His mode of adjustment may cause him to seek certain satisfactions, but the means of achieving these satisfactions vary so much from one person, with one set of aptitudes and in one set of circumstances, to another person with other abilities and in another situation, that the prediction of interest patterns from modes of adjustment is hardly possible. Because of the stability of the hereditary endowment and the relative stability of the social environment in which any given person is reared, interest patterns are generally rather stable; their stability is further increased by the multiplicity of opportunities for try-outs, identification and social approval in the years before adolescence. By adolescence most young people have had opportunities to explore social, linguistic, mathematical, technical, and business activities to some extent; they have sought to identify with parents, other adults, and schoolmates, and have rejected some and accepted others of these identifications; self-concepts have begun to take definite form.   For these reasons interest patterns begin to crystallize by early adolescence, and the exploratory experiences of the adolescent years in most cases merely clarify and elaborate upon what has already begun to take shape.   Some persons experience significant changes during adolescence and early adulthood, but these are most often related to endocrine changes and less often to changes in self-concept resulting from having attempted to live up to a misidentification and to fit into a inappropriate pattern.   Vocational interest patterns generally have a substantial degree of permanence at this stage: for most persons, adolescent exploration is an awakening to something that is already there. (406)

At this point it seems wise also to call attention to two possible dangers in interpretation of patterns on the *SVIB*.   One of these concerns the danger of interpreting a pattern of maladjustment as a stable occupational pattern.   A person who is withdrawing because of emotional upset may reject the Group V (Social Welfare) and Group IX (Business Contact) scales on the *SVIB*.   After successful therapy such a person may reverse this pattern and show high scores on scales for these occupations dealing with people.   Conversely, a person who cannot solve such emotional problems will sometimes compensate to such an extent that it results in a Social Welfare pattern which is not a valid occupational one.

The other danger is in the interpretation of a pattern of interests developed in a very restricted environment as a stable occupational pattern. A boy brought up in a prominent family with a traditional history as business leaders in a community may show a pronounced pattern on the *SVIB* scales for business detail and business contact occupations as a freshman entering college.   If after he has been in college for some time he retakes the *SVIB*, he may then show a moderate pattern on the Group V scales (Social Welfare) with lowered scores on the business scales.   At this point his pattern is really beginning to represent his own interests, rather than those to which he was exposed in the restricted family environment.   The original scores might be considered a reflection of family interests, not his.   The counselor should interpret these successive testings very cautiously over a period of time until retests appear stable enough that no further changes occur.   Another example of such change in interests is the gifted student from the small community who can do most things well; yet he shows no pronounced interest pattern as he enters a university.   Here again the counselor must wait and see what develops on periodic retests before any sound interpretation can be made.

Ginzberg, Ginsburg, Axelrad, and Herma (1951), as a result of studying the interests of boys from the upper socio-economic level and in the top bracket of mental ability, stated that vocational interests pass through three developmental periods: ages 6–11, fantasy; 12–17, tentative; and 18 and beyond, realistic. In the first period the individual, as typical with children, sees himself doing all sorts of things as an adult. In the second stage he starts selecting a vocation and, as this stage goes on and he matures, he passes to the final stage. With advancing age vocational choices become more realistic and are made on sounder bases. According to the authors of this theory, vocational choice, since it is based upon all that one has undergone before, is basically irreversible, but there has to be compromise as vocational choice consists of a balancing of subjective aspects of an individual with the opportunities and restrictions of daily living.

This theory has been taken to task by other psychologists (see Darley and Hagenah, 1955, Super, 1953) for disregarding all past research, the statistical naïveté of the theory, and its basic lack of validation.

In another approach Kitson (1942) wrote that vocational interests develop through experiences. It follows that an important task of the counselor is to aid the client in obtaining experiences that will help him in making a vocational decision.

Briefly then these are the ideas the psychologists have set down when they speculated upon the nature of interests. A comprehensive summary of these theories and the research basic thereto is found in Chapter V of Darley and Hagenah (1955). Hahn and MacLean (1955) summarize the research and theorizing on vocational interests succinctly when they write:

1. Interests are an aspect of personality shaped by both hereditary and environmental factors.

2. Long-range, stable, occupational interests emerge during the early teens, but mature interest patterns are not fixed for most individuals until an age of approximately twenty-five years.

3. Interests are not necessarily closely related to aptitudes or abilities.

4. Interests probably cannot be created *de novo* and in a short time merely by the classroom presentation of varied and vicarious experiences to youth. Such exposures may possibly, however, start the development of a new zone of interest, help fix existing interests, or uncover latent ones.

5. A strong motivation toward certain types of occupational or avocational behavior is expressed by a wide number of responses to an extremely wide range of stimuli.

6. Interests, as aspects of personality and as employed by the general clinical counselor, involve both acceptance and rejection of possible lines of activity. For example the typical worker with processes and things (mechanical interests) obtains interest scores which are negatively related to scores which measure a liking for persons and social situations.

7. The estimated, judged, or measured interests of secondary school and college students in an occupation seem to them to be and in fact often

are quite unrelated to the training program they must take to prepare them for employment in the occupational family in which they have an identified dominant interest.

8. A legitimate interest in an occupational outlet often has little effect on grades earned in the curriculum leading to that outlet. Much of the training in a medical school may be largely quite unrelated to the particular aspects of medical practice toward which the interest is expressed.

9. Vocational and avocational interests appear to run in similar directions for a large proportion of individuals.

10. The interests of individuals tend to be less varied with increasing age. (201–202)

In reading the literature about vocational interests, the student is apt to become concerned with the loose use of terms. Super (1949) brought a semblance of order to the classification of interests when he proposed the following four types.

First there are *expressed* or stated interests. These are the verbal professions of an individual in an activity. Research has shown this type to be quite unreliable.

Second are the *manifest* interests. Super feels that these are synonomous with participation in an activity or an occupation. As measures of interests they may or may not be valid. Probably most high school students who participate in the school's dramatic offerings do so because of an interest in dramatics. It is possible though that one of the boys is involved merely because of a girl who is there.

Third are the *tested* interests. These are the same as Fryer's objective interests. The assumption here is that high scores on an achievement test in a specific subject, or one related to a particular job, are related to an interest in that subject matter or job. Again this may or may not be so. Some people achieve in academic situations because of past behavior and conditioning. A high grade results sometimes with no interest, even aversion, simply because a person sees himself as a good student.

Fourth are *inventoried* interests. These are the ones most frequently encountered by the counselor and the type obtained from an inventory like the *Kuder* or the *Strong*. In the counseling situation, the counselor should as far as possible try to obtain information on all of these different types of interests, for as usual the more different types of information collected about the client, the more valid the insights into his behavior and problems.

Kuder, Strong, and others who have developed interest inventories have used names for areas of interests or occupations through which they expressed the results of their inventories. For example, they used "scientific," "artistic," "outdoor," "chemist," and the like. Cottle (1951) as the result of an extensive factor analysis of data including both scores on the *Kuder* and *SVIB* showed that these factors were bipolar in nature.

By this is meant that a preference for a type of work is associated with the rejection of another type of work. These bipolar factors used by Cottle are:

1. Preference for activities concerned with people and the communication of ideas.   vs.   1. Preference for activities dealing with things and objects.

2. Preference for activities involving business contact with people.   vs.   2. Preference for activities of a scientific and technical nature.

3. Preference for activities of an abstract and creative nature.   vs.   3. Preference for activities of a routine, concrete, organized business detail nature.

4. Preference for working for people for their presumed good as in Social Welfare, or for dealing with people and language in social situations.   vs.   4. Preference for activities that are nonsocial in nature, and are carried on in relation to processes, machines, and techniques.

5. Preference for activities resulting in prestige or the esteem of others.   vs.   5. Preference for activities resulting in tangible, productive satisfaction.

Extensive use of this classification has been made in a publication of the U. S. Department of Labor, *Estimates of Worker Trait Requirements for 4000 Jobs* (1956). It will readily be seen that one pole of each of these factors is related to activities of a linguistic nature which revolve around working with people. Those on the left side of the page illustrate this. The other pole of each factor, as shown on the right side of the page, is related to activities of a nonlinguistic nature revolving around working with processes, related machines, and routine activities. Thus overall descriptions of occupations and clients in terms of linguistic versus nonlinguistic activities appear more meaningful in counseling than the fragmentary and confusing terms of masculinity versus femininity of interests. A further implication is involved in the linguistic-nonlinguistic concept. It may be possible eventually to show by statistical processes that previous attempts to describe individuals and vocations in terms of patterns of field and level of interest and ability were basically sound.

Present consideration of this in the light of techniques of factorial analysis involves three limitations. First, the problem to be solved is limited by the method used. That is, the chief purpose of a factor analysis method like Thurstone's centroid analysis is to account for the primary interest factors in a given number of tests or variables. On the other hand, a Spearman analysis is designed to produce a general factor and one or more specific factors. Thus the nature of interest factors is determined in part by the factorial method chosen. A second limiting element is that the nature and number of tests used in a factor analysis also in part determines the factors operating and therefore the relationship that can be found.   In other words, the more different combinations of related interest tests or other variables that can be used in research, the more interest factors are apt to appear in these research studies.   A third limiting factor would be the population sample chosen.   Some interest factors have seemed to transcend populations, while others appear unique to a given sample or population.   Thus it can be seen that the factor analysis method chosen, the variables combined for purposes of investigation, and the population sample will be limitations on the nature and number of interest factors that emerge from a given study.

The factorial studies performed on the *SVIB* and *Kuder* must be considered in light of these statements.   The factors which have emerged in studies of the *SVIB* and *Kuder* are a result of the method, the peculiar combination of variables, and the samples used in a given study.   They are not necessarily the only factors present, nor are the variables without high factor loadings invalid.   The interest variables with low or zero factor loadings in one study may have high loadings on new factors when combined with new variables in another study.

An illustration of this would be the factorial analysis of the *Minnesota Multiphasic Personality Inventory* (MMPI), *Strong, Kuder Preference Record—Vocational,* and the *Bell Adjustment Inventory* performed by Cottle (1951).   In this study of 400 male veterans, high relationships between the two personality inventories were found, as were high relationships between the two interest inventories.   However, little relationship between the personality inventories and interest inventories was found.   This would seem to be indicating little overlap between personality and interest inventories.   Yet when a sub-sample from this group was selected on a criterion of high versus low scores on the masculinity-femininity scale of the *MMPI*, significant relationships between certain scales of the interest and personality inventories were found which could logically be expected to be related.   Thus it would seem that the heterogeneity of the sample of 400 veterans was masking relationships, which were found when a sub-sample was selected on a criterion that reduced these wide differences by emphasizing a given difference in the sub-sample.   Thus development of interest theory and evaluation of research into the measurement of interests must be interpreted in view of the limitations of the data and of the methods being used.   Failure to substantiate counselor hypotheses developed from empirical evidence may be a function of the experimental design of the research rather than evidence that such hypotheses cannot be substantiated.

THE EVALUATION OF INTERESTS

The appraisal of an individual's interests provides some of the most important and valuable information for the counseling situation.   It should be no surprise then to find out that over the past forty years certain psychologists have devoted considerable time and effort to the study of this aspect of personality. Interests are important in achievement. This fact alone makes them almost invaluable to the counselor. However, in addition to this, results obtained from interest inventories may motivate students in getting concerned about their educational and vocational future; they may serve as guideposts for the use of the counselor in the counseling interview, and they may provide information that to a great extent explains the social and emotional adjustment of an individual.

In the evaluation of interests it is most convenient to divide interests into two types, general and vocational, and consider the determination of each separately. By general interests are meant that type related to success in the classroom, those related to the avocational use of spare time, and those related to an individual's overall development. This separation is purely arbitrary and somewhat artificial.

EVALUATION OF GENERAL INTERESTS

Interests of this type are most conveniently evaluated by the use of questionnaires, check lists, the writings of students, and measures of achievement.

The questionnaire

The interest questionnaire is one of the most useful tools of the counselor. Basically it consists of a series of questions covering such items as the subject or subjects liked most in school and those liked least. Sometimes these questions are followed by others asking the clients to give a reason for each answer. Related questions ask the client in which subjects best and poorest grades are or were achieved. If the client is a college student, similar questions are constructed about high school educational experiences. Other questions may be related to the difficulty that the various subjects offer. Also the client may be asked to indicate which subjects seem most practical and those which seem to have no significance in respect to personal educational goals. After the questions on subject matter are exhausted these can be followed by items related to extracurricular activities. Further information is obtained by questions concerning type of activities, degree, awards, and the like. Following this part of the questionnaire there are usually items covering such questions as the types of magazines and books that the client reads. Perhaps a client is asked to note the names of a half dozen books recently read or to list articles read in the magazines. The same sort of questions are also asked about newspapers. The reading interest may then be followed by items related to both television and radio programs and the movies.

Interest questionnaires also contain items on the individual's hobbies, spare-time activities, and perhaps study habits. Questions related to the client's future, covering the type of work to be undertaken, responsibilities, and possible future salary are frequently encountered on these instruments. Actually what they measure depends upon those things that the user of the instrument feels significant for the counseling situation.

The counselor should be aware that an interest questionnaire is an important time-saver from the counseling point of view. There is actually no reason why the client should be asked all of the above questions in an interview when they can be obtained from the client prior to the interview. Questionnaires like these can be completed by the client simultaneously with forms that contain biographical data.

Check lists

Check lists are made up of groups or series of items that cover various types of activities. Topics such as "books," "magazines," "radio and television programs," "extracurricular activities" and the like are included. The constructor of the check list makes as comprehensive as possible a listing under each of the categories. The client then completes the list by checking those carried on. It must be emphasized here that these checks made by clients may not necessarily be valid. They may be a result of the person's concept of the social desirability of the response. The client knows that it is socially respectable to read magazines or books, to attend concerts, to listen to symphonies, and to read certain of the better magazines. A person may distort the responses to the list to produce socially desirable or acceptable responses. It is also possible that in some sub-cultures it is considered socially undesirable or sissified to do certain things or carry on various activities. Rather than depart from the group values and attitudes, certain individuals will not mark various activities that they carry on. Eliminating social desirability from responses can be controlled to a certain extent by not only asking individuals to tell which books or magazine articles are read but also asking them to write a sentence or two describing or summarizing what was read. Failure to check items for a socially desirable reason can sometimes be overcome by establishing rapport and having the clients understand the use of responses to these items.

Another type of check list was developed for use in the Eight Year Study (see Smith and Tyler, 1942). This consists of items that cover the usual academic subjects of the curriculum. In making one of these the teacher or teachers in the various academic areas may each be asked to construct items related to activities in their area. Typically this would result in groupings such as biological sciences, physical sciences and mathematics, literature, music, art, social sciences, and the like. If fifteen or twenty items are written in each of these areas, arranged in random order, and assembled into an inventory a comprehensive check list of activities related to the academic areas results. Typical of these items are the following: "to write stories," "to make chemical compounds," "to make an insect collection," "to sing in a glee club or choir," and "to take part in a class discussion of literature."

There is no hard and fast line which separates check lists from questionnaires. As a matter of fact, many questionnaires are made up in part of check lists. This is especially so in the coverage of reading, listening, and leisure-time activities.

Student's writings

A very useful technique in obtaining information about interests is by the use of a student's writings, especially those of an autobiographical nature. The general use of this tool was discussed in Chapter 2. Here consideration will be given only to information related to interests that may be obtained by this technique. When the client is asked to write an autobiography, usually an outline is furnished indicating the various points that the counselor wishes covered. Such a piece of writing is referred to as being structured. Usually the client is asked to write about hobbies, interests, past employment, and future vocational plans. The latter gives not only an indication of the area in which the client wants to work, but also an indication of level of aspiration or motivation of a given client.

Achievement

As noted earlier, interests are related to achievement. From the viewpoint of learning, interests are an important aspect of the learning situation. In general one might conclude that one does best in learning in those activities in which there is an interest. Downie in an unpublished study collected inventoried interest data on the freshmen class of a large engineering school. Four years later the members of the class were studied and divided into three groups. One large group, "the successful group," consisted of those individuals who were obtaining their bachelor's degrees in engineering in normal time, that is, four years after being freshmen. The second group consisted of individuals who were also graduating, but in another school of the same university in which the engineering school was located. The third group was made up of those who had withdrawn from the university. The first and third groups consisted of about 300 individuals each and the second group of about ninety men. The third group was made up of those who withdrew voluntarily from school for various reasons other than academic deficiencies. They had not been dropped.

In summary it was shown that those who were obtaining degrees in engineering scored significantly higher on the scientific and computational scores of an interest inventory administered to them as freshmen than the other groups. The students in the second group most of whom were obtaining degrees in a liberal arts curriculum scored significantly higher on the literary key of the same inventory. The third group, being much more heterogeneous in composition, had no clear-cut pattern but there was a trend for these to be high in the mechanical area of the inventory, which has less to do with total requirements of an engineering curriculum. Counselors have noted empirically that engineering students with a high pattern on Group IV of the *SVIB* also tend to drop out of an engineering curriculum.

Unfortunately as with all other human variables, the relationship between interests and achievement is complicated by the fact that some individuals succeed in a given area in spite of their measured or stated interests. For example, take two college students of equal academic ability both of whom are taking a required course in freshman chemistry and both of whom are known to have no interest in chemistry. As a matter of fact, their interest may be described as abhorrence. One of these students obtains an A for his work in both semesters of the course. The other receives an F and three years later may still not have passed the course. Any counselor soon runs into behavior of this type and begins to wonder. Some students are so conditioned as a result of the educative and life processes that, given any academic or learning situation, they tend to perform as they have in other similar situations in the past. Hence if a student sees himself as an A student, that type of behavior is continued in new courses regardless of interest in them. Other students of equal ability learn or study more selectively. Interests are important to them. Then it follows that personality factors, particularly self-concept, are related to the integrating of interests and achievement. It might be noted that even the A student described here will probably take no more chemistry courses once the required ones are out of the way.

Strong (1943) in his book on the vocational interests of men and women summarizes a large amount of research on this relationship between academic success and scores on interest inventories. None of this will be repeated here other than to note that such correlation coefficients are usually low, with practically all of the coefficients ranging between $-.40$ and $+.40$. Highest positive correlation coefficients were obtained between achievement and scientific and linguistic interests. The negative ones were found in the areas of business and sales interests and in the area referred to as social welfare. Strong (1943) summarizes all this as follows:

> All this suggests the following hypothesis: If a student has sufficient interest to elect a course, his grade will depend far more on his intelligence, industry, and previous preparation than on his interest. Interests affect the situation, however, in causing the student to elect what he is interested

in and not to elect courses in which he is not interested.   When a student discovers that he has mistakenly selected a course in which he finds little interest, he will finish it about as well as other courses, but he will not elect further courses of a similar nature.   Because of this situation it is difficult to obtain a real measure of the relationship between interest and scholarship, since those with less than a fair amount of interest in the subject seldom take the course at all.   (528)

One test, the *Michigan Vocabulary Profile Test* (published by the World Book Co.) has been constructed to measure interests by the method of measuring achievement.   This test consists of eight sub-tests, each made up of 30 items covering human relations, commerce, government, physical sciences, biological sciences, mathematics, fine arts, and sports. The rationale behind the test is that a high score on any one of the sub-tests indicates an interest in that area.   Not many studies have been published using this test and those that have, as might be expected in the light of the previous discussion, have not too well demonstrated the validity of such a concept.

THE EVALUATION OF VOCATIONAL INTERESTS

By far the largest amount of research and publication in the area of interests has been done in relation to vocational interests and the majority of this has been related to the *Strong Vocational Interest Blank*.   Other major inventories in use today as previously noted are the *Kuder Preference Record—Vocational* (published by Science Research Associates), the *Allport-Vernon-Lindzey Study of Values* (Houghton Mifflin Company), the *Occupational Interest Inventory* (California Test Bureau), and the *Brainard Occupational Preference Inventory* (The Psychological Corporation).

The Strong Vocational Interest Blank

This vocational interest inventory consists of 400 items to which the client responds by marking (L) like, (D) dislike, and (I) indifferent. The scale consists of eight parts: (I) Occupations; (II) School Subjects (from algebra to zoology); (III) Amusements; (IV) Activities (such as repairing a clock, writing reports, and methodical work); (V) Peculiarities of People (progressive people, pessimists, foreigners); (VI) Order of Preference of Activities (selecting from sets of ten activities the three that would be enjoyed most and the three that would be enjoyed least); (VIII) Comparison of Interests between Two Items (outside work versus inside work); and (VIII) Rating of Present Abilities and Characteristics ("Am quite sure of myself," "Am approachable," and "Win friends easily"). There is a form for men and a form for women.   Most of the research has been carried out using the men's form and all that follows will pertain to that form unless otherwise stated. The women's blank will be discussed later.

In the manual Strong (1945, 1959) notes that since changes in interests are considerable between the ages of 15 and 20 as shown by his own research experience, the inventory should not be used with individuals who are less than 17 unless these individuals are especially mature. He further adds that because of their youth the interest scores of boys under twenty are apt to be lower than they will be five or ten years later. Darley and Hagenah (1955) state that the inventory can be used with ninth and tenth grade students with I.Q.'s of 105 or more. Forbes and Cottle (1953) showed that the average reading difficulty level of the Strong based upon five techniques of measuring reading difficulty was 11.4 and on the Forbes formula devised specifically for standardized tests, the readability level was college sophomore. This indicates that the vocabulary of the inventory is too difficult for a large part of the high school population. For responses to be valid, the individual has to know terms like psychology, physiology, and physics. The same is true for the various occupations such as social worker, labor arbitrator, and civil engineer. There are many in high school who do not know what these terms mean. The writers feel that this instrument is best used with sophisticated bright upperclassmen in high school and with university students and adults.

At the present time the *SVIB* is scored for more than 40 different occupational keys and for 3 non-occupational scales (see Figure 10.1). This depends somewhat upon the counseling needs in a given setting. Hand scoring is difficult and laborious because a separate key has to be used for each of these scales and the responses to each item are weighted from plus 4 to minus 4 in the light of which of the 3 possible responses the client made. At the present time, to avoid scoring these tests by hand or locally by the use of scoring machines, the completed blanks are sent to centers that have an electronic scorer that is capable of scoring these and printing the results very rapidly. Hankes' Testscor in Minneapolis is an example of such an agency.

Results are recorded in letter grades, A through C. Strong (1943, 1959) states that a letter grade of A means that the individual has the interests of individuals successfully engaged in that occupation. A C rating means that individuals do not have such interests. The other ratings, B+, B, and B—, mean that the person probably has those interests but one can not be as certain of the fact as he can with the A ratings. A scores include just under 70 per cent of the norm group, the B ratings about 26 per cent of the norm group, and the C scores, the remainder (Strong, 1943:66). A T-score of 40, which is the beginning of the B+ range, is achieved by 82 per cent of the criterion group in each occupation. Ninety-seven per cent in the occupation score above the middle of the shaded or chance area (see Figure 10.1).

STRONG VOCATIONAL INTEREST TEST-MEN

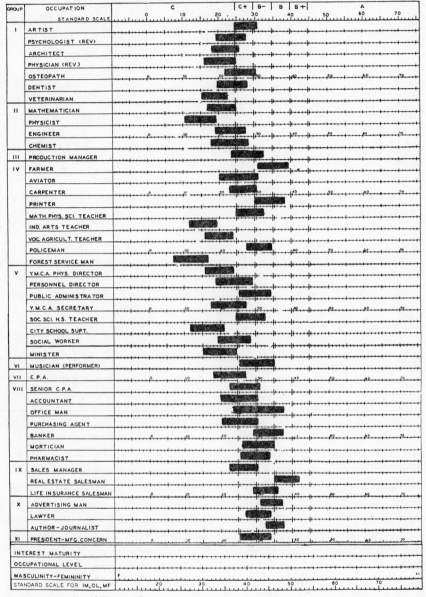

Used by permission of Testscor, Inc.

Fig. 10.1. Profile sheet for the Strong Vocational Interest Blank for Men.

In setting up the keys for the various occupations Strong placed those items in a key for a specific occupation that significantly separated successful men in that occupation from professional "men-in-general." Success was defined as earning a certain salary per year, length of experience in the occupation, level of training obtained, and the like. "Men-in-general" referred to has meant several things to Strong. At first it meant all the other successful professional men who completed the blank but who were not considered in the group for whom the key was being made. Later it was revised to include a fair representation of business and professional men earning $2500 and above per year in the later 1930's. It must be remembered that these would be considerably higher salaries today. A client then who receives an A rating for a specific occupation such as physician has responded to the items as successful physicians did in Strong's sample.

The counselor should become familiar as rapidly as possible with the *SVIB* profile sheet that will be used in the agency—such as that shown in Figure 10.1. These occupations are arranged in groups based upon correlation among interest scores of the different occupations (Strong, 1945). In daily usage these different groups are referred to by special names, such as I, scientific; II, technical; V, social welfare; VIII, business detail; IX, business contact; and X, linguistic.

At the bottom of Figure 10.1 are the three non-occupational scales. The first of these is known as the Interest Maturity or IM scale. Strong (1943) defined this as the quantitative measurement of the differences in interests of 15-year-old boys in contrast to men between the ages of 23 and 27. On the basis of his research Strong showed that there is relatively little difference in mean scores on most occupational scales after 25 years of age. He also showed that there is either a distinct rise or a distinct fall in score between 15 and 25 years of age, the direction being associated with whether the scale score was negatively or positively related with the IM scale. Strong also showed that there was a relationship between the stability of the interests of adolescent boys and their scores on the IM scale, those with the higher IM scores having the more stable interests. According to Strong, therefore, the IM scale separated those with the interests of a 15-year-old from those with more mature interests. Darley (1941) stated that interest maturity was defined as reflecting the "well-organized, socially sensitive, generally mature, tolerant, insightful individual." Stordahl (1954) and King (1958) found no relationship between stability of interests and IM scores. Such research forced Darley and Hagenah (1955, p. 45) to conclude that the IM scale is "not a clear index of growth or change of interest patterns; it is, however, a possible index of general maturity of outlook." Research by Rhodes (1956) on effect of response set indicates that high IM scores are a function of the preponderance of like responses over dislikes and counseling experience has shown a high score is most closely associated with Group V and an interest in the social sciences.

The second of these scales is referred to as the Occupational Level or OL scale. Strong originally described this as a scale that contrasted the interests of unskilled men with those of business and professional men earning $2500 per year and up. Darley (1941) indicated that this scale gave a measure of a man's level of aspiration. In his words he stated "the degree to which the individual's total background has prepared him to seek the prestige and discharge the responsibilities growing out of high income, professional status, recognition, or leadership in the community." Kendall (1947), Gustad (1952), and Ostrom (1949-a-b) have shown the relationship of the OL scale to achievement in the university, to staying power in school, and to interest patterns in certain areas. Gustad (1954) showed that primary interests (see below) in the verbal-linguistic fields were associated with high OL scores, whereas low OL scores went along with primary interest patterns in the technical fields. Rhodes has shown that these occupational differences are at least partially a function of tendency to respond with "like" or "dislike," respectively (1956). Darley and Hagenah (1955) report highest OL scores associated with primary interest patterns in the business contact and linguistic areas, next in size those in the biological and physical sciences. Primary patterns in the social service and business detail areas had OL scales at the mean (50). Primary interest patterns in the technical area had a mean OL score of 43, considerably below the mean on the scale itself. Barnett et al. (1952, 1953) reported studies which tended to cloud the picture somewhat. However, the evidence seems to point out that this index is a useful and meaningful one showing a client's level of aspiration in cases in which the score is either high or low and when interpreted in the light of differences among the various occupational groups. Actually observation in a counseling situation indicates that high scores on Occupational Level are achieved by marking few items in the Indifferent category and are associated with high scores in managerial, sales, and promotional occupations.

The third of these special keys is referred to as the Masculinity-Femininity or MF scale. As originally determined by Strong the purpose of this scale was to separate the interests of men and women. Darley (1941) described masculinity-femininity as "a continuum based upon the extent to which an individual's attention is held by technical, depersonalized, manipulative, concrete activities or objects in his environment (masculinity) or by cultural, aesthetic, personalized, symbolic, appreciative activities or objects, in his environment (femininity)." Darley and Hagenah (1955) showed high MF scores on the men's blank for individuals whose primary interest pattern was in either technical or physical science areas. Those whose primary interest patterns were in business detail and business contact had MF scores just below the mean, while those with primary patterns in the biological sciences were below the mean. The individuals with patterns in either the social-service or linguistic areas were considerably below the mean on the MF scale.

In summary, masculine interests which, as indicated previously, might better be called nonlinguistic interests, reflect an interest in things and processes. Most typically the interests of the engineer or mechanic are of this type. On the other hand feminine or linguistic interests are associated with an interest in people, and attempts at communication, such as written or spoken verbal activities. Clergymen, counselors, clinical psychologists, and poets have typically feminine interests. The counselor should note that this continuum of interest as now considered has nothing to do with the *physical* dichotomy of sex. Males may have feminine interests and females likewise may have masculine interests. Sexual deviation or abnormality is *not* the personality aspect measured by this scale. Graphically this can be depicted by two overlapping distributions, one for each sex, ranging from masculinity to femininity, with the most feminine males overlapping in score the distribution of the most masculine females.

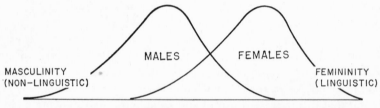

Fig. 10.2.   Overlap of interests between the two sexes.

Darley (1941) described the patterns used in evaluating interests on the Strong inventory. A primary pattern is one in which a preponderance of A and B+ scores occur within an interest group. For example an A in both "social worker" and "social science high school teacher" and a B+ in "personnel director" would constitute a primary pattern as all three are in the group V or social welfare area. Secondary patterns are made up of a preponderance of B+ and B scores in a group and tertiary patterns are composed of primarily B and B— scores. Rejection patterns exist when the preponderance of scores for a given grouping of interest fall to the left of the chance area on the profile sheet. On Figure 10.1 this chance area for each occupation consists of the blackened area. Any score falling in this blackened area could have been this high by chance alone. A score to the left of the area is known as a rejection. For an individual to obtain a score in this part of the sheet he has to reject definitely activities related to the given occupation. Only three per cent of men in a given occupational criterion group score below the middle of this shaded area. Thus a score below the shaded area is quite unlike that of most persons in the given occupation. The alert counselor regards scores on this side of the profile sheet as of equal importance with significant scores to the right of the darkened area. Too often these rejection scores are overlooked.

Hagenah reports (Darley and Hagenah, 1955) the result of analysing the *SVIB* profiles of 1000 freshmen at the University of Minnesota. She found that 193 or 19.3% of these students had no primary interest pattern, 410 had a single primary interest pattern, 303 had two or a double primary pattern, 88 had three or a triple pattern, and three individuals had four primary patterns. In a similar analysis of secondary patterns, 260 were found to have no secondary pattern, 429 a single, 234 a double, and 42 a triple secondary pattern. In terms of patterns of rejection, 64 individuals had no rejection pattern, 399, two, 251, three, and 47, four rejection patterns. In a further analysis of the same data Hagenah reports the simultaneous occurrence of primary and secondary patterns, primary and rejection patterns, the different types of primary patterns for these freshmen, different secondary patterns, and different rejection patterns. The counselor will find that this use of patterns is most helpful in explaining the results of the inventory to the client. Hagenah's work also points up the fact that there are many students who have no primary interests and some without any secondary ones in addition. Some beginning counselors are startled the first time that this situation appears in a real case. A similar study dealing with superior students is reported by Stewart (1959).

Methods are needed for handling patterns or profiles of individuals and of groups in research with interest and personality inventories. Cronbach and Gleser (1953) discuss the problems involved in such an approach. They stress the point that one method will provide one part of the answer and another method will provide another part. So far there is no simple way to substantiate clinical subliminal cues about this area of pattern analysis. The present systems for handling profiles on the *SVIB* do not include ways of showing both similarity in profiles and differences in height between the profiles at the same time.

In the case of the *SVIB* it is the pattern of high and low occupational and non-occupational scores together which helps differentiate curricular or occupational choices. A high score on the Production Manager scale along with high scores on other managerial scales and a moderate masculine pattern on the non-occupational scales may be pointing toward the technical aspects of factory management, while a low score on this scale, high scores on other managerial scales, and a feminine pattern on the non-occupational scales may point toward the personal contact aspects of business management. High occupational scores on scales for engineer, chemist, and sales manager may be pointing toward technical sales in chemical engineering, while high scores on scales for engineer and chemist and low scores on the business contact and business detail scales may be pointing toward research aspects of chemical engineering. (It should be noted here that there are many other data which are added to these and the choices is not made on *SVIB* scores alone.) This illustrates why the combination of acceptance and rejection or like and dislike is important in interpreting the total pattern.

As was noted earlier much research has been carried on using this interest inventory. Strong and his students have been instrumental in doing a large amount of this work. Strong (1953, 1955) reported on a study that began in 1930 when a group of Stanford University freshmen were administered his inventory. In 1949 a follow-up study was made of these same freshmen, the inventory readministered, and their occupations engaged in at that time studied. Strong reported that half of these students continued in the occupation of their early choice, thirty per cent changed to an occupation correlating .71 to .00 with their original choice, and twenty per cent changed to an occupation quite unrelated to their original choice (correlation of —.01 to —.71). When transformed into a validity coefficient this produces an r of .69. He further notes that at the age of 18.7 years half of these freshmen had selected occupations that they finally entered or one very close to it. From this he infers that many of these must have made their vocational choice while in high school and thus it follows that vocational counseling is a necessity in any high school. Those individuals who changed their occupations did not select an occupation with as high a prestige value as those who did not change. Also individuals who changed their occupation to occupations correlating from .71 to —.71 with their original choices scored lower both in 1930 and in 1949 on their average interest score than those students who either did not change or who changed to a very closely related occupation.

In another study, Stordahl (1954) considered the results obtained from testing and retesting a group of metropolitan and non-metropolitan boys with a time gap of 2 to 2.5 years between the administrations. He found that the relationship between their scores obtained from the two testings to be high with an over-all average for both groups in the low .70's. On examining the letter ratings he found that the C's were the most stable, with 68% of the C's on the first testing being C's on the second. The A's were next, with 60% being the same from test to test. The intermediate letter ratings were less stable. In the same research he studied the permanence of the different interest patterns. Again he found that the extremes were the most permanent, with 58% of the primary patterns and 81% of the "no patterns" being identical on the retest. Counselors should note then that clients should be informed that intermediate scores on the SVIB can move in either direction on a retest, but that the extreme scores are apt to change very little. It would be highly unusual for a rejection to become a score like those of successful persons in a given occupation and vice versa.

In another study conducted with students at Yale, Trinkaus (1954) studied a group first tested in 1935–36 and then retested in 1950, a period of approximately 15 years. His results were very similar to those obtained by Strong with Stanford students. Specifically he found that both A and C scores were more stable than B scores and that of the first two the more stable were the C's. From this he concluded that the counselor should pay more attention to extreme scores and that he should place more confidence in the stability of the low ones than in the high ones. He also noted that the B scores are more safely interpreted as an indication of future weakening rather than of the strengthening of an interest in a specific occupation.

In another study Powers (1954) reported an average Pearson r of .69 on the vocational scale for a group of 109 individuals tested in 1931 and again in 1941. McArthur (1954, 1955) studied 63 Harvard men who were tested first in 1939 and again in 1953, over a fourteen year interval. In general his results confirm those from other studies with the exception that the SVIB was of considerably less value in prediction when used with boys from private schools than with graduates of public schools. He suggests that his study and many others, mostly unreported, offer evidence that these private school graduates have values and needs that differ considerably from those of public school graduates. All of this research conducted with the SVIB suggests that the SVIB is a valid instrument when used with the groups for which it was developed. When compared to other psychometric devices such as intelligence tests, it holds up excellently and from the viewpoint of stability and prediction fares even better. There is no question that the Strong Vocational Interest Blank is one of the best and most useful instruments among those that the counselor uses.

The Strong Vocational Interest Blank for Women

This inventory is very similar in both its make-up and scoring to the men's form. It differs in that there are keys for a smaller number of occupations and of the non-occupational keys only the FM scale is present. A high score on this latter scale means femininity for women and a low score is a masculine score. This is the reverse of the MF scale for men. The use of this inventory has varied considerably from place to place. Strong recommends that women be tested only with the women's blank.

Since there is some evidence (Seder, 1940; Stewart, 1959) that the vocational interests of successful professional women do not differ greatly from those of successful men, women are administered the men's blank in some counseling bureaus. In other clinics women are administered both blanks, the men's blank with its additional scoring keys acting as a supplement to the women's blank. Most of the research done with the SVIB has been done with the men's blank. In the eyes of some coun-

selors this is a very important reason for using this form in preference
to the other.   There is a complicating factor in the women's blank in
that the housewife scale correlates high with nurse, elementary school
teacher, office worker, and stenographer, with these coefficients ranging
from .59 to .80.   Factor analyses of this form has lead Super (1949) to
conclude that there is a home-vs.-career factor present, most strongly
related to the housewife scale, negatively related to various careers for
women, and not found in similar factor analyses of the men's blank.   The
old problem of the woman's being a homebody or a career girl is involved
with the use of this form of the SVIB and this tends to lower the usefulness of the women's blank in appraising the vocational interests of women
when compared to effectiveness of the men's blank with males.

Limited attempts at pattern analysis have been made with the women's
SVIB.   In general there is a tendency for counselors to expect women
to score high on the scales in the middle of the profile (housewife, elementary teacher, office worker, stenographer-secretary, and business education teacher).   More important vocationally are clusters of scores
in the linguistic occupations toward the top of the profile, or clusters
of scores in the nonlinguistic occupations toward the bottom of the
profile.   Usually the women's SVIB is used with some other measure
of interests in order to get further clarification and a sort of cross-
validation.   *The Kuder Preference Record—Vocational* is one of these
other measures.

The Kuder Preference Record—Vocational; Form C

This interest inventory published by Science Research Associates is
made up of approximately 500 items representing all types of interests
arranged in a set of three or triad like the following:

1. A. Design bird houses ....( )
   B. Sell bird houses ....( )
   C. Live in bird houses ....( )

The clients goes through the inventory selecting from each three the one
liked most and the one liked least.   This provides six possible scoring
combinations for each triadic item.   Since some of the activities require
special training, the respondent is to assume ability to do any of the
listed activities.   In any case a choice must be made even when all are
liked or disliked equally.   Males and females use the same inventory
with different norms and profiles available for each sex.   There are two
forms of this edition of the inventory, CM in which the responses are
placed on an answer sheet for scoring with the IBM scoring machine
and CH which uses the pin-punch method of scoring.   In an attempt to
enhance the validity of the instrument, a list of words and phrases is

printed on the back of the direction page defining words and phrases that might be unfamiliar to the client. Appearing here are such words as "data," "psychologists," "erosion," "linoleum block," and the like.

Scores are reported for ten areas of human activities: Outdoor, Mechanical, Computational, Scientific, Persuasive, Artistic, Literary, Musical, Social Service, and Clerical. In addition to these there is a verification or V score which is acceptable when it is within the range of 38–44. If it is higher than 44, it means that the client has marked or punched too many answers, since the highest possible score is 44. When the V score falls between 33 and 37, this is considered to be within the doubtful range and questions should be asked to determine whether the respondent understood the directions, has difficulty in reading comprehension, answered the items carelessly, or actually has interests that are different from others. A score of 32 or less according to Kuder (1956) reflects a number of omissions or there is reason to doubt the value of the answers given. It is recommended that the inventory be readministered emphasizing the importance of following directions carefully.

The counselor will find the *Kuder* useful in describing *areas* or *fields* of general activity with two types of clients—the young individual who has made little or no decision about his vocational choice and the individual who has made a choice and wishes some means of verifying it. In this latter case cross-validation against the *SVIB* is often done in terms of scores on the *SVIB* group keys. Scoring of the inventory is very easy, so easy as a matter of fact that often the subject is allowed to score the answer sheet and to plot the profile on the blanks provided. In scoring the *Kuder*, the answer pad is opened and the number of pinholes appearing in small circles are counted for each key. These raw scores are then entered on the profile sheet. Of course, this method of scoring can be carried out only when the pin-punch answer sheet is used. Very conveniently, the filling out of the *Kuder* takes about one class period. The next period that the client has free can be spent in scoring and profiling the results.

Any score at the 75th centile or higher is taken as evidence of a significant interest in a particular area. The manual contains a list of suggested occupations for each of the areas of interest. These lists are arranged from the professional occupations down to the unskilled ones. Suppose that a boy has a high score on the Outdoor key. In the manual he will find suggested occupations which he may wish to use to find some additional information from a library of occupational information or some other occupational source. Frequently a client has two or more significant high scores. In this case there are suggested occupations for these combinations of interests also. These are limited and rather naïve suggestions which deal only with the meaning of high scores.

To take into account Fryer's suggestion of acceptance-rejection pat-

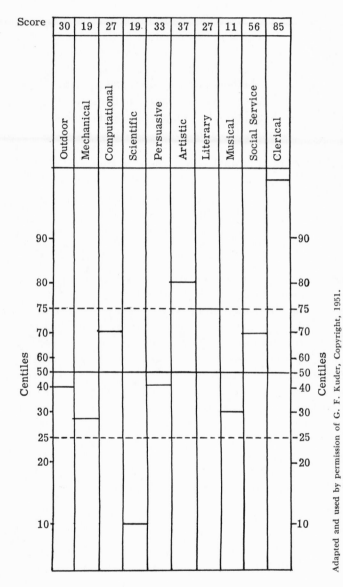

Score

| 30 | 19 | 27 | 19 | 33 | 37 | 27 | 11 | 56 | 85 |

Outdoor · Mechanical · Computational · Scientific · Persuasive · Artistic · Literary · Musical · Social Service · Clerical

Centiles

Fig. 10.3. **Kuder Preference Record, Vocational. Profile for a female.**

248

terns, the counselor should also pay especial attention to scores that are below the 25th centile. These are the so-called rejection scores and for an individual to obtain such a score it is necessary to mark items related to a particular area of vocational interest "dislike" every time that one of these items appears. A knowledge of what an individual dislikes is just as important as those things that are liked. These are interpreted in terms of patterns of high *and* low scores. An example of this is the tendency of engineers to score high on computational and scientific scales and to score low on the literary scale. Another example is the tendency for people in business contact work to score high on persuasive and low on scientific scales. The counselor will also find that there are individuals who have no significant high or low points. When the profile is made up of scores all of which are near the middle, probably the best conclusion is that the interests of the client are not yet developed and suggest a retest in a year or so. Kuder (1956) also suggests that rarely one may encounter an individual whose interests are equally balanced in all ten fields. Also he notes that a profile of no peaks may be that of an individual whose interests are in the field of personal service or manual labor. Figure 10.3 shows a Kuder Form C profile.

The development of this instrument was quite different from that of the *SVIB*. It may be recalled that Strong used criterion groups of successful individuals in different occupations. Items which separated these so-called successful individuals in one occupation from professional men-in-general went to make up the key for that specific occupation. In the *Kuder*, the author built items and then constructed keys on the basis of item analysis results. The first key that Kuder developed was a literary key. This was done merely on the basis of the logical appearance of the items. After scoring a group of papers with this key an item analysis was made. Those items which correlated significantly with the literary scores were kept for the literary key. These items that did not relate significantly with the literary key were further treated and analyzed until a series of almost pure scales was developed. As a result of the procedure described above there are ten scales which by construction are internally similar and not highly related to each other.

Research carried on with the *Kuder* since World War II has been considerable. A current edition of the manual lists well over 200 articles reporting such research. Any attempt to summarize these here would be pointless. That this inventory has both reliability and validity cannot be doubted in the light of many of these studies and in counseling experience with it. Studies have shown that the *Kuder* and *SVIB* administered to the same individuals frequently produce similar results. However, it might be noted that the *Kuder* has a reading level much lower than the *SVIB*—8.7 vs. 11.4 for the *SVIB* (Forbes and Cottle, 1953). It also, unlike the *SVIB*, is not geared to professional workers or the groups just below these. That is, it covers a much wider range of occupational activities. (It might be added that there is really no instrument that significantly separates the vocational interests of the semi-skilled and unskilled workers.) The *Kuder* then is very useful in dealing with high school and junior high school students. It can be used just when these young people are beginning to pay attention to work and their future. Over the high school years the instrument may be used again and again to measure growth and development in vocational interests. It is also useful with adults of limited intelligence or education who would have no use for the information covered by the *SVIB*. Form C of the *Kuder* is another of the counselor's most basic tools.

Form D of this inventory (Kuder, 1956, 1957) appeared in 1956. This differs from the previous editions in that separate scores for specific occupations are provided instead of the general area keys. At the present time scoring keys are available for a number of occupations. While Kuder has not defined success as Strong did, he apparently secured groups of successful individuals by asking persons from the membership rosters of the American Psychological Association, the American Academy of General Practice (for physicians), the American Institute of Electrical Engineers, and the like to complete the Form D blank as a criterion group.

The Occupational Interest Inventory (Lee-Thorpe)

This inventory (California Test Bureau) was produced in two forms, Intermediate for junior high school, and Advanced for high school students and adults. Part I of the inventory is made up of 240 paired items, each describing a vocational activity. The examinee selects the one of each pair that he prefers. From this part of the inventory, six field of interest scores are obtained—Personal-Social, Natural, Mechanical, Business, The Arts, and The Sciences. In addition to these a score for each of three types of interest is also obtained—Verbal, Manipulative, and Computational. Part II is made up of 30 items in sets of 3's, each set containing an activity that can be classified as being high, medium, or low in the hierarchy of vocational interests. This section produces a level of interest score. The inventory can be administered in less than a school period and is easy to score. Forbes and Cottle (1953) found the advanced form to have a reading difficulty level of 9.5.

This instrument has in the past been strongly and very adversely criticized for being put on the market with almost no validation studies provided. In the past few years some studies have appeared and the instrument now merits some consideration by the counselor. One study (Lindgren and Gilberg, 1955) consisted of a correlation of all keys on this with the conventionally scored occupational and non-occupational keys of the *SVIB*. In general for the occupational keys these correlations were what might be expected. Level of Interests on the Lee-Thorpe did not correlate significantly with Strong's OL key, but did with his IM key at the 1% level. In another study Roeber (1949) correlated scores on the *Lee-Thorpe* scales with those of the *Kuder, Form B*. This form differs from Form C in having no Outdoor key. Here again there were significant relationships among keys that one would expect to be measuring similar vocational interests. Downie observed this high similarity between Kuder and Lee-Thorpe when both are administered to clients at the university level.

The manual (Lee and Thorpe, 1956) contains other validation data. MacPhail (1954) showed very significant profiles for university students in three curricula—B.A., B.S. in Chemistry, and B.S. in Engineering. Congdon and Jervis (1958) analyzed the profiles of graduates in Agriculture, Liberal Arts-Verbal, Liberal Arts-Scientific, and Technology based upon scores obtained as freshmen 4 years earlier. The profiles for individuals in the four areas all differed significantly. The counselor may find this instrument a valuable adjunct to either the *Kuder* or the *SVIB*.

Another interest inventory released by the California Test Bureau is the *Picture Interest Inventory*. This one differs from all those previously discussed in that the client reacts to pictures instead of words. Part I consists of 53 triads of pictures each one depicting an individual performing a type of work. The client on the answer sheet marks the one that he likes most and the one that he likes least. Part II is made up of 30 similar pictures to which the respondent reacts individually on a "Like"-"Dislike" basis. The fields of interest measured are very similar to those measured by the Lee-Thorpe. In the manual the author (Weingarten, 1958) reports significant correlations with the scores of the different fields on his manual with corresponding scores on similar or related fields of the *SVIB*, *Kuder*, and *Lee-Thorpe*. It seems that such an inventory as this should remove the effects associated with a poor reading vocabulary on the evaluation of interests and become increasingly useful with the growing numbers of nonlinguistic clients. The author suggests that this inventory also removes the "halo effect" that is associated with words used to identify the professional vocations.

The *Study of Values*

This short scale of values or interests as they might be called consists of 45 items. The first 30 of these are pairs which are to be evaluated in terms of preference or no preference for one over the other. The last 15 items are each completed by 4 statements. These statements are to be ranked on the basis of appeal to the respondent. This instrument was constructed for college students and is usually so used. Forbes and Cottle (1953) showed that it had a reading difficulty level of 12.7, which makes it more difficult to read than all of the others discussed in this section, except possibly the *SVIB*.

This inventory is based upon the writings of Spranger (1928), in which he discusses the types of men based upon their personalities, these being to a great part reflections of their interests and vocational activities. His types are: the *Theoretical*, dominant interest is the discovery of truth (scientific); the *Economic*, characteristically interested in that which is useful; the *Aesthetic*, seeing the highest value in form and harmony (artistic); the *Social*, love of people (social service or welfare); the *Political*, interested primarily in power; and the *Religious*, whose highest value is unity, seeking to comprehend the cosmos as a whole.   Naturally many men are mixtures of these types.

The counselor may find this inventory useful with university students when used with one of the other inventories. Research shows that it separates students in different curricula from each other. It can be used then in exploring the different fields of interests and also in educational counseling in selecting a curriculum in line with the individual's interests. Much research has been carried out both with this revision (see Alport, *et al.*, 1951) and the original, attesting to the instrument's validity. This research has been summarized by Dukes (1955).

The Brainard Occupational Preference Inventory (Form R)

This inventory, published by The Psychological Corporation, is intended for the educational-vocational counseling of individuals from grade 8 to adulthood. The inventory is relatively short, consisting of 120 items and requiring about 30 minutes for administration. There are 20 items covering each of the following fields: commercial, mechanical, professional, aesthetic, and scientific. The 6th field consists of agriculture for males and professional and personal service for females. The 20 items in each field are distributed among 4 sub-fields. For example, the commercial field consists of 5 items each, covering accounting, clerical work, selling, and business management. One tends to wonder about the reliability and validity of such scales.

Centile norms are presented for boys and girls in grades eight through twelve. Reliabilities run from the .70's to the .90's for the various fields at different grade levels. Correlations are presented between *Brainard* scores and *Kuder* scores and the usual expected positive and negative relationships among scales are in evidence. Other than this, there is very little evidence of validity, and any counselor using this inventory would have to develop validity or demonstrate it in his local situation.

Scoring is relatively simple, being done by hand or by machine, the client's responses being placed on IBM answer sheets. While this edition is an improvement over earlier forms of the inventories, much validity data still must appear before the counselor can use the inventory with the confidence with which some of those previously discussed may be used.

SUMMARY

The counselor considering evidence of a client's interests is often so engrossed with the results obtained from vocational interest inventories that the more diversified evidence of total client interests may be overlooked. Admittedly, the evidence secured from vocational interest inventories can be derived in no other fashion, especially the comparison with the interests of professional persons furnished by the two *SVIB* blanks. At the same time, this information must be synthesized with the general picture of linguistic or nonlinguistic interests developed from the client's stated interests, information about hobbies and other leisure activities, school classwork and extra-class activities, work experience, and family background. The non-test information comes from autobiographies, personal data forms, themes, school records, observation, and the initial interview which were discussed in previous chapters. Synthesis of these data with those about general interests secured from check lists, questionnaires, and some measures of achievement, such as the *Michigan Vocabulary Profile Test*, will provide a much more valid and stable pattern of the general interests of a given client.

When vocational interest inventories are used they should be carefully chosen in terms of client needs, such as stated vocational plans and norms appropriate for the age and group in which the client will be functioning. It is absurd to use the *SVIB* with high school freshmen, particularly with those who will never seek professional level occupations. The choice of these inventories should also encompass the characteristics considered in selecting any test. Unless data on validity and reliability are available, the test should only be used experimentally until these have been provided by the publisher. Research published on a given test should be studied and evaluated to seek further evidence of the usefulness of that inventory.

There are unique characteristics of a given test which may affect its desirability, such as the high cost of scoring of *SVIB* answer sheets. This comes to about a dollar per individual. Different inventories may be chosen according to the specific needs of groups or individuals. A class exploring the world of work and their own vocational interests might best take and score the *Kuder* to see what it shows about them.

Keep in mind that these vocational interest inventories, although considered among the best constructed and most useful of psychometric instruments, are still paper and pencil tests and do have limitations. That they can be falsified or distorted, there is no doubt. Many studies have been made in which students have been asked to complete an inventory from the viewpoint of a certain vocation or interest (for example, see

Longstaff, 1948). This points out that use of these vocational interest inventories in selection and employment programs may be highly questionable without adequate safeguards. Since the alert individual can produce the interest profile that is desired, probably these inventories should be used only as clinical instruments in vocational counseling. There does not seem to be any really valid reason why a client would desire to fake the results of these inventories when that client understands and accepts the purposes and goals of the *voluntary* counseling situation. Where counseling is *required,* scores on interest inventories can take on a different meaning.

REFERENCES

Allport, G. W., P. E. Vernon, and G. Lindzey. *Study of Values,* Revised Edition. Boston: Houghton Mifflin Company, 1951.

Barnett, G. J., I. Handelsman, L. H. Stewart, and D. E. Super. The occupational level scale as a measure of drive. *Psychol. Monogr.,* 1952, *66,* No. 10 (Whole No. 342), 1–37.

Barnett, G. J., L. H. Stewart, and D. E. Super. Level of occupational interest: deadweight or dynamism? *Educ. Psychol. Measmt.,* 1953, *13,* 193–208.

Bordin, E. S. A theory of vocational interest as dynamic phenomena. *Educ. Psychol. Measmt.,* 1943, *3,* 49–65.

Carter, H. D. The development of vocational attitudes. *J. Consult. Psychol.,* 1940, *4,* 185–191.

Congdon, R. G., and F. M. Jervis. A different approach to interest profiles. *J. Counsel. Psychol.,* 1958, *5,* 50–55.

Cottle, W. C. A factorial study of the Multiphasic, Strong, Kuder and Bell Inventories using a population of adult males. *Psychometrika,* 1950, *15,* 25–47.

Cronbach, L. J., and G. C. Gleser. Assessing similarity between profiles. *Psychol. Bull.,* 1953, *50,* 456–473.

Darley, J. G. *Clinical aspects and interpretation of the Strong Vocational Interest Blank.* New York: The Psychological Corporation, 1941.

Darley, J. G., and T. Hagenah. *Vocational interest measurement.* Minneapolis: University of Minnesota Press, 1955.

Dukes, W. F. Psychological study of values. *Psychol. Bull.,* 1955, *52,* 24–50.

Forbes, F. W., and W. C. Cottle. A new method for determining readability of standardized tests. *J. Appl. Psychol.,* 1953, *37,* 185–190.

Fryer, D. *The measurement of interests in relation to human adjustment.* New York: Henry Holt and Company, 1931.

Ginzberg, E., S. W. Ginsburg, S. Axelrad, and J. L. Herma. *Occupational choice: an approach to a general theory.* New York: Columbia University Press, 1951.

Gustad, J. W. Academic achievement and Strong occupational level scores. *J. Appl. Psychol.,* 1952, *36,* 75–78.

——. Vocational interests and socio-economic status. *J. Appl. Psychol.*, 1954, *38*, 336–338.

Hahn, M. E. and M. S. MacLean. *Counseling Psychology.* New York: McGraw-Hill Book Company, Inc., 1955.

Kendall, W. E. The Occupational level scale of the Strong Vocational Interest Blank. *J. Appl. Psychol.*, 1947, *31*, 283–288.

King, L. A. Factors associated with vocational interests profile stability. *J. Appl. Psychol.*, 1958, *42*, 261–264.

Kitson, H. D. Creating vocational interests. *Occupations*, 1942, *20*, 567–571.

Kuder, G. F. *Kuder Preference Record—Occupational, Form D.* Chicago: Science Research Associates, 1956.

——. *Kuder Preference Record—Vocational, Form C.* Chicago: Science Research Associates, 1956.

——. A comparative study of some methods of developing occupational keys. *Educ. Psychol. Measmt.*, 1957, *17*, 105–114.

Lee, E. A., and L. P. Thorpe. *Occupational Interest Inventory.* Los Angeles: California Test Bureau, 1956.

Longstaff, H. P. Fakability on the Strong Interest Blank and the Kuder Preference Record. *J. Appl. Psychol.*, 1948, *32*, 360–369.

Lindgren, H. C., and R. L. Gilberg. Interpreting occupational interest: the relationship between the Lee-Thorpe Occupational Interest Inventory and the Strong Vocational Blank for Men. *Cal. J. Ed. Res.*, 1955, *6*, 15–21.

MacPhail, A. H. Interest patterns for certain degree groups on the Lee-Thorpe Occupational Interest Inventory. *J. Appl. Psychol.*, 1954, *38*, 164–166.

McArthur, C. Long-term validity of the Strong interest test in two subcultures. *J. Appl. Psychol.*, 1954, *38*, 346–353.

——, and L. B. Stevens. Validation of expressed interests as compared with inventoried interests: a fourteen year follow-up. *J. Appl. Psychol.*, 1955, *39*, 184–189.

Ostrom, S. R. The OL Key of the Strong test and drive at the twelfth grade level. *J. Appl. Psychol.*, 1949, *33*, 240–248.

——. The OL Key of the Strong Vocational Interest Blank for Men and scholastic success at the freshman level. *J. Appl. Psychol.*, 1949, *33*, 51–54.

Powers, Mabel H. *A longitudinal study of vocational interests during the depression years.* Ph.D. dissertation, University of Minnesota, 1954.

Rhodes, G. S. *An investigation of response sets in the Strong Vocational Interest Blank for Men and response set effects on scores of selected SVIB scales.* Unpublished Ed.D. Dissertation, University of Kansas, 1956.

Roeber, E. C. The relationship between parts of the Kuder Preference Record and parts of the Lee-Thorpe Occupational Interest Inventory. *J. Ed. Res.*, 1949, *42*, 598–608.

Seder, M. A.   The vocational interests of professional women.   *J. Appl. Psychol.*, 1940, *24*, 130–143, 265–272.

Smith, E. R., and R. W. Tyler.   *Appraising and recording student progress.*   New York: Harper & Brothers, 1942.

Stewart, L. H.   Interest patterns of a group of high-ability, high-achieving students.   *J. Couns. Psychol.*, 1959, *6*, 132–139.

Stordhal, K. E.   Permanence of interests and interest maturity.   *J. Appl. Psychol.*, 1954, *38*, 339–340.

———.   Permanence of Strong Vocational Interest Blank scores.   *J. Appl., Psychol.*, 1954, *38*, 423–427.

Stranger, E.   *Types of men.*   New York: Stechert, 1928.

Strong, E. K.   *Vocational Interest Blank for Men.*   Palto Alto, Cal.: Stanford University Press, 1945.

———.   *Vocational interests 18 years after college.*   Minneapolis: University of Minnesota Press, 1955.

———.   *Vocational interests of men and women.*   Palo Alto, Cal.: Stanford University Press, 1943.

———.   Validity of occupational choice.   *Educ. Psychol. Measmt.*, 1953, *13*, 110–121.

———.   *Strong Vocational Blank—Manual.*   Palo Alto, Cal.: Counseling Psychologists Press, 1959.

Super, D. E.   *Appraising Vocational Fitness.*   New York: Harper & Brothers, 1949.

———.   A theory of vocational development.   *Amer. Psychologist*, 1953, *8*, 185–190.

Trinkhaus, W. K.   The permanence of vocational interests of college freshmen.   *Educ. Psychol. Measmt.*, 1954, *14*, 641–646.

U. S. Department of Labor, Bureau of Employment Security (USES).   *Estimates of Worker Trait Requirements for 4000 Jobs.*   Washington, D.C.: U. S. Government Printing Office, 1956.

Weingarten, K. P.   *Picture Interest Inventory.*   Los Angeles: California Test Bureau, 1958.

11

Evaluation of other personal

data

ONE PART OF THE PROCESS OF COUNSELING IS HELPING A CLIENT GET TO know how he feels about himself and various aspects of his environment. This is the affective or emotional part of the psychological triumvirate of cognition, motivation, and affect. The previous two chapters have reviewed the various ways of helping a client collect and evaluate data about aptitudes and abilities, and about interests. This present chapter will review the various remaining tools and techniques the counselor will use to evaluate aspects of client personality prior to and during counseling interviews.

Several of these techniques for the evaluation of social and emotional adjustment have already been described. Chapter 2 contained a discussion of personal documents and their use in counseling. Chapter 2 also discussed the use of sociometric techniques as methods of identifying the individual who has emotional or adjustment problems. In Chapter 3 there was a discussion of observational techniques including the use of anecdotal records and rating scales.

In this chapter, attention will be paid to two other aspects of the appraisal of client personality—adjustment and attitudes. The review for the counselor here will cover, first, the structured personality or adjustment inventories. The use of these instruments results in scores for various named components of personality. They usually are used to describe what kind of behavior occurs, but do not tell *why* it occurs. The latter part of this chapter will present check lists, or problem check lists, followed by the so-called projective techniques or the unstructured and semistructured instruments used in studying adjustment. The chapter will conclude with a discussion of attitudes and their importance in counseling. These latter topics are ways of finding out why a client behaves in a certain fashion.

THE NATURE OF ADJUSTMENT

In general it may be said that personality inventories measure that which is very conveniently referred to as adjustment. What is meant by this term *adjustment*? What problems arise from the consideration and use of the term? Psychologically, adjustment is the process that an individual goes through when giving varied response patterns to changes in environment. All active, living organisms are constantly making adjustments to various aspects of their physical, social, and mental environment. As a result of the adjustment processes, tension is reduced and the so-called "normal" condition results.

There seems to be little disagreement as to what adjustment is. Values become associated with the adjustment process and descriptions of the well-adjusted individual result. This well-adjusted individual receives various descriptions depending on who is doing the describing. The description may be the relatively consistent individual behaviorally, one who controls emotional behavior, conforms to the mores of the group, becomes increasingly more mature, adapts to reality situations, and the like (see Tindall, 1955). All of this is fine in describing some sort of an ideal or imaginary man, but actually, adjustment is relative to the society in which an individual resides and the time when the individual lives in that culture. What is considered a desirable form of adjustment in one culture or cultural subgroup may be considered an illegal practice in another. Any book on cultural anthropology is filled with examples of this when the social practices of the primitive societies are described. Even within one culture, practices and mores are in a constant state of change. A consideration of the attitudes toward the use of tobacco and alcohol, the role of women, and the role of religion in daily living will point this out. It is difficult to state exactly what "normal" behavior is, if, indeed, it exists at all. "Normal" may be defined here as within the range of socially acceptable behavior at a given time.

Another aspect of adjustment is that it is quite an individual matter. What is considered to be good adjustment for one individual may be the worst sort of adjustment for another. It is important that the counselor know how the client feels about adjustment problems. If certain aspects of behavior seem unimportant to the individual, even if they are atypical as measured by a personality inventory or by other group norms, then it follows that the counselor should not make issues of them. It is only when these aspects of behavior become important to the individual that there are problems. Since desirable adjustment is relative and individual, it is questionable whether the norms that accompany many of the adjustment inventories are of any value. This is particularly true when the inventory was administered six months or more previous to the interview.

While much has been written on desirable adjustment by teachers and psychologists in the past several decades, it does not follow that all such workers feel that an attempt should be made to force all into a common mold in respect to adjustment. There is a growing feeling that much of this is so much nonsense; the point is made by Lindner (1952) that real progress in human affairs often comes about from the actions of those individuals who differ in their behavior from the group and its mores. Many famous scientists of the past are excellent examples of this. The inference from Lindner's statements would be that emphasis on *good adjustment for all* would lead to a nation of mediocrity and ensuing dullness.

HISTORY OF PERSONALITY APPRAISAL

Personality or adjustment has been studied and evaluated since early times when man first began to reflect upon himself and his world. The ancients in the Near East related the movements and locations of the stars and planets to human personality. The ancient Greeks classified men into types on the bases of the different colored "biles" and "humors." Where the analysis of behavior through the use of palmistry and physiognomy arose is difficult to tell. These also go back to primitive times. Body type has long been associated with personality types as witnessed by the clichés such as the jolly fat man, the quick-tempered redhead, or by the following from Shakespeare: "Let me have men about me that are fat; sleek-headed men and such as sleep o'nights; yond' Cassius has a lean and hungry look; . . . such men are dangerous." (*Julius Caesar*, Act I, Sc. II.) Even today there are still studies going on in which body size and shape is related to aspects of adjustment (see Sheldon, 1942). In the Eighteenth Century phrenology made its appearance. The use of handwriting (graphology) to evaluate personality is most widely used today by nonprofessional individuals. So for over 2,000 years many devices were developed in an attempt to describe man's personality and those factors that affect it. It is interesting to note that practically all of these old and ancient techniques are still in use today and probably will continue to be because of the difficulty of measuring and defining personality and adjustment in precise terms.

Late in the Nineteenth Century and at the beginning of the current one, attempts were made to measure personality and adjustment "scientifically." Among the first of these techniques to appear were the free-association techniques of Jung. In this method, words are presented to the client and he is told to respond to the stimulus with the first word or phrase that comes into his head. The nature of the response, whether common to a group or unique to the individual, speed of response, and the like were analyzed. During World War I, as was previously noted, psychometric evaluations were made on a very large group of men for the first time.   In an attempt to screen out the misfits to prevent their induction into the military service, R. S. Woodworth constructed his *Personal Data Sheet*.   This was the first personality inventory and it differed little in make-up, content, and types of responses used in filling it out from many that are used today.   In this inventory, Woodworth attempted to put a psychiatric interview onto a piece of paper to save the time of having every inductee examined by a psychiatrist.   After the war, this and similar inventories were used in educational and business situations. The results obtained with them were disappointing when compared to those for intelligence as measured by the *Army Alpha* which was developed at the same time.   Reliability and validity were difficult to ascertain because of the nature of the instruments and the variables.   Since then the acceptance and use of these adjustment inventories has been of a rather varied nature.   Periods of rejection have been followed by periods of acceptance when a new "star" appeared on the horizon.   Today as shall be pointed out later there are many of these available for use by the counselor.

In 1921, another technique appeared that was to create a revolution in the appraisal of personality, this being Rorschach's *Ink-Blot Test*. This date may be considered as the real beginning of the projective or unstructured phase in the measurement of adjustment.   The activities of psychologists in World War II and in the decade after this war resulted in much research on the *Rorschach* and also in the development of other projective techniques that will be discussed later.

STRUCTURED PERSONALITY INVENTORIES

A personality inventory consists of from 100 to 500 or more of items like these:

Do you daydream frequently?

Do you often have dizzy spells?

Do you always tell the truth?

Do you like the opposite sex?

Usually the client responds to the items by marking them "*Yes*" (Y), "*No*" (N), or (?) "*can not tell.*"   On several of them there are but two choices, "*Yes*" or "*No.*"   Most of these inventories are of such a length that they can easily be completed in an hour when the examinee operates at normal speed and responds to the items as they immediately strike him rather than giving thought to each item.   Typically scores are presented for a series of traits or characteristics.   Profiles are commonly used in reporting the results of these inventories.   In using the inventories it is assumed that personality may be broken down into traits and that these traits have variability, that is, vary in amount possessed from individual to individual. It is further assumed that there is a certain amount of stability of these traits within the individual. Actually traits may be classified as *charcter* traits, which are fairly stable, and *mood* traits, which fluctuate from time to time.

The user of a personality inventory should seriously consider the following every time such a document is used:

1. *Are the responses of this individual to the items candid?*
   Getting sincere or candid responses is one of the major problems with the use of these inventories. The nature of the items is not disguised and any but the extremely dull person has no trouble in figuring out what the item is attempting to measure. In any society there are certain standards that are set up relating to behavior. Most individuals know what these are. In responding to the items on the inventory, examinees often offer the responses that they feel are demanded by their society, rather than revealing their own feelings and behavior. Frequently the examinee may see himself differently from the way others do. Thus, a perfectly candid response may be at variance with societal evaluations. In addition there is the problem that the examinee does not know who is going to have access to the results and thus marks the inventory in a defensive manner without being really aware of doing so. Many of the items are of a very personal nature or reflect an indication of antisocial behavior. This may produce a response set in the individual which causes these items to be answered in an erroneous fashion. These various response sets have been explored by factor analytic methods by Broen and Wirt (1958). They found in examining eleven kinds of response sets that three factors accounted for the common variance among these response sets. These three factors they described as (1) a tendency to agree with the item versus denial, evasiveness, or indecision; (2) a tendency to disagree with assertions versus evading the questions; and (3) a tendency to list or check many adjectives describing behavior. This last factor Broen and Wirt feel may be most characteristic of adolescence. When he has no idea who is going to see his paper, an examinee thinks twice before he answers such questions candidly. Part of these effects can be dissipated if the counselor explains that the chief interest is in scores and not in item responses. It helps also if the counselor has established good rapport prior to testing and the examinee knows the results are a confidential matter.

2. *Does the individual understand the questions and does he understand himself to the extent that he has insight into his own behavior so that he could mark the inventory candidly if he so desired?*
   Research like that of Forbes and Cottle (1953) has shown the relative readability indices for the more widely used of these inventories. In general, the vocabulary level of these when compared with interest inventories and intelligence tests tends to be rather low, fifth and sixth grade level being typical. Even at that there are many individuals in any high school who will find the words on some of these inventories unknown to them. A perusal of the catalogs of the different test publishers will show that one can obtain inventories of this type for use in the primary grades. The writers feel that children at that level of development are in no position to answer these inventories, especially when, as in some cases, each

of the items has to be read to the child individually. The writers further feel that any of these inventories used below grade 13 should only be used in a one-to-one testing situation after careful explanation of the purpose to which the scores will be put.

3. *What exactly do the results that have been obtained mean?*
It was previously noted that there was no average type of behavior that is considered desirable for all. Actually the results are meaningless unless it is ascertained how the client feels about his behavior. There is a rather old inventory that gets at this problem. This is the *Minnesota Inventory of Social Attitudes,* composed of two parts, *Preference* (P) and *Behavior* (B), and published by The Psychological Corporation. The idea behind this instrument is that there is no adjustment problem when scores on the two parts are approximately at the same level. For example, in Figure 11.1, Individual A is low in preference and low in behavior, no real prob-

SCORES ON MINNESOTA INVENTORY OF SOCIAL ATTITUDES

	5th %ile	50th %ile	95th %ile
Social Preference	A B	C D	E
Social Behavior	A D	C	B E

Fig. 11.1. Scores of individuals *A, B, C, D,* and *E* on the Minnesota Inventory of Social Attitudes.

lem exists as long as he is doing that which he is contented to do. He appears to have no great interest in getting involved in social activities and his behavior score seems to show that he does not engage in many social activities. He has no problem until he discovers girls. On the other hand, consider Individual D who has a high preference score and a very low behavior score. He would like to do many things, yet he does very little and problems arise. Such a pattern frequently characterizes a college freshman coming from a small town to a large university campus. Individual C has a pattern like that found with salespersons in a store, while the pattern of Individual E is like that of the more aggressive door-to-door salesman. The pattern shown for Individual B of high behavior and low preference may be indicating withdrawal tendencies and deserves rather careful investigation by the counselor for further evidence of adjustment problems. Individuals A and E may also be exhibiting tendencies toward abnormal behavior which should be checked carefully by the counselor.

4. *What is the reliability of these inventories?*
In general the reliability of these instruments tends to run in the .80's, just slightly lower than the reliability coefficients for intelligence and achievement tests. These coefficients, however, refer to the entire score made with the instrument. As has been pointed out, usually the total score is broken down into a dozen or more sub-scores. In some cases the number of items in one of these subtests may be as small as eight.

Reliability, being a function of the length of a scale, is apt to be quite low in such situations. Then it follows that, although the entire scale may have acceptable reliability, the sub-scales do not. This makes the use of many of the so-called diagnostic profiles quite questionable. Pauline Pepinsky's discussion of reliability of sociometric devices (1949) applies to these inventories also. She points out that part of the problem is created because each measurement is really of a changed individual and this tends to reduce reliabilities. Even reliabilities computed from a single administration are not too satisfactory. Most one-test reliabilities assume the items are of the same category and value. In personality inventories this assumption is highly questionable.

5. *What is the validity of the inventory?*
   As with all instruments of appraisal, it is important that criteria be used in determining the validity of the instrument. One of the major problems with adjustment inventories is that of obtaining adequate criteria against which to validate. Those that are most frequently used are the ratings of teachers, psychologists, psychiatrists, or supervisors in an industrial setting. It so happens that the reliability and validity of many of these ratings may be low as was pointed out in Chapter 3. Other aspects of validity were discussed in 1 and 2 above. Finally it may be added that the use or misuse of these has a lot to do with validity. When these instruments are kept in the clinic or counseling part of the agency or used as screening devices to pick out those who are emotionally disturbed or are used with an individual client after rapport has been established and the client understands how the proper completion of the inventory will contribute to helping solve the problems, then the results may be quite valid. However, these inventories are widely used in industry both in the hiring of personnel and in the promotion of employees within the plant. Since there is no question that the results of these can be falsified, the results are questionable and this is really a misuse of these inventories. Whyte (1956) in *The Organization Man* suggests that, when asked for comments about the world, the respondent give the most conventional, run-of-the-mill, pedestrian answer. He further states that when one is in any doubt about the most desirable answer to any item the respondent reflect an attitude which includes that he loves both his father and his mother, but his father a little bit more, that he never worries much about anything, that he does not care much about books or music, and that he loves his family, but does not let them or their problems interfere with the work of the company. The psychological literature has much research related to the validity of these instruments. Summaries are found in Ellis (1946, 1953), and Ellis and Conrad (1948). It should be noted, however, that some of the studies quoted by Ellis may have questionable experimental designs and may not be reflecting the real validity and reliability of the inventories.

The builders of the newer inventories have attempted to improve the validity of their instruments by the use of different item types, using different methods of response, or by establishing so-called validation keys. Certain of these improvements will be mentioned when particular inventories are discussed. In the pages that follow these inventories will be described under the heading of the older, conventional types, factorial inventories, and the newer approaches using item analysis techniques with criterion groups and attempts to control response set.

THE OLD-TYPE INVENTORIES

In respect to the types of items included in these inventories and to the types of responses used, these inventories are very similar to the original Woodworth *Personal Data Sheet*. Two publications of the Stanford University Press are excellent examples of this type. They are the *Bernreuter Personality Inventory* and the *Bell Adjustment Inventory*. The first of these, the *Bernreuter,* is made up of 125 questions which are responded to on a *Yes-No?* scale. Item responses are weighted, increasing both the time and complexity of scoring. Four traits are purportedly measured—neuroticism, self-sufficiency, introversion, and dominance. Flanagan (1935) factor-analyzed the scale and reduced it to two factors— self-confidence and solitariness. It should be noted here that such a factor analysis holds only for the sample on which it was computed and may not hold for other population samples unless it can be demonstrated they are from a similar population.

The *Bell Adjustment Inventory* consists of two forms, a student form and an adult form. The first of these is made up of 140 items which when completed result in four scores—health, home, social, and emotional adjustment. The adult form has an additional scale measuring vocational adjustment. It is possible through use and research to develop added meaning to these scores by identifying patterns of scores connected with various traits. However, it would appear more profitable to devote such research to newer types of inventories. In contrast to the *Bernreuter,* the *Bell* is very easily scored as the item responses are not weighted. At the present time the *Bell* and *Bernreuter* should be used for no more than screening devices.

A much newer series of inventories than the above is the *California Tests of Personality,* issued by the California Test Bureau. The current revision (1953) consists of two forms that cover five different levels: primary, elementary, intermediate, secondary (grades 9 through college), and adult. Each of these inventories is divided into two parts, one which measures "self-adjustment" and the other, "social adjustment." Scores for both of these parts, a total score, and a score for each of six components making up the two sub-tests are obtained. There are 180 items on the adult scale, 15 items being allocated to each of these 12 different traits. On the lower forms of the inventory the number of items on the different sub-tests decreases. Administering, completing, and scoring the inventory are each easy and simple. There is one characteristic of the items on this inventory that separates them from that of many of the other inventories and this is that the items consistently ask the examinee how he feels about this or that as opposed to the other approach which asks whether one does or does not do certain things. Some clinicians consider the responses to individual items very valid and meaningful in themselves even though there may be questionable validity to the total score. The same publishers also issue the *Mental Health Analysis* of similar format in four levels including from grade four through adulthood. The two major breakdowns of the scores are into *Assets* and *Liabilities*. The writers feel these two inventories are more useful as *individual* tests with persons at the elementary school level after proper rapport has been established with examinee *and* parents, but of very limited value in the primary grades.

FACTORIAL INVENTORIES

Certain psychologists have developed personality inventories as a result of factor analyzing existing inventories, using items of their own making, or a combination of both. Guilford has produced a whole series of such inventories, the current edition of which is known as the *Guilford-Zimmerman Temperament Survey* (issued by the Sheridan Supply Co.). Thurstone similarly produced his *Temperament Schedule* (Science Research). R. B. Cattell on the basis of his factorial investigation produced a 16-factor personality inventory. Workers at the University of Minnesota have developed the *Minnesota Personality Scale* (The Psychological Corporation) which appraises 5 different personality factors. One of these factorial inventories will be described in detail.

The *Guilford-Zimmerman Temperament Survey* consists of 300 items that measure 10 traits. These are listed below with several terms under each to give an indication of the nature of the trait:

G—*General Activity.* Energy, vitality, enthusiasm vs. slowness of action, and inefficiency.

R—*Restraint.* Serious-mindedness, persistence, self-control vs. carefree, excitement-loving, impulsive.

A—*Ascendance.* Self-defense, persuading others, bluffing, leadership vs. submissiveness, hesitation in speaking, and avoiding conspicuousness.

S—*Sociability.* Many friends and acquaintances, liking social activities and contacts vs. few friends and acquaintances, shyness, dislike of social activities.

E—*Emotional Stability.* Evenness of moods, interest, and energy, optimism, cheerfulness vs. fluctuation of moods, pessimism, gloominess.

O—*Objectivity.* Being "thick-skinned" vs. hypersensitiveness, suspiciousness, self-centeredness.

F—*Friendliness.* Toleration of hostile action, acceptance of dominance, and respect for others vs. belligerence, hostility, resistance to domination and contempt for others.

T—*Thoughtfulness.* Reflectiveness, interest in thinking, mental poise, observation of self vs. interest in overt activity, and mental disconcertedness.

P—*Personal Relations.*   Tolerance of people and faith in social institutions vs. faultfinding habits, suspiciousness of others and self pity.

M—*Masculinity.*   Interest in masculine activities and vocations, hardboiled vs. interest in feminine activities and vocations, easily disgusted, sympathetic, romantic interests, great interest in clothes and styles.

The items on this inventory are all stated in the affirmative rather than in question form and they all use the second-person pronoun.   Guilford feels that the use of the direct statement makes possible more simple and direct ideas.   Also the avoidance of the first person singular would make the items seem less personal to the examinee and less like a cross-examination.   Both, he feels, should increase the validity of the responses.   Items are responded to on a "*Yes*," "*?*," and "*No*" scale.   The nature of these items is such that they may be used with high school students with little fear of repercussions, if proper precautions are taken.   In general this is a well-made inventory, useful with both high school and college youth.

It is easy to administer, score, and profile.   The profile has positive traits at the top and negative traits at the bottom.   One way of spotting forged or falsified profiles is to note whether most of the scores are a standard deviation or more above the mean.   Such a "good boy or good girl" profile usually indicates the person who is trying to fake a good score.   Jacobs and Schloff (1955) have suggested falsification scales for the *GZTS*, but these do not seem any more effective than the observation of preponderance of high scores just suggested.   More than 3 items left unanswered among the 30 in each scale tend to invalidate that scale.   However, the counselor can make a tentative interpretation of the scale by indicating the band of raw scores within which the actual score would be.   Items scored on any scale only act to raise the score.   Therefore, the actual score, if all items had been answered, would be between the obtained score and a score indicated by adding the omitted items to the obtained score.   Such a procedure has the advantage of allowing some interpretation of scores and still indicating that the obtained score represents a band rather than a pinpoint on a scale.   This inventory, like those discussed previously, is probably best used as a screening device roughly to identify traits unique to a given individual as contrasted to others and to get a preliminary measure of ability to relate to others.

OTHER TYPES OF INVENTORIES

The Minnesota Multiphasic Personality Inventory

This inventory, the *MMPI* as it is usually called, is published by The Psychological Corporation.   It was constructed as a screening instrument to aid physicians in the identification of abnormal emotional states in order that they might make referrals to a psychiatrist.   Items on it were obtained from earlier inventories, texts, and forms used in psychiatric examinations. Items are responded to on a "True," "False," or "Cannot say (?)" basis. For most scales, items were chosen on the basis of their ability to produce differing responses between a psychiatrically diagnosed criterion group and a normal group without history of psychological abnormalities. The items are scored in the direction of abnormal responses. Except for three scales (the K-scale, Mf, and Si, social introversion), there was no attempt to attach meaning to low scores. Actually there are two forms of the inventory, an earlier one consisting of 550 cards which the examinee separates into three piles as he responds to the items and a later booklet form made up of 566 items answered on the conventional IBM answer sheet. There are other adaptations such as a shortened form made up of the first 366 items plus any K-scale or Si-scale items beyond item 366, and an edition in Braille.

Scores are reported using standard T-scores with a mean of 50 and a standard deviation of 10. Results are plotted on a profile sheet. Interpretation consists of analyses of these profiles or patterns. To assist with this Hathaway and Meehl (1951) have produced an atlas containing a large number of coded profiles and brief case histories of almost a thousand patients arranged according to similarity of profile. This atlas is used as an aid in the interpretation of the profile of the client.

Scales on this inventory are classified into two types: validity scales and clinical scales. The validity scales are the result of the concerns of psychologists in trying to get valid responses with these instruments and of the numerous studies showing the fakability of such inventories. The four *validity* scales are:

1. *Cannot say* (?). This is the total number of items placed in the *"cannot say"* category. The manual (Hathaway and McKinley, 1945) states that high ? scores (100 or more) invalidate the test, and that scores between 70 and 100 indicate that the individual's actual scores would deviate even more if he had not used the question category so freely in completing the inventory. Actual use of the booklet form produces few unanswered items.

2. *Lie scale* (L). The purpose of this scale is to pick out those individuals who attempt to falsify their score by selecting responses that appear socially or morally desirable. A high lie score indicates that the true value of the other scales may actually be higher than indicated by the obtained scores. This scale, together with the K-scale, tends to identify various response sets.

3. *Validity scale* (F). This scale is used to determine if the inventory was taken and scored properly. Originally high scores were taken to indicate that the subject was careless, did not understand the items, or that scoring and recording errors were made. Later research showed that a high score on this scale was identified with a psychosis or deliberate faking.

4. *Correction scale* (K). This scale is referred to as a "suppressor" meaning that it is supposed to increase the effectiveness of the clinical scales in diagnostic work. There is little evidence outside of the statements of the authors that this scale performs this function. (See Cottle, 1953.) A score on the K-scale by itself, when high, may indicate the defensive person trying to appear normal and a low score a self-critical individual or an individual trying to make himself appear abnormal. The most recent profile for the test only accounts for the effect of high scores (defensiveness) on K, and "corrects" selected scales for the effects of such defensiveness.

Below a brief description of the 10 basic *clinical* scales is given.

1. *Hypochrondriasis* (Hs). A deviant high score indicates abnormal amount of concern over bodily functions. A T-score between 60 and 70 indicates the person who is somewhat more concerned about physical symptoms than most people but who may not necessarily be "abnormal" in this respect.

2. *Depression* (D). A high score on this scale indicates poor morale and feelings of uselessness and pessimism when it is the single high score. When it appears high along with other variables, the different patterns indicate various psychological states. The most common one is a high score on D and Pt which identifies the individual under more than usual psychological tension. The height of these two scores is usually an indication of the degree of tension the individual feels.

3. *Hysteria* (Hy). A subject with a high Hy score is considered to be like patients with various types of hysteria symptoms. A T-score between 60 and 70 may be reflecting the person who tends to "clutch" in pressure situations and who lacks self-confidence.

4. *Psychopathic deviate* (Pd). A high score on this scale according to the manual indicates an individual with an absence of deep emotional response, an inability to profit by experience, and a disregard of social customs. A T-score between 60–70 indicates the individual who dislikes rules and regulations and having to conform. This may be evidenced in behavior, however, by refusal to conform (rebellion) or by conformance accompanied by covert resentment.

5. *Masculinity-femininity* (Mf). This scale measures the tendency for an individual to have the basic interest pattern of the opposite sex. Cottle (1953) summarized the research on this scale as follows: college males tend to score higher than the general population; a high score for men means an interest in people, language, and ideas whereas a high score for women indicates an interest in mechanical, scientific, and computational activities; and certain vocational groups such as seminarians and music education students tend to have high scores on this scale; a high score *sometimes* is found with evidence of homosexuality.

6. *Paranoia* (Pa). A high score on this scale according to the manual associates the individual with a group of patients characterized by suspiciousness, oversensitivity, and delusions of persecution. Scores between 60 and 70 usually indicate the person who reads more into what others say or do than they intend. This is usually accompanied by difficulties in interpersonal relations.

7. *Psychasthenia* (Pt). This scale is supposed to measure the similarity of individuals to patients having phobias or compulsive behavior. A score between 60 and 70 characterizes the individual who prefers routine or organized activities which follow the same pattern. Such a score may indicate the worker who persists until the work is completed and it acts as a check on the *Hypomania* score.

8. *Schizophrenia* (Sc). This scale according to the manual measures responses characterized by bizarre and unusual thoughts or behavior. A score between 60 and 70 seems to be characteristic of the individual who uses solitary recreation to get away from the "present."

9. *Hypomania* (Ma). A high score on this scale is stated to indicate an individual with marked overproductivity of thought and action most of which is never carried through to completion.

10. *Social Introversion* (Si) A high score characterizes the individual who prefers activities carried on alone or with a few people. A low score seems to describe the individual who likes to meet and deal with people in groups.

It might be noted again that there is no general agreement about the meaning of extremely low scores on any scale except K, Mf, and Social introversion.

Over the years considerable research has been carried on with this scale. Cottle (1953) summarized the research done on it between 1940 and 1950 and in the last chapter indicated some more extensive interpretations when using the inventory with normals. One of the important aspects of the research on this instrument has been the development of new scales. Some of these additional scales are called *socio-economic status, dominance, responsibility, neuroticism,* and *prejudice.* As a matter of fact, psychologists have developed scales for all sorts of conditions by comparing how the responses of members of the group being studied differ from another group. Items to which the responses differ significantly between groups go to make up the new scale which is scored in the desired direction and cross-validated with a second group supposedly having the same psychological status as the first criterion group. Summaries of these research articles are found in the manual accompanying the inventory or in the later volumes of Buro's *Mental Measurements Yearbooks.*

As has been mentioned earlier, the usual procedure in studying scores on this inventory is by analyzing profiles. Psychological behavior is not simple and usually can be attributed to multiple causation with multiple effects. Hence, most of the scores to the individual scales have limited meaning by themselves, but become very significant when considered as part of a profile or pattern. The *Atlas for the Clinical Use of the MMPI* serves as a guide for the analysis and interpretation of these profiles. Over the years certain profiles have appeared so frequently that they have been given common names.

The literature shows that several studies have found a neurotic factor and psychotic factor in research with the *MMPI*, but it should be borne in mind that other studies may produce additional factors. It is significant for the counselor that general agreement in several studies on the existence of a neurotic and a psychotic factor in the *MMPI* is supported also by imperical observations from counseling itself. The *MMPI* scales with highest factor loadings on the neurotic factor are *Hypochondriasis, Depression,* and *Hysteria.* Experience in counseling has already shown these three scales to be related and highest among the patterns on the clinical scales in the psychoneurotic and psychosomatic illnesses. They have been named the "neurotic triad." The position of the *Depression* scale in the pattern of the neurotic triad, highest with psychoneurotics and lowest with psychosomatic illnesses, seems to be a key in diagnosis and prediction of results of counseling and psychotherapy. Counseling evidence indicates this neurotic triad may be related to jobs of a cyclical nature which are characterized by highs and lows of production.

The psychotic factor has highest loadings on the *Paranoia, Psychasthenia,* and *Schizophrenia* scales of the *MMPI* with abnormals. (With normals *Pa* often seems to be a part of the neurotic factor.) These three scales have been identified in counseling with the name "psychotic triad" and have been found most prominent in clients with psychotic tendencies. Here, as in the case of the *Depression* scale in the neurotic triad, the position of the *Psychasthenia* scale seems to reflect the amount of tension present and hence gives an estimate of response to counseling or psychotherapy. Counseling observations indicate that some rise on the *Pt* scale ($T = 55$–65) of the normal individual appears characteristic of the worker who performs well in a routine, repetitive situation and who sticks with a job until it is done.

An example of a part of the problem involved in interpretation of *MMPI* profiles will illustrate the difficulty in handling profiles. Certain of the clinical scales of the *MMPI* are referred to by Welsh (1952) as "character" scales, namely *Hysteria, Psychopathic deviate,* and *Hypomania;* while others are called "mood" scales, such as *Hypochrondriasis, Depression,* and *Psychasthenia.* By this Welsh means that the character scales remain fairly constant in the repeated measurement of an individual, while the mood scales may fluctuate according to the amount of psychological pressure operating on this individual at a given moment. Unless the counselor is aware of the difference between these two kinds of scales in the *MMPI,* it is difficult to see similarity in an individual's profile from a test taken when he feels more secure or at ease and in one taken when he feels under tension. At first glance the profiles will appear widely different. It is only as character scales are compared for two or more test administrations to the same person that similarities begin to emerge. It is only when the client discusses with the counselor possible causes of variation in tension, that causes of variation in the mood scales from test to test for that client are at least partially explained.

Problems such as these are involved in the meaning of patterns of scores on the *MMPI*. It is necessary to operate from the hypothesis that people are more alike than they are different, if identification of group patterns for job families is to be made. In this instance such gross patterns as the over-all masculinity or femininity of interests in personality data are useful to describe jobs of a mechanical-scientific nature versus those dealing with people. At the same time attention must be devoted also to the minor deviations from average in a given individual profile in order to identify individual differences noted in people in a particular job or school curriculum. On the *MMPI* these minor deviations from average show how a given individual tends to behave and thus what job choices might be most suitable. The counselor should note here that the balance of the total pattern shown by significant high and low scores is the element which usually gives meaning to the pattern and indicates the psychological balance of personality traits within a given individual. Cottle and Powell (1951) have demonstrated that to secure a normal profile it is necessary to have the integrating effect of a human personality. A normal profile is not secured by random methods of answering the *MMPI*.

In the *MMPI* it is this balance of high and low scores which indicates a normal adjustment. An example of this would be a score on the *Psychopathic deviate* scale which is high accompanied by high scores on the neurotic triad. In this type of profile there frequently appears to be sufficient pressure from the neurotic elements to prevent a severe character disorder. Another example would be a rise on *Psychopathic deviate* and *Hypomania* accompanied by a social extroversion score which is balanced by a slight rise on the *Psychasthenia scale*.

This inventory has been demonstrated over and over to be an effective tool for the screening of the emotionally disturbed from a group. High scores in almost any combination are an indication of some abnormal behavior. In this way it has been used in universities, industry, and the military services. Research by Forbes and Cottle (1953) showed that the reading level was 5.4 by an average of five formulas of readability. This would indicate that it could be used with younger clients except for one fact. Many of the items are of nature that they would be considered highly objectionable by student and parents. This is especially true of some of the items related to sexual and religious behavior. Research indicates that this inventory has been used with some success in vocational and educational counseling. Certain vocational groups have been shown to have typical profiles. However, the research on this aspect of the *MMPI* is quite limited and few generalizations can be drawn. It must also be reiterated that the individual scales cannot be used alone for differential diagnosis.

Reliability of the individual scales as reported in the manual tends to be in the .70's. Cottle (1950), using correlations between scores on the individual or card form versus the group or booklet form, showed coefficients on the clinical scales ranging between .51 and .92 for males and between .34 and .91 for females with a median between .79 and .80; a week was the maximum time between the two administrations. When this inven-

TABLE 11.1

RELIABILITY COEFFICIENTS FOR CARD vs. BOOKLET FORM
OF THE *MMPI* WITH 100 COLLEGE STUDENTS

	N	L	K	F	Hs	D	Hy	Pd	Mf	Pa	Pt	Sc	Na
r_{cb} Males	68	.51	.79	.77	.72	.65	.65	.81	.83	.53	.92	.90	.78
r_{cb} Females	32	.34	.72	.72	.91	.69	.83	.79	.79	.63	.87	.82	.75
r_{cb} (Product Moment)	100	.46	.76	.75	.81	.66	.72	.80	.91	.56	.90	.86	.76

tory is used by a professionally competent person, there is evidence that it has validity. Results obtained with it agree with other evidence contained in the case history. Ellis (1946), Ellis and Conrad (1948), and Ellis (1953), in summaries of the validity of personality inventories, showed that of all these inventories the *MMPI* consistently appears to show the most evidence of validity. It might be noted that Ellis, especially in his 1946 study, set up exceptionally high standards for acceptable validity.

It must be emphasized that the counselor should learn to use this instrument under supervision. The *MMPI* should be considered a highly professional instrument, the interpretation being complex and learned only through use in a training situation. Like the *Binet, Wechsler,* and some of the projective methods a casual reading of manuals or looking at profiles or case studies is not considered to be adequate for the beginning counselor to achieve competence in the use of the inventory.

FORCED-CHOICE TECHNIQUES

In the 1930's Kuder began experimenting with the forced-choice technique in the development of his vocational interest inventory. The form and use of forced-choice items was illustrated in Chapter 10 under the discussion of the *Kuder Preference Record.* During World War II and in the period shortly thereafter this technique was applied to personality inventories. The general feeling was that the use of the forced-choice technique reduced the ability of the individual taking it to falsify the results. Since this is most important when these inventories are used in employment and promotion practices, it is not strange that the original research with the use of this technique in adjustment inventories began in an industrial or military setting. For example, Jurgensen (1944) developed a so-called *Classification Inventory* for industrial use. Shipley, et al. (1946) developed the *Personal Inventory* for psychiatric use in the Navy. Each item of this inventory consisted of two parts and the respondent had to select the one that best described him. These items were paired on the basis of social acceptability but differed on the basis of their frequency of choice when used with the so-called normals and the disturbed. Jurgensen's differed from this in that the items were in triad form similar to the Kuder with the respondent selecting the one that he most and least preferred. The main objective as has been pointed out with this technique was to decrease the likelihood of falsifying or fudging the results. Edwards and Thurstone (1953) applied the psychological scaling methods to the equating of items on the basis of equal social acceptability. In the *Personal Preference Schedule (PPS)*, Edwards (1953) (1954) describes methods that he used in equating the pairs of items making up the *PPS* on the basis of the degree of social acceptability of each.

The research on this alleged claim of lowering fakability by advocates of forced-choice inventories is far from conclusive. In a recent study Linden (1958) administered the *Guilford-Zimmerman Temperament Survey* to groups of university students, in its original form and in two forced-choice forms, one made up of three responses per item and the other of two parts to each item. Each form was given under normal administering conditions and then for each form the respondents were asked to make themselves appear as they would under certain described circumstances. The forced-choice forms were put together using methods suggested by Edwards for assuring that the different parts of each item had equal social acceptability. In brief, Linden produced results that were inconclusive. In general, it was more difficult to fake responses on the three-part forced-choice form of the inventory than on the other two. Faking seemed related to the scales, for on some scales it was possible to shape the results to the respondent's desires on all three forms.

The Edwards Personal Preference Schedule will be discussed as an example of a forced-choice type of inventory supposedly balanced for response set. According to the manual the instrument was designed to measure a number of relatively independent variables that were obtained from a list of manifest needs developed by H. A. Murray et al. (1953). This inventory measures 15 of these needs:

1. *ach*   *Achievement:* to do one's best, to be successful, to do a difficult job well.

2. *def*   *Deference:* to get suggestions from others, to find out what others think, to let others make decisions.

3. *ord* *Order:* to have work neat, to plan in advance, to keep files neat and orderly.

4. *exh* *Exhibition:* to say witty things, to tell clever jokes, to be the center of attention.

5. *aut* *Autonomy:* to be independent of others, to say what one thinks about things, to criticize others, to avoid responsibilities.

6. *aff* *Affiliation:* to be loyal to friends, to participate in friendly groups, to share and to do things with friends.

7. *int* *Intraception:* to analyze one's motives and feelings, to understand how others feel about things, to predict the behavior of others.

8. *suc* *Succorance:* to receive a great deal of affection from others, to be helped by others, to have a fuss made by others when not feeling well.

9. *dom* *Dominance:* to be a leader, to argue for one's point of view, to settle arguments, to supervise, and to tell others how to do things.

10. *aba* *Abasement:* to feel guilty when one does something wrong, to feel timid and inferior, to feel better when giving in.

11. *nur* *Nurturance:* to help friends when they are in trouble, to treat others with kindness and sympathy, to have others confide in one.

12. *chg* *Change:* to do new and different things, to experiment, to try new jobs, to move about the country.

13. *end* *Endurance:* to keep at a job until it is finished, to work hard at a task, to avoid being interrupted while working.

14. *het* *Heterosexuality:* to associate with members of the opposite sex, to be in love with one of the opposite sex, to read books about sex.

15. *agg* *Aggression:* to attack contrary points of view, to make fun of others, to become angry, to blame others when things go wrong.

In addition to the above there is a *consistency* variable based upon a comparison of the number of identical responses made in two sets of the same 15 items. A *consistency score* of 10 or higher is considered by Edwards to indicate that the subject is not responding to the items on the basis of chance alone.

In building the inventory, Edwards compared each of the above traits with every other trait two times. The maximum score then for any given variable is 28. The respondent goes through the 225 pairs of items making up the inventory and from each pair of items selects the one that he believes most characteristic of himself. The inventory is rather long and university students require about a full period to complete it. Scoring is straightforward, with hand-scored or IBM answer sheets available.

Reliability coefficients reported in the manual show that this type of inventory is neither more nor less reliable than the usual form. A table of intercorrelations among the 15 variables shows that, in general, these intercorrelations are quite low, the highest—.46 between *Affiliation* and

Nurturance—being quite atypical. Validity is demonstrated in the manual by showing correlations between the different scales of the *EPPS* and *Guilford-Martin Personnel Inventory* and the *Taylor Manifest Anxiety Scale*. Significant correlations in the expected direction were obtained for the scales where it would be expected. The *EPPS* seems to add a lot of information to the counseling situation. Users of the inventory in counseling situations feel that it gives excellent insights into the make-up of the client. It is expected that in the years to come this instrument will be accepted as one of the most useful and valid for the counselor.

Allen (1957), using 130 university students administered both the *MMPI* and *EPPS* to them. Intercorrelations were then run between the various scores obtained upon the two instruments. Of the 630 correlations 69 were significant at the 5% level and 21 at the 1% level. All of these significant coefficients, however, were quite low, indicating that these two inventories are in general measuring rather different aspects of personality.

In another study Merrill and Heathers (1956), as a result of administering the same two inventories to another college group, concluded that since the intercorrelations among the various keys of the two instruments are not high, both are useful in the counseling situation. They state that while the *EPPS* indicates the relative strength that an individual gives to certain needs, the *MMPI* shows degrees of responses similar to well-defined clinical groups. They point out that data from one inventory supplement those from the other just as information from the *Allport-Vernon-Lindzey Study of Values* supplements data obtained from the *SVIB*. In another study Dunnette et al. (1958) correlated scores on the *EPPS* with 11 group scores from the *SVIB* and with the 18 scores obtained from the *California Psychological Inventory* (an instrument similar to the *MMPI*). A large number of rather low but significant correlations resulted. The authors concluded "To a great extent then, the correlations shown among scales in this study are reflections of tendencies to be dominant, confident, and sociable on the one hand as opposed to tendencies toward permissiveness, dependency, and individualistic activities on the other."

Specific examples of structured personality inventories have been discussed; these may be considered as samples of a large group of such inventories. The reader who wishes information on others should consult Anastasi (1954), Downie (1958), the later editions of Buros, and the catalogs of the various test publishers. Again it must be emphasized that these are useful to the counselor when they are used correctly. Much of the evidence of lack of validity that has been produced has come about because of their misuse. This section will be closed with a summary from Meehl (1945) in which he points out that the responses to the items on these inventories are not important as facts, but as indicators as to how the client feels about the items. It is not important whether the client does or does not have frequent colds when compared to others. What is important here is that such an individual feels that he has frequent colds and is thus concerned about his health. The cumulative effect of the responses to such items as this leads to the identification of these individuals with abnormal concern about their health.

PROBLEM CHECK LISTS

Problem check lists differ from structured inventories mostly in the method in which the client responds to the items on them and in the method of scoring. In one of the most widely used of these check lists, the *Mooney Problem Check List,* published by The Psychological Corporation, the client is confronted with a list of problems covering varying areas of adjustment and is asked to read through the list carefully and to underline those statements he feels are problems. When he has finished the check list, he is told to go back and draw a circle about the number in front of those problems he feels are bothering him most. Actually there are no scores for this check list. Since the problems are arranged in groups representing similar problems, a summary may be made of the number of problems checked in each of the areas. But here the scoring ends. There are no labels to attach to the individual on the basis of his profile nor are there profiles based upon so few items that they are unreliable.

The Mooney Problem Check Lists

In the current revision of the Mooney check lists, four forms are available: C, College; H, High School; J, Junior High School; and A, Adult. In the College and High School forms there are 330 items, 30 in each of the following areas:

I   Health and Physical Development (HPD)
II   Finances, Living Conditions, and Employment (FLE)
III   Social and Recreational Activities (SRA)
IV   Social-Psychological Relations (SPR)
V   Personal-Psychological Relations (PPR)
VI   Courtship, Sex, and Marriage (CSM)
VII   Home and Family (HF)
VIII   Morals and Religion (MR)
IX   Adjustment to College or School Work (ACW) (ASW)
X   The Future: Vocational and Educational (FVE)
XI   Curriculum and Teaching Procedure (CTP)

The Junior High School form is made up of 210 items, 30 in each of 7 areas. The items are arranged on a six-page folder with the items systematically arranged in groups. For example, the items appraising the Health and Physical Development area occupy the top five positions in each of six columns. The number of items marked in this area is easily summed and the number checked by the client inserted into a space at the right. Items making up each of the other areas are all arranged in like fashion.

After the client responds to the items, he is asked if he feels that the items that he checked actually present a good picture of his problems. He is then asked to summarize his problems in his own words. There is adequate space on the back sheet of the check list for this. Finally he is asked if he would like to talk about these problems with some member of the staff, and, if he does, with whom would he like to carry on this discussion.

The items for these check lists were obtained from such sources as the analyses of paragraphs written by 4000 high school students in which they described their personal problems, the review of 5000 cards itemizing the personal-educational needs expressed by students in grades 6, 9, and 12, an intensive analysis of expressed problems of 250 students in grades 7 through 12, analysis of case histories and counseling interviews, and the like. The authors used the following criteria in selecting the items for the lists (see Mooney and Gordon, 1950): (1) phrased in the language of students; (2) short for rapid reading; (3) self-sufficient as individual phrases; (4) common enough to be checked frequently in a large group of students or serious enough to be important in an individual case; (5) graduated in difficulty from relatively minor to major concerns; (6) vague enough in rather personal or delicate situations to enable the student to be able to check the item and still feel that he can conceal his problem in later conferences if he chooses to do so; and (7) centered within the student's own personal orientation. Such an approach in item construction and selection assures that the instrument has content validity. Research has also demonstrated that these check lists possess both concurrent and predictive validity.

Reliability coefficients reported in the manual are above .90. These were obtained by successive readministrations of the inventory to the same individuals and hence are coefficients of stability. This is the only type of reliability coefficient that can be correctly obtained for an instrument of this type.

In using this check list the counselor should, after frequency counts of the different areas have been entered into the proper spaces, note the areas of greatest and least concentrations of problems. The client's summarizing statement should be read and similarities and discrepancies looked for.   Then the counselor should examine other data on the client, interrelate all the material, and then decide the direction that the counseling situation might most profitably take.   Mooney and Gordon (1950) note in the manual that ". . . it is clearly necessary to evaluate the problems marked by the individual in terms of his particular environmental and psychological situation and in terms of the particular circumstances under which the *Problem Check List* was given.   Only then can interpretation result in a realistic appreciation of the individual's problem world and, subsequently, in guidance that is appropriate in concrete situations.   Merely counting the problems is not enough for these purposes."

These check lists are also very useful in screening out those individuals who are in need of considerable counseling or possibly psychotherapy. The authors suggest that this can be done using the total number of items checked on the entire list, the number of items marked in a particular area, responses to particular items, and the client's statement as to whether or not he would like to discuss the results of the inventory with a staff member.

In summary, these *Mooney Problem Check Lists* are both reliable and valid indicators of clients' problems.   They have the additional advantage over personality inventories that the client is not forced to respond to the items.   There is a permissive atmosphere about these that creates an attitude such as, "Here is a group of problems that individuals like yourself have."   "Would you care to check over those that are your problems and talk about the results with a counselor?"   The client, if he feels that he does not wish to do this or if he feels that his problems are of no importance, then does not make a lot of responses that in the end would be worthless.   The other value is that since there are no scores, there can be no labels that can be placed upon an individual.   It is all too easy for uninformed individuals to take the results from some personality inventories and associate certain terms as paranoid, schizophrenic, psychopath, and the like with an individual.   It must be recalled that it is yet to be demonstrated that these inventories are capable of use for differential diagnosis.

SRA Youth Inventory

The SRA Youth Inventory, Form A (Remmers and Shimberg, 1949) is a check list consisting of 298 items covering the following areas: (1) My School; (2) After High School; (3) About Myself; (4) Getting Along with Others; (5) My Home and Family; (6) Boy Meets Girl; (7) Health; and (8) Things in General.   This check list resulted from an investigation conducted by the Purdue Opinion Panel on the problems of high school youth.   Teen-agers in both urban and rural schools located all over the United States were asked to write anonymous essays about their problems. These essays were examined and analyzed by the members of the Purdue

Opinion Panel and finally the items making up the SRA *Youth Inventory* emerged from the study.

As with the *Mooney Check Lists*, the client goes through the list marking those problems that he feels are related to him. This inventory differs from the *Mooney* in that centile norms for urban and rural boys and girls are available for each of the areas measured by the check list. In addition to the above scores there is a *Basic Difficulty Score* that is based upon 109 items that are felt by psychologists to be most indicative of basic personality problems. When this check list is used as a screening device, it is suggested that these *Basic Difficulty Scores* be obtained for all students and that those students with the highest scores be the first scheduled through counseling.

Form S, the revised edition of the SRA *Youth Inventory* (Remmers and Shimberg, 1956), is very similar to the original edition except in the manner of making the responses to the items. The authors have established what they call an intensity dimension. Each item is followed by three squares of decreasing size and a 0. The instructions tell the respondent to mark the largest square if the statement is felt to be one of his most serious problems, the middle size box, if it is a moderate problem, the smallest box if the statement is a small or occasional, and the 0 if the statement does not express the way he feels. An intensity score is obtained by multiplying the number of marks in the largest squares by three, those in the second size boxes by two, and the number of checks in the smallest boxes by one, and summing all three products. Since both of these check lists are used similarly to the *Mooney* in screening and counseling, it is unnecessary to repeat what was previously mentioned about usage.

Adjective Check List

Another type of check list is exemplified by the *Adjective Check List* developed by Gough (1955). This list consists of 300 adjectives ranging from "absent-minded" to "zany." The client is told to go through the check list rapidly and to place a mark in front of each one that he feels to be self-descriptive. The check list is scored for fourteen scales covering such variables as "originality," "good judgment," "likeability," "rigidity," and "social poise and presence." In scoring the check list attention is paid not only to those adjectives that have been checked, but also to those that were not checked. For example, on the "originality" scale the directions are to score one point for each of eight adjectives that is checked and one point for each of thirty-four adjectives that is not checked. In the manual data are presented showing reliability coefficients somewhat lower than those usually obtained with the typical adjustment inventories. Also studies are reported showing relationships with other techniques used for appraisal of personality. At the present time the evidence points to this adjective check list as being a useful research instrument. It is simple, short, and, in the words of the author, "non-threatening."

PROJECTIVE TECHNIQUES

The various techniques that are grouped under this heading are all similar in that an ambiguous stimulus of one sort or another is presented to the client and he is required to make a free response to this stimulus. These methods are referred to as being unstructured, semi-structured, or free-response in their makeup and use. The general idea underlying all of them is that it is hoped by the examiner that the client will bring out significant statements and feelings that may offer the examiner insight into the client's behavioral problems.

Included under this general heading of projectives are such devices as the *Rorschach* or ink-blot test, the *Thematic Apperception Test (TAT)*, sentence, paragraph, and story completion techniques, word association, analysis of drawings and paintings, play analysis, the autobiography, diary, and essay, and the responses to various test situations such as the *Rosenzweig Picture Frustration Test*. In the pages that follow no attempt will be made to discuss these various techniques in any detail. A few that the counselor might be able to use will be described. The student who wishes to read about these instruments in detail is referred to Abt and Bellak (1950), Anderson and Anderson (1951), or Bell (1948). The general problems associated with projectives and their use in counseling will also be considered.

Most projectives are individual tests requiring the presence of the examiner to record the responses of the examinee. To collect the data and especially to analyze them require that the examiner be trained in each of the different methods. To be able to use the *Rorschach,* the psychologist finds that he has to take several graduate level courses or attend a workshop or seminar conducted under one of the *Rorschach* specialists. Responses are interpreted under guidance just as with the *Stanford-Binet*. There is a little difference here, however, and that is that the various specialists seem to have different ways of interpreting the same responses. Projectives are more customarily used as basic tools by the clinical psychologist. In his training he takes courses that enable him to use these devices. The counselor should not attempt to interpret them unless this extensive training has been completed. The counselor should, however, know the function these devices perform and be able to use the information from the protocols provided by the clinician who administered the instrument.

As was noted earlier in this chapter, projectives have been around for some time, beginning with the word association techniques that go back to Jung and with the *Rorschach* test in 1921. In clinics many are used daily and thousands of articles have appeared in the journals discussing them over the years. Probably their popularity is great because of their general makeup. They are novel, interesting, and diverting from the viewpoint of the client, and clinicians *feel* that they *work*. In taking one of them the client's attention may be diverted from other immediate problems.

When one applies the usual criteria for an acceptable test to projectives, one is apt to find that these devices fall far short of standards of acceptance. When reliability is studied, very little is found except for discussions of scorer reliability, such as have been associated with the use of the essay examination in the classroom for the past 50 years. The validation studies are no better. Many of them are statistically naïve, with the experimenter making no attempt to cross-validate his results. Cronbach (1949) summarized this research on the validity of the *Rorschach* by saying that of the results or differences reported significant at the 5% level, the majority were probably due to chance. Kelly (1954) makes one of the most apt summaries of the use of these techniques when he says: "The curious state of affairs wherein the most widely (and confidently) used techniques are those for which there is little or no evidence of predictive validity is indeed a phenomenon appropriate for study by social psychologists." On many of these instruments normative data are either absent or very often of a very poor quality. The builder of a projective device frequently uses, as norm groups, patients in clinics or hospitals. Little attention is paid to individuals whose behavior is within the normal range. Thus, unless the clinician is quite well-adjusted personally and has considerable information about normal behavior, each interpretation by a different clinician may vary for the same series of responses.

Rorschach

In the space below some of the more frequently encountered projectives will be described briefly. Probably the most popular of all such instruments is the *Rorschach*. This consists of a series of 10 cards each of which contains a large ink-blot on a white background, 5 in black and 5 in colors. The client is asked to tell what he sees. Responses are recorded and then analyzed by one of several current methods. In general, uniqueness of response is what is felt to be of most psychological significance. There are several formal scoring systems used, but no general agreement on scoring has been reached.

TAT

The Thematic Apperception Test (TAT), consists of a series of cards, some for men, some for women, and others that are responded to by both sexes. On each card is an ambiguous picture such as might be used to illustrate a story in one of the popular magazines. The client is asked to tell a story about each of the pictures as each is handed to him. Specifically he is asked to tell what he feels has happened and what is going to happen. These stories are then evaluated according to the manual (Murray, 1943) and an evaluation made usually on the bases of themes that tend to recur from picture to picture.

Sentence completion

Typical of sentence completion techniques is the *Rotter Incomplete Sentences Blank* (Rotter and Rafferty, 1950). This instrument consists of 40 so-called stems like the following:

I need ....

Best friends ....

Women ....

The client filling out the blank is to complete each of the sentences in such a way as to express his real feelings.

The manual contains scoring examples for males and females separately. Responses are scored on a 7-point scale with values ranging from 6 to 0. The most undesirable responses have the highest values. For example, to the stem "at bedtime," the response "I become depressed" receives 6 points; "I am tired" (a neutral response) receives 3 points, and "I go to sleep right away (an example of the most positive type of response) receives 0 points. Samples such as these are prepared for the evaluation of the student's responses. Scoring is not difficult and it does not take long for a scorer to become adept at assigning values to various sentence responses. A high score is a reflection of poor adjustment and a low score of desirable status. Split-half reliability coefficients in the low .80's are reported for the *Rotter* in the manual. Validity has been demonstrated by differences between mean scores of individuals rated adjusted and those rated maladjusted.

Rotter and Rafferty (1950) summarized the general advantages of their blank in the manual by noting that: (1) there is freedom of response; (2) there is some disguise of the purpose of the test; (3) group administration is efficient; (4) no special training is needed for administration; (5) scoring is quite objective; (6) time of administration is short; and (7) the method is flexible in that new stems may be made for different purposes. As disadvantages, the authors note that (1) machine scoring is impossible; (2) disguise is not as great as with the other projectives; and (3) with uncooperative, illiterate, or disturbed subjects insufficient response material often results. It is felt that this listing of advantages and limitations adequately covers all similar blanks.

The chief purpose of a blank like this is to serve as a screening device to pick out those individuals from a group who are in need of counseling. Of the different projectives, this is one that meets criteria used as standards in selecting tests.

Similar to these sentence completion tests are others referred to as paragraph or story completion. In general, they are the same as those described except that, instead of the stem consisting of a word or two, a paragraph or story is started and the client asked to finish it.

The remaining projective techniques such as play diagnostic methods, analysis of paintings and drawings, situational tests, and others have value to the clinical or child psychologist, but have little to offer the counselor. Most of the research that has been done with the use of projectives in the counseling situation is concerned with the use of the *Rorschach*. Patterson (1957) reviews and summarizes this research adequately and concludes that in the light of the known reliabilities and validities they have little to offer the vocational counseling situation. Studies that claimed success with the *Rorschach* in vocational or educational prediction failed to hold up under cross-validation. In others it was shown that simple paper and pencil tests did a much better job and, of course, were much cheaper in time and costs. He concludes that "The widespread use of projective techniques, and their enthusiastic acceptance and extension in all areas of applied psychology, with so little critical analysis of their value is amazing." The counselor should remember that there are much better instruments meriting further research and development. When we know more about the *SVIB*, the *SCAT*, the *DAT*, and the *MMPI*, perhaps then, if the projectives still exist in that remote time, their value in vocational counseling might be investigated.

ATTITUDES

Attitudes are usually defined as the tendency to react toward or against an object or value. Attitudes arise from daily experiences. They may be likened to a potential that is built up within the individual and, when the proper stimulation is presented, is released as the individual responds in a certain manner. Consider politics for example. Suppose that an individual is a Democrat. When a political stimulus is presented as in a political discussion, the Democrat responds in a particular way that reflects those feelings and opinions that he has about the Democratic Party. These are his attitudes. Attitudes are either learned from the personal experiences one has or are unconsciously adopted from his social environment. Children tend to reflect the same religious, political, and racial attitudes as their parents as a result of this social inheritance. Interests are very similar to attitudes. As a matter of fact, they may be considered as a special type of attitude. Attitudes may best be thought of as comprehensive, including, along with those aspects of an individual that are usually considered as attitudes, other concepts such as interests, values, mores, appreciations, and the like.

In the pages that follow only a brief discussion of the evaluation of attitudes will be presented. Anyone who wishes to pursue the topic in detail should see Remmers (1954) or Edwards (1957). Summaries of the techniques used in attitude appraisal are found in Cronbach (1960) and Downie (1958).

The measurement of attitudes began in a scientific manner with the work of Thurstone (see Thurstone and Chave, 1929). Thurstone and his students at that time constructed scales for the measurement of attitudes toward many concepts, especially those of a controversial nature —attitudes toward war, evolution, and Prohibition, for example. While these early scales are dated and mostly useless today, the technique used by Thurstone is frequently encountered. Thurstone's method involves the writing of a large number of items about the attitude under study. These should be variable enough to cover all shades of opinion. These items are next presented to a number of judges (Thurstone said at least 50) and these judges are asked to sort these items into 11 piles, the pile at one extreme reflecting the most favorable attitude and that at the other end, the most unfavorable, with the neutral attitude being represented by the center pile. Since it is assumed that these piles are equally placed along a continuum, this method is known as that of equal appearing intervals. Each item is given a scale value on the basis of the median value assigned to it by the judges. When much disagreement prevails on an item, it is discarded. Each item ends up with a specific value and the scale is constructed by selecting a series of 20 or more items that cover a wide range of scale values. For example, below are several items from the scale *Attitude toward the Law* with respective scale values:

The law is more than the enactments of Congress; it is a sacred institution. 10.5, highly favorable attitude.

Some laws command our respect while others are mere regulations. 6.1, neutral attitude.

The law is just another name for tyranny. 0.8, highly unfavorable attitude.

In completing a Thurstone-type scale, the respondent goes through the items and places a mark in front of those with which he agrees. The scale values of these are taken, the median of them computed, and this average, falling somewhere between zero and eleven, will give an indication of the examinee's attitude toward the object in question. In each of the manuals are norms for translating these medians into qualitative terms.

Likert scales

The major difficulty with the use of Thurstone's scales is that they are laborious and time-consuming in their construction. This is especially true in reference to obtaining a large number of competent judges for each scale and in the amount of time spent in evaluating the items by the judges. Likert (1932) developed another method that does not have this limitation. After items reflecting various degrees of the attitude toward the object in question have been written, the respondent answers each item on a five-point scale: "strongly agree," "agree," "undecided or no opinion," "disagree," and "strongly disagree." Favorable items have a value of 5, 4, 3, 2, and 1 ranging from "strongly agree" to "strongly disagree." Unfavorable items are scored in a reverse fashion with values of 1, 2, 3, 4, and 5 ranging from "strongly agree" to "strongly disagree." A high score then would reflect a favorable attitude toward the attitudinal object. After administering the items on the experimental form of the scale, an item analysis is made and those items that correlate highest with the total score are retained and become the next form of the scale. The construction of a scale like this is very simple. Studies have shown that the correlation between scores, when the same attitude is appraised by both the Thurstone and Likert method, is very high. It is not strange then that a good share of modern attitude testing is done with scales of this type. Items on both the *Minnesota Teacher Attitude Inventory* and the *Minnesota Inventories of Social Attitudes* are of this type (both published by The Psychological Corporation).

Other techniques

Many of the techniques that have been previously discussed may be used for evaluating attitudes. For example, both the autobiography and the essay may be structured to cover attitudes. Sentence and paragraph completion have been used to evaluate attitudes such as social and racial ones. Observational techniques implemented by both anecdotal records and rating scales are very useful methods. There are a few standardized scales available, but these are not too numerous. Check lists of one type or another may offer evidence of attitudes. A new method referred to as "error-choice" disguises the purpose of the scale (Kubany, 1953). With this technique a test is constructed, made up in part of a group of items that are very simple and that have a correct answer. Mixed with these is another group of items that have no correct answer. Both of the alternatives offered as answers are wrong, one erring in one direction and the other in the opposite direction. The score consists of the individual's responses to these items; if he tends to select the responses going in one direction, this is taken as his attitude toward whatever the scale is measuring.

The chief issue with the use of instruments to measure attitudes is that of validity. The psychological and educational literature is full of studies that reveal validity coefficients of zero or thereabouts. *In simple language this usually means that there is no relationship between what individuals say they would do (their attitudes) and their behavior.* The causes of such poor results are varied depending upon the technique used and the user. Measurement of attitude has to be divorced from other types of measurement; sometimes it has been administered as part of an achievement test. Just the hint of a grade will cause the real attitudes to be concealed, and socially desirable ones (at least from the viewpoint of the teacher) substituted. Then the attitudes of an individual may be classified as private and public attitudes. An individual has no objection to letting others know about his public attitudes, but private attitudes are another matter. These make up one's own very intimate religious, political, sexual, or other attitudes. There are times when many do not wish to reveal them and feel that what they are is nobody else's business. Another problem is that sometimes the attitudinal object is so general that the respondent can easily agree that it is desirable. However, when specifics that make up the general attitude are responded to, the respondent reacts differently to them. In other words, although favoring internationalism, when the various things necessary for internationalism are investigated, the respondent opposes them. Good rapport with the respondent, more disguised scales, and the evaluation of the more public attitudes may do a lot toward the attainment of acceptable validity and the avoidance of socially-acceptable responses and other kinds of response sets. Combining observation and attitude measurement may help also.

A knowledge of a client's attitudes is important in counseling. Different attitudes are associated with different occupations. Even within an occupation, attitudes differ depending on what the individual is doing. For example, elementary teachers reflect attitudes different from those of high school teachers when their attitudes are measured by the *Minnesota Teacher Attitude Inventory* (see Downie, 1958) and the *Experimental Attitude Scale* (see Ashlock and Cottle, 1958). There is no question that similar attitudinal differences can be found in many vocations. Among various vocations the differences are even more pronounced. For example, consider the attitudes of contrasting groups such as socialworkers and policemen, labor organizers and plant managers or supervisors, research physicists and clinical psychologists. Attitudes then are another important aspect of the counseling situation. It can also be shown that attitudes differ between teachers and counselors.

Socio-economic status

It has been previously mentioned that scores made by clients should be interpreted in the light of what is known about the client's socio-economic background. The effects of environment on intelligence test scores have been noted. Information about the client's background may be collected in various ways. In some school situations, especially in smaller schools, certain teachers have entrance to the homes of some of the students. This is especially true of the home economics and agriculture teachers. In hospitals or other agencies, social workers gather such data. With other groups it is almost impossible to know about background without asking the client personally. Occupation of parent has been used as one method of evaluating this. However, when one uses this approach, the counselor soon becomes frustrated as there is first the problem of candidness of the client's response and secondly that of the meaninglessness of it. If the response is "machinist," this can cover many occupations of varying degrees of skill responsibility. The same for "railroad worker," which covers everyone from track walker to president.

In an attempt to obtain valid measures of background, various score cards and scales were developed. For example the obsolete *Sims Score Card* was made up of a series of items covering the education of the parents, occupation of parents, physical aspects of the home, and the like. Responses were filled in by the student. *The American Home Scale* (Psychometric Affiliates) is similar, measuring four areas: cultural, aesthetic, economic, and miscellaneous. Both of these can be easily distorted by the respondent's giving socially desirable answers. Warner, Meeker, and Eells (1951) have developed an index of status based upon occupation, source of income, housing, and dwelling area of the individual being evaluated.

Another approach in this area is the *Sims SCI (Social Class Identification) Occupational Rating Scale* (World Book Co.; see Sims, 1952). This consists of 42 occupations ranging from professional worker down to the most unskilled type of laborer. The examinee responds to each of these on the basis of feeling that individuals in each of these occupations are in a higher (H), lower (L), or the same (S) social class as compared to the examinee's own family. Completion and scoring of this instrument require only a very few minutes. The cost is very low. At the present time, not much research is available on this scale, but evidence presented in the manual points to a possible useful inventory for the evaluation of socio-economic status.

SUMMARY

In dealing with the results obtained with personality or attitude inventories, the counselor must be extremely cautious. These are very useful instruments, but in using them it is very important to know something about the conditions under which the clients completed the inventories. It is important to know whether or not the client understood the purposes of the inventory taken and accepted the fact that the results would be most useful to him and the counselor in the ensuing counseling situation when the inventory is filled out properly and carefully. Unless the counselor knows something about the response set or motivation of the client when taking the inventory, results are apt to have little validity. Only on some of these inventories are there built-in devices aimed at detecting invalid or falsified responses.

The counselor should also freely use some of the other available instruments in collecting data concerning a client's adjustment. Perhaps in this area of human behavior more than in any other, it is most desirable to have as many evaluations as possible, hoping that data obtained by the inventory when used along with information collected by other techniques or from other sources will lead to a better and more valid picture of the client's personality patterns and problems.

REFERENCES

Abt, L. E., and L. Bellak. *Projective psychology.* New York: Alfred Knopf, 1950.

Allen, R. M. Relationship between the *Edwards Personal Preference Schedule* variables and the *Minnesota Multiphasic Personality Inventory* scales. *J. Appl. Psychol.,* 1957, *41,* 307–311.

Allport, G. W. The use of personal documents in psychological research. *Social Science Research Bulletin,* No. 49, 1942.

Anastasi, Anne. *Psychological testing.* New York: The Macmillan Company, 1954.

Anderson, H. H., and G. L. Anderson. *An introduction to projective techniques.* Englewood Cliffs, N. J.: Prentice-Hall, Inc., 1951.

Ashlock, R. A., and W. C. Cottle. An experimental scale on attitudes. *U. of Kansas Bull. of Educ.,* 1958, *2,* 106–109.

Bell, J. E. *Projective techniques.* New York: Longmans, Green, 1948.

Broen, W. E., Jr., and R. D. Wirt. Varieties of response sets. *J. Consult. Psychol.,* 1958, *22,* 237–240.

Cottle, W. C. Card vs. booklet form of the *MMPI. J. Appl. Psychol.,* 1950, *34,* 255–259.

———. *The MMPI, A Review.* Lawrence, Kansas: School of Education, University of Kansas, 1953.

———, and J. O. Powell. The effect of random answers to the *MMPI. Educ. Psychol. Meas.,* 1951, *11,* 224–227.

Cronbach, L. J. *Essentials of psychological testing,* 2nd ed. New York: Harper & Brothers, 1960.

———. Statistical methods applied to Rorschach scores: a review. *Psychol. Bull.,* 1949, *46,* 393–429.

Downie, N. M. *Fundamentals of Measurement.* New York: Oxford University Press, 1958.

Dunnette, M. D., W. K. Kirchner, and JoAnne DeGidio. Relation among scores on the *Edwards Personal Preference Schedule,* the *California Psycho-*

logical Inventory, and *Strong Vocational Interest Blank* for an industrial sample. *J. Appl. Psychol.,* 1958, *42,* 178–181.

Edwards, A. L. *Personal Preference Schedule, Manual.* New York: The Psychological Corporation, 1954.

———. *Techniques of attitude scale construction.* New York: Appleton-Century-Crofts, 1957.

———. The relationship between the judged desirability of a trait and the probability that the trait will be endorsed. *J. Appl. Psychol.,* 1953, *37,* 90–93.

———, and L. L. Thurstone. An internal consistency check for scale values determined by the method of successive intervals. *Psychometrika,* 1953, *17,* 169–180.

Ellis, A. Recent research with personality inventories. *J. Consult. Psychol.,* 1953, *17,* 45–49.

———. The validity of personality questionnaires. *Psychol. Bull.,* 1946, *43,* 385–440.

———, and H. S. Conrad. The validity of personality inventories in the military service. *Psycho. Bull.,* 1948, *45,* 385–426.

Flanagan, J. C. *Factor analysis in the study of personality.* Stanford University, Cal.: Stanford University Press, 1935.

Forbes, F. W., and W. C. Cottle. A new method for determining readability of standardized tests. *J. Appl. Psychol.,* 1953, *37,* 185–190.

Gough, H. G. *Reference handbook for the Gough adjective check list.* Berkeley, Cal.: University of California Instit. of Personality Assessment and Research, 1955.

Hahn, M. E., and M. S. MacLean. *Counseling Psychology.* New York: The McGraw-Hill Book Company, Inc., 1955.

Hathaway, S. R., and P. E. Meehl. *An atlas for the clinical use of the MMPI.* Minneapolis: University of Minnesota Press, 1951.

Hathaway, S. R., and J. C. McKinley. *Minnesota Multiphasic Personality Inventory, Manual.* New York: The Psychological Corporation, 1945.

Jacobs, A., and A. Schloff. Falsification scales for the *Guilford-Zimmerman Temperament Survey.* Los Angeles, Cal.: The Sheridan Supply Company, 1955.

Jurgensen, C. E. Report on the *Classification Inventory,* a personality test for industrial use. *J. Appl. Psychol.,* 1944, *28,* 445–460.

Kelly, E. L. Theory and technique of assessment. *Ann. Rev. Psychol.,* 1954, V, 281–310.

Kubany, A. J. A validation study of the error-choice technique using attitudes on national health insurance. *Educ. Psychol. Measmt.,* 1953, *13,* 157–163.

Likert, R. A technique for the measurement of attitudes. *Arch. Psychol.,* N.Y., No. 140, 1932.

Linden, J. D. *The development and comparative analysis of two forced-choice forms of the Guilford-Zimmerman Temperament Survey.* Unpublished Ph.D. dissertation, Purdue University, 1958.

Lindner, R. L. *Prescription for rebellion.* New York: Rinehart and Company, 1952.

Meehl, P. E.   The dynamics of structured personality tests.   *J. Clin. Psychol.*, 1945, *1*, 296–303.

Merrill, R. M., and Louise B. Heathers.   Relations of the *MMPI* to the *Edwards Personal Preference Schedule* on a college counseling center sample. *J. Consult. Psychol.*, 1956, *20*, 310–314.

Mooney, R. L., and L. V. Gordon.   *The Mooney Problem Check Lists, Manual.* New York: The Psychological Corporation, 1950.

Murray, H. A.   *Thematic Apperception Test, Manual.*   Cambridge, Mass.: Harvard University Press, 1943.

———, et al.   *Explorations in personality.*   New York: Oxford University Press, 1953.

Patterson, C. H.   Use of projective tests in vocational counseling.   *Educ. Psychol. Measmt.*, 1957, *17*, 533–555.

Pepinsky, Pauline.   The meaning of "validity" and "reliability" as applied to sociometric tests.   *Educ. Psychol. Measmt.*, 1949, 9, 39–49.

Remmers, H. H.   *Introduction to opinion and attitude measurement.*   New York: Harper & Brothers, 1954.

Remmers, H. H., and B. Shimberg.   *SRA Youth Inventory, Form A, Manual.* Chicago: Science Research Associates, 1949.

———. *SRA Youth Inventory, Form S, Manual.*   Chicago: Science Research Associates, 1956.

Rotter, J. B., and J. E. Rafferty.   *The Rotter Incomplete Sentences Blank, Manual.*   New York: The Psychological Corporation, 1950.

Sheldon, W. H.   *The varieties of temperament: a psychology of constitutional differences.*   New York: Harper & Brothers, 1942.

Shipley, W. C., F. E. Gray, and N. Newbert.   The personal inventory.   *J. Clin. Psychol.*, 1946, *2*, 318–322.

Sims, V. M.   *Sims SCI Occupational Rating Scale.*   Yonkers, N.Y.: World Book Company, 1952.

———. The essay examination as a projective technique.   *Educ. Psychol. Measmt.*, 1948, *8*, 15–31.

Strang, R. A.   *Counseling technics in college and secondary school.*   New York: Harper & Brothers, 1949.

Thurstone, L. L., and E. J. Chave.   *Measurement of attitudes.*   Chicago: University of Chicago Press, 1929.

Tindall, R.   Relationships among indices of adjustment status.   *Educ. Psychol. Measmt.*, 1955, *15*, 152–163.

Warner, W. L., M. Meeker, and K. Eells.   *Social class in America.*   Chicago: Science Research Associates, 1949.

Welsh, G. S.   An anxiety index and an internalization ratio for the *MMPI*. *J. Consult. Psychol.*, 1952, *16*, 65–72.

Whyte, W. H.   *The Organization Man.*   New York: Simon and Schuster, 1956.

12

The counselor's research

IN THE PREVIOUS CHAPTERS DISCUSSION CENTERED ABOUT THE USE BY THE
counselor of established tools and techniques in gathering information
about the clients that he meets. In this chapter consideration will be
given to another important tool of the counselor—research.

Many counselors develop a concept of research during their student
days that is hardly conducive to being research minded. In the words
of Rummel:

> Research, as the typical college student understands the term, is a rela-
> tively long investigation carried out primarily in libraries with the results
> presented in a highly documented paper of some length. (1958:3)

As is readily apparent, research is much more than this. In the same
work Rummel notes that research includes all specialized and thorough-
going investigations in which educated people engage. The chief purpose of research should be to answer questions that arise with the counselor as he carries on his daily activities. Very simply, research is an
attempt to find out new things, to study new uses of those tools and
techniques already possessed, and to investigate the truthfulness or validity of the existing procedures.

Research is a way of thinking. John Dewey (1933) set forth five
steps through which one goes in solving a problem: (1) a felt need;
(2) the statement of problem; (3) a statement of the hypothesis; (4)
collection of data; and (5) the testing of the hypothesis in the light of
the collection data and the drawing of a conclusion. These are the same
steps that the counselor or any other individual goes through when
carrying on research. It should follow that there is nothing esoteric or
mysterious about research. It is basically another use to which the
counselor can apply the tools and techniques previously discussed in
this book to enhance his skill as a counselor, and in the long run to add
to the improvement of the counseling process. It is not the purpose of
this chapter to present detailed information on research techniques in

education and psychology. Hillway (1956), Rummel (1958), and Selltiz et al. (1959) each contains much important information on research methodology in the social sciences. In this chapter types of problems for research associated with counseling and some illustrations of research methods will be presented.

It is simpler to discuss in detail research with which one is familiar. Then it is possible to show step by step how the research developed so that the reader can have a better understanding of the process. For this reason the writers hope the reader will pardon the use of research in which the writers have had a personal interest. Such studies are used only as examples of some things a counselor could do to answer questions raised by work with clients. This chapter is not intended as a complete coverage of all research in the area of counseling, only to give selected illustrations.

Many counselors avoid research activities, perhaps being overcome with the awesome connotation of the term in this scientific age. Such fears are groundless, although research does take time. If any research is to get done, the counselor should see that a certain part of his time is budgeted for it, and he should be determined to see that time so allotted is actually spent in carrying on research. It is very easy to give up this time to other seemingly more important activities.

The veteran counselor has no trouble finding topics for research, but with the student counselor and the beginner this may not be the case. Working in an area of specialization and thus becoming an expert is bound to lead to many of the unanswered questions in that area. This, then, is a primary source of research ideas. Reading the research of others as reported in journal articles, monographs, theses, or books should lead the thoughtful counselor to problems for research. New ideas in any of these may lead the counselor to see if they would actually work in his own agency. Another source for research ideas is the dissatisfactions arising within the counselor's work. Certainly days come when he feels that a given technique or method could be improved to provide more effective results. Then there is the generalized wondering that any intelligent counselor should have as to whether or not the entire counseling or guidance program is contributing anything to the welfare of the clients and, if so, exactly what. In the pages that follow an attempt will be made to show how research may be carried out by the counselor. Once a piece of research is started, other problems often seem to stem from it endlessly.

In carrying on any research project, the counselor has first to see if what he wishes to do is feasible, or perhaps practical. There is no point in starting out on a piece of research that cannot be finished because of the time involved, the money needed for financing, or the inaccessibility of the data. Frequently a research worker starts out to collect data and soon finds that his subjects do not cooperate by answering his questionnaire or by completing his tests or scales. Some research plans require that respondents spend several hours in filling out the forms. The easiest way for the subject to handle such documents is to throw them into the wastebasket. The counselor should also determine ahead of time if he can manipulate the data after he obtains them. Frequently the amount of data becomes so large that it must be placed on IBM cards for analysis. Such a procedure is expensive in terms of time and money. Finally the counselor should see if he really can analyze the data. Most important here is whether or not he has the statistical background necessary for working his data and interpreting his results correctly.

APPROACHES TO RESEARCH

A large part of the research carried on in counseling has been directed to evaluation studies. Dressel (1953) lists three major approaches to such research. First, he notes the study of the counseling process itself. Here are included studies of the amount of client participation in the counseling process, counselor activity in the counseling situation, and the like.

Second, he lists studies in the outcomes of counseling. Much of the research carried out is of this type, perhaps because it is the easiest to carry on. Such topics as improvement in school work, improvement in social and emotional adjustment, changes in attitudes, and vocational selection and placement are frequent titles for research studies in this category. Often the client is asked to evaluate the outcomes of counseling himself, showing how it helped him or failed to do so.

Third, Dressel notes that much research is based upon data derived from the use of tests and other techniques. This research is mostly related to the use of the various instruments and their validity. Related to this is the development of agency norms to replace those supplied by the publisher of the instrument used. Each measurement device used by an agency should be evaluated and statistics compiled concerning its usefulness to the agency.

In the pages that follow, various types of research problems will be taken up. First of these are the evaluation studies. While it is easy enough to give lip service to the evaluation of counseling and guidance services, when one begins to carry on such a study he soon runs into a number of troubles. In any evaluation procedure in education the first step is to determine the objectives of what is being evaluated. This in itself is a huge and sometimes very difficult task. Usually the major objectives of a course of study or of an entire educational experience are determined by the discussions and debates of experts. When these individuals are finished, the resulting stated objectives, while imposing and impressive, actually cannot be evaluated because of their broad, general nature.   For example, an objective of counseling might be stated as "satisfactory vocational or educational adjustment."

A little thought will show the difficulty involved in trying to evaluate this objective of satisfactory vocational adjustment.   First the terms have to be defined and these definitions agreed upon.   Then the nature of the kinds of evidences to be used and their sources have to be determined. As has been stated many times by evaluation experts (Smith and Tyler, 1942), these broad general objectives have to be stated in terms of human behavior.   Specifically in this case, how does the individual who is well-adjusted behave vocationally?   After these behaviors have been determined, methods have to be devised to evaluate or measure such behavior. This calls for the construction of practical, valid, and reliable tests and other evaluation tools to be used in the appraisal process.   And finally there has to be an analysis and then a synthesis of these fragmented evaluations into a whole.

As Rushong (1953) has summarized it, counseling is essentially a learning situation.   Those techniques that have been developed for the evaluation of the outcomes of other learnings must be used when counseling is evaluated.   Otherwise, the results of the so-called evaluations are meaningless and useless.

The major obstacle in setting up a functional evaluation program is in the obtaining of valid evaluative criteria.   Many past research studies have used improvement in grades, better adjustment, more social participation, and the like as evaluative criteria.   As previously stated, such terms as these are not desirable because of their vagueness.   Take the phrase "better adjustment."   If in a group of individuals each was asked to tell what "better adjustment" meant to him, it is highly possible that there might be as many different explanations of the term as there were participants.

Travers (1949) separates the types of evaluative criteria used in counseling into two groups: subjective and objective.   Included as subjective criteria are the satisfactions an individual obtains from his job, an assessment of his personal adjustment including both his social life and emotional status, and the general satisfactions that the client feels with the counseling process.   The first of these criteria Travers dismisses as useless because evaluative instruments have not yet been developed which can be used to produce valid appraisals.   As far as satisfaction goes, he noted that this also is of little value as a measure of counseling effectiveness, because people tend to be satisfied by, and feel that they have been helped by, the most useless types of quackery.

Travers feels that these subjective criteria are generally unsatisfactory. He then enumerates his objective criteria, which include grades, income, job stability, tenure, completion of educational or vocational plans, life goals, and the like.   Even these objective criteria have to be used with caution. One of the most common objectives of educational counseling is to improve a student's grade point average. This is frequently shown to happen. The student's grades do improve, but the question is really whether this is a result of changes that have been brought about in the counselee or the result of the counselor's helping the student select easier courses and professors with the more generous grading practices. The second of these is hardly a valid criterion to be used in evaluating counseling. In regard to these objective criteria, Travers notes that many of these goals are long term ones and hence, to be valid, evaluation activities must be carried on over a long period of time. In other words, the approach should be longitudinal rather than cross-sectional. A much more inclusive listing of evaluative criteria is found in Benson (1949).

A second type of research that the counselor carries on may be classified as *follow-up*. While this is a type of an evaluation study, it is a rather specific and distinct one. Unless the counselor knows what has happened to the clients who have passed through the agency in which he works, it is rather difficult to feel well satisfied about the job that the agency is trying to do or to know exactly which kind of procedures to continue and which to curtail or eliminate. An example of this would be the follow-up of graduates and school dropouts which is carried on by most schools. This type of research program shows the kinds of placement in jobs and in further schooling that have been achieved by the people who have left that school. This in turn indicates possible revisions of the curricular or counseling program of the school.

One of the simplest ways to conduct a dropout study or a follow-up study of this nature is to enlist the help of the current graduating class in a follow-up of those who left school the preceding year. This has the advantage of acquainting most of next year's school-leavers, the present graduating class, with the kinds of information needed, and some of the difficulties involved, in follow-up procedures. It acquaints them with the purposes of a follow-up survey to which they may later be asked to respond and makes them more aware of the value of such a program to the school. The most useful procedure is to contact, either by use of 'phone or house-call, the people who left school the preceding year. If this cannot be done the kind of information needed might be placed on a return postal card as the next best way of getting the information. A postal card survey limits the kinds of information to be requested and makes it necessary also that statistical procedures be fairly simple in order to handle this limited information. One technique is to have the high school seniors who are helping with the survey compile a list of those people who left school the preceding year, breaking it down into those who went directly into jobs and those who went on to further education. Then different kinds of postal card questions can be developed for each group. Members of the group who have gone to work can be asked questions like those indicated in Form 12.1, while those in the group who have gone on to higher education could be asked questions like those indicated in Form 12.2. These are short and simple questions adapted to a postal card survey. Of course, more elaborate follow-up questionnaires might be used.

Another way of surveying graduates and drop-outs other than by mail or by personal interview is through telephone solicitation. Any of these methods offer specific advantages. The direct interview produces the information with more certainty than any of the others. An economy of time would be secured by a structured series of questions for this interview which would be the same for each interviewer and each person being interviewed. This produces a standardization highly useful in the statistical handling of the information which is collected. If direct interviews are not possible, a combination of mail and telephone interviews for those who do not respond to the information requested by mail can be used. It should be noted here that a double postal card signed by someone who is known to the recipient is more frequently returned than is one with an impersonal message or signed by someone unknown to the recipient of the questionnaire. Experience indicates that mailing long questionnaires with return stamped envelopes is the poorest method of conducting a survey of school-leavers.

A procedure such as this obviously requires careful planning, not only to get the kinds of information which are useful to the agency, but to insure a way of asking for this information which will give as much freedom of response as possible and at the same time be as easy to handle statistically as the information permits. A careful tryout of preliminary forms of a follow-up survey will indicate many of the places where the survey can be improved in terms of securing a clear, useful response. In addition, a tryout will make it possible to see whether the statistical techniques proposed for handling these data will actually do the job.

A third type of research is related to the counseling process itself. In these days of increasing enrollments, counselors may find themselves using more and more group techniques in preference to individual ones. Then it follows that an investigation should be made to see which of the two approaches is more effective. In a similar fashion, the so-called directive as opposed to the client-centered approach might be compared.

A fourth important area of research for the counselor is in the development of local school norms, the special norms required for rehabilitation clients, and the job description required for work in a given plant or office. The development of such norms and the statistics for use with them are matters which should be given serious consideration by a counselor in a given agency. For example, it is highly important to begin as soon as possible the development of longitudinal information that will

Postal Card Follow-up For Employed/Form 12.1 Graduates.

1. What was your first full-time job after leaving school?

2. For what firm?

3. Are you on a different job now? What?

4. From which of the following did you learn about your job(s)?
   _____ Family or friend   _____ Private employment agency
   _____ School   _____ State employment agency
   _____ Found it myself   _____ Other (Explain)

5. Do you plan any other schooling?

6. Can we help you in any way in planning jobs or training?

7. Name:

8. Address:

1. What school did you attend after leaving high school?

2. What course did you take there?

3. Are you enrolled there now?   Same course?

4. Where did you learn about the school?

5. Can we help you in planning schooling or locating a job?

6. What activities are you in at school?

7. Name:

8. Address:

be collected and interpreted over relatively long periods in the history of an agency.

An example of this is the collection of information on the *General Aptitude Test Battery* of the United States Employment Service. Information collected over a period of time could be highly useful to an agency, but when collected on a given group of people it must be set aside until those people have held various kinds of employment successfully or unsuccessfully. Then the successful workers can be contrasted with the unsuccessful workers in a given occupation to give a pattern of scores which might then be described as characteristic of successful workers and lacking in unsuccessful workers.

One method of obtaining local norms is to follow a given group through an agency or through various kinds of work and educational activities outside the agency in order to see what happens to this group at various stages. Too much of the research available at the present time has been developed on a given group at a given age. The results are generalized to other groups who are older or younger on the assumption that they will resemble the original group at the same age. This is not necessarily so and the only assumptions which can be made are those which are based upon a knowledge of the behavior of a given group of individuals at various points in their school and work career. Generalizations can be made only after the same group has been studied at age 15, at age 20, at age 25, and so on. Only then is it possible to see what changes take place over a period of years. Then it is not necessary to generalize about the kind of behavior a given group of 15 year olds will exhibit at age 25 from the behavior of current 25 year olds who may have no relationship to the group of 15 year olds being predicted.

The problems involved in the development of specific local norms have been described in Chapter 7. Other problems connected with the development of local norms have also been described in Chapter 6. There seems to be no need for extended discussion of these at this point.

A fifth and very useful area of research is related to the various tools of the counselor. For example, in predicting academic grades, which does the better job, a long battery or a short twenty-minute intelligence test? It is an accepted fact that clients can cheat on personality inventories. Can a typical inventory be changed to another form such as the paired-comparison form, and this cheating at least be lessened? Should bright senior high school girls be given the women's form of the *Strong Vocational Interest Blank* or does the use of the men's blank provide adequate and valid information? Suppose the *Kuder Preference Record —Vocational* is used with all freshmen. The counselor might be interested in knowing what profiles are associated with successful completion of the various school curricula. These are just a few of the many research problems that an alert counselor might find worth carrying on.

Closely related to the above is the development and compilation of new information of use to the agency from the clinical hunches or subliminal cues which the counselor develops through work with clients. Research to add information in each of these areas does not have to be difficult or involved. It should be an outgrowth of the experiences the counselor undergoes in the agency. It should be a result of the kind of questions which appear normally in the course of the counselor's day. Also questions should be of a nature which will add information to the counselor's store of knowledge about counseling and make it possible to do a better job with clients.

A sixth area in which research effort should be expended is in a survey of placement opportunities available to the clients of the agency. Whether it is a public school, an employment service, or a rehabilitation agency makes little difference. The sources of placement available to the agency need to be explored periodically and re-evaluated, and possible new placement sources discovered. In the public schools this involves an exploration of employers' needs and an exploration of the school resources which will supply those needs. An example of this is the Committee Report (1949) of a questionnaire developed by a group of interested personnel in the Kansas City Public Schools to survey entry jobs in the greater Kansas City area.

This survey had three objectives: first, to locate sources of entry jobs available for individuals leaving school; second, to assemble data describing entry jobs including the training and personal qualities which employers desire in entry workers; and third, to make these data available for use in each of the schools in the greater Kansas City area. In order to do this a questionnaire had to be developed which could be used for interviewing employers and certain common techniques for interviewing these employers had to be developed through experimental interviewing. These techniques had to be thoroughly understood by relatively untrained people who would do the interviewing in the greater Kansas City area.

Some of the recommendations suggested for undertaking interviews of this nature are indicated as follows by the committee:

1. Know thoroughly the purpose of the survey and what information you want to secure. Make sure the employer understands it also.

2. Listen courteously to any extraneous information offered.

3. Take careful notes, putting additional information on the reverse of the sheet.

4. Maintain an objective attitude, and express no opinions of your own.

5. Observe plant safety requirements.

6. Schedule visits at the convenience of the employer. Be sure to keep the appointment.

ENTRY JOB INFORMATION

Job Title .... D.O.T. Code .... Date ......
Job description ....
No. employed .... No. entering each year ....
Name of firm .... Address ....
Kind of business .... Type of product ....
Firm representative reporting .... Title ....

A. Years of school required:
....

B. Academic ability required:
1. High ....
2. Medium ....
3. Low ....

C. Work is:
1. Heavy ....
2. Inside ....
3. Outside ....
4. Hazardous ....
5. How ....
....

D. Personal qualities:
1. Accuracy ....
2. Neatness ....
3. Honesty ....
4. Initiative ....
5. Reliability ....
6. Appearance ....
7. Promptness ....
8. Leadership ....
9. Tact ....
10. Aggressiveness .....
11. Alertness ....
12. Speed ....
13. Other ....

E. Exposure to:
1. Temp. change ......
2. Moisture ....
3. Fumes ....
4. Dust ....
5. Other ....

F. Physical requirements of job:
1. Sedentary ....
....

2. Active ....
3. Other ....
....

G. Physical requirements of person:
1. Weight ....
2. Height ....
3. Eyesight ....
4. Hearing ....
5. General Health .....
6. Sex ....
7. Age preferred ....
8. Other ....

H. Mechanical abilities:
1. Finger dexterity .....
....
2. Manipulative skill ....
....
3. Space perception ....
....
4. Other ....

I. Technical knowledge:
1. Blueprints ....
2. Mechanical ....
3. Math. ....
4. English ....
5. Spelling ....
6. Other ....

J. Clerical abilities:
1. Typing ....
2. Dictation ....
3. Bkkpg. ....
4. Filing ....
5. Switchboard ....
6. Office machines .....
....
....
....

K. Training available:
1. On job ....
....
2. Elsewhere ....
....

L. Responsibilities:
1. Handle money ....
2. Records ....
3. Equipment ......
4. Follow orders only .
....
5. Others ....

M. Contacts:
1. With public ....
2. Other workers ....
3. Letters ....
4. Telephone ....
5. Other ....

N. Employment:
1. Permanent ....
2. Part-time ....
3. Seasonal ....
4. Daily hours .....
5. Start time ......
6. Wages:
   a. By ....
   b. Amt. ....
7. Pay period ....
....

O. Promotion:
1. Possible ....
2. Not likely ....
3. Time ....
4. Next job ....
....
....
....

Committee Report (1949:328). Reproduced by permission.

7. Follow a common procedure for collecting and recording information.

8. Be sure you know the "what, how, why, and skill involved" in each entry job before terminating your interview.

9. Know the various occupations in the industry to be surveyed.

10. Know how to check and evaluate accuracy of information offered.

11. Don't interrupt workers.

12. Treat all information as confidential. Discuss no other firms you may have visited.

13. If you are a trainee in interviewing, let the experienced interviewer control the interview.

14. Remember that you are collecting information—not evaluating firms.

15. Express your thanks for the time and effort the employer has given. (Committee Report, 1949:327)

As a result of the interview experiences of this group in Kansas City, a form for listing entry job information during employer interviews was developed. This form is shown as Form 12.3. It indicates the types of information that employers and interviewers felt was important in trying to bring to individuals starting their first jobs a description of the kinds of characteristics such entry jobs require.

Some of the findings of this particular study of entry jobs conducted in 1949 are quite applicable to today's job market and show the factors teachers and counselors should bear in mind when considering employer needs in entry jobs. The most important of them are suggested by the Committee Report (1949:330):

1. Nearly all firms have some type of entry jobs and are anxious to hire young people as they leave school.

2. Most employers prefer to hire high school graduates, though graduation is not a universal requirement.

3. Most employers place great emphasis on desirable personality traits, proper attitudes, and good work habits.

4. According to employers, the ability to get along well with employers, fellow workers, customers of the firm, and others is the most important factor in job success.

5. Employers claim that many young employees lack proficiency in the use of such fundamentals as arithmetic, spelling, English, and legible hand-writing.

6. Employers also claim that many young people have apparently had no training in doing independent, logical thinking.

A seventh area of research would be to make an investigation of the population from which an agency's client came. It has been observed that the clients of a given agency tend to resemble each other very closely.

For example, the type of client entering a large Veterans Administration Hospital is apt to come from a certain socio-economic group, to have a more or less similar level of educational attainment, and to engage in occupations of similar levels and fields. A survey of several hundred entering patients will give the counselor an excellent overview of what his counselees are like, what their needs are, and how the counseling program may be adapted to serve them best. A similar survey or study would also be most useful for the high school and university counselor.

An eighth and final type of investigation (and a necessary one) is a study of the sources for referral. No counselor is equipped to handle all types of clients. Neither does he have the time to do so. When cases arise that are outside his domain, he should know exactly where this individual client might best be referred for help. Then it follows that the counselor should be acquainted with all of the community agencies in his city. He should not only know what they do in respect to cases and therapy but he should have established effective relationships with each. The counselor should even go beyond his own city, and include the clinics associated with the public and private universities within his state.

EXAMPLES OF RESEARCH

Some of the problems involved in conducting research may be illustrated by attempts to evaluate a practicum for counselors which has been conducted at the University of Kansas in variations of its present form for approximately 12 years (Cornwell, 1959). It presents certain problems of evaluating the kinds of experience offered in interviewing. These problems could be grouped under two headings, one involves the responsibility of the supervisor to the counselor in practicum and to the volunteer client being used to provide the counselor with necessary experience in interviewing. The other phase of evaluating a practicum program involves a judgment of the actual procedures carried on in that practicum by the supervisor in evaluating and teaching the counselor in training.

In the beginning counseling practicum at the University of Kansas the supervisor sat in on every interview. The counselor-trainee carried 10 cases and received two semester hours of graduate credit for this work. The trainee was a person concluding the work required for the Masters degree or beginning work on a Specialist or Doctoral degree. The cases handled were those of volunteer high school seniors who were concerned with appropriate educational or vocational choices after they left high school. This emphasis on educational-vocational choice tended to reduce the number of factors which the beginning counselor must handle in this first experience at interviewing and counseling. In order to find cases volunteers were solicited either in local high schools or in schools in which the counselor works as a teacher. These volunteer clients received the same services as ordinary counseling cases. At least two interviews were held with each client. The first interview was directed toward the validation and expansion of information from a biographical data form, from school records, and any other available sources of information about the client. At the end of this initial interview the client and the counselor decided what other information was necessary for more adequate educational or vocational choices. This usually required the use of interest inventories and various aptitude tests. Following the initial interview, other interviews were held as deemed necessary to help the client secure information and make adequate educational and vocational choices.

The supervisor conducted the initial interview with the first client as a demonstration for the counselor and the first interview in the second series following the initial interviews to demonstrate interpretation and synthesis of case data. All these interviews were recorded after the permission of the client had been secured. The recordings were also used by the neophyte counselor to identify places in the interview where the supervisor felt it was necessary to participate or point out counselor idiosyncrasies which must be changed. The recordings tended to give a fairly clear picture of the areas the supervisor felt important to explore and why the supervisor felt it necessary orally to enter the interview. The counselor also used the recordings to avoid taking notes in the interview. This permitted more concentration during the interview on the client and less on the mechanics of note-taking or summarizing.

The presence of the supervisor in each interview did not seem to have an adverse effect upon the progress of the interview. However, since this was only an impression gathered over a period of time by the supervisor, it was necessary to check it through some sort of program of evaluation. Periodic oral checks with the counselor and the client tended to support this observation, but actual results of research conducted apart from the practicum were needed to find out what client and counselor felt was really happening. This was the first aspect of the practicum covered in Cornwell's investigation (1959).

Another aspect of the situation which needed investigating was that dealing with the effect upon the client and the counselor of recording the interviews. A third area was that dealing with the effect of the surroundings in which the interviews were being held. Some of these interviews were held in school classrooms, others in any unused corner that the school could provide, still others were held in regular counseling rooms in a given local school, or at the Counseling Bureau at the University of Kansas. The answers to these and other questions were needed from a research project rather than from subjective judgments made by the people supervising counseling practicum or the people who had observed what was happening in the counseling practicum program. For this reason questionnaires were developed which would try to get at these questions about the counseling practicum.

The questionnaires used were the combined product of pilot studies, discussions in counseling seminars, and in the class meetings held in connection with this practicum. The actual questions asked of the practicum counselor are shown in Table 12.1 together with the results of responses of 43 counselors to these items. As far as possible a negative, a positive, and a neutral response were included for each item, so that there were three degrees of responses possible for each item. In the construction of the questionnaire itself, these options were randomized so that the effect

TABLE 12.1

RESULTS OF QUESTIONNAIRE COMPLETED BY 43 COUNSELORS WHO HAD COMPLETED THE HIGH SCHOOL COUNSELING PRACTICUM AT THE UNIVERSITY OF KANSAS GUIDANCE BUREAU

Question	Total Answers	Per Cent of Response
1. Has the course proved helpful to you?	43	
a. It was as helpful as any of the other courses I took	11	26
b. It helped me apply the knowledge I gained in other courses.	31	72
c. In actual work situations it has not been helpful.	1	2
2. Was it helpful to you to have the counseling supervisor participate in each interview (present at all times) in the first Practicum?	43	
a. I felt it cut down on my effectiveness as a counselor.	10	23
b. The presence of the supervisor gave me the security I needed for my first interview.	23	53
c. The presence of the supervisor made no difference.	10	23
3. Was the method of participation by the supervisor helpful in improving your counseling?	39	
a. It was helpful for the supervisor to do the first interview, so I would have a broad pattern to follow.	32	82
b. It would have been more helpful for the supervisor to have done the second interview following the discussion of my first interview.	4	10
c. Some other method of suggestions and supervision would prove more helpful.	3	8
4. Did you gain enough additional help in the Practium class meetings to warrant continuing them?	41	
a. I got some help; they could be held once or twice during the course.	14	34
b. They were helpful and should be continued as they were scheduled.	27	66
c. I could have spent my time to better advantage.	0	0
5. How did the class of trainees affect you?	40	
a. I resented or felt threatened by their comments.	2	5
b. I felt that what they said was of minor importance.	8	20
c. I found their comments quite helpful.	30	75

TABLE 12.1 (Continued)

Results of Questionnaire Completed by 43 Counselors Who Had Completed the High School Counseling Practicum at the University of Kansas Guidance Bureau

Question	Total Answers	Per Cent of Response
6. Did it disturb you to have the recordings of your interviews played in class?	34	
a. I was a little disturbed at first but found the comments helpful.	31	91
b. I do not think this is helpful as it is too disturbing.	0	0
c. All the recordings were about the same. I did not get much out of listening to other people's recordings.	3	9
7. Did you feel that the use of the tape recorder in interviews was helpful?	43	
a. I felt I could remember the important points about the interview.	1	2
b. I found it very helpful not only in picking up points about the interview, but in helping me correct undesirable verbal habits.	42	98
c. I felt it hindered me in my effectiveness; it made me too self-conscious.	0	0
8. Were the surroundings in which you did your counseling satisfactory?	43	
a. The surroundings were not conducive to good counselor training.	4	9
b. The surroundings did not affect me.	16	37
c. The surroundings were not perfect, but were as good as possible.	23	53
9. In terms of semester hours preparation, where in the training of counselors should Practicum be offered?	42	
a. After 16 or 20 hours preparation (Master level)	36	86
b. After 28 or 30 hours preparation (Specialist level)	5	12
c. After 56 or 60 hours preparation (Doctoral level)	1	2

(Check as many opinions as necessary)

10. If the procedure in Practicum were changed, which of the following should be eliminated?	48	
a. Counseling supervisor participating in each interview	14	29
b. Tape recorded	0	0
c. Playing of trainee recordings in class	3	6
d. Practicum class meetings	2	4
e. Having interviews at local schools	4	8
f. No major changes	25	52
g. Others	0	0

Cornwell, 1959:39–42.

of marking at one extreme or another of the grouping of item options would be minimized.

In the same way, items were constructed for the questionnaire to be sent out to clients who had completed counseling in the practicum program between 1953 and 1959. The questions in the final form of the questionnaire sent out to these former clients are shown in Table 12.2 together with: (1) the responses for the total group of 130 clients responding; (2)

TABLE 12.2

RESULTS OF QUESTIONNAIRE COMPLETED BY 130 CLIENTS IN HIGH SCHOOL COUNSELING PRACTICUM AT THE UNIVERSITY OF KANSAS GUIDANCE BUREAU FROM 1953–1959

Question	Total Response	Per Cent	1953–1955 Response	Per Cent 1953–55	1956–1958 Response	Per Cent 1956–58
1. Did you feel free to discuss and ask questions in the interview?	130		43		87	
a. I could talk only about things connected with school or a job.	17	13	10	23	7	8
b. I could talk about anything.	108	83	30	70	78	90
c. It was hard to discuss almost everything.	5	4	3	7	2	2
2. How did working with a counselor and a supervisor affect you?	130		43		87	
a. The supervisor (Third) person made it difficult to talk.	10	8	6	14	4	5
b. The supervisor (Third) person made no difference.	80	62	28	65	52	60
c. The supervisor (Third) person made me feel more comfortable.	40	31	9	21	31	36
3. Did you feel that the counselor was genuinely interested in you and the things you talked about?	130		43		87	
a. I felt the counselor was interested in helping me work out the best solution to my problem.	105	81	28	65	77	89
b. The counselor did not seem genuinely interested in me or the things I talked about.	5	4	3	7	2	2
c. I felt like the counselor was just doing the job assigned.	20	15	12	28	8	9
4. Did the presence of the supervisor make you feel that your interview was important?	130		43		87	

TABLE 12.2 (Continued)

RESULTS OF QUESTIONNAIRE COMPLETED BY 130 CLIENTS IN HIGH SCHOOL COUNSELING
PRACTICUM AT THE UNIVERSITY OF KANSAS GUIDANCE BUREAU
FROM 1953–1959

Question	Total Response	Per Cent	1953–1955 Response	Per Cent 1953–55	1956–1958 Response	Per Cent 1956–58
a. The presence of the supervisor make me feel that the counselor did not know very much.	5	4	1	2	4	5
b. I felt they were combining their efforts to help me.	80	62	20	47	60	69
c. I had no feeling on the matter.	45	35	22	51	23	26
5. Did you feel at ease in the first interview?	130		43		87	
a. I was nervous during the entire interview.	5	4	4	9	1	1
b. I felt a little nervous at first but soon got over it.	114	88	35	81	79	91
c. The interview was almost over before I felt at ease.	5	4	2	5	3	3
d. I was not nervous at all (added by counselees when answering questionnaire).	6	5	2	5	4	5
6. Did the fact that the interview was recorded affect you in any way?	130		43		87	
a. I forgot all about it once I started talking.	53	41	13	30	40	46
b. I held back information because I knew it would be recorded.	1	1	1	2	0	0
c. I thought at times about the recorder but did not care.	76	58	29	67	47	54
7. Did you feel free to refuse to have the interview recorded?	130		43		87	
a. I thought it was silly but did not care.	2	1	2	5	0	0
b. I was perfectly willing to have the interview recorded.	127	98	40	93	87	100
c. I did not want the recording made but did not feel free to refuse.	1	1	1	2	0	0
8. Were the office surroundings such that you felt free to talk?	130		43		87	
a. The room seemed close and crowded.	8	6	5	12	3	3
b. I did not notice the surroundings enough for them to affect me.	104	80	36	84	68	78

TABLE 12.2 (Continued)

RESULTS OF QUESTIONNAIRE COMPLETED BY 130 CLIENTS IN HIGH SCHOOL COUNSELING PRACTICUM AT THE UNIVERSITY OF KANSAS GUIDANCE BUREAU FROM 1953–1959

Question	Total Response	Per Cent	1953–1955 Response	Per Cent 1953–55	1956–1958 Response	Per Cent 1956–58
c. The surroundings made me feel free and relaxed.	18	14	2	5	16	18
9. Was the material explained clearly in the interview?	130		43		87	
a. The part of the material I did not understand was explained again when I asked questions about it.	101	78	33	77	68	78
b. I did not understand what was said to me.	0	0	0	0	0	0
c. The counseling supervisor used different words to explain the material so I could understand.	29	22	10	23	19	22
10. Did the interview and follow-up letter cover most of the questions you had?	130		43		87	
a. I found out some things I did not know. I guess it was worth the effort.	32	25	14	33	18	21
b. I felt that nothing had been accomplished. It was not worth the effort.	2	2	1	2	1	1
c. I feel I know now what I am capable of doing. All high school senior boys and girls should have the opportunity to go through this procedure.	96	74	28	65	68	78
11. Did you understand the use of the recorder?	130		43		87	
Yes.	119	92	38	88	81	93
No.	11	8	5	12	6	7

Cornwell, 1959:30–36.

clients in the 1953 to 1955 group; and (3) clients representing a 1956 to 1958 group. This latter division was made to see whether any items would be answered differently by earlier groups of clients than by more recent clients.

The results shown in Table 12.2 indicate relatively little difference between the groups of clients in the early part of the program and those more recent clients. Most of the differences in responses which exist appear to be the result of changes in the practicum program which have tended to produce a better relationship between the client, the counselor, and the supervisor participating in the practicum interviews. In general

Table 12.2 seems to indicate that clients felt free to talk about anything they wished in the series of practicum interviews. Approximately 60 per cent of the clients felt that the presence of the supervisor as a third person in the interview made no difference. Another 30 per cent felt that the supervisor made the client feel more comfortable, so that only 10 per cent or less of the clients responding indicated that the supervisor as a third person in the interview made it more difficult to talk in the interview. (It should be noted that Table 12.2 shows that significantly more of the clients from the early group were adversely affected by the presence of the supervisor since 14 per cent of those indicated a negative reaction and approximately 5 per cent from the later group indicated an adverse reaction.)

About four-fifths of the clients felt that the counselor was genuinely interested in helping them work out the best solution possible. Approximately 60 per cent of the clients felt that the supervisor and the counselor were combining efforts to help (a significantly larger number from the later group felt this was true than those in the early group of clients). Another 35 per cent who had no feelings about the relationship between supervisor and counselor left only 4 per cent who had negative feelings about the presence of the supervisor in the interview, according to their responses to item 4.

In response to item 5, about whether the clients felt at ease in the first interview, the bulk of respondents (88 per cent) indicated that they were a little nervous at first but soon got over this feeling, and 5 per cent voluntarily added the response that they were not nervous at all. In response to a question dealing with tape-recording the interviews, 41 per cent said they had forgotten all about the recorder once the interview began, and another 58 per cent said they thought at times about the recorder but did not care that it was used. This left only one person who said information was held back because the interview was being recorded. Ninety-eight per cent of the respondents to the questionnaire said they were perfectly willing to have their interviews recorded.

In the item dealing with counseling surroundings 80 per cent said they did not notice the surroundings enough to affect the counseling interview or client feelings.

Seventy-eight per cent felt that a second explanation by the counselor of material which was not clear at first eliminated any difficulties the clients encountered in understanding what was discussed in the interviews. Another 22 per cent said that the presence of the counseling supervisor who used different words to explain material made it easier to understand the material. No respondent answered the option which said, "I did not understand what was said to me." The other item dealing with the interview and follow-up letter covering information useful to the client produced a response of 75 per cent of the clients saying that they felt now that they knew more about what they should be doing educationally and vocationally. They felt that this was a worthwhile experience for all high school senior boys and girls. Another 25 per cent said they had found out some things they did not know and felt it may have been worth the effort. Only two of the 130 clients felt that it was not worth the effort that they had expended.

Table 12.1 not only indicates the items which were answered by 43 counselors completing the beginning practicum at the University of Kansas but also gives the distributions of these responses. In the first item 72 per cent felt that this practicum helped them to apply knowledge gained in other courses, while only one person felt that the course had not been helpful later in an actual work situation. Thirty-three indicated that the presence of the counselor supervisor in each interview either gave security to the counselor or made no difference, while 23 per cent felt that this cut down their effectiveness as a counselor. In a further discussion of the method of participation by the supervisor, 32 felt that it was helpful for the supervisor to do the first interview so that they would have a broad pattern (subject to their own adaptations) to follow in succeeding interviews. Only three felt some other method of suggestions and supervision would have proven more helpful. Group discussions or classes connected with practicum were felt to be important by the 41 people responding to this item and no people felt that this time could have been spent to better advantage during the practicum. Only two of the 40 counselors responding to item 5 made negative comments indicating they resented or felt threatened by the playing of their recordings during the class meetings of practicum counselors. Of the 34 counselors responding to the items dealing with the playing of recordings in class, 31 indicated they were somewhat disturbed by this but ultimately felt the comments helpful, while another three felt they did not get much out of listening to other counselor's recordings. No counselors indicated that this was too disturbing to be helpful, as far as the 34 counselors responding to this item were concerned. It should be noted, however, that 9 of the counselors who had completed this practicum failed to answer this item and may have had some negative feeling about the playing of their recordings in a class group of the counselors taking practicum the same semester.

As far as the use of tape recorder in the interviews was concerned, 42 of the 43 counselors felt that it was very helpful not only in picking up points about the interview but in helping them understand and correct undesirable verbal habits. None felt that this hindered his effectiveness or made him too self-conscious. Fifty-three per cent of these counselors in practicum felt that the surroundings for the counseling interview were as good as possible, and another 16 or 37 per cent felt that the surroundings had not affected them. Only nine per cent felt that the surroundings were not conducive to good counselor training. Item 9, dealing with the number of semester hours of preparation prior to the practicum experience may have been somewhat biased by an overloading of counselors taking this practicum who had only obtained a Master's degree. But 86 per cent of the respondents indicated that a minimum of 16 to 20 hours' preparation was sufficient for counseling practicum to be offered to beginning counselors. This fits the practical situation of schools hiring counselors with only a Master's degree. Item 10 made it possible for recommendations to be made by these counselors from the beginning practicum about the practicum procedures that should be changed or eliminated. Twenty-nine per cent felt that the counseling supervisor participating in each interview could be changed or eliminated and 52 per cent felt that no major changes were needed in the practicum program at the present time.

These data indicate the responses of a group of counselors and clients about their feelings concerning interviews conducted in a counselor practicum sequence. It was possible for them to respond anonymously to a person other than the one who was conducting the practicum course. Thus they were free to indicate their real response, handicapped only by whatever positive feelings they may have felt toward the person who supervised this practicum program. These results within the limits indicated show one series of expressions about questions many counselors have asked. These questions deal with the effect of the circumstances under which counseling takes place, the effect of recording of counseling interviews, and the effect of presence of a supervisor in such counseling interviews. The preponderance of responses in the direction indicated in Tables 12.1 and 12.2 seem to overshadow any personal relationships the supervisor and the counselor in practicum may have had upon the clients or the effect the supervisor himself may have had upon the counselors in the practicum program. This is one illustration of a way in which an evaluation of counseling programs may be conducted.

THE DEVELOPMENT OF A DESIGN FOR NEW RESEARCH

As the counselor gains experience, many of the activities that take place in preparation for counseling and during counseling interviews raise questions which can be answered only by a personal or agency research program. Many beginning counselors are quite concerned about the way in which a research problem develops and the method by which a research design is drawn up. As has been pointed out, research should develop naturally from the questions which arise in a counseling program. Simple, practical research designs can best grow out of such questions. An attempt will be made to illustrate, using the steps undertaken by a counselor in developing a scale to identify potential dropouts before they leave school.

A survey of the literature on dropouts over a period of years indicated that there are many ways of describing people who leave school. This problem is unique as far as the counselor is concerned in that these dropouts can be described only after they have left school. At the time this study was begun there was no way of identifying dropouts before they left school so that something could be done to help them, either in better placement in activities while they remained in school or in better placement in jobs or other training when they left school. As a consequence, 15 characteristics that seem to describe most dropouts were used as a basis for developing inventory items that would center about these characteristics. There were about 10 items for each of the characteristics and these items were combined into a 150 item scale called *The Life Adjustment Scale #1*, described in the work reported by Herrman and Cottle (1958).

Since it was possible to leave school in Kansas at the end of eighth grade or at age 16, whichever came first, *The Life Adjustment Scale #1* was administered to all eighth and ninth grade pupils in a large city school system. A pilot study was conducted earlier by Havens (1955), which indicated that the dropout rate in smaller cities was so low, or the accounting system for tallying dropouts was so inadequate, that work on dropouts in the smaller cities of Kansas did not seem useful. (Kansas has a very low dropout rate among the 50 states.) As a consequence, Herrman administered *The Life Adjustment Scale #1* to 1,834 eighth and ninth grade pupils in a large Kansas metropolitan area. Later these groups were followed up and the dropouts were identified. It was found that 3 semesters and one summer later 61 boys and 53 girls had dropped out of school. The answer sheets for these individuals were matched with those for an equal number of boys and girls drawn by use of a table of random numbers from the remainder who had stayed in school. (It is easier in comparing proportions and computing statistics if equal numbers of experimental and control groups are contrasted because simpler statistical techniques exist for handling equal numbers.) A description of these dropout groups indicated that the boys ranged in age from 13 to 17 with a mean of 14.7 and that the girl dropouts ranged in age from 13 to 16 with a mean of 14.2. The age of the group of boys who stayed in school ranged from 13 to 15 with a mean of 13.8 while that for the stay-in girls was 13 to 17 with a mean of 13.5. The dropouts tended to be older than those individuals who stayed in school as has been shown by most of the other dropout studies which have been conducted.

When these two groups had been selected, other statistical techniques were used to compare the responses of the boy dropouts versus the boys who stayed in school and the girl dropouts against the responses of girls who stayed in school, on each of the 150 items of the inventory. Using the IBM answer sheets of the contrasting groups, a complete item count of the responses of each group to each item was made with the graphic item count mechanism of the IBM test scoring machine. The count for boy dropouts and boy stay-ins, girl dropouts and girl stay-ins, was made separately. Then the number of dropouts and stay-ins of each sex answering a specific item *true* was converted into proportions of the total group of dropouts or stay-ins for each sex. Guilford (1954) has provided a table which allows the reading of phi coefficients from proportions of two *equal* samples responding to test items. (See Guilford, 1954:431; or Downie and Heath, 1959:176.)

The phi coefficient for each item was used to evaluate the item's usefulness in discrimination between the two groups within each sex. Items that discriminated at the .01, .05, and .10 level of confidence were selected to use as items characteristic of boy or girl dropouts, respectively. These items were used in making a scoring key which was keyed in the direction of dropout responses. There were 60 items which differentiated between the boy groups at this level of significance, and there were 58 items which differentiated between the girl groups. The choice of the 10 per cent level of confidence was made because there were 11 items at this level common to both boys and girls out of a total of 28 common items. It has also been found in previous research with this type of scale and item that an item at the 10 per cent level might be significant at a higher level of confidence in succeeding studies and this would prevent the dropping of items which might be of use as the research continued.

These statistical procedures identified a total of 90 items out of the basic 150 which differentiate responses of dropouts from those of boys or girls who stay in school. In a preliminary attempt to validate these items, a small group of 20 girls and 20 boys who had dropped out of school in another city of Kansas were matched with a randomly selected equal number of boys or girls who had stayed in the schools of that city. Significant differences were found for the dropouts versus those who stayed in school between these validation groups of boys or validation groups of girls. This was done by the use of variance ratio (F tests) to determine that dropout and stay-in groups had similar variability. (The variance is the square of the standard deviation.) Then t tests were used to judge the significance of difference between the means of the dropout versus the stay-in groups. Statistical processes are simplified if the dropout and stay-in group are equal in number. The F test is no more than the ratio of the two variances (Downie and Heath, 1959). If no differences in variances are found, a t test for testing the significance of the difference between two means is made as outlined in Chapter 6.

Epps and Cottle (1958) report on a follow-up of the original data collected by Herrman in December, 1954. In the more recent study the ninth graders had been graduated from high school and the eighth graders in the study were beginning seniors. Thus, most of the people in the study have had considerable opportunity to leave school, and relatively few of those remaining would leave school if their behavior was similar to those previously studied. The list of school-leavers, other than those reported in the Herrman and Cottle study, was composed of 146 boys and 152 girls who dropped out after Herrman's original dropout group had been studied. Their responses were matched with an equal number of answer sheets of boys and girls drawn from the remaining stay-in group by use of a table of random numbers. Both groups ranged in age from 13 to 17 years when tested in the eighth and ninth grades. The mean age for the dropout boys was 13.9, while that for the boys who stayed in school was 13.6. The mean age for the dropout girls was 13.7, while that for the girls who stayed in school was 13.5. Thus it is evident that there is little difference in age between these two groups.

Again, item analysis techniques were used to identify items differentiating between dropout and stay-in responses for boys and girls. The itemized process for doing this is shown as follows:

1. Collect data.

2. Run Item Count. Score both true and false items. Need four runs to complete count since only 45 questions can be scored at one time.

3. Tally count and group columns as indicated.

	111111111111	
Question 1	111111111111	
		(Tally dropout and
	111111111111	stay-in groups sep-
Question 2	111111111111	arately by sex)

4. Make table of proportions and convert both dropout and stay-in groups in terms of proportion of true responses.

5. Use Guilford (1954) or Downie and Heath (1959) to look up phi coefficients.

6. Test for significant of phi coefficients by using the following formulas (Guilford, 1954):

$$phi_{.01} = \frac{2.576}{\sqrt{N}} \qquad\qquad phi_{.10} = \frac{1.645}{\sqrt{N}}$$

$$phi_{.05} = \frac{1.960}{\sqrt{N}}$$

These are the values of the phi coefficient significant at the three levels.

7. Cut scoring stencil and score papers.

8. Make frequency distribution and find mean and variance.

9. Do F and t tests of significance between experimental dropout and stay-in groups as check.

10. Score papers of validation dropout and stay-in groups. Do F and t tests in the same fashion as in steps 8 and 9.

This study reported by Epps and Cottle (1958) found 79 items which were able to differentiate potential dropouts from pupils who stayed in

school. This compares with 89 items found in the study reported by
Herrman and Cottle (1958). Forty-one of the items were common to
both studies. These items were composed of those dealing with concern
about conditions in the home, the school, economic stress, and personal
feelings of the student toward environment. At least in this scale sex
differences in item response do not seem as important as might be expected, because one-third of the total items in each study were common
to both boys and girls in the study.

This experimental scale has proven to be efficient in identifying the
potential dropouts in this study. When scored either on the keys from
the Epps and Cottle study, or with keys composed of items common to
both studies, a comparison of the scores of dropout groups with those for
corresponding stay-in groups showed that the dropout groups had significantly higher scores. A statistical comparison of the variances indicated that the ranges of scores for each of the paired groups was similar
in all but three cases, so that the difference was solely a difference in
means.

An interesting point is that the first study conducted about the time
most of these pupils had reached the end of ninth grade found more
significant items than the second study when most of the students had
reached graduation. Since the groups in the second study were more
than twice the size of the first dropout group it might have been expected
that more significant items would appear with the larger group of dropouts because the larger groups presented a greater possible variety of
items which would reflect their reasons for leaving school. Also, because
of the fact that the group was larger, the level of significance required for
each item would be lower. A comparison of these two studies indicated
that the dropout groups in the later studies were not as different from
the stay-ins as were the groups in the original studies. The dropouts
in the groups reported by Herrman and Cottle were so different from
those who remained in school that they left school as soon as it was
legally possible to do so. This was done either at the end of the eighth
grade, or within a year of that time. In the second sample reported
by Epps and Cottle, those who eventually dropped out had been suffi-
ciently similar to those who had stayed in until graduation that many of
them remained in school close to three of the four necessary high school
years. Consequently, the dropouts in the second study were more like
the boys and girls who stayed in school until graduation; it was more
difficult to show differences, and there were fewer differences.

These two studies offered sufficient evidence that potential dropouts
could be identified; hence *The Life Adjustment Scale #1* was revised
into a scale called *The School Interest Inventory* with 108 items which
had differentiated between dropouts and stay-ins in the earlier studies.

Forty-two linguistic or nonlinguistic items were added in place of items which appear to be only padding in the early studies. At the present time *The School Interest Inventory* (Cottle, 1959) has been administered to boys and girls in grades 8 through 12 in a number of large metropolitan suburban areas in Eastern Kansas. A number of studies are under way attempting to identify those items that will differentiate between the responses of boys and girls to the scale. It is anticipated that more than the original 42 linguistic-nonlinguistic items will show such differentiation. If this is possible it may indicate a way in which boys and girls at the ninth grade level may be helped to make curricular choices during high school.

The way in which this is to be undertaken is as follows:

1. Clean and check the markings on the IBM answer sheets so that only those answered properly will be tallied by the IBM item counter.

2. Sort the papers by grade and sex, equalizing randomly the number in each grade group by sexes. That is, if there are 130 papers for boys in grade nine, there should be 130 papers for girls. If there are more girls than boys, their papers should be reduced to 130 by pulling at random the number necessary to do this. If the boys outnumber the girls, the reverse should be done in order to reduce the number of boys' answer sheets to equal that of the girls.

3. Do item analysis by grade and by sex separately.

4. Check for differences within sex by grade according to each item. This is done by computing the significance of differences in percentages using a nomograph prepared by Lawshe and Baker (1950). If there are no differences between the boys in each grade, then the boys from each grade can be combined into one group of boys. The same procedure would be followed for the girls. If there are no differences, the various grades of girls can be combined. If there *are* differences the grades will have to be treated separately to see which items differentiate between boys and girls in grade nine and between those of ten, eleven, and twelve, respectively.

5. Obtain the phi coefficients by items between sexes, making sure that the N for each sex is equal, as indicated in item 2 above. These phi coefficients are computed in the same manner as indicated early in this chapter.

6. Pick the items differentiating between the sexes and punch these into a scoring key according to the differentiation in the boys' direction and this key would be called a "nonlinguistic scale."

7. Score the papers of both boys and girls. Check to see by the use of both *F* and *t* tests that there are no differences between either groups of boys *or* groups of girls in this study, but that there are differences between the boys *and* girls in each of the groups. This is a check on the accuracy of the process thus far, because by construction this scale must differentiate between boys and girls.

8. Select an additional set of papers on this nonlinguistic scale. This makes up the validation group.

9. Do F and t tests between experimental and validation groups. There should be no difference between the score of boys in the experimental and the validation groups nor should there be differences between the girls in the experimental and validation groups. However, if the scale is to work effectively there should be differences between the boys in the validation group and the girls in the validation group. This is evidence that the scale works.

This is an illustration of how curiosity about things appearing in previous research and in past experience may combine with a need for identifying such individuals as potential school dropouts or a need for differentiating between a linguistic and a nonlinguistic group to give a counselor clues to needed research. It also illustrates how experimental designs of this nature can be constructed without a great deal of difficulty. The main problem involved in any research carried on by the counselor is the amount of time it takes, and the effort it may be to find this time in a busy schedule where there are too many clients for each counselor.

SUMMARY

This chapter has attempted to show how various kinds of counseling research can contribute to the information needed prior to counseling and can contribute to counseling itself to make that counseling more effective. The kinds of research which have been considered are those dealing with: a follow-up of agency clients; the placement of agency clients in further education or in jobs; the construction of local norms, and statistics necessary to do this in order to make the work with clients more effective on a local basis. It has also discussed the way in which attempts can be undertaken to evaluate the counseling program itself, and, lastly, some examples of how new research can contribute information of value to the counselor and the client.

REFERENCES

Benson, A. L. *Criteria for evaluating guidance programs in secondary schools.* Washington, D.C.: U. S. Office of Education, 1949.

Cornwell, H. *Reactions of clients and counselors to a beginning counseling practicum.* Unpublished Specialist project, the University of Kansas, 1959.

Committee Report. A proposed survey of entry jobs in the greater Kansas City area. *Occupations,* 1949, *27,* 326–331.

Cottle, W. C. *The school interest inventory.* Lawrence, Kansas, 1959.

Dewey, J. *How we think.* Boston: D. C. Heath and Company, 1933.

Downie, N. M. *Fundamentals of measurement.* New York: Oxford University Press, 1958.

———, and R. W. Heath. *Basic statistical methods.* New York: Harper & Brothers, 1959.

Dressel, P. L. Personnel services in high school and college. *Occupations*, 1951, *29*, 331–340.

――――. Some approaches to evaluation. *Personnel and Guidance Journal*, 1953, *31*, 285–294.

Epps, M. M., and W. C. Cottle. Further validation of a dropout scale. *The Vocational Guidance Quarterly*, 1958, 7, 90–93.

Froehlich, C. P. *Evaluating guidance procedures: A review of the literature.* Washington, D.C.: U. S. Office of Education, 1949.

Guilford, J. P. *Psychometric methods*, Second Edition. New York: McGraw-Hill Book Company, 1954.

Havens, N. H. *A study of the answers one year in advance to the Life Adjustment Scale by students who drop out or remain in four Kansas high schools.* M. Ed. report, the University of Kansas, 1955.

Herrman, W. L., and W. C. Cottle. An inventory to identify high school dropouts. *The Vocational Guidance Quaterly*, 1958, *6*, 122–123.

Hillway, T. *Introduction to research.* Boston: Houghton Miffin Company, 1956.

Lawshe, C. H., and P. C. Baker. Three aids in the evaluation of the significance of difference between percentages. *Educ. Psychol. Measmt.*, 1950, *10*, 263–270.

Pepinsky, H. B. Some proposals for research, *Personnel and Guidance Journal*, 1953, *31*, 291–294.

Rushong, H. D. Present status and trends in the evaluation of counseling. *Educ. Psychol. Measmt.*, 1953, *13*, 418–430.

Rummel, J. F. *An introduction to research procedures in education.* New York: Harper & Brothers, 1958.

Selltiz, C., et al. *Research methods in social relations.* New York: Henry Holt and Company, 1959.

Shoben, E. J., Jr. Some problems in establishing criteria of effectiveness. *Personnel and Guidance Journal*, 1953, *31*, 287–291.

Smith, E. R., and R. W. Tyler. *Appraising and recording student progress.* New York: Harper & Brothers, 1942.

Travers, R. M. W. A critical review of techniques for evaluating guidance. *Educ. Psychol. Measmt.*, 1949, *9*, 211–225.

Williamson, E. G., and E. S. Bordin. Evaluation of vocational and educational counseling: A critique of the methodology of experiments. *Educ. Psychol. Measmt.*, 1941, *1*, 5–24.

Index

321